ECONOMIC INEQUALITY~~~

in the

UNITED STATES

ECONOMIC INEQUALITY

in the

UNITED STATES

Lars Osberg

M. E. SHARPE, INC.
Armonk, New York / London

Design: Angela Foote

Library of Congress Cataloging in Publication Data

Osberg, Lars, 1946-
    Economic inequality in the United States.
    Bibliography: p.
    Includes index.
    1. Income—United States. 2. Income distribution—United States.
3. Equality—United States. I. Title.
HC110.15082   1983   339.2'2'0973   83-15382
ISBN 0-87332-234-7
ISBN 0-87332-259-2 (pbk.)

Printed in the United States of America

For
EDITH SPENCER OSBERG
and
GUSTAV LAWRENCE OSBERG
—in gratitude

CONTENTS

PREFACE

The aim of this book is to combine a description of the extent of economic inequality in the United States with a discussion of some of its causes and some of its implications. However, economic incquality is a vast topic, one which has become highly specialized and subdivided and sometimes very technical. My hope is that this book can serve to consolidate some essential parts of the literature and that it will prove useful to general readers interested in the issues surrounding economic inequality as well as to students of both economics and sociology courses. To my mind, the study of economic inequality is one of the most fascinating and important areas of economics—if some of the readers of this book develop a greater interest in the values, the facts, and the causes of economic inequality, this book will have accomplished its purpose.

In chapter organization and in occasional sections of text this book resembles my earlier book, *Economic Inequality in Canada*, Butterworths, 1981, and I must confess that at one point I thought that there would be a much greater resemblance between the two. They differ, not only because significant new literature has appeared in the last two years but also because of the many differences one finds between two very similar societies. Indeed, one of the most fascinating issues in the study of inequality is why nations differ in their degree of inequality and what the implications of these differences are. For the most part, however, this book focuses on the United States, since this nation alone provides enough material to fill several much larger volumes.

In writing a book of this sort, however, one accumulates debts in many directions. Many of the ideas developed in this book were first inflicted on students in classes in labor economics and income distribution and poverty at Dalhousie University and the University of Western Ontario. Their comments and questions over the past seven years have forced the clarification of many points, even if the original presentation may have been more obtuse.

I would also like to express my appreciation to the Dalhousie University Research and Development Fund—whose financial support enabled me to obtain the valuable research assistance of Kevin Reilly. To

Monique Henderson, Mary Simms, and Jura Smith fell the burden of coping with both manuscript and author. I am not sure which was the greater stress, especially in the latter stages, but I know that I am grateful for their help. I also owe a great deal to the many colleagues who have been so generous with their own research, their time, and their comments. I hope I am not missing too many—when I thank especially Robert Comeau, John Cornwall, James Davies, David Donaldson, Edgar Friedenberg, Christian Marfels, Dan Radner, Pat Ruggles, Al Sinclair, Fred Wien, and Ed Wolff. Finally, Ann Kearns deserves special thanks for the many errata she detected before it was too late. However, since I did not always take all the advice which was offered to me I cannot implicate any of the above in the final product, for which I take sole responsibility.

Although some additional references were included in galley revisions, the manuscript was essentially completed in June 1982.

ECONOMIC
INEQUALITY—
in the
UNITED STATES

1 INTRODUCTION

1.1 Equality—A Value or a Description?

Few areas of economics are as contentious as a study of economic inequality and, in part, this is because at the same time that "equality" is for many a deeply held value about how society should be, "inequality" is a description of how society is. The most straightforward definition of economic inequality is probably "differences among people in their command over economic resources" (although to be useful one must be more specific about which economic resource and how it is measured). In this book, we do not enter the debate on whether society *should be* economically equal or unequal or how a "just" degree of economic inequality should be defined. Rather, the emphasis here is on description and analysis—description of the extent of economic "inequality" and analysis of its causes. The omission of a full discussion of what "ought to be" is not due to any view that it is an unimportant topic; the omission arises solely because there is more than enough material involved in the description and analysis of economic inequality to fill this, or indeed a much larger, book.

Most people's interest in the extent and causes of inequality stems, however, from the value which they place in "equality." Such a value is traced by many writers to religious roots, that "all men are equal in the eyes of God," since regardless of "superiority in the arts which bring wealth and power, judged by their place in any universal scheme, they are all infinitely great or infinitely small" (Tawney, 1952:38). The value of equality finds expression in such classic statements as the American Declaration of Independence: "We hold these truths to be self-evident, that all men are created equal, that they are endowed by their Creator with certain unalienable Rights, that among these are Life, Liberty and the pursuit of Happiness." "Equality" is thus a very powerful ideal, closely connected to (but not identical with) the criteria of "equity," "fairness," and "justice" by which we judge the moral authority of existing and potential social institutions.

3

But what does "equality" mean? If it means "equality of result" in the economic sphere, is this equality of annual income, of lifetime income, or of lifetime "utility," which includes nonmonetary rewards? If it means "equality of opportunity," is this an "equal start" in any race, however defined? Or is it an "equal start" in a contest whose prizes are set to maximize the utility of the least well-off participant (Rawls, 1971)? Or is it the conception that although people "differ profoundly as individuals in capacity and character, they are equally entitled as human beings to consideration and respect, and that the well-being of a society is likely to be increased if it so plans its organization that, whether their powers are great or small, all its members are equally enabled to make the best use of such powers as they possess" (Tawney, 1952:35)?

Each of these conceptions of "equality" would lead to a very different "ideal society." There is a world of difference, for example, between a society which defines "equal opportunity" as identical expenditure on the education of all children and one which defines it, as Tawney does, to mandate compensatory educational programs for the handicapped and the disadvantaged. If "equality" is one's goal, it clearly matters a great deal how one defines it.

A major theme of Chapters 2 and 3 is, however, that for the purposes of description and analysis it also matters a great deal how one defines the extent of inequality. Pure "description," uncontaminated by values, is probably an unobtainable goal. There are many empirical definitions of economic "inequality," each of which emphasizes more or less heavily particular aspects of inequality. As Chapter 2, section 2 points out, some statistical measures emphasize more heavily differences between the extremes and the middle groups of a distribution, while some emphasize more heavily inequality among the middle groups. Some variables (such as wealth, Chapter 3) are distributed more unequally than other variables (such as income, Chapter 2). Which variable, and which measure, one chooses to describe will clearly affect one's perception of economic "inequality." In Chapter 2, we focus on the distribution of annual income, whereas Chapter 3 discusses the distribution of economic power, of wealth and riches, and of lifetime income. One's view of which variable is the most important to study depends, at least partially, on one's values— i.e., on which definition of "inequality" as a description of where society *is* makes most sense in terms of one's conception of "equality" (i.e., where society *should be*).

Indeed, definitions are important even if one does not value "equality" and wishes only to analyze the reasons why annual earnings of full-year, full-time employees varied in 1981 between $7,000 and $22,550,000[1] or why the top 0.5% of the population own roughly 20% of the nation's wealth (see Table 3.1). There are a variety of explanations of these phenomena, and some variables (such as "economic power" and its inequality) may be crucial components of one theory although they do not "make sense" in the context of another. Indeed, even the "facts" one selects to explain are intimately related to one's theoretical perspective. Some "facts"—such as the inequality of lifetime consumption annuities as described by Irvine (1980) or the rate of surplus value as described by Wolff (1979b)—are understandable only within a particular theoretical context. Other "facts" (such as the inequality of "wealth" or "riches"— see Chapter 3) may have subtly different definitions whose rationale depends partially on the theory they are part of and whose measurement produces different perceptions of the extent of the economic inequality around us. Since it is a truism that the personal acquaintances of most people tend to be other people with similar habits, attitudes, and backgrounds, these differences in theoretical perspective can have important practical consequences. Given a sufficiently circumscribed set of personal experiences it is quite possible (and quite comforting) for an individual to believe that "most" people are "like me." If the logic of a theory, reinforced by the comforts of complacency, overwhelms an individual's other sources of information, he or she may be convinced that economic inequality is "really" quite small and not worth troubling about.

Such a perception does not, of course, alter the reality which faces other people. Low income is a fact of life for many Americans but our perception of the extent of "poverty" will be influenced by which definition of a "poverty line" we choose to adopt. Chapter 4 outlines these methods of defining "poverty" (which are ultimately based on differing analyses of the nature of deprivation) and argues that there are good grounds for seeing "poverty" as *relative* to the average living standards of the rest of society. The issue of poverty is, therefore, inextricably linked to the inequality which exists in the lower half of the income distribution. On the other hand, such issues as the inheritance of property are of primary importance for the upper tail of the income and wealth distributions. Since economic inequality has several aspects, no single measure of inequality is likely to be appropriate for all purposes.

1.2 Economic Theory—The Problem of Choice of Perspective

It is far from easy to separate values from descriptions and descriptions from analyses. It is, however, essential to try if one is to make an informed choice among the various research traditions which seek to explain economic inequality. A major theme of Chapters 5 through 11 is that a variety of explanations exist—Chapter 5 discusses alternative explanations of the division of national income between the owners of "labor" and "capital" while Chapters 6 through 9 present critical summaries of the different theories available of the determination and distribution of labor earnings (Chapter 10 offers a summary) and Chapter 11 examines the acquisition of property.

In Chapters 6 through 10, a distinction is drawn between theories which explain the determination of individual earnings and those which explain the distribution of earnings. It is argued that only under particular assumptions can a theory which explains, for example, why a union member or a more highly educated individual usually receives a relatively higher salary be directly generalized to a theory of the impact of unionization or a general increase in education on the distribution of earnings (see sections 6.3.3, 8.2.2, and 9.1). To some extent, the issue is the familiar one of a distinction between partial and general equilibrium analysis. It makes sense, when looking at how education or unionization will affect an individual, to assume that the market demand for goods and for education (either as a credential or as a productive input) remains unchanged. It makes much less sense to assume that a general change in the distribution of education or a general increase in union membership will leave market values unchanged; thus generalizations concerning the impact of the distribution of education or unionization on the distribution of earnings require a general equilibrium approach—i.e., both a theory of supply and one of demand. A theory of earnings determination can, therefore, explain why the earnings of two individuals are unequal but it may not be able to explain the "inequality" of earnings—i.e., the distribution of earnings of the entire population.

Chapter 6 discusses "chance" as a theory of earnings distribution and the role of ability and socioeconomic background in earnings determination. Chapter 7 concerns racial and sexual differences in earnings. Chapter 8 presents the "human capital/neoclassical" perspective on individual and family earnings, on the distribution of earnings, and on the intergenerational transmission of earning power. It emphasizes the role of individual choice in earnings determination. Chapter 9 outlines the "neo-institutional" and "radical" views—it emphasizes the importance of constraints. In some respects the differences among these theories are very profound—as can be seen in Chapter 13's discussion of public policy to deal with inequality. In some respects, however, their differences are surprisingly slight since as bodies of applied theory their predictions must conform to the same underlying empirical events of the real world. Some events therefore acquire a different terminology in different theories, but retain the same consequences. One can, for example, assert that the advantages children from upper income families have when they enter primary school (see section 6.3) are due to early human capital investments in "child quality" by their parents (see section 8.4) or to their "class background" (see section 9.4)—either way they tend to do better in school as a result. Given the great differences in theoretical starting points and methodologies, it is extremely interesting that the "neoclassical" and "radical" analyses agree on two important predictions—that left to itself a capitalist market system will produce *neither* equality of outcome *nor* equality of opportunity in the labor market. Indeed the very distinction between "equality of opportunity" and "equality of outcome" is somewhat misleading in any society which lasts over more than one generation and in which the resources acquired by parents can be passed, without redistribution, to children.

1.3 Other Issues

Anyone who starts writing a book on economic "inequality" will inevitably acquire a certain humility by its end. The topic is as vast as any in economics, and with considerably more implications than most for a wide range of other disciplines. Psychology, biology, and genetics tell us of the "inequalities" we can expect to find in the human organism; sociology and politics emphasize the inequalities in the relationships of human social animals; history reminds us that the inequality of the present is conditioned by the inequalities of the past, while ethics points out that as moral beings we all must make judgments on inequality. All of these disciplines remind us that "economic man" is but one of humanity's dimensions and in all of these disciplines inequality has been greatly studied—often with frequent reference to economic inequalities. One cannot, and should not, avoid making some connections to these other disciplines in a book on economic inequality but, for the most part, they have been left as unexplored avenues.

Even within economics, "inequality" is so broad a topic that any discussion that does not spread over several volumes will leave many stones unturned. There is no discussion here, for example, of regional or international inequalities, very little on the impact of trade unions on inequality, and nothing on economic inequality in noncapitalist societies. Even among those subjects which are discussed, it is apparent that any of them could well have received far more extensive treatment, and every reader will have his or her candidates for the ones which should have. The selection of topics and emphases is entirely the responsibility of the author—in addition to that of the determination of labor earnings, the issues of property, of growth, and of government intervention seemed to him the most important.

Chapters 6 through 10 emphasize the determination and distribution of earnings because that is the primary source of income for most American families. Chapter 11 discusses the acquisition of property—the theory and evidence surrounding both the "life-cycle" view that most families acquire their property by individual saving from labor earnings and the radical view that most property is inherited. However, although the tenor of discussion is markedly different, there is no basic disagreement on empirical predictions between "radical" and "neoclassical" positions. As an empirical matter, there is no necessary contradiction between the two views if a relatively small minority of families own a very large chunk of the nation's wealth (and inherit most of it) while the rest of the population (i.e., the majority of families) save their wealth (if any) from labor earnings, as appears to be the case. The *ethical* issue involved is that of the justification of the social institution of private property since private property as a reward for individual exertion and private property as an inherited birthright have often been viewed somewhat differently.

Chapter 12 discusses the link between economic inequality and economic growth and development. Sociologists and political scientists would argue that the link is profound, that unequal societies which lack an ideology to legitimate inequality face a continual tension between institutionalized values and social reality which may be politically and socially destabilizing. Economists, on the other hand, have tended to talk of "trade-offs" between equity and efficiency, between growth and redistribution. International comparisons, however, do not indicate any clear tendency for more unequal societies to grow faster. Indeed, most of the rest of the OECD (Organization for Economic Cooperation and Development) nations have both more growth and more equality than the United States.

In the early 1980s, the tax and transfer policy of the U.S. government became less redistributive from rich to poor, partly in the hope that this would spur further growth. Whether it will is doubtful. Chapter 13, therefore, considers the current impact of government policies on the distribution of income and the potential impact of a number of alternative policies. It will be seen that great disagreements exist about the desirability of particular policies—disagreements which stem from different conceptual understandings of the economy and in particular from the debate outlined in Chapters 8 and 9. One is therefore brought back to the problem of choice, since one must choose which analysis of the economy appears most reasonable if one wishes to advocate particular policies to affect it.

Since the distribution of economic resources reaches into every facet of economic life, the analysis of inequality can scarcely help but be a complex issue—which ought to tell us to avoid like the plague simplistic slogans. Slogans, however, have pervaded the discussion of economic inequality, presenting false choices and obscuring common insights. If this book assists in the more exact evaluation of choices and in a greater dialogue of ideas, its purpose will have been well served.

NOTE

[1]*Forbes* magazine (May 1982) reports that S. Ross of Warner Communications earned $22.55 million in 1981. Forty hours per week × 50 weeks × $3.50 per hour yields $7,000 per year.

2 INEQUALITY IN MONEY INCOME

In this chapter, we examine the distribution of annual money income among households. Any discussion of distributional issues must begin by defining:

(a) distribution of what?
(b) distribution among whom?
(c) distribution how measured?

Section 2.1 therefore presents the definitions of "income" and "household" which are necessary to get the discussion under way; section 2.2 examines alternative measures of the extent of inequality, while section 2.3 compares the current inequality of the American income distribution with that prevailing in other nations.

One should state at the outset that money income inequality is only a part of economic inequality. Statistics on the distribution of annual money income among existing households present only a snapshot of a complex and moving process. Some things (such as noncash fringe benefits, wealth, or leisure) are left out of the picture entirely, some things (such as income or family composition) may change drastically before the next snapshot is taken, and still other aspects of the picture (such as rental incomes) are very blurred and out of focus. These omissions are the subject of Chapter 3, but as we shall see there is plenty of complexity even in the snapshot which income distribution statistics present.

2.1 Definitions

2.1.1 What Is Income? Economists usually distinguish between wealth and income by arguing that the former is a stock and the latter is a flow, but underlying *both* is the broad concept of "control over the use of society's scarce resources" (Simons, 1938:58). Wealth is then the total extent, at a point in time, of an individual's access to resources. Income (minus consumption) is the amount by which wealth changes during a given period of time. Or, as Hicks put it, income is "the maximum value a

9

person can consume during a period and still be as well off (as wealthy) at the end of the period as he was at the beginning" (Hicks, 1946:75). "Income" can thus come to a person in many ways—as cash, as goods, as services for which one does not have to pay, as gifts, or as increases in the value of assets which one already owns.

A broad concept of income would come close to measuring flows of economic welfare but this is extremely difficult to measure in statistical surveys. In practice, the Bureau of the Census estimates "money income"—i.e., receipts from wages and salaries, net income from self-employment, dividends, interest, royalty and net rental income, Social Security and welfare payments, pensions, and miscellaneous incomes such as alimony. Excluded from this measure of income are inheritances, gifts, capital gains or losses, the value of fringe benefits, income in kind (such as free meals, living accommodations, or food and fuel produced for one's own use), or the value of food stamps or government services received during the year. The great advantage of using Bureau of the Census data on money income to measure income distribution is their availability. The disadvantage is that one cannot be sure that omissions at the upper end of the income scale (e.g., capital gains and executive "perks") balance omissions at the lower end of the income scale (e.g., medical services received by the elderly)—and, to the extent that they do not balance, published statistics on money income shares will disagree with more comprehensive measures.

2.1.2 Distribution among Whom? In this chapter we refer primarily to the distribution of money income among *households*. Households are the focus because a concern with the distribution of current economic welfare implies a concern for the distribution of potential consumption. If income is pooled within a household for the purposes of consumption, which may not always be the case, then the household is an appropriate focus. If income is typically not shared among unrelated cohabiting individuals then the family is a more appropriate focus. As we shall see, it makes a difference whether one chooses households or families as the appropriate recipient unit.

A household is defined as all the persons occupying a housing unit—i.e., a separate living quarters with either a separate entrance or separate cooking equipment. A household can thus consist of a single person, a family, a family plus unrelated individuals or a group of unrelated individuals. A "family" is defined as "two or more persons related by blood, marriage or adoption and residing together." In March 1981, there were 82,368,000 households in the United States, of which 18,936,000 were one-person households, 60,309,000 were composed entirely of family members and 3,123,000 were composed partially or wholly of unrelated individuals.

There are no single "always correct" answers to the questions of which recipient unit and which measure of income to choose. A concern with the distribution of economic well-being would imply that one should examine the distribution of income from all sources among *consuming units*—families *may* share consumption, but not all households do.[1] However, a concern with discrimination in the labor market would imply that one should examine the distribution of earnings among individual employees. The choice of whether to use individuals, family units, or households therefore depends on the question at issue.[2]

The economic well-being of a household with a given income clearly depends on how many mouths there are to feed with a given income;[3] hence, a particularly important distinction is that between families and unattached individuals. Table 2.1 presents separately income distribution data for families, households, and unattached individuals. In part because many unattached individuals are either young people who have not fully entered the labor market or older people who have left it, and partly because there is, by definition, only one earner, the average income of unattached individuals is very much below the average income of families. Income inequality among all households is therefore somewhat greater than income inequality among families of two or more people. The "household" concept cannot, however, capture the economic inequality within those families or households where income is not shared. On the other hand, some fraction of unattached individuals may be able to lay claim, in practice, to family resources, although they may not share a common dwelling unit—hence, their true economic resources may be understated by a focus solely on personal income. One cannot, however, *ignore* unattached individuals since many unattached individuals who have no family (e.g., elderly single women) are among the poorest people in American society. The "household" is an imperfect compromise as a consumption unit, but at least it counts everybody somewhere.

If we compare income distribution statistics across countries and over time we have, however, to remember the social trends which shape household composition. In some cultures the extended family is the norm—grandparents typically residing with one of their married children and children usually remaining at home until their own marriage. Family income may then be contributed by, and shared among, three generations. Aggregate statistics will, as a result, show a relatively small number of unattached individuals, whose incomes are typically low—thereby complicating comparisons with societies like the United States, where the nuclear family is the norm.

Within the United States, analysis of trends in inequality is complicated by social trends such as the rise in divorce rates. Many people are familiar with the drastic change in individual economic well-being that typically accompanies marriage breakdown, and these micro-events have their counterparts at the level of aggregate statistics. A divorce or separation means that a family unit, size *n*, with two potential earners becomes two units—usually one single-person household and the other a

Table 2.1

U.S. Households, By Type and Total Money Income in 1980
(number in thousands, households as of March, 1981)

Total Money Income	All Households	Family Households					Nonfamily Households					
		Total	Type of Family				Single-Person Household			Multiple-Person Household		
			Married Couple	Male Householder, Wife Absent	Female Householder, Husband Absent	Total	Total	Sex of Person		Total	Sex of Householder	
								Male	Female		Male	Female
All Races												
Total	82,368	60,309	49,294	1,933	9,082	22,059	18,936	7,253	11,683	3,123	2,025	1,098
Under $2,500	2,511	1,203	570	44	589	1,307	1,277	450	827	31	20	11
$2,500 to $4,999	7,172	2,407	1,031	63	1,312	4,765	4,678	1,069	3,609	87	58	29
$5,000 to $7,499	6,832	3,694	2,239	164	1,291	3,138	2,957	878	2,080	181	98	83
$7,500 to $9,999	6,176	3,851	2,655	163	1,033	2,325	2,099	762	1,337	226	138	88
$10,000 to $12,499	6,509	4,345	3,239	158	948	2,164	1,906	766	1,140	258	160	99
$12,500 to $14,999	5,734	4,141	3,218	147	776	1,594	1,337	548	789	257	156	101
$15,000 to $17,499	5,817	4,339	3,530	162	647	1,477	1,209	591	618	268	163	105
$17,500 to $19,999	5,147	4,093	3,400	131	561	1,054	828	427	402	226	125	101
$20,000 to $22,499	5,522	4,476	3,853	146	477	1,046	780	460	320	267	194	72
$22,500 to $24,999	4,495	3,840	3,347	151	342	654	473	283	190	181	122	59
$25,000 to $27,499	4,432	3,863	3,480	124	259	569	398	289	109	171	113	58
$27,500 to $29,999	3,330	2,975	2,730	76	169	355	191	141	49	164	105	59
$30,000 to $32,499	3,418	3,035	2,800	75	160	383	217	150	67	166	104	62
$32,500 to $34,999	2,408	2,175	2,032	38	105	233	110	73	37	123	86	37
$35,000 to $37,499	2,316	2,125	1,976	37	111	191	98	80	17	93	55	39
$37,500 to $39,999	1,624	1,510	1,399	50	60	114	50	27	23	64	47	18

$40,000 to $44,999	2,766	2,557	2,389	72	97	209	84	71	13	125	98	27
$45,000 to $49,999	1,759	1,615	1,533	33	49	144	62	46	16	82	60	21
$50,000 to $59,999	2,128	1,969	1,868	50	52	159	79	55	24	80	60	19
$60,000 to $74,999	1,222	1,128	1,087	25	16	95	51	45	5	44	38	6
$75,000 and over	1,051	967	916	25	26	84	53	43	10	31	23	7
Median income—dollars	17,710	21,162	23,180	18,775	10,830	9,456	8,162	11,527	6,690	20,264	21,217	18,350
Mean income—dollars	21,063	24,118	26,171	21,743	13,480	12,711	10,981	14,347	8,891	23,199	24,301	21,165
Income per household member—dollars	7,720	7,328	7,831	7,626	4,336	10,688	10,981	14,347	8,891	9,930	10,277	9,266
Mean size of household	2.73	3.29	3.34	2.85	3.11	1.19	1.00	1.00	1.00	2.34	2.36	2.28
Number with earnings—thousands	65,724	52,151	43,396	1,711	7,043	13,573	10,656	5,415	5,241	2,917	1,907	1,010
Median earnings—dollars	18,913	20,867	22,752	17,483	10,304	12,497	11,423	13,716	9,923	19,264	20,462	17,062
Mean earnings—dollars	21,402	23,101	25,029	19,951	11,991	14,873	12,984	15,424	10,464	21,776	23,073	19,327
Mean number of earners	1.78	1.92	1.97	1.81	1.63	1.23	1.00	1.00	1.00	2.06	2.07	2.06

Source: U.S., Department of Commerce, Bureau of the Census. Current Population Reports (C.P.R.), Series P-60, No. 132. Washington: U.S. Government Printing Office, Table 9.

household of size n-1. Since women face lower wages in the labor market than men (see Chapter 7) and usually gain custody of the children, the larger household typically has the lower income, one which is, per capita, *very much* lower than predivorce income. (Now-single males, of course, have much higher per capita incomes.) The Aid to Families with Dependent Children program (AFDC) mitigates some of the financial consequences of separations and many divorced people subsequently remarry after a few years, but rising divorce rates nevertheless produce increasing numbers of low-income family units and increased family income inequality. Orcutt, Caldwell, and Wertheimer (1976) compared the impact of divorce rates which remain constant (at the 1974 level) over the period 1975 to 1984 with the impact of divorce rates that rose over the same period by the average percentage increase of the early 1970s. Rising divorce rates imply an increase of 1.8 million in the number of female-headed family units. Since this type of family is the least well-off in U.S. society, 4.5 million additional people could be expected to suffer a 40% drop in per capita income if divorce rates continue to increase—implying a powerful trend to increasing family income inequality.

2.2 Measuring the Inequality of Income

2.2.1 Quintile Shares An "obvious" way of measuring the inequality in the income distribution at any point in time is to calculate the share of the total income of a society which is received by the "poor" and by the "rich." If we lined up the whole population in order of income from poorest to richest and then divided the line into five equal groups, each group would be called a "quintile." Table 2.2 gives the share of different quintiles of households in total income by households and by family. An equal distribution of income would imply that each quintile received 20% of total income—i.e., the poorest 20% of households would receive 20% of the total income, as would the richest 20% of households. By contrast, one can note that during the period in which these statistics have been collected the share of the poorest 20% of households has remained roughly constant at around 4.2% of total income while the share of the richest 20% of households has remained roughly constant at around 44% of total income—if anything there has been some tendency to a recent decline in the share of the poorest 20% of households.[4] Statistics on the 1930s are fragmentary but appear to indicate a somewhat higher level of income inequality—i.e., income inequality appears to have decreased during World War II.

This constancy of income share since World War II should be something of a surprise since a great deal has happened in the American economy in the last thirty years. Real per capita personal income has considerably more than doubled, the labor force participation of married

Table 2.2

Income Shares of Americans
Family Units by Quintiles
(share by households in parentheses)

	Poorest 20%	2	3	4	Top 20%	Top 5%
1980	3.8 (4.1)	9.7 (10.2)	16.4 (16.8)	24.8 (24.8)	45.3 (44.2)	17.0 (16.5)
1979	3.8 (4.1)	9.7 (10.2)	16.4 (16.8)	24.8 (24.7)	45.3 (44.2)	17.4 (15.8)
1978	3.8 (4.3)	9.7 (10.3)	16.4 (16.9)	24.8 (24.7)	45.2 (43.9)	17.3 (16.6)
1977	3.8 (4.3)	9.7 (10.3)	16.5 (16.9)	24.9 (24.7)	45.2 (43.8)	17.3 (16.6)
1976	3.8 (4.3)	9.9 (10.4)	16.7 (17.0)	24.9 (24.7)	44.7 (43.6)	17.1 (16.5)
1975	3.9 (4.3)	9.9 (10.4)	16.7 (17.1)	24.9 (24.7)	44.5 (43.4)	17.0 (16.3)
1970	3.6 (4.1)	10.3 (10.8)	17.2 (17.4)	24.7 (24.5)	44.1 (43.3)	16.9 (16.8)
1965	3.6	10.6	17.5	24.8	43.6	16.6
1960	3.2	10.6	17.6	24.7	44.0	17.0
1955	3.3	10.6	17.6	24.6	43.9	17.5
1950	3.1	10.6	17.3	24.1	44.9	18.2
1947	3.5	10.6	16.8	23.6	45.5	18.7
1947	5.0	11.0	16.0	22.0	46.0	
1941	4.1	9.5	15.3	22.3	48.8	
1935/36	4.1	9.2	14.1	20.9	51.7	
1929	12.5 (poorest 40% combined)		13.8	19.3	54.4	

Sources: 1929-47—U.S., Department of Commerce, Bureau of the Census. *Historical Statistics of the United States*, Part 1, Series G319-G324. Washington: U.S. Government Printing Office, p. 301.
1947-80—Bureau of the Census, C.P.R. Series P. 60, No. 121 (Households), No. 123 (Families), No. 132 (Households and Families).

women has more than tripled, the number of families composed of only one person has increased dramatically, and, recently, inflation has played havoc with money wage rates and the returns from different assets. All these factors could be expected to affect income shares. Having two family members in paid employment, for example, pushes the money income of many families into the middle-class range. The rise in female labor force participation therefore tends to decrease inequality, if measured in money income terms. Measured in terms of economic well-being, however, the decrease in inequality is far less, since working in the labor market means a decrease in time available for other things—goods that were previously produced at home (e.g., meals, child care) must now be purchased (see Chapter 8, section 8.4). On the other hand, some of the increase in single-person households might mean that income inequality is now overstated since it may be a sign of affluence that young workers or retired parents set up their own (low-income) household rather than continue to live at home.

Table 2.2 gives a fairly good picture of the income shares of Americans but it requires five numbers to describe the income distribution at any given point in time. This method could be improved by examining the shares of each decile (i.e., each 10%) of the population, but that would require even more numbers. All these numbers can appear confusing if one is looking for an answer to the seemingly simple question of whether income inequality is "greater" or "less" now than in 1950 or "greater" or "less" in the United States than in Britain or Germany. Economists yearn to answer such seemingly simple questions and have therefore been fascinated for years with the search for an index of inequality which could summarize the income distribution in a single number.

2.2.2 The Gini Index of Inequality One of the most popular indices of the extent of inequality was also one of the earliest proposed. In Figure 2.1, if one graphs the cumulative percentage of households along the horizontal axis and the cumulative percentage of income received by those households along the vertical axis, one has what is known as a Lorenz curve (Lorenz, 1905). In fact, Table 2.2 enables us to find five points on the Lorenz curve for 1980 since A is the point where the poorest 20% of households received 4.1% of total income, B is the point where the poorest 40% of households received (4.1 + 10.2 =) 14.3% of total income, C is the point where the poorest 60% get (14.3 + 16.8 =) 31.1%, D represents the fact that the poorest 80% of households receive (31.1 + 24.8 =) 55.9%, and E represents the fact that the bottom 95% get 83.5% of total income. If Table 2.2 were the only source of data we had available, we could draw an approximation to the Lorenz curve (i.e., a polygon) by simply connecting the points O, A, B, C, D, E, and Y. Such an approximation would be rather crude and clearly could be improved if data were available on a larger number of income intervals. Where the incomes of individual respondents are reported, the Lorenz curve can be drawn exactly.

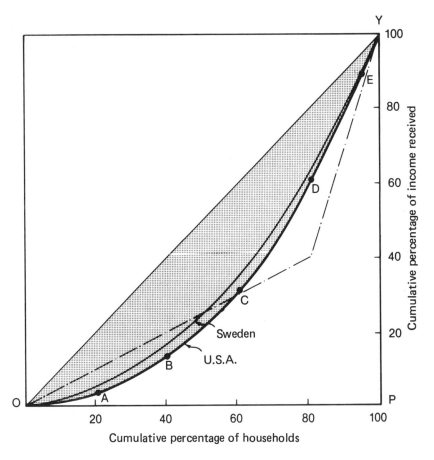

Figure 2.1 THE GINI INDEX OF INEQUALITY

Corrado Gini (1912) proposed that the extent of inequality in a society might be measured by the ratio of the area between the Lorenz curve and the line OY (shaded in the diagram) and the area of the entire triangle OPY. If everyone had equal incomes, each quintile of the income distribution would receive exactly 20% of total income and the Lorenz curve would coincide with the diagonal OY. Then the shaded area would disappear and the Gini index would be 0. By contrast, a situation of "perfect inequality" where one person had all the income and everyone else had none would imply that the Lorenz curve lies along the line OP for virtually all its length and the area between it and the diagonal would be almost exactly equal to the area of the entire triangle OPY—hence the Gini index would be very close to one. The real world falls between these two extremes—in 1980 the Gini index for the distribution of money income among American households was 0.4.[5] The Gini coefficient for Sweden is 0.346 and the Lorenz curve for Sweden lies entirely inside the

U.S. Lorenz curve. Thus, one can say unambiguously that the Swedish income distribution is more equal than America's. Unfortunately, this unambiguous situation is relatively rare and it is more common for the Lorenz curves of different societies (or the same societies at different points in time) to intersect. In this case interpretation of the Gini coefficient becomes much more problematic—as the following example (admittedly extreme) may indicate.

Suppose there were a society (call it "Adanac") in which the top 20% of households all had annual incomes of $63,189 while all other families had annual incomes of $10,531. This would mean that the bottom 80% of households share equally 40% of total income (each of the bottom four quintiles getting 10%) while the top quintile shares equally the remaining 60% of total income. These figures have been picked so that average income of Adanac ($21,063) is the same as the average income of American households in 1980. Remembering that each of the bottom four quintiles of Adanac receives 10% of total income, one can compare its income distribution with the 1980 U.S. distribution (see Table 2.2). Both the poorest and the richest quintile would receive a larger share of total income in Adanac than in the United States—the poorest quintile would get 10% instead of 4.1% and the richest quintile would get 60% instead of 44.2% (the top 5% would lose, getting 15% in Adanac versus 16.5% in the United States). The second quintile would be approximately equally well-off but the third and fourth quintiles would be significantly less well-off. Is Adanac more "equal" or "less equal" than America? The Lorenz curve for this mythical society is drawn as the dashed line in Figure 2.1 and one can note that it lies above the U.S. Lorenz curve over approximately the bottom three quintiles before crossing and lying below it for the remainder. One might well think that a society where 20% of households have incomes six times the incomes of the remaining 80% would be a much more unequal society than the United States—but in fact the numbers in this example have been chosen so that the Gini coefficient of this mythical society is 0.4, i.e., the same as America's! Societies which are very similar in terms of average income and Gini coefficient can have very different income distributions.

One may adopt the Gini index as an indicator of the extent of income inequality, but the interpretation which one places on it will depend on the mechanism which produced that distribution of income and the values by which one judges both the mechanism and the ensuing distribution. A caste society in which the top 20% of households were able to pass their incomes of $63,189 on to each succeeding generation while all other households inherited an annual income of $10,531 would be judged by most to be extremely unfair. If the income distribution of Adanac were determined by a truly random lottery in which each person had the same 20% chance of winning an income for life of $63,189, it would be more "fair" in the sense that all individuals at least had an equal opportunity of joining the privileged classes. In both the above examples annual income is a good indicator of total lifetime income, but where this is not the case income inequality may be a poor indicator of the extent of economic inequality.

In our society, old people are generally poorer than average but in African societies which are organized along an "age set" principle old people enjoy much greater status, authority, and income than average. If Adanac were organized along the principle that the youngest 80% of the population had annual incomes of $10,531 while the oldest 20% had annual incomes of $63,189 the Gini index of inequality of *annual* incomes would still equal 0.4—even though (assuming equal lifetimes) each person could expect, eventually, to become wealthy and everyone would, over his or her lifetime, receive the same total income. This example may be as unrealistic as Adanac but it illustrates the importance of looking beyond annual income to broader ideas of economic inequality (i.e., Chapter 3).

In many cases, a picture is "worth a thousand words" and a useful picture of the American income distribution is that of Figure 2.2. In it, annual dollar income is shown along the horizontal axis and the percentage of all households which are in that income class is measured vertically. As is typical of income distribution in most countries, the resulting graph shows a large hump concentrated among lower incomes and a long tail extending out to the right denoting the small percentage of households which receive high annual incomes. Indeed, one cannot both preserve the scale of the diagram and include everyone in it as those households with incomes as high as $100,000 or $200,000 (although only a small fraction of the entire population) are simply off the page entirely! The dividing lines between the income quintiles of Table 2.2 are marked in Figure 2.2 as A, B, C, D, and E.[6] One can note that the bottom four quintiles span intervals of more or less $7,000 each but the top 20% includes everyone from associate professors to multimillionaires. It takes only a few very high incomes to pull up the arithmetic average of incomes fairly substantially; hence average income $(\bar{Y})$ is approximately $3,000 higher than median income Y_M (the income which separates the poorest and richest halves of the population). Jan Pen (1971) paints a fascinating "word picture" of the income distribution of individuals when he likens it to a parade of people whose height is proportional to their income and who all must pass a certain point in an hour. It takes 48 minutes before one sees marchers of average heights (income) and the parade grows with agonizing slowness until giants of 27 feet loom up at 1 minute to go. From then on, their height increases with dizzying rapidity—in the last few seconds of the march come businessmen and executives 100 feet tall while the final marcher (a multimillionaire) is some thousands of feet high.

More concretely, the 1980 data indicate that 20% of households had total money incomes less than $7,478; 40% had incomes under $14,024; 60% were under $21,500; 80% were under $31,480; and 95% were under

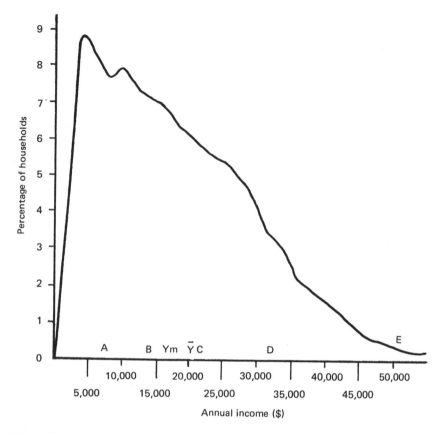

Source: Bureau of the Census, C.P.R. *Money Income of Households, Families, and persons in the United States*, p. 60, No. 132, 1980, p. 11.

Figure 2.2

$50,661 (Bureau of the Census, *P-60, No. 132*, Table 5). Since hourly wages are more familiar to many people, one can calculate that if each household had one earner (and no income from any other source) a "normal" 2,000 hours per year (= 50 weeks per year × 40 hours per week) would mean that the bottom quintile would consist of those earning $3.74 per hour or less, while the next quintile's wages would lie in the range $3.75 to $7.00, and the third and fourth quintiles would range up to $10.75 and $15.75 per hour respectively. Of course, in reality the bottom quintile is heavily dependent on transfer payments and the number of earners and hours worked differs greatly across households. Especially in the lower quintile (the poverty population) many households are composed of retired people or mothers with young children (see Table 4.5). Many households in the middle-income groups are there only because they have two (or more) earners. Unemployment, even for part of the year, means that wages which might appear high on an hourly basis (e.g., in construction) must be spread over slack periods as well. And, of course, in thinking in terms of hourly wages one must remember that households differ in size and what is "good money" to a college student who lives at home or shares rent with roommates is bare subsistence if the same wage must support a family.[7]

   2.2.3 The Coefficient of Variation Those who have a statistical background will recognize Figure 2.2 as a frequency distribution and perhaps will wonder if a statistical measure such as the variance of this distribution can be a good index of the inequality in it.[8]

   Unfortunately, the variance of the income distribution is not a particularly good measure of inequality. Most economists have argued that a measure of income inequality should be "scale free" in the sense that it should be unaffected by equiproportionate changes in all incomes (such as might occur if inflation affected everyone equally) or by changes purely in the size of the population (such as might occur if two separate, identical, societies were merged). One can, however, "normalize" the variance so that it is unaffected by such changes by dividing its square root by the average income. The resulting measure is called the "coefficient of variation."[9] Like the Gini coefficient, the coefficient of variation is unaffected by "scale." Both measures also have the desirable characteristic that they decrease (i.e., show less inequality) if income is transferred from a richer individual to a poorer individual.[10]

   Using the idea of transfers, let us examine the responsiveness of the Gini ratio and the coefficient of variation to changes in the income distribution which occur at different points in the income distribution. Hypothetically, consider two possible transfers: (a) a transfer of $100 of annual income from the Smith family, who have an annual income of $100,000, to the Jones family, who have an annual income of $99,000; (b) a transfer of $100 in income from the Gray family, annual income $18,000, to the White family, annual income $17,000. Since the coefficient of variation is calculated from the variance, which in turn depends on the *absolute difference* between an individual family income and the average income, and since the same *size* of transfer ($100) is involved in both cases, both transfers would produce the same size of change in the coefficient of variation. The Gini ratio, however, depends on the Lorenz curve, which expresses the *cumulated percentage of income received by households*. Hence the size of the change in the Gini ratio is affected by the number of households who have incomes between the incomes of those who are involved directly by the transfer. Since very few households have incomes in the range $99,000 to $100,000 while a great many are in the range of $17,000 to $18,000, the Gini ratio will decline by considerably less if $100 is transferred from the higher income Smiths to the high income Jones than if $100 is transferred from the low income Grays to the lower income Whites. If, therefore, one wishes to measure the extent of changes in the inequality of income distribution one must remember that the Gini ratio is more sensitive to changes which occur in the middle ranges of the income distribution than among the very poor or the very rich, while the coefficient of variation is more sensitive to changes in the upper income ranges.

The choice of a measure of income inequality cannot, therefore, be "value free." In addition to the problem of choosing which economic variable (e.g., income, earnings, or wealth) and which population (e.g., households, individuals, or family units) one is concerned with, there is also the problem of which statistical measure one wishes to use to summarize the inequality of that variable among that population. Basically, one must "choose one's index of inequality to be sensitive to changes (in the income distribution) of that type with which one is primarily concerned" (Champernowne, 1974: 806) since different indices of inequality will emphasize more heavily changes in different parts of the income distribution.[11]

2.2.4 Theil's Index of Inequality If you knew that a society contained one hundred households and had an equal distribution of income, you would not be surprised to learn that each family received 1% of total income. "Surprise" is a key concept in information theory since when a message is completely predictable it conveys no information (i.e., does not surprise). When a message tells you something you did not already know (i.e., surprises you) it conveys information. Similarly, when income is equally distributed or nearly so, income for any individual is predictable. When income is unequally distributed, however, it is less easy to predict the income of any randomly chosen individual and a message which tells us what that individual's income is has information content. Theil (1967:90-134) has therefore proposed that the inequality of income distribution be measured with the aid of some concepts developed in information theory to measure the average information content (surprise) of a series of messages.[12]

Often, income distribution data are available only on a group basis— i.e., one knows that the n individuals in a society are divided into g groups where N_g denotes the number of people in group g and Y_g denotes the average income of that group. The formula for the Theil index of inequality then becomes somewhat more complex.[13] But one of the great advantages of the Theil index of inequality is its property of decomposition, i.e., the straightforward way in which inequality in a total society can be broken down into the components of inequality which exist between and within different social groups.[14] In fact, Shorrocks (1980), Cowell (1980), and Marfels (1972b) have independently shown that if one wishes a measure of total inequality (1) which can be decomposed into between-group inequality and within-group inequality, (2) which is "scale free," and (3) which respects the principle of transfers, only the Theil measure will do.

Like the Gini ratio and the coefficient of variation the Theil index satisfies the "principle of transfers" in that a transfer of income from a richer to a poorer person implies a decrease in the index. The size of the change in the Theil index of inequality for any given transfer of income, however, depends on the changes in the *ratio* to average income of the incomes of the individuals involved in the transfer. If we consider, again, a $100 transfer between two high-income families and compare it to the effect of a $100 transfer between middle-income families, the same dollar transfer will cause a small change in the ratio of high incomes to the average and a larger change in the ratio of low incomes to the average.[15] The Theil index, like the Gini index, is therefore most sensitive to movements in the middle part of the distribution.

2.2.5 Atkinson's Measure Implicitly, the choice between the Gini ratio, the coefficient of variation, and the Theil index as measures by which to rank the inequality of societies inevitably implies value judgments. Of course, if one is comparing two societies whose Lorenz curves do not cross (i.e., the Lorenz curve for one lies completely inside the Lorenz curve of the other) Atkinson (1970) has shown that the choice of an inequality index is relatively unimportant since they will all give the same ranking. A choice of inequality index is important, however, when Lorenz curves intersect, as they commonly do. Out of sixty-six comparisons of countries, Atkinson found that in fifty cases the Lorenz curves crossed. This implies that the choice of inequality index may reverse the ranking of societies; e.g., measured by the Gini index of inequality the Netherlands may be seen as more equal than Sweden, but measured by the coefficient of variation Sweden may seem more equal than the Netherlands. Choosing among these two indices of inequality in such a case will necessarily involve a value judgment, as we will wish to use the coefficient of variation if we consider inequality between the middle class and the very rich to be especially important while we will wish to use the Gini index if we wish to give more weight to the inequality among the middle classes.

Atkinson has argued that, since value judgments are unavoidable, we should make them more explicit—i.e., specify our "social welfare function." In particular, he argues that one might want to be specific about the degree of "inequality aversion" with which one approaches the issue of the income distribution. He sees "inequality aversion" as the price which society is willing to pay in order to decrease income inequality. Atkinson argues that if we are considering taking one dollar from a rich person and giving a proportion x to a poor person (the remainder being lost in the process—for example, in administering the transfer), we ought to ask, "At what level of x do we cease to regard the redistribution as desirable?" If all the income lost by the rich actually gets to the poor (i.e., $x = 1$) then anyone at all concerned about inequality sees redistribution as desirable. If only a small fraction (say 20%) gets to the poor, presumably only those who are very concerned about inequality will see the transfer as desirable. "What is crucial is how far one is prepared to let x fall below 1 before calling for a stop" (Atkinson, 1973:49). Another way of putting it is to say that society would be equally well-off if all incomes were the same, even if these equal incomes were only x percent of current average income. If we argue for a low value of x, we are highly "inequality averse"—i.e., we believe society would be equally well off with an equal distribution of income, even if its average were only (for example) two-thirds of current average income.

Notice that we have introduced the idea of "society's" having different degrees of welfare. Economists often argue that "social welfare" depends on the incomes of the individuals which make up a society and that the way in which social welfare depends on individual income can be expressed as a "social welfare function."[16] If we prefer one society to another solely because its index of inequality is lower, one can see this as implicitly saying that the social welfare of the first is greater than that of the second. Our ranking, however, may depend on the index of inequality which we chose—hence the choice of index implicitly involves a choice of a social welfare function.

Atkinson's measure of inequality requires that we should specify ϵ— our degree of "inequality aversion."[17] Specifying a high value of ϵ implies that we are most concerned with the share of the bottom end of the income distribution, while specifying a relatively low value of ϵ means that we are particularly sensitive to changes in distribution at the top end.

2.3 International Comparisons

The various measures of section 2.2 may indicate how much income inequality exists in a society but by themselves they are mere numbers and cannot say whether this degree of inequality is "a lot," or "a little." Such statements are relative ones and involve a comparison either between the inequality of this society and that existing in other societies or between current inequality and past or possible future inequality. Comparisons between countries that are broadly similar in level of economic development and social organization (i.e., rich and capitalist) are helpful in answering such "reformist" questions as whether it is possible to make changes in the income distribution, within a familiar social and political framework. More fundamental questions, e.g., the impact socialism would have on the income distribution, cannot be answered with statistics alone.

Even comparisons of inequality among capitalist countries are, however, fraught with many difficulties. Countries differ slightly in the definitions they use of income and of household.[18] They differ as well in the extent of coverage of their population and of income which their statistical authorities succeed in achieving. Errors and omissions also differ in importance. When a survey of households is conducted (as by the Census Bureau), poor memories or modesty may prevent some respondents from giving an accurate answer as to their annual income. Where taxes are concerned, natural modesty tends to be reinforced by a certain financial incentive. Several studies have found (e.g., Projector and Weiss, 1966) upper-income groups tend to understate their income rather more than lower-income groups largely because some *types* of income are particularly susceptible to being understated (e.g., income from rents, dividends, one's own business, or professional employment are poorly reported—salaries are generally fairly accurate).

One can check these suspicions of underreporting by adding up the income which individuals do report and checking the total against aggregate estimates of income from GNP statistics. Sawyer (1976) and Stark (1977) have conducted extensive comparisons of the estimates of income distribution in developed economies. Comparing the coverage of income achieved in those countries which use large-scale labor force surveys as a data source, Stark (1977:210) concluded, "The overall coverage of total personal income ranges from 76 percent for the American data to 84 percent for the Australian and Canadian sources respectively. The American survey is particularly deficient with respect to incomes from rent, dividends and interest. This may cause some understatement in the degree of dispersion." Sawyer (1976:513) found that American statistics succeed in counting 98.3% of wage and salary income, 91.1% of entrepreneurial income, and 45% of property income in the income distribution statistics. By comparison with other countries (with the exception of France) the United States does relatively poorly in capturing capital income in its income distribution statistics.

In a sample survey such as the Current Population Survey (C.P.S.), reported money income may not equal actual money income if some types of respondents are undersampled, or if respondents make mistakes in estimating income, or if they conceal some income from interviewers. Radner (1981a, 1981b) has recently checked the money income reported by respondents to the Current Population Survey of the Bureau of the Census by comparing their responses to income reported for tax purposes. He used a statistical match of respondents to the 1972 Current Population Report and the 1972 Statistics of Income File from individual tax returns. In aggregate, money income was underreported to the C.P.S. by about 12%, but there were striking differences by income type. On balance, he concluded that the C.P.S. underestimated wages and salaries by 3%, Social Security by 3%, self-employment income by 24%, government transfer income by 42%, and property income (interest, dividends, rent, royalty, and trust) by a whopping 135%. Since property income is highly concentrated among the more affluent, he concluded that the C.P.S. underestimated the share of the top 5% by about one-tenth, and overestimated somewhat the shares of the fourth through ninth deciles.

Comparisons across societies of the distribution of family money income are also affected by variation in family size and structure (see Kuznets, 1976). Societies differ widely in such social norms as the appropriate age at which children should leave home to establish separate households and in the degree to which aged parents reside with their married children or separately. Different social norms and differences in the cost of maintaining separate households cause the proportion of single-person households to differ very widely among nations—from a low of 6.6% in Spain to high of 45.4% in the Netherlands (Sawyer, 1976:18). Since small households tend to have considerably lower incomes than average, a society which has a large proportion of single-person households will tend to have an income distribution which shows a large number of households at low income levels. Its distribution of economic welfare may, however, be just as equal as a society where young workers and older retired people stay in the family unit and add their (low) incomes to the household total. Correcting for such differences in the distribution of household size, we present in Table 2.3 the results of Sawyer (1976)[19] for the OECD nations (also adjusted for the impact of direct taxes). He cautions, "It is only when the international differences are large that unequivocal statements on intercountry degrees of inequality can be made." His caution arises partly because of the statistical deficiencies of the data (such as the underreporting of capital income in the United States) and partly because it was impossible for him to account for variations in the impact of indirect taxation and government expenditure across nations.

Nevertheless it is fairly clear that the Netherlands, Sweden, and Norway are the most equal of the OECD nations while the most unequal are France and Spain. Rankings of inequality are often ambiguous.[20] By the Gini index of inequality, the Netherlands is the most equal but by the coefficient of variation measure (which emphasizes high incomes) Sweden is. Using Atkinson's measure with a low ϵ value (i.e., emphasizing the middle and top end of the distribution) we infer that Canada is more equal than Germany but if we emphasize the inequality between the poor and the rest of society (high ϵ) Canada is more unequal than Germany.

In terms of "inequality rankings" if we use measures such as the Gini, Theil, or Atkinson (where $\epsilon = 0.5$) only France, Spain, and Germany were more unequal than the United States in the early 1970s. Using the measure most sensitive to the "upper tail" of the distribution, the coefficient of variation, the United States tied with Japan, behind France, Germany, and Spain. On balance, among these eleven countries, the United States was, in the early 1970s, among the more unequal, particularly insofar as inequality reflects the condition of the poor.

A particularly noteworthy difference is that in America the poorest 20% of households are considerably less well-off than that group is in the social democracies of Western Europe. The fraction of national income

Table 2.3
International Income Inequality—Posttax, "Standardized" Household Size

| | Year | Share of Income Received by Income Quintiles | | | | | Inequality Indices | | | Atkinson | |
		1	2	3	4	5	Gini	Theil	C.V.*	$\epsilon = 0.5$	$\epsilon = 1.5$
Australia	1966/67	4.8	12.2	17.8	24.1	40.9	.354	.091	.065	.106	.329
France	1970	4.2	9.7	16.2	22.8	47.1	.417	.126	.081	.143	.401
Germany	1973	6.5	10.3	14.9	21.9	46.3	.386	.110	.078	.118	.299
Japan	1969	7.1	12.4	16.8	21.7	41.9	.336	.084	.068	.092	.247
Netherlands	1967	9.1	14.5	17.5	22.5	36.3	.264	.050	.050	.057	.167
Norway	1970	6.6	13.0	18.9	24.7	36.9	.301	.064	.055	.076	.236
Spain	1971	4.2	10.2	16.8	24.0	45.0	.397	.113	.076	.132	.383
Sweden	1972	7.3	14.1	19.0	24.7	35.0	.271	.051	.048	.063	.201
United Kingdom	1973	6.1	12.2	18.4	24.0	39.3	.327	.076	.060	.088	.261
U.S.A.	1972	4.9	10.9	17.5	24.6	42.1	.369	.097	.068	.113	.338
Canada	1972	5.2	12.0	18.0	24.2	40.5	.348	.087	.063	.103	.320
Average		6.0	12	17.5	23.5	41.0					

Source: M. Sawyer, July 1976: Tables 10, 11.
*Coefficient of variation calculated from decile shares.

going to the poorest 20% in Sweden in 1972 was, for example, 48% higher than that fraction in the United States. The least well-off quintile in the Netherlands received a share of national income fully 85% greater than that it would receive in the United States. These are large differences, especially from the point of view of the poor.

Stark (1977) omitted Spain, the Netherlands, and Norway from his list of comparisons but included Ireland. His emphasis was on trends in the distribution of income within each country and on comparison of income distribution figures drawn from a similar statistical basis. Comparing the taxation statistics of the United States, the United Kingdom, Germany, Ireland, and France, he concluded that the distribution of all taxable incomes in the United States is markedly more unequal than elsewhere, "with a long run trend to increased dispersion" (1977:215). Comparing the distribution of income across consuming units for the United States, the United Kingdom, and Canada, he found that neither the United States nor Canada showed a trend toward equality in the 1970s and there is too little data to discern any U.K. trends. The level of inequality was less in the United Kingdom than in Canada, and less in Canada than in the United States (1977:219). Finally, Stark examined the distribution of posttax personal income by household, unadjusted for household size. Again, he found a trend to increased U.S. inequality since 1968. In this comparison of eight countries, he found France to be the most unequal and the United States the second most unequal, measured either by the Gini index or by the share of income of the top quintile or by the share of income of the poorest 20% (1977:224).

2.4 Summary and Conclusions

(1) Definitions are important in a study of inequality. Different definitions of what is being distributed among whom will affect our perceptions of the extent of inequality. For example, measuring inequality of annual money income among households measures only one aspect of economic inequality, but even here the use of a "household" concept rather than a "family unit" concept will indicate an apparently lower degree of inequality. In the text we have used the household concept but this measure does not reveal inequalities of consumption within households. The "correct" definitions with which to organize data depend entirely on what question one wants to ask of the data, but unfortunately most researchers have no feasible option but to use data in the form in which they are presented.

(2) Examination of income quintile data reveals that the distribution of money income among households has remained fairly constant over the post-World War II period. This is a surprising and highly important finding, since a great deal has happened over the same period which might have been expected to change the income distribution.

(3) Detailed examination of income distribution statistics may reveal some differences (or no differences) but in general one should be very cautious of such statements as "country X is more equal than country Y" or "country X is more equal (or unequal) now than it was some years ago." It may be that such statements are unambiguously true but it may also be the case that they depend on the use of a particular measure of inequality and would be contradicted by other measures of inequality. The Gini coefficient, like the Theil index, is more responsive to changes in distribution among the middle classes while the coefficient of variation emphasizes more heavily inequality between the top and the middle of the income (or wealth) distribution. Atkinson's measure may be specified so as to emphasize either the high or the low end of the distribution. The Theil measure of inequality should be used when one wishes to "decompose" aggregate inequality into that inequality which exists within groups and that inequality which exists between groups. In analyzing inequality, one should therefore choose the measure of inequality which is most sensitive to the type of inequality in which one is primarily interested— and that choice must depend, again, on the issue at hand.

(4) One must, as a consequence, remain somewhat cautious about the conclusions of studies which examine only one measure of inequal- ity—e.g., the Gini index. Conclusions based on a single index of inequal- ity—for example, on tax incidence (Reynolds and Smolensky, 1977) or the distribution of earnings capacity (Garfinkel and Haveman, 1977)—are useful and should not be ignored, but a different index of inequality might yield a different result. For example, using the Gini index, Blinder's simulation study (1974: 119–140) concluded that inherited wealth had a very small impact on aggregate inequality—but inherited wealth is likely to be an important factor only for the upper tail of the income distribution and changes in the upper tail are poorly captured by a Gini index. Use of a different measure (e.g., the coefficient of variation) would indicate inheri- ted wealth to be more important. How much more important we do not as yet know.

(5) Comparing income distributions internationally is made more difficult by the considerable differences in statistical sources and social structure which exist, even among developed capitalist nations. Never- theless it appears that most measures of inequality would place the United States "among the more unequal" of OECD nations—a degree of inequal- ity which is particularly high when we emphasize the share of total income going to the poor.

NOTES

[1]In fact, neither do all families share consumption. Pahl (1980) has argued that there may be great *within-family* inequality in families which practice an "allowance" system in which a fixed sum is made available to the wife each month for household purchases while the husband spends the remainder. However, there is very little reliable data on intrafamily economic inequality. Concentration on *family* income levels assumes that "one cannot be

poor in a rich family" and implicitly sets intrafamily inequality at zero. This is a bad assumption, but an inescapable one, given current data.

[2]Suppose that instead of talking of the distribution of income among *households,* we had focused on the distribution of income among family units (families plus unrelated individuals). We would then have counted unrelated individuals living in households as separate, one-person family units. Since there were 3,123,000 households all of whose members were unrelated, a distribution of income among *family units* would count these 7,297,000 people as being one-person family units—whose average income was $9,930. As it is, they are counted as 3,123,000 households, with an average income of $23,199. A distribution of income among *family units* therefore displays more inequality than a distribution among households, since counting households means that several low-income individuals are added together into one medium-income household.

[3]We consider this issue again in Chapter 3, section 3.5.3

[4]One can note that, when the top 5% receive 16.5% and the bottom 20% get 4.1%, the incomes of the top 5% are roughly 16 times that of the bottom 20%, on average.

[5]The Gini coefficient can be calculated as equation (2.1). For a further discussion, see Marfels (1972a), or, for a generalization of the Gini index, see Donaldson and Weymark (1980).

(2.1)
$$G = \frac{1}{2\bar{Y} \cdot n \cdot (n-1)} \cdot \sum_{i}^{n} \sum_{\neq j}^{n} |Y_i - Y_j|$$

where: (1) Y_i and Y_j are the incomes of the ith and jth family units,
(2) $\bar{Y}$ is the average income, and

(3) n is the number of family units.

[6]The income shares of various groups can be read off Figure 2.2. For example, if the total area under the graph represents 100% of personal income, the area under the graph over the interval OB then represents the share of total personal income received by the bottom 40%.

[7]High rates of inflation render the dollar figures cited here inappropriate quite rapidly—but since the overall income distribution has changed relatively little, a rough approximation of current values can be obtained by "scaling up" by the rate of inflation.

[8]The variance of a distribution is calculated as equation (2.2).

(2.2)
$$\text{Var}(Y) = \frac{\sum_{i=1}^{n} (Y_i - \bar{Y})^2}{n}$$

[9](2.3)
$$\text{CV} = \frac{\sqrt{\text{Var}(Y)}}{\bar{Y}}$$

[10]This is known as the "principle of transfers." Obviously, the transfer of income must be less than half the original difference between their incomes, as otherwise the transfer would simply reverse the original inequality (see Cowell, 1977:62).

[11]It is worth noting that some measures of inequality that have been proposed are completely insensitive to certain sorts of transfers. For example, measures of inequality such as the "Kuznets" measure which are based on the relative mean deviation do not change at all when income is transferred from a poor person to a richer one, as long as both individuals are on the same side of the average income level. Worse still, a measure such as the variance of the logarithm of income may actually show the perverse result of an apparent decrease in inequality when a transfer of income occurs from a rich person to an even richer one and for that reason is a poor indicator of the extent of income inequality—which does not prevent it from being widely used (e.g., Chiswick and O'Neill, 1977). In the text we consider only measures of income inequality which satisfy the "principle of transfers." None of these measures can, however, escape the problem of Adanac vs. America—that very different societies may appear the same if we use only one number to measure their inequality. Love and Wolfson (1976), Sawyer (1976), Rossi (1979), Cowell (1977), and Champernowne (1974) provide surveys of the characteristics of alternative income inequality measures.

[12]When data on individual income are available the Theil index of inequality is calculated as equation (2.4).

(2.4)
$$R = \frac{1}{n} \sum_i \frac{Y_i}{\overline{Y}} \log \frac{Y_i}{\overline{Y}}$$

[13](2.5)
$$R = \sum_g \frac{n_g \overline{Y}_g}{n \overline{Y}} \cdot R_g + \frac{1}{n} \sum_g n_g \frac{\overline{Y}_g}{\overline{Y}} \log \frac{\overline{Y}_g}{\overline{Y}}$$

Fortunately, this equation has the easy interpretation that the first term in it represents the inequality which exists within group g (R_g), weighted by that group's share of total income, and the second term in it represents the inequality which exists between groups, calculated by the Theil formula. (If we only have data on the income of groups we are often forced to assume incomes within that group are identical—e.g., $R_g = 0$). Up to this point, we have been quite general—the total population could be divided into G groups on the basis of income intervals, regions of the country or age or sex of household head.

[14]Neither the Gini ratio nor the coefficient of variation can be easily decomposed into between-set and within-set components of inequality. Thus, when Paglin (1975) attempted to decompose the trend of total inequality in the United States by age groups he asserted that his "Paglin–Gini" index allowed one to distinguish between the intrafamily variation in income over the life cycle and interfamily variation in lifetime income (the latter being of greater normative interest). However, the so-called "Paglin–Gini" ratio was based on an incorrect decomposition of the Gini index—as Nelson (1977), Danziger, Haveman, and Smolensky (1977), and others were quick to point out. As a result, it does not deserve serious consideration.

[15]Example: if average income is $18,000, $100 transferred to someone with a $90,000 income means their income changes from 5 to 5.0055 times the average—a 0.11% change in the ratio. A $100 transfer to someone with $36,000 income represents a change from 2 to 2.0055 times the average—a 0.27% change in the ratio.

[16]In Atkinson (1970) the social welfare function is required to be "additively separable and symmetric"; i.e., social welfare depends not on who is well-off but only on the amount of individual utility, and the utility of an individual depends only on his own income and not on that of others. This formulation rules out envy or altruism, and, one must say, imposes social values of its own. Some (e.g., Sen, 1979; Dasgupta, Sen, and Starrett, 1973) have therefore criticized this formulation of a social welfare function, arguing that if utility is really *only* dependent on one's own income, why does "society" care about inequality?

[17](2.6)
$$I = 1 - \left[\sum_{i=1}^{n} \left(\frac{Y_i}{\overline{Y}} \right)^{1-\epsilon} \cdot \frac{1}{n} \right] \frac{1}{1 - \epsilon}$$

where

(2.7)
$$X = \frac{1}{2^\epsilon}$$

[18]A concise summary of U.S. data on income distribution and of comparable data sources for other countries is provided by Stark (1977).

[19]Note that by adjusting for family size we eliminate the difference between income inequality calculated on a "household" or "family" basis.

[20]The inevitable delays of reporting are particularly frustrating with these statistics since one would expect that the posttax income distributions of France and Spain in 1970/71 reflect partially the policies of their governments in the preceding decades. Both the Gaullist regimes of postwar France and the Franco regime of Spain (1936-1975) were avowedly right-wing and notably inegalitarian in social policies. In 1981 and 1982 France and Spain elected socialist governments, but one will have to wait to see the impact of these new governments on their countries' income distribution. By contrast, many have argued that recent U.S. policies will accentuate inequality and diminish the share of the poor—e.g., Reuss, 1981.

3 ECONOMIC INEQUALITY

3.1 Introduction

Chapter 2 discussed the distribution of annual money income among family units and households but for many purposes this is an inadequate description of inequality. Economic inequality can be broadly conceived of as differential command over resources, but there are many different types of resources. The aspect of economic inequality which we choose to emphasize will affect our perception of the extent of inequality; it will color our understanding of its causes and, as we will see in Chapters 8 and 9, it will "fit" with only some of the explanations of inequality which exist.

In this chapter, section 3.2 discusses the distribution of economic power while section 3.3 concerns the measurement of the inequality of wealth and of riches. Section 3.4 is a brief summary of evidence on long-term trends in the distribution of wealth. Section 3.5 considers the adjustments for omitted types of income, family size, and lifetime income which can be made to the income distribution statistics of Chapter 2. Section 3.6 is a brief international comparison and section 3.7 is a summary and conclusion.

All of these topics are highly controversial. Data limitations are particularly important elements of the controversy underlying the discussion of economic power and of wealth. In addition, the inequality of lifetime consumption has not been directly observed. The estimates which we discuss of behavior over time are extrapolations from cross-sectional evidence on differences at a point in time and may not be reliable. This chapter does not, naturally, provide the last word on any of these issues since they have a depth and a history which renders final resolution impossible for many generations to come, but it does attempt to outline the main features of current debate.

3.2 Economic Power

Imagine yourself as the chief executive officer of one of America's top 200 corporations. Perhaps your company is not as big as Exxon, with

32

its $103 billion in annual sales, or General Motors, with its 746,000 employees, but as a middling large major enterprise it employed roughly 44,000 people in 1980 and had sales of some $3.4 billion.[1] As chief executive officer you are responsible for $2.7 billion in assets with a net income of $188 million, but your business activities are not limited to only one company. Your company is extensively involved in joint ventures with other members of the top 200[2] and you and your colleagues are often invited to sit on the Board of Directors of other major corporations.[3] As a member of the Business Round-Table, the Chamber of Commerce, and various industry associations you and other chief executives often meet with senior government figures to present your point of view on the economic issues of the day. With your annual income in the $600,000+ range, you have, over the years, acquired a considerable portfolio of assets and are now a wealthy man.[4] You often mix business with pleasure in such businessmen's gatherings as the Knickerbocker Club or the annual Bohemian Grove encampment (Domhoff, 1974).

Your decisions matter, to many people. Local politicians all over the country stress to you the favorable business climates of their areas, in the hope that new investments and new jobs will be directed to their jurisdictions. Some of your employees worry that lower labor costs in your operations overseas will mean plant closing and layoffs here in the United States. Your subordinates know that their chances for promotion, or perhaps for keeping their job, depend on your judgment of their ability. You have power—but you know that that power is far from absolute. Should you make too many money-losing decisions, your bankers may become restive and uncooperative or, in an extreme case, you may find the stock of your company is bid down in price and your company becomes vulnerable to a takeover bid. If your employees are unionized, your hiring and firing decisions may be impeded by a collective agreement—and even if they are not unionized you realize that arbitrary decisions now may sometimes have future costs in morale and productivity. Government also imposes constraints on your operations, only some of which can be avoided with the aid of the legal department. Above all, there is "the market," to which your attitude is ambivalent. On ritual occasions, such as a Chamber of Commerce speech, you are fond of stressing that the market for capital governs your access to resources and the market for your product determines the survival of your company.[5] However, when you walk into the office in the morning neither you nor anyone else is silly enough to pretend that your decisions do not matter.

Economic power is thus difficult to define and even more difficult to measure. A dictionary definition of "power" is "control, authority, or influence over others" (Webster's) and clearly you have authority and control over the thousands of your company's employees, based on your power to hire or fire, to promote or demote. Power in your corporation is clearly unequally distributed since your subordinates have no corresponding degree of control over you. "Influence," either inside or outside the corporation, is necessarily a more elusive concept. In its practical application it is full of subtle nuances. A company's Board of Directors has the formal legal power to hire and to fire senior management and to set corporate policy. "Outside" directors who are not simultaneously officers of the company usually comprise a majority of board members— but effective control usually rests with the more informed "inside" directors, who set the agenda, who determine the selection of new board members, and who can sometimes force the resignation of uncooperative directors.[6] In formal terms a company may be subject to regulation by government agencies whose powers are potentially enormous; in practical terms the agency may be so underfunded as to be ineffectual or so co-opted by long and intimate contact as to be essentially "captured" by the industry in question. In addition, those who are *really* powerful do not usually have to spell out what they want done in a particular instance, since it is worth the while of their subordinates to anticipate their responses and not to take actions which conflict with their known policies. In many cases, therefore, the *observed* exercise of power, the explicit instruction issued or the sanction administered, is evidence of failures of communication or perhaps of challenges to authority much more than it is evidence of the extent of authority. One must therefore distinguish between real and nominal economic power and between the existence and the exercise of that power.

In addition one must be conscious that corporate power is important only in some sectors of the economy. Large firms dominate transport and communications, manufacturing, mining, and the financial sector in the United States[7] but they play a smaller role in trade, services, construction, and agriculture. The 100 largest manufacturing firms control roughly one-half of all U.S. manufacturing assets (Herman, 1981:192) while the top 500 industrials as a group employed some 15.9 million people in 1980, or roughly 64% of all those employed in goods production. If one counts financial firms and utilities as well, the stock of the largest 122 corporations comprised 41% of the market value of all outstanding common stock in the United States in 1976 (U.S., Congress, Senate, 1978b:1). Whatever way one counts it, the largest U.S. corporations are extremely large and important organizations—larger, in many instances, than the economies of entire countries. Moreover, when we examine the influence of major corporations on, for example, local governments we must be aware that their influence will be proportional to the *fraction* of economic activity in that area which they control. If you control a payroll of 3,500 jobs you may be just a face in the crowd in New York City but in Spencer, Iowa (population 10,000) you will be the life and death of the town. To have a large degree of political influence in a major metropolis you will have to make alliances and influence other employers to your point of view; in a smaller center things will tend to be simpler.[8]

Overwhelmingly, major American corporations are not controlled by owner-managers; hence, definitions of "economic power" which are based on ownership are not really appropriate to the United States. In other countries major domestic corporations tend to be controlled by identifiable families or other ownership groups. Nyman and Silberston (1978:77) concluded, for example, that "ownership interests control, in one way or another, the majority of large U.K. industrial companies."[9] In the United States, however, the "Pujo Committee" (chaired by Congressman A. P. Pujo of Louisiana and famous for the questioning of J. P. Morgan on banking) of 1913, Berle and Means in 1932 and, most recently, Herman (1981) have all found the ownership and the control of large U.S. corporations to be two very distinct and separate issues.

Among the top 200 nonfinancial corporations of 1974, Herman (1981:58) found only three that were controlled by identifiable families or individuals with a majority stock holding and a further twenty-nine with some degree of minority ownership control. He classified 82.5% of major U.S. nonfinancial corporations as "management-controlled." Even blocks of stock which are worth quite a lot of money may, for these very large corporations, be a small fraction of shares outstanding and, as Herman puts it (1981:53), "wide diffusion (of share holdings) does not increase the power of holders of small blocks of stock: it enhances the power of whoever controls the proxy machinery." Strategic position is thus key to corporate control. In access to and control of information, in control of the proxy votes of small shareholders at corporate meetings, and in influence over the selection of new board members and high-level management, current top management has a control which cannot be effectively challenged by the diffused mass of small shareholders. Even in companies with a past history of family control, the growth of a company has often meant a need to attract outside equity capital or to merge with other businesses, with a consequent diminution of the relative importance of family share holdings. When succeeding generations of the founding family differ in their interest in company management and in their personal investment plans, their wealth and their involvement in management becomes dispersed over a number of endeavors—leaving management in effective control.

Herman argues, however, that the separation of ownership and control does not necessarily mean that the behavior of large firms will change. Both the ideology of the business community and the organizational constraints of systems of profit center accounting may impel paid managers toward behavior consistent with profitable growth just as surely now as when these large firms were owner-controlled.[10] Even owner-controlled firms face, after all, the problem of how to prevent "organizational slack" and "expense preference" from emerging. The difference for managerial firms is that they are governed by an essentially self-selecting coalition of senior management, and one must examine the constraints to which this coalition is subject if one is to estimate their degree of economic power. Let us, then, use as a working definition of "economic power" "that authority, control, or influence over others that arises from one's position in economic organizations" and examine the constraints to which such authority, control, or influence may be subject.

What one might call the "Chicago" position argues that economic power is so constrained by market forces as to be practically meaningless—amounting only to the power to make bad business decisions and be driven forthwith[11] from the marketplace. In this view, a perfectly competitive market with no externalities and no distortions offers no alternative but profit-maximizing behavior—i.e., a unique course of action. The consumer, or rather consumers in aggregate, determine through decentralized individual decisions what will sell and those who do not provide it at minimum cost go bankrupt. Hence, economic power in anything but a very transitory sense is not an issue.

This may be a reasonable picture of life in the small business sector but great size and the diversification of activities across many lines of business of the "top 200" offer a long period of protection against the implications of past "bad" decisions in any one area. Clearly, good financial results for the corporation as a whole tend to mean that management is given a free hand, while economic difficulties will attract the attention of bankers and stock market analysts. Nevertheless, Herman argues, "Even in this case, however, managerial control over the flow of information to outside directors and outside financial interests, its influence over board members derived from personal or business relationships, and fears of disruption and open conflict frequently allow managerial survival and continued domination of the succession process under conditions of proven managerial ineptitude (1981:29).[12] Indeed, many have wondered if the great size of the largest corporations, and the consequences their bankruptcy would have for the national economy, do not mean that, effectively, they cannot be allowed to fail. In recent years, for example, Chrysler and Lockheed were saved from financial collapse by government loans while Ford and General Motors have been rescued from superior quality, lower priced foreign competition by the imposition of import quotas on Japanese autos.

The constraints facing very large firms are not the same as those that face small firms. Competition is likely to be that of the tactical pursuit of market share, based largely on product development and advertising strategy, rather than the pure price competition of atomistic markets. Corporations may invade the traditional market of a competitor, but at the risk of attracting a counterattack in their own traditional markets.[13] If corporate conglomerates have activities in many industrial sectors, these "wars" can be costly while reciprocal selling to each other's subsidiaries can be both secure and profitable, producing a pattern of what Mueller (1977:471) calls "conglomerate mutual interdependence and corporate forbearance." Effective competition within an oligopoly may then run in cycles, with periods of intense struggle followed by longer periods of price leadership and "live and let live."

Ever since the time of the great financiers of the late 1800s (notably J. P. Morgan), there has been great interest in the roles played by major banks in corporate concentration and coordination (see Carosso, 1970). Kotz (1978, 1979) has recently identified four major groups of investment banks[14] and argued that financial control remains an important part of the American corporate scene. Although investment banks may not directly own a large fraction of corporation stock, they often vote the shares of personal trusts and pension funds for which they are trustee, which, together with a long-term banking relationship, may give bankers an important degree of long-term influence.[15] Usually, however, bank trust departments are passive investors (Herman, 1981:114-161) whose authority is latent rather than active and whose influence lies in a collective definition of the rules of the game and the appropriate goals of business enterprises—i.e., "the bottom line."[16] Nevertheless, the major financial institutions, especially when acting in concert, have an enormous potential power that may come into the open should a company's operating results deteriorate sufficiently.

The opinions of key bankers and company directors can be communicated and given joint effect through the interlocking directorships of major corporations. The 1978 Senate study examined the extent to which the directors of the 130 largest U.S. corporations in 1976 sat on each other's Board of Directors or met on the board of a third enterprise. Examining in particular the 13 largest, they found 240 direct interlocks and 5,547 indirect interlocks. They argued "in a truly arm's length free enterprise economy one would expect to find large companies relatively independent of each other. After all they have enormous resources with which to buy and sell on a competitive basis. The computer analysis here, however, raises serious question as to whether such corporate independence really exists among these companies" (U.S. Congress, Senate, 1978a:29).

Communication, discussion, and the harmonization of opinion is also facilitated by linkages through joint ventures (at home and abroad), joint membership of government advisory committees and trade and business organizations, and joint use of the same law and accounting firms.[17] In addition, corporate leaders tend to be of the same sex, age, and race and to share the same educational background—Dye and Pickering (1974:914) demonstrated that 55% of the presidents and directors of major corporations obtained their first degree at twelve Ivy League institutions.

As one introductory text on U.S. politics and government puts it, "the most striking fact about national leadership is how few people are directly involved in it" (Prewitt and Verba, 1979:216). These authors argue that one should think of roughly 4,000 to 5,000 leaders in business, government, and major civic institutions. As we have seen, the links among major business decision makers are many and varied but, as Lundberg (1968:308) puts it, "There is, of course, no 'plot'. There are certain shared attitudes and ways of doing business in a small continually consulting group and these are reflected in the public behavior of the corporations." As the business press puts it, there is a "business and investment community."

But does this group have any "power"? Galbraith (1967) argues that the power of senior management has been usurped by the "techno-structure" and that the power of large corporations is balanced by the clout of big unions and big government. Union membership has, however, declined markedly in recent years while effective government action has often been neutralized by more effective political lobbying.[18] Top management has always had the power that comes with personnel selection and with the choice of priorities and operational criteria. Middle management experts may define the details but they are selected by, and operate within the context set by, top management.

A "political economy" perspective therefore sees fewer effective constraints on economic power since it sees middle managers as having little independence of action and views government as essentially subject to the manipulations of large corporations. This perspective expects that individuals will use all the resources at their command, both political and economic, to advance their interests, which are both political and economic. The economically powerful have, in this view, some conflicting interests, such as which company should get approval to build a pipeline, and some common interests, such as opposition to a redistribution of wealth. Their aim in politics is to ensure that government is in the position of arbitrating their conflicting interests while safeguarding their common interests. The "political economy" viewpoint then sees great economic power as inevitably conveying political influence. Campaign contributions, corporate lobbying,[19] the potential rewards which a business career can offer people after their civil service or political career, personal influence and elite friendships, and the ability to withhold or divert investment from areas where jobs are needed—these all give political leverage to those who possess economic power.

3.3 The Inequality of Wealth

It is fairly easy to *describe* the extremes of wealth distribution. At the top of the wealth pyramid are a few hundred families, some famous and some reclusive, such as the Mellon, Du Pont, Rockefeller, Ford, Weyerhauser, Guggenheim, Pew, Getty, or Hunt families. These families have assets of several hundred million, and occasionally several billion, dollars.[20] At the other end of the scale are the nameless millions who have greater debts than assets. In between are the many millions of "middle-class" Americans whose most important possessions are usually such physical assets as consumer durables, cars, or houses but who may, if they are somewhat better off, in addition have a small portfolio of stocks, bonds, or other financial assets. As one moves up the wealth pyramid from the middle-class through the "well-off" to the truly rich, the typical portfolio of assets owned changes rather dramatically—from a portfolio almost exclusively composed of physical assets to a portfolio largely composed of financial assets. One would therefore like to know not only how unequally net worth is distributed but also how the particular assets which make up America's wealth are distributed among the population.

Accurate measurement is, however, made more difficult in the United States by the absence of a regular, comprehensive survey of the assets and liabilities of the American people. Survey data have been infrequent (Projector and Weiss, 1966; Lininger, Vaughan, and Whiteman, 1981) or generated incidentally as a by-product of other studies. Surveys also suffer from the general problem that the rich are too few in number to be adequately captured in a general probability sample of the population and may understate their assets even if they are located as respondents.[21] To estimate the wealth share of top wealth holders, one can examine the estate tax returns which are left by the wealthy when they die (estate tax multiplier method—section 3.3.1). However, survey data in some form are essential if we are to estimate the distribution of wealth among the bulk of the population (section 3.3.2) and ingenious researchers have combined data from several sources to produce "synthetic" data bases which are representative of the bulk of the population (Wolff, 1982). Neither of these two different methodologies, alone, is totally satisfactory, but together they give a reasonable picture. We will consider each in turn—the results of both are broadly consistent.

3.3.1 The Estate Tax Multiplier Method: Estimates of the Share of the Very Rich In any given year, a certain fraction (Pa) of those people of age a die. If they leave an estate, the worth of that estate is evaluated in the United States (and in the United Kingdom) for inheritance taxes. If death is random each decedent can then be seen as "representing" a certain number of living persons $(1/Pa)$, and the size distribution of estates can be adjusted for the number of living fortunes which each represents to give an estimate of the size distribution of total wealth. For example, if $1/1000$ of 30-year-olds and $1/10$ of 87-year-olds generally die every year, it is assumed that, for each estate left by a 30-year-old, one thousand other similar living people have assets of the same amount as the estate and for each estate left by an 87-year-old ten living people have assets of the same size. Adding up the estimated wealth of all age groups gives the total wealth distribution of the society.

Of course, the probability of death (Pa) depends on more than just age and to give an accurate picture of how many living people a decedent "represents" one must be as accurate as possible in estimating death probability. Since males and nonwhites have lower life expectancies, Pa must be calculated separately by race and sex. Since wealthier individuals tend to live longer, Pa must be adjusted for social class (U.K.) or size of estate (U.S.) (See Harrison, 1979:9).

Corrections are also necessary to account for the fact that wealth for estate tax purposes is not quite the same as wealth for the living. Some assets (such as pensions) may cease on death while some (e.g., life insurance policies) may change in value. Other assets, such as an ongoing business, may be worth less in the open market than as a going concern. Other corrections must be made for property held jointly with one's spouse, but a major problem with the estate multiplier method is that most people leave either no estate at all on death or an estate that is too small to be evaluated for estate duty purposes. The minimum exemption has been raised and lowered over the years, but it has never been so low as to bother the vast majority—from 1916 to 1954 the number of estates subject to tax as a fraction of all estates was as low as 0.5% and as high as 2.47%, but more normally was around 1% to 1.5% (Lampman, 1962:29). During the 1970s as many as 4% may have been required to file returns (see Smith, 1973).

The estate multiplier method is therefore best able to estimate the share of top wealth holders in total wealth, since their total wealth (as derived from the estate multiplier method) can be expressed as a fraction of the nation's total wealth (as derived from balance sheet totals and national income figures). Table 3.1 presents some recent estimates of the share of top wealth holders.

These estimates can be contrasted with the earlier work of Lampman (1962:24), who estimated that the share of the top 0.5% of persons was 29.8% of personal sector wealth in 1922, 32.4% in 1929, 25.2% in 1933, 28.0% in 1939, 20.9% in 1945, and 19.3% in 1949. Smith and Franklin (1974:162) sum up: "The distribution of wealth (1) became significantly more equal in the 1930's and early 1940's, two periods of massive government intervention in the marketplace and (2) has remained essentially unchanged since 1945."[22] The year of greatest measured wealth equality appears to have been 1949, which may have been followed by an increase in wealth inequality during the early 1950s and a gradual decline to current levels. A clear trend is apparent in the declining share of all corporate stock held by the very rich—in 1953 the top 1% owned 86.3% of corporate stock; by 1972 this was reduced to 56.5%. However, even in 1972 the value of common stock held by the top 1% comprised some 54% of their total net worth—which implies that fluctuations in the stock market are very important to the estimated net worth of top wealth holders in any particular year.[23]

The estate tax methodology involves, however, a crucial presumption—that the wealthy do not anticipate their demise with sufficient

Table 3.1
Share of Top Wealth Holders in Personal Wealth

ASSET	1953 Percentage Held By—		1958 Percentage Held By—		1962 Percentage Held By—		1969 Percentage Held By—		1972 Percentage Held By—	
	Top 0.5 Per-cent	Top 1 Per-cent	Top 0.5 Per-cent	Top 1 Per-cent	Top 0.5 Per-cent	Top 1 Per-cent	Top 0.5 Per-cent	Top 1 Per-cent	Top 0.5 Per-cent	Top 1 Per-cent
Total assets	21.2	26.7	20.4	25.5	20.7	26.2	19.3	24.4	18.9	24.1
Real estate	10.3	15.5	10.1	15.1	10.3	15.3	9.8	14.4	10.1	15.1
Corporate stock	77.0	86.3	66.6	75.4	53.3	62.0	44.0	50.8	49.3	56.5
Bonds	45.3	52.6	36.0	41.4	35.1	40.6	47.6	53.4	52.2	60.0
Cash	13.1	18.0	10.4	15.2	10.4	15.3	9.7	14.3	8.5	13.5
Debt instruments	24.1	32.1	28.6	37.3	32.0	42.3	30.2	40.9	39.1	52.7
Life insurance	10.2	14.1	9.4	14.1	7.6	11.4	6.6	10.8	4.3	7.0
Trusts	85.4	91.7	85.1	92.1	(NA)	(NA)	85.8	92.3	80.8	89.9
Miscellaneous	5.6	8.9	6.3	7.9	10.5	13.9	7.4	10.9	6.8	9.8
Liabilities	15.2	20.7	12.9	16.8	15.2	19.4	13.6	18.0	12.5	16.2
Net worth	22.0	27.5	21.7	26.9	21.6	27.4	20.4	25.6	20.4	25.9
Number of persons, million	0.8	1.6	.87	1.74	.93	1.87	1.01	2.03	1.04	2.09

Sources: U.S., Department of Commerce, Bureau of the Census. *Statistical Abstract of the United States,* 1979. Washington: U.S. Government Printing Office, p. 740.
Smith and Franklin (1974: 166).

foresight to avoid death duties. Gifts made just before death, i.e., within three (U.S.) or seven (U.K.) years of death, have been taxed as part of the estate. However, the Grosvenor family of England still owns the 12,500 acres of Cheshire which they acquired in 1068 and 300 of the 500 acres of downtown London which they obtained in 1677. As Gerald Grosvenor, Sixth Duke of Westminister, who made his first will at 18 and whose family fortune of between 200 million and 500 million pounds is safely in the hands of eleven family trusts, puts it, "The whole concept is planning ahead in case I fell in front of a number eight bus" (Cunningham, 1979). Where succession duties are heavy, "estate planning" can become a minor art form where lawyers and accountants create intricate mazes of foundations, fiduciary trusts, lifetime interests, and trusts between grandparents and grandchildren whose ultimate aim is to ensure that each generation dies legally penniless yet materially comfortable. Cooper (1979) details some of the intricacies of preferred stock recapitalization, charitable split interest trusts, and other devices which have enabled some families of immense wealth (e.g., the Du Ponts, with a fortune of roughly $500 million) to reduce estate taxation to nuisance levels. He concludes that the U.S. estate tax has been largely a voluntary tax, paid only by those who do not really want to avoid it. Titmuss (1962, Chapter 5) earlier reached a similar conclusion for Britain. One must therefore suspect that an unknown fraction of the wealth of the rich escaped Table 3.1.[24]

This unreported fraction of wealth will increase over time if, as appears likely, increasing estate tax rates, greater tax sophistication, and/ or declining urges to voluntary tax compliance produce increased estate tax avoidance. In addition, the measured share of top wealth holders is not immune from such social trends as a rising divorce rate. Typically, most of the wealth of a household is in the name of the male, implying that the estates of married men are considerably greater than those of married women (see Brittain, 1977:32-41). When divorce rates are low, males will therefore tend to die in possession of most of the household's wealth (much of which is usually left to the spouse). Higher divorce rates imply, however, that more households divide their assets while both spouses are still alive, implying lower wealth for the male when he eventually dies and an *apparent* deconcentration of wealth holdings, as measured by the estate tax methodology.

3.3.2 The Distribution of Wealth in General Discussion of the inequality in wealth holdings in the population as a whole requires reliable information on the wealth of the poorer 96% of the population, but since they do not generally file estate tax returns, some sort of survey data is essential. Unfortunately, the United States does not have a regular series of household surveys on this issue. Some surveys have been done,[25] but they have been small and infrequent, with differing questions and methodologies. Survey evidence on wealth distribution suffers, in general, from the problem of "response error" since assets or liabilities may be forgotten or not revealed. American survey evidence suffers, in addition, from small sample size.[26] As a result, estimates of the wealth share of top wealth holders are potentially sensitive to sampling variability. Since relatively wealthy people are a small percentage of a small sample they are very few in number, in these data sets, and estimates of their share can be influenced by the idiosyncracies of the particular few who are sampled.

As a result, the more detail one asks for on the American distribution of wealth, the more unreliable the numbers become. The consequence is that one is forced to rely on aggregate measures of wealth inequality, and the most popular one has been the Gini index. Using data from early 1953 and early 1962 and examining individual cohorts, Lansing and Sonquist (1969:50) concluded that "the distribution of wealth remained stable for these age groups during the period." They argued "there are no substantial differences between cohorts, between age groups or between years." The Gini coefficients ranged from 0.69 for the group aged 25 to 34 in 1953 to 0.62 for those aged 55 to 64 in 1962. Of course, when one adds together the wealth distributions of different age groups to get the overall wealth distribution, the Gini index will increase—the Federal Reserve study of Projector and Weiss (1966:110) estimated the Gini index of consumer units to be 0.76 in late 1962 (see Table 3.2). Wolff (1982) has pieced together evidence from a variety of sources and estimates the Gini index of personal disposable wealth to be 0.720 in 1969. The top 1% of households owned 30.8%, the top 5% owned 49.2%, and the top 20% owned 73.9% of all household disposable wealth (defined as salable assets of all sorts minus liabilities).

Greenwood (1983) has recently merged income tax microdata with census files. Her estimate of the Gini index of net worth (all items with durability and realizable cash value less all debts), as distributed among families, was 0.81 in 1973. She comments that the poorest 35% of American families have no measurable wealth, the poorest 75% own, in total, only 11.2% of net wealth, but the upper 10% hold almost 70% of net wealth (including 93% of corporate stock).

Personal disposable wealth is, however, made up of a number of different types of assets, whose distribution among the population varies greatly. Almost everyone has some consumer durables, household inventories of food or clothing, and some cash or demand deposits—these assets are substantially more equally distributed than assets in general. Equity in owner-occupied housing is, likewise, not only a huge part of America's personal wealth;[27] it is also relatively widely held in the community—some 64% of households having some equity in a home by 1979. These types of assets (durables, cash, personal bank accounts, and equity in owner-occupied housing) are what Wolff (1982) has called "life cycle wealth"[28] since they are very widely held and family holdings tend

Table 3.2

Wealth Inequality Over Time

Thirteen Colonies 1774, United States 1962 and 1973 (percentage shares of wealth, by decile)

	All Potential Wealthholders TPW 1774	Free Wealthholders		Consumer Units Wealth 1962	Net Wealth, Families 1973
		TPW 1774	NW 1774		
Percentage share held by:					
100th percentile (richest 1%)	15	13	15	34*	32.6
99th percentile (next richest 1%)	9	7	8	8	9.8
98th-96th (next richest 3%)	17	15	16	11	15.1
Tenth decile (100th-91st, richest 10%)	56	51	55	62*	69.8
Ninth decile	18	17	18	16	13.8
Eighth decile	12	11	11	7	7.3
Seventh decile	8	8	7	6	4.5
Sixth decile	4	6	5	4	2.6
Fifth decile	2	3	3	3	0.9
Fourth decile	1	2	2	2	0.1
Third decile	—	1	1	—	—
Second decile	0	1	—	—	—
First decile	0	—	-2	—	—
Mean	£199.1	£252.0	£237.3	$20,982	$37,657
Median	£ 47.7	£108.7	£ 83.8	$ 6,721	$ 9,595
Gini coefficient	0.73	0.66	0.73	0.76	0.81

Sources: A. H. Jones (1980: 289), Greenwood (1983).
*Figures questioned (see Jones, 1980: 261, 437).
Notes: 1 £ Sterling in 1774 = $54.26 in 1978. TPW = total physical wealth. NW = net wealth.

to increase with age. He estimated the Gini index of life-cycle wealth to be 0.585 in 1969. In 1979, Pearl and Frankel estimates indicate such assets to be roughly 50.7% of all assets of the household sector (1981:Table 2).

The other half of personal wealth, which can be called "capital wealth," is *much* more unequally held. It consists of bonds and securities, corporate stocks, commercial real estate and rental property, business and trust fund equity, and the cash value of life insurance policies. Some types of assets, such as trust funds, are extremely rare (concerning about 1% of the population), but even more familiar assets, such as corporate stock, are in practice pretty narrowly held. Wolff (1982:47) estimates some 15.9% of households had some corporate stock in 1969 while Pearl and Frankel put the fraction of households owning stock or mutual funds at 19.5% in 1979 (1981:Table 1). Even among those who do own stock the inequality of holdings is rather large—as Table 3.1 indicates, the top 1% have over half of all stock holdings. Overall, the Gini index for capital wealth was estimated by Wolff to be 0.881, and, as he notes, its distribution was "essentially independent of age" (1982:6).

The assets underlying life-cycle wealth and capital wealth can be disposed of by the individual who owns them and hence can be called "personal disposable wealth." In addition, it has been argued by Feldstein (1976) that the expectation of future receipts from Social Security should be counted as part of wealth—a procedure which decreases measured wealth inequality since Social Security entitlements are gained by most people in paid employment. However, the *size* of the reduction in measured inequality is quite sensitive to the methodology chosen. If one counts *contributions* it is not particularly large—the Gini index of personal disposable wealth plus the cumulated value of Social Security contributions was 0.684 in 1969 (Wolff, 1982:47). If one counts *expected benefits* one must presume that benefit schedules will remain unaltered and *are expected by all to remain unaltered* (which, today, rather implies that nobody reads the newspapers).

3.3.3 The Distribution of "Riches" Most students consider discussion of definitions to be a bore and accept them uncritically, impatient to get on to the "real thing." This is a great mistake as apparently quite subtle differences in initial wording are magnified by their subsequent logical development into very different perceptions of the world around us. Greenwood's estimates imply that a family with more than $16,713 of net wealth in 1973 was in the top 40% of the wealth distribution (1983:31). This is a sum that could be accounted for by a car, a few consumer durables, a small bank balance, and some equity in a home. It is likely that many of those who are in fact in the *top 40%* of the wealth distribution do not consider themselves to be "rich." Indeed, they may well consider themselves to be "just getting by."

When most people talk of "the rich," they usually appear to mean other people who have a large amount of money (or assets which can be converted to money) which they can spend as they wish. They do not generally mean "ordinary" people (e.g., a high-school teacher?) who bought "ordinary" houses in the early 1970s and then watched their paper wealth increase dramatically as housing prices rose. Confronted with an economist's challenge that such a person is now wealthy if only he or she would sell the old house, such a high-school teacher is apt to respond that a person would only have to buy another one, since we all have to live somewhere. Suppose, therefore, that we had defined "riches" as an individual's stock of discretionary purchasing power, which might seem an unobjectionable, commonsense idea underlying wealth. We would then have had to define the difference between "discretionary" and "nondiscretionary" and we might well have adopted the idea that "nondiscretionary" expenditures on assets are those expenditures which are necessary for subsistence or socially required by one's occupation or work role.

To highlight the difference between a conception of "riches" and of "wealth" consider the example of a 60-year-old person who has $100 worth of furniture and clothing and a pension of $20 per month for the next fifteen years and no other assets or liabilities. An economist who calculates this person's wealth would usually add to the $100 worth of physical assets the present value of the pension entitlement, which at 10% discount would be roughly $922, for a total wealth of $1,022. Noneconomists, however, might protest that on a pension of $20 per month this person is unlikely to survive very long and that a hundred dollars worth of clothing and furniture is minimal enough that nothing could reasonably be sold to finance consumption. "Riches" would therefore be a negative amount. Adding the current market value of assets and the present value of future income to get "wealth" does not take account of the maintenance cost of humans.

In addition, some occupations require the ownership of tools (e.g., mechanics) or expensive clothing (e.g., secretaries). More importantly, some occupations, such as fishing or farming, require the possession of assets for which a rental market may be poorly developed. These assets may be worth a great deal if sold, yet the owner cannot sell without fundamentally changing his or her occupation and life-style. Hence, the owners have a relatively small stock of purchasing power which can be used for personal consumption. The extent to which other ownership patterns are socially required would be a gray area of such a definition, but gray areas also exist in the computation of income in kind or of "wealth" in the standard definition. If we adopted the stock of discretionary purchasing power held by an individual as our idea of "riches" we would probably have to exclude from its measurement the "transactions balances" and the inventory of household supplies which we use from day to day, the transportation element of the cost of the automobiles which get us to work, and some fraction of the value of our housing stock.

We would be asking, in effect, What assets do people have *over and above* those assets which are necessary to reproduce their labor power from day to day, rested, fed, and at their customary place of work? Since most of the assets of the poorer half of households are of exactly these types, the resulting distribution of "riches" would be more unequal than the distribution of "wealth."

3.4 Long-Run Trends in the Distribution of Wealth

Piecing together the story on the historical evolution of wealth inequality in America is something like detective work; one has to use what evidence is at hand. Jones searched the probate records of estates settled in 1774 at a sample of county courthouses of the original thirteen colonies. She used the estate multiplier method to estimate the level of wealth, and its inequality, on the eve of the War of Independence. In the census of 1850, 1860, and 1870 individual respondents were asked questions about their personal wealth—these records have been examined by Gallman and Soltow. Following the introduction of an estate tax in 1916, estate-tax records became available and were used by Mendershausen (1956) and Lampman (1962). Since these data all have their deficiencies, and these deficiencies are quite different, there is quite a bit of room for debate. However, Jones's succinct conclusion probably has a reasonable degree of consensus: "For a general statement, it would seem that the most likely pattern of change in the United States as a whole over the past two centuries was: (1) some increase in wealth inequality to 1860-1870, (2) possibly continued to a somewhat higher degree of concentration, which may have peaked around 1890 or 1929 or 1940, (3) a mild downdrift in inequality to the 1950's and (4) little change since, at least among top wealthholders" (1980:273).[29]

Jones's work with the probate records of wills filed at county courthouses in 1774 has at least one advantage over the more recent estate multiplier studies—since there was no estate tax at the time, there is no reason to expect underestimates of estate size to occur. However, in common with current studies, she had the problem of estimating the wealth of the very poor, who have no estate at all. In addition, since in 1774 slaves and indentured servants were considered to be "property," part of the net worth of slave owners was in fact composed of other people. In Table 3.2, column 1 is most nearly comparable to present-day wealth statistics since it includes all people as "potential wealth holders" but counts slaves as having zero wealth and slave owners as having wealth which includes the market value of their slaves. "Total physical wealth" then includes the value of land and buildings, slaves and servants, and nonhuman portable physical assets. "Net worth" refers to total physical wealth plus financial liabilities. By 1870, the Gini index of wealth among adult males had increased to 0.83 (Soltow, 1975). As Jones concludes, "The wealth inequalities in the thirteen colonies were about on a par with those in the United States nearly two hundred years later, and somewhat less than those prevailing one century later" (1980:317).

Gallman (1969) estimated that the richest 2,000 American families in 1890, some 0.16% of all families, held 9.6% of total domestic assets, up from 5.2% in 1840. The share of the top 1% of adult males, however, was reduced from 35% of wealth in 1860 to 27% in 1870, probably largely because of the emancipation of slaves. Both Jones (1980) and Williamson and Lindert (1980) report that wealth inequality and the share of top wealth holders varied from region to region and period to period in the United States, but it is clear that great wealth and substantial wealth inequality have long been part of the American scene.

However, it is the dynamics of wealth acquisition which interests many people. Some of the wealthy of the early 1800s (e.g., the Du Ponts) have retained and expanded their wealth through succeeding generations, but many have not (see Lebergott, 1975). There has been both some circulation of elites and a general increase in wealth over the last two hundred years.[30] Soltow (1971) concentrated on the distribution of wealth among the population in Wisconsin, with detailed examination of the distribution of wealth within a number of counties and within the city of Milwaukee and calculated the Gini index of the wealth distribution to be 0.77 in 1850, 0.75 in 1860, and 0.74 in 1870 (1971:9). Since the census records for 1850 to 1870 listed individuals by age and by origin, Soltow was able to identify which groups in the population had assets and which did not. The poorest groups in the Wisconsin population of 1850 to 1870 were the young foreign-born who did not have land. The wealthiest groups in the population of that time were older native-born farmers and city merchants. Older men typically had more wealth than younger men and the second, native-born generation of immigrant families typically had more wealth than the first generation. Since Norwegian immigration was highly important in this area of Wisconsin, Soltow compared the average wealth of Norwegian-born individuals in four counties in Wisconsin in 1860 with the wealth of Norwegians as revealed in the Norwegian census of the similar period—as one might expect "the advantage clearly lay in Wisconsin" (1971:95).

As a result, although the wealth distribution was unequal, it was a wealth distribution within which there was a substantial individual mobility and one in which even the poorest (the foreign-born) had substantially more wealth than those in their country of origin. Average wealth in Wisconsin was growing at a per capita rate of between 1 and 2% a year but individual wealth typically grew much faster as individuals moved up the relative distribution of wealth over time. As a result, "a system of extreme inequality at a point in time could be tolerated because of the obvious increases in expected and real wealth values over time" (1971:43). Contrary to many impressions, the initial allocation of land in

Wisconsin (or in the thirteen colonies earlier) was far from equal. Those early settlers who brought capital with them were able to purchase large landholdings and acquire very great wealth. Immigrants, however, also acquired substantial wealth over their own life cycles and could look forward to even more growth during their children's lifetime.

As Soltow concludes, "Wealth inequality, particularly among upper wealth groups, has changed very little in Wisconsin since settlement. How could this happen in a state which originally had free land? . . . The basic reason is that there was such large inequality at the time of settlement. The need for large numbers of hired farm laborers, the inefficiency in finding suitable land, and the large number of foreign-born left a large propertyless group at any point in time. Strong economic growth meant that there were some rich native-born families who, on the average, had been accumulating at a handsome rate perhaps for generations" (1971:13). As farm laborers acquired a "stake" and became farmers and as their native-born children inherited wealth, a family could expect to prosper. This is, therefore, a picture of a pyramid which is continually growing at the base, pushing the peak ever higher. However, such upward mobility for all is only possible as long as there is continual inflow of the poor foreign-born. Once large-scale migration ceases, the dynamics of the wealth distribution change—it is no longer possible to have both a constant distribution of shares of wealth and upward relative movement for most families.

3.5 Adjustments to Measures of Income Inequality

In Chapter 2 we distinguished between income as a flow, and wealth as a stock, of command over goods and services. Annual money income (as defined by the Bureau of the Census) is, however, only part of one's total income, omitting, in particular, "in-kind" income in the form of government transfers or fringe benefits paid by employers, and capital gains. One would like to know how much, and in which direction, the omission of these items alters our perception of the amount of income inequality. In addition, since the economic welfare of a household depends not only on its current income but also on its future income and the number of people among whom that income is shared, one would like to know how different the inequality picture would look were one to take account of differing family size and expected future income. If one were very ambitious, one would try to sum up all these influences in a single "true" measure of income inequality—but such a single number would be subject not only to the value judgments implicit in the choice of a single inequality index (see Chapter 2) but also to the value judgments hidden in a great many "not-so-technical" decisions such as the alternative weightings of family size, the valuation of transfers, the base periods for capital gains, estimates of income variability, etc. The approach adopted here is, therefore, simply to present separately the available evidence on the magnitude and direction of each of these issues, leaving the reader the task of overall evaluation.

3.5.1 Omitted Income: In-Kind Transfers, Fringe Benefits, and Capital Gains Money income received includes cash transfers and payments from government but excludes government-financed services such as schooling, Medicare or Medicaid, or in-kind transfers such as food stamps or subsidized housing. Since these programs have some tendency to be targeted to groups with low average incomes (such as Medicare for the elderly) or are subject to an incomes test (such as public housing or food stamps), they are an especially large fraction of the incomes of the poor. In Chapter 13 we discuss the role of government in income distribution in more detail but here we can state the conclusion—if one includes the cost of in-kind government transfer programs in measured income, inequality is reduced. Smolensky et al. (1977:24) calculated that the Gini index of household income inequality as conventionally defined was 0.398 in 1970; if one had included the cost of in-kind government transfers to households as part of income the Gini index would have been 0.371 (and the share of the poorest 20% would have risen from 5.2% to 6.5%).[31]

"In-kind" government transfers are a particularly large fraction of the incomes of the poor, but the poor tend to receive relatively little in *private* in-kind transfers or "fringe benefits." In aggregate, such elements of employee compensation as employer-paid life, accident, disability, and health insurance or employer contributions to pension and retirement plans have grown slightly more rapidly than government social welfare expenditures—rising from 5.2% of wages and salaries in 1966 to 10.5% in 1979 (Smeeding, 1981:5).[32] These benefits are far from equally distributed—indeed the majority of employees were not covered by an employer-paid pension in 1979. Coverage tends to increase with income and to be particularly poor for part-time and part-year workers. In addition, the value of a fringe benefit such as a pension plan or life insurance is higher, the higher was one's income while employed. Smeeding (1981:44) therefore found that, when one includes the value of fringe benefits, measured inequality tends to increase. Whereas the Gini index of inequality of money wages and salaries among private employees was 0.4529, the Gini index of wages and salaries plus the value of fringe benefits was 0.4667. The share of the poorest 20% of all workers fell from 2.4% to 2.1% while the share of the best-off quintile rose from 47.3% to 48.4%[33] As Smeeding notes, "Moreover, if we could include measures of other job perks and noncash compensation normally enjoyed by professionals, managers and administrators in our estimates, we suspect that an even more unequal distribution of compensation would result" (1981:46).

Government in-kind transfers may ameliorate poverty at the low end of the income distribution, private fringe benefits may accentuate wage inequality among the middle groups of the distribution, but capital gains are an income source that is of greatest importance to high-income groups. After all, a change in the market value of assets or liabilities is important only to the extent that one has substantial assets or liabilities. Possession of assets yields returns both in current interest or dividend payments (which are counted in census money income) and capital gains (which are not). Both sorts of returns produce an increase in the purchasing power of wealth holders and should be included in a discussion of the impact of wealth on the distribution of income. Capital gains (and losses) on the stock market are especially important for upper-income groups, since as we saw from Table 3.1 this ownership is heavily concentrated. If the average value of stocks falls, the owners of stocks will, on average, realize losses on their holdings—since the people at the top of the distributions of income and wealth have such a large fraction of stock ownership, the inclusion of capital gains and losses in a measure of income distribution will then mean that measured inequality will show a decrease. Over a longer period of time, however, stock market gains have tended to dominate losses; thus, including capital gains will mean that the measured share of upper-income groups tends to increase.[34] Bhatia (1976) has shown that over the period 1960 through 1964 the inclusion of capital gains on stocks would have increased the Gini index of the U.S. income distribution by about 5%. A single year's measurement of the wealth distribution (and especially the share of the top 1%) is, however, highly sensitive to year-to-year vagaries in the stock market.

Where there are capital gains, however, there are also capital losses. During inflationary times, for example, holders of real assets get capital gains as the prices of those assets rise in money terms but holders of currency have capital losses, since a dollar now buys less. If we think of "pure" capital gains in the economy at a given point of time, i.e., the change in household wealth arising purely from changes in relative prices, then it must be the case that capital gains, in aggregate, balance capital losses, in aggregate. To put it a bit differently, "pure" capital gains/losses are purely redistributive.

However, capital gains as they appear in the marketplace are not "pure," since they measure the change in the market value of an asset over a period of time and the asset may have changed in nature over that period. A car will, for example, change in market value over a year partly because of pure changes in relative prices and partly because it becomes a different commodity, with more rust, higher mileage, etc. Similarly, corporate stocks will change in market value partly because a given company's assets at a point in time change in relative value and partly because these assets (e.g., technical processes, factories, or ore bodies) change over time. One cannot, therefore, exclude capital gains from a discussion of economic inequality[35] but neither can one count the gains without allowing for the losses.[36]

3.5.2 Inflation Capital gains (and losses) can be especially important in an inflationary environment. If inflation is unanticipated it will benefit those who hold most of their wealth as real assets (such as houses or land) and those who have debts with fixed monetary value and interest costs (e.g., people owing money on mortgages). People who have assets (such as a pension entitlement) which are fixed in dollar amount will tend to lose. Since most of the poor have relatively little debt (presumably because few institutions will lend to them) they are unlikely to benefit much from the depreciation of the real value of debt. The decline in the real value of pensions income will, however, affect older people very heavily. Their decline in welfare will be greater if inflation in the prices of necessities (e.g., heat and food) is greater than inflation in the general price index.

Of course, in the longer run expectations and behavior become adjusted to inflation and if inflation is correctly anticipated its distributional consequences may almost disappear.[37] The main issue is the speed and accuracy with which expectations of inflation adjust. If inflation is correctly anticipated mortgage interest rates will, for example, rise to reflect these anticipations—this interest rate rise will erode the benefits of borrowing to buy real estate and will increase the earnings of the pension funds which invest in mortgages. Fully anticipated inflation has few long-run impacts on the real economy. Unanticipated inflation is another matter. Unanticipated inflation imposes on everyone a giant lottery wherein some (e.g., homeowners) gain and some (e.g., pensioners) lose.

Nordhaus (1973) argued that, under a variety of assumptions regarding the macroeconomic structure of the economy, inflation, either a "one-shot" increase in prices or a continual increase in prices, is an equalizing factor in the long-run distribution of economic welfare. Wolff (1979a) found that in the 1969-1975 inflation in the United States (which was largely unanticipated) the largest gainers were homeowners with large mortgages. Since the real value of stocks fell relative to other assets and since these are largely owned by top wealth holders, this inflationary period saw a decline in wealth inequality (an effect that could be expected to be temporary, lasting only until inflationary expectations and interest rates rose). Minarik (1979) examined the impact of inflation on the U.S. *income* distribution in the 1970s (comprehensively defined to include capital gains, etc.) and found that inflation hurt primarily upper-income groups—while low-income households suffered only small losses and the gains and losses of middle-income groups roughly balanced. These studies thus agree in the broad conclusion that inflation is an equalizing influence. Tables 2.2 and 3.1 indicate, however, that, although increases in the price level imposed substantial gains and losses on particular individuals, *in the aggregate* the distributions of income and wealth underwent very little change in the 1970s, which may perhaps be due to the balancing *disequalizing* policies of monetary restraint and high unemployment which were adopted to combat inflation. In practice, the quasi-random reshuffling of individual fortunes has probably been the most important consequence of inflation.

3.5.3 Family Size and Average Income Inequality in annual income among households tells only part of the story, since such statistics do not take account of differences in household size. If our focus is the distribution of economic well-being we ought to account in some way for the obvious fact that a given income goes further if spread among fewer people. One possibility is simply to divide household income by the number of people in the household and then compute the distribution of per capita money income. However, this is likely to understate the welfare of people who live in larger households, since there are some "economies of scale" involved when several people pool their consumption (e.g., they may be able to buy in bulk, share the use of an indivisible commodity such as a telephone, etc.). We therefore need to use some set of budget equivalences, such as the family needs standard developed by Mollie Orshansky to define the official poverty line (see Chapter 4, Table 4.1). Table 3.3 is drawn from Hoffman and Podder (1976) and presents the distribution of 1973 money income among households who were interviewed in the Panel Study of Income Dynamics as well as the distribution of money income relative to estimated needs of a family of that size.

The inequality index for annual money income in Table 3.3 differs from that reported in Chapter 2 because Table 3.3 reports the income distribution among those families which had the same head in all seven

Table 3.3

**Income Inequality Measures
Adjusted For Family Size**

	1973 Income	1973 Income/Needs	Seven-Year Average Income	Seven-Year Average Income/Needs
Quintile Shares				
Share poorest 20%	4.6%	5.8%	5.5%	6.7%
2	11.1	11.2	12.2	12.5
3	17.6	17.6	18.1	17.5
4	24.4	23.4	24.2	23.3
Share richest 20%	42.3%	42%	39.8%	39.8%
Gini coefficient	.379	.361	.345	.331
Coefficient of variation	.766	.758	.669	.680
Theil index	.107	.098	.087	.081

Source: Hoffman and Podder (1976: 338).

years, 1967 to 1973, and it is therefore not completely representative of the American population as a whole. Table 3.3 can, however, still be used to assess the impact of a longer time period or correction for family size on income distribution statistics.[38] Since an individual household's income may fluctuate considerably from year to year, part of the inequality in annual incomes reflects these temporary fluctuations. Column 3 of Table 3.3 therefore presents statistics on the distribution of average household income over the seven-year period 1967 to 1973 and column 4 reports the distribution of the average income/needs ratio. Clearly, averaging income over a longer period and deflating household incomes for different household sizes produces measurements of income inequality that are lower than those reported for the distribution of annual money income among all households. Whether these changes are "small" or "large" is, however, largely a matter of opinion.

3.5.4 Lifetime Income Up to this point we have been, for the most part, simply counting the income and the wealth of current households. This has the great advantage of concreteness. Corrections may be required for incomplete surveys or biased responses but fundamentally we are concerned with a currently observable entity. We have, however, omitted "human wealth," or the prospects of future earnings which an individual is likely to receive. If, for example, we look only at people's current wealth and income we might see a bus driver and a medical intern as being in the same economic position—but the latter can look forward to a very much higher income soon after beginning practice. Their economic expectations are thus fundamentally different. If it is frequently true that families have low incomes now because they are now investing in "human capital" (see Chapter 8) but they will have high incomes in future years when this investment "pays off" then we will overestimate the degree of "true" inequality if we look only at their current incomes.

Unfortunately there is no known way of predicting the future with certainty. In order to estimate the inequality of lifetime earnings we must forecast the earnings individuals are likely to receive in future years as well as how these earnings will be combined within families. Total future earnings plus current wealth give the total resources which a family will have available over its lifetime. Out of these resources, a family can finance a certain amount of consumption. If it is the fully informed, forward-looking, utility-maximizing family of neoclassical economic theory it will choose an optimal pattern of lifetime consumption, which implies a program of asset accumulation while working and of dissaving while retired of the sort discussed in Chapter 11.

One can then think of the "utility equivalent annuity" defined as the constant amount of income, received for the rest of one's life, which would give you the same utility as your current stock of wealth and the varying earnings which you can actually expect. To estimate the inequality of "utility equivalent annuities" one must make some assumptions about the nature of utility functions and likely future labor earnings. One must also have available comprehensive data on the wealth holdings of households. Nordhaus (1973) used the 1962 Federal Reserve survey of U.S. families and computed the distribution of per capita utility equivalent annuities. He concluded, "As would be expected, the comprehensive measures of economic welfare are more unequally distributed than income but less unequally distributed than wealth. The reason is that annuity incomes are (complicated) functions of both labor income and wealth" (1973:477). However, when Irvine (1980) used the 1970 Canadian Survey of Consumer Finance, he reached a different conclusion. He argued that the distribution of lifetime consumption annuities was unambiguously more equal than the distribution of money income, showing a Gini index that was 10% lower and even greater differences in the Atkinson index or coefficient of variation. Similarly, Blewett (1982) used 1968 to 1978 data from the Panel Study on Income Dynamics to decompose the aggregate inequality in effective consumption (allowing for different family size) into year-to-year inequalities for particular persons, inequalities among persons of similar age, and inequalities over the life cycle of people of different ages. He argued that it is intracohort inequality (i.e., among people of the same age) which has the most ethical relevance but such inequality is substantially less than annual money income inequality.

Two factors may imply that "lifetime" income exhibits less measured inequality than annual income. In Chapter 8, Figure 8.1 illustrates the case where earnings paths cross—e.g., some occupations may have relatively low pay to start and high pay later on. In addition, variations from year to year may mean greater income inequality in any given year than if incomes were averaged over a number of years. (If, on the other hand, some individuals commence working with a low salary, which stays low, while others start with a high salary, which gets higher, inequality in annual earnings may be less than inequality in lifetime earnings.)

The simulation model of Davies (1980:23) again used Canadian data and examined the distribution of the present value of lifetime financial resources of young couples (see Chapter 11). His base run estimate was that the top quintile would receive, from market earnings and inheritances, 40.4% of the lifetime resources available while the bottom quintile would receive 5.3%. Irvine's methodology started from characteristics of respondents to the 1970 survey but ignored the possibility of inheritance. He estimated the share of the top quintile in lifetime consumption annuities to be 36.0% and the share of the bottom quintile to be 6.8%. Looking simply at annual money income in Irvine's sample, one would have said that the share of the top 20% of families was 38.5% and the share of the poorest 20% of families was 5.3% (Irvine, 1980: Tables 2 and 4). The underlying difficulties of earnings estimation, representativeness of the samples, and data reliability ought to caution us against placing too exact an interpretation on these numbers; rather, they ought to be seen as approximate estimates. Hence, it is the stability of shares of total income, after a very complex series of manipulations, which is their most remarkable aspect. It appears that, in most studies which find lifetime market earnings (or lifetime financial resources available or lifetime consumption annuities) to be more equally distributed than annual money income, the difference is not very large.

Even, however, if we include current earnings, future earnings, and future inheritances as well as the value of current wealth and even if we then adjust for family size before prorating consumption over a lifetime— even then we will not have the full picture. We will not have the full picture because we will not have included the value of "home production" or productive activity that does not pass through the market.[39] This home production can be extremely valuable—Gronau (1980) estimates that the value of a housewife's work is an average of 60% of family pretax money income. It is particularly important to consider when we examine trends in inequality. Sometimes reference is made to the "increased number of working women" in recent years but this is a gross slander since women have always worked. What has changed in recent decades is the *form* of female work, from being almost entirely unpaid work in the home to being, in the majority, paid work in the labor market. The increasing trend to paid work has been particularly important for families in the lower-middle- to middle-income ranges, as one would expect when a husband's low wage increases the chances of a wife's paid work. Had this trend not occurred, had the labor force participation of women remained constant from the 1950s to the 1970s, measured inequality of money income would have been higher in the 1970s. Danziger (1980) notes that the Gini index of inequality for white couples' incomes in 1977 was some 6.4% lower when one includes the wife's earnings than when one does not.[40]

3.6 International Comparisons

Comparisons of wealth inequality across countries are made extremely difficult by the differing degrees of bias created by the use of different methodologies. Some countries rely on the estate tax multiplier method, some have developed surveys (of varying administrative reliability), and some have records on wealth tax collections. Harrison (1979) was so impressed by the data deficiencies that despite collecting data on some ten countries he refused to list it all in the same table since that would imply a degree of comparability he felt to be unwarranted. He did, however, feel that the data on the United States, Britain, and Canada could be compared—Table 3.4 presents his results and those of Davies (1979a).

Table 3.4

The Distribution of Wealth—Comparisons

	Share of the Top		
	1%	5%	10%
U.S.A. 1969 (individuals)	25.1%	43.7%	53.0%
Britain 1970 (individuals)	30.1%	54.3%	69.4%
Canada* (1970)	18.8%	42.9%	57.1%

Sources: Davies (1979a, Table 10). Harrison (1979).
*U.S. and British data drawn from estimates of individual wealth computed by estate tax multiplier method; Canadian data from adjusted household wealth survey—household wealth then divided by number of adults present.

3.7 Summary and Conclusions

1. To answer the question, How much economic inequality is there? one must first specify:
(a) inequality of what?
(b) inequality among whom?
(c) inequality how measured?
In considering inequality of economic power, of wealth, of riches, and of adjusted income we ought first to ask the question, Why do we want to know? Each of these topics can be considered a different dimension of inequality, and the dimension one emphasizes should depend largely on the problem at hand. Those interested in political science or the political economy of policy formulation will probably be most interested in the distribution of economic power. Those interested in social class attitudes will emphasize lifetime income and consumption. Tax specialists, on the other hand, may emphasize the distribution of annual money income. No one variable, no single criterion of inequality, is likely to be optimal for all possible questions.

2. In examining the influence of measures of inequality of including or excluding something such as fringe benefits, lifetime income, or wealth one often reads statements such as "inequality is decreased by . . ." or "inequality increases when. . . ." Here, however, we have tried to refer as much as possible to *measured* inequality since it is worth reminding ourselves that only the measurement is changing in all these exercises; the reality remains unaffected. Whether one measure or another produces higher or lower measured inequality is, therefore, an entirely separate issue from the ethical one of whether inequality is "too high" or "too low." Whatever one's ethical views, it is clear that inequality of economic outcomes will not "disappear," even after the most complex of manipulations.

3. Ethical concern with inequality is focused just as much on the *trend* of inequality as on the *level* of inequality. However, since the most sophisticated economic studies (e.g., Nordhaus, Wolff) have been done only recently and have not been replicated for a number of different years one cannot really answer the question that is most interesting to many— i.e., What is the *trend* of measured inequality of lifetime utility/consumption? Is it increasing, decreasing, or remaining constant? It is by this sort of global question that many judge existing social and political institutions but unfortunately, we cannot as yet prove that movements (or lack of movements) in each of the dimensions of inequality are correlated or necessarily linked.

Those figures that are available show a roughly constant level of aggregate wealth inequality (as measured by the Gini index)[41] in the United States over the period 1774 to 1969. However, there may have been a fairly substantial decline in the share of top wealth holders during the Great Depression/World War II period. Certainly, there has been a substantial change in the dynamics of wealth acquisition during the transition from an agrarian frontier society to an urban industrial society.

As regards income from market work, Henle and Ryscavage (1980) noted a "slow but persistent" trend to greater inequality among the earnings of men over the period 1958 to 1977, while female earnings inequality showed no real trend. Smeeding (1981) has noted that, since fringe benefits are correlated with money wages and have increased relative to money wages, this trend would be accentuated if the value of fringe benefits were counted as part of employee compensation.

Individual returns from market work thus do not show any trend toward equality. When these individual returns are combined within households, one must consider as well trends in household size and composition and the increasing monetization of female labor, plus the influence of government transfers. The constancy of the distribution of annual money income among U.S. households (Chapter 2) is thus attained by the balancing of opposing tendencies. Divorce and the separation of the young and the old from larger households swells measured inequality; increased cash and noncash transfers and government services have mitigated inequality but the increase in female labor earnings, which tends to reduce measured (money) inequality, overstates increases in family economic well-being. Most authors in the field would probably agree with Blinder's summary statement: "when we consider the distribution of economic welfare—economic equality as it is commonly called— the central stylized fact is one of *constancy*" (1980:416).

NOTES

[1]Figures given are median sales and employment of the top 200 industrials—all figures are taken from the *Fortune* listing of May 24, 1981, pp. 322-349.

2The median company of the top 200 in 1980 in terms of sales was National Steel of Pittsburgh, which was linked by nine joint ventures, chiefly in iron ore production, to eleven other major steel producers—see Herman (1981:210).

3The Senate subcommittee on Reports and Accounting (U.S., Congress, Senate 1978:890) found, for example, that the directors of A.T. & T. sat on the boards of 26 of the other top 130 companies in the United States and met the directors of a further 66 of the top 130 while sitting on the boards of third companies.

4See *Forbes* magazine, May 1982 and 1981, for the names and salary details of chief executive officers.

5However, "the market" is not what sets your salary; rather, it is set by a compensation committee of fellow directors and, as *Fortune* magazine puts it, "Most directors on compensation committees probably have an urge to be agreeable about questions of pay" (*Fortune*, December 12, 1982, p. 45). As a result, "In the upper reaches of corporate America, the market frequently does not seem to work. In a totally rational world, top executives would be paid handsomely for first-class performance, and would lose out when they flopped. But to an extraordinary extent, those who flop still get paid handsomely" (op. cit., p. 42).

6See Herman (1981); for a case study see *Fortune*, October 1981.

7In 1975 there were for example 217,354 manufacturing firms in the U.S.—448 of them had assets of over $250 million, and these 448 comprised 72.5% of all assets in manufacturing (Herman, 1981:189).

8At the federal level, exerting political influence can be a complex exercise in influence and coalition building—see Fenn (1979).

9Osberg (1981) and Niosi (1978) reached a similar conclusion for Canada.

10Whether "profitable growth" is strictly "profit maximizing" is often a rather difficult thing to know, ex ante, in a world of uncertainty if one is interested in "long-run" profits.

11Clearly, market processes must work quickly if the Chicago position is to deserve our attention, since the "long run" is little consolation to individuals with finite lives.

12The example he cites is Penn Central.

13As when BIC entered the disposable lighter and razor markets, and Gillette riposted with an entry into ball-point pens. *New York Times*, Nov. 4, 1982.

14Chase Manhattan, Morgan Guarantee, Mellon National Bank, and Lehman, Goldman, Sachs.

15Kotz (1978:97) argued that 59 of the "top 200" nonfinancial corporations were wholly or partially under financial control.

16Whether this influence is benign is another issue. Hayes and Abernathy (1980) are among those who have argued that excessive emphasis on short-term return-on-investment calculations lies behind inadequate commercial R & D (research and development) and low U.S. productivity growth.

17For a detailed examination of ties among oil companies and a control sample of large industrial firms, see Herman (1981:209). Domhoff (1974) and Lundberg (1968) have documented the links which run through clubs and social gatherings.

18Herman (1981, Chapter 5) gives examples of such ploys as the underfunding of uncooperative regulatory agencies or the mobilization of congressional pressure.

19*Dun's Review* (1978:32), for example, refers approvingly to "the increasingly sophisticated and successful lobbying efforts of big business—as evidenced by such recent Congressional victories as defeat of labor law reform and the passage of legislation to reduce the capital gains tax."

20It is extremely difficult for outsiders to get accurate or complete information—but see Lundberg (1968) or *Forbes*, September 13, 1982.

21For a discussion of wealth survey methodology see Davies (1979a, 1979b).

22Smith and Franklin (1974:163) note that their methodology "understates the degree of concentration in any given year but is consistent and permits comparisons over time."

23Table 3.1 refers to the top 0.5% and top 1% but, if one broadens the analysis to the top 4% of the adult population, Smith (1973) found that they owned 37% of private gross assets and 33% of net worth in 1969. Their assets included 63.3% of corporate stock, 78.4% of state and local bonds, and 39.5% of business assets.

24Whalley (1974) used stamp duty statistics in the United Kingdom to estimate that perhaps 7% of wealth passing between generations was as tax exempt gifts and thus escaped estate duty. This exempt wealth is "probably" concentrated among the top percentiles.

Cooper emphasizes that such outright gifts are only one of the many tax avoidance methods and have the significant disadvantage, unlike trusts, of a surrender of control.

[25]Notably several 1950s versions of the Survey of Consumer Finance of the University of Michigan (see Lansing and Sonquist, 1969), the 1962 Survey for the Federal Reserve Board of Financial Characteristics of Consumers (Projector and Weiss, 1966), and the 1979 ISDP [Income Survey Development Panel] panel (Lininger, Vaughan, and Whiteman, 1981).

[26]Some 3,500 in the 1950-1962 Michigan survey, 2,557 households for the Federal Reserve study, and 7,000 for the ISDP panel.

[27]Pearl and Frankel (1981) estimate that equity in owner-occupied housing was 39.4% of all recorded personal wealth in 1979, up substantially from 30% in 1962.

[28]One should not confuse this with the "life-cycle savings model" of Chapter 11. These assets, and especially housing, are typically not dissaved in old age, due to their great illiquidity.

[29]Williamson and Lindert describe the period 1860 to 1929 as "a high uneven plateau of wealth inequality" (1980:59). They use a style of language which emphasizes the changes in wealth inequality before and after this period. Soltow (1971), on the other hand, emphasizes the continuity of wealth inequality.

[30]There have been spurts and lags but Jones (1980:307) estimates the average compound annual rate of growth of per capita wealth to be 1.3%, from 1774 to 1973.

[31]A slightly different calculation which evaluated in-kind transfers at "cash equivalent" values and adjusted for taxes produced a drop in the Gini index to 0.372 (1977:40).

[32]The shift to untaxed fringe benefits as a form of compensation is often explained by rising marginal tax rates. In addition, legally required employer payments (to Social Security, unemployment insurance, etc.) have risen from 5.7% of wages and salaries to 9.1%.

[33]Inequality in wages among employees dominates other inequalities for the middle bulk of the population but it excludes the extremes—those poor people who are out of the labor force and those who are rich enough to live on income from capital. The figures cited above include part-time employees—if we count only full-time, full-year workers the share of the bottom quintile of employees is higher (roughly 8%) but the impact of counting fringe benefits is the same—i.e., an increase in measured inequality.

[34]The favorable tax treatment of capital gains (see Chapter 13) also tends to produce schemes—such as stock options for executives—which have the effect of classifying employee compensation as capital gains.

[35]As Blinder (1980:449) does.

[36]As Beach (1981) does.

[37]Nordhaus (1973:492) estimates the "tax on real balances" (i.e., the economic cost of economizing on the use of money balances) which is due to a 1% rise in the anticipated inflation rate to be roughly $0.30 per capita per year.

[38]Lazear and Michael (1980) have demonstrated that alternative ways of deflating household income for household size make relatively little difference for households with two to five members, but they make a much larger difference for single-person households. Their preferred methodology involves estimating the changes in expenditure induced by changes in family size and they argue that the Orshansky scale of budget equivalencies (used here and in Chapter 4) understates considerably the needs of single-person households, which implies that it understates the fraction of the population living in absolute poverty by some 2.4%.

[39]See Chapter 8, sections 8.2.5 and 8.4. Murphy (1982) demonstrates that the valuation of household work is very sensitive to the technique of valuation employed, but by any technique is very large—between 31.6 percent and 59.5 percent of money GNP, in aggregate.

[40]Wives' earnings in 1974 were very poorly correlated with their husbands' earnings (.11 for whites) but their earnings were a larger fraction (20%) of family money income for all poor families than for better off families (4%) (Danziger, 1980).

[41]Recall from Chapter 2 that the Gini index is most responsive to changes in the *mid-range* of the wealth distribution.

4. POVERTY AND INEQUALITY

Material welfare has no significance except in its relation to men's feelings and as an element in the psychological state called happiness. And the extent of a man's happiness depends on the number and intensity of the desires which he is able to satisfy relative to the number and intensity of those which he is not able to satisfy. . . . in the search for material welfare, our modern civilisation under conditions of industrial progress is continually manufacturing new and previously unwanted sources of pleasure, so that the old luxuries become the new necessities, alike for those who can and those who cannot afford them. Hence where there is a great inequality of purchasing power, a continuous increase in the statistical total of goods and services produced per head will no doubt enable a larger and larger proportion of the people to satisfy certain wants, but will, equally certainly, increase the number of wants which the majority desire to satisfy, and only the minority can.

JOSIAH C. WEDGWOOD
The Economics of Inheritance (1929)

4.1 Introduction

What is the relationship between inequality and poverty? Has an increasing GNP largely eliminated poverty? Or is a redistribution of income necessary to reduce the distinctions between "rich" and "poor" in society? In this chapter, we consider alternative definitions of "poverty" and the connection between these concepts of poverty and the concept of inequality. We examine the problem of "measuring" poverty and we discuss, briefly, who "the poor" are and some of the consequences of their poverty.

4.2 Defining the "Poverty Line"

There is no real agreement on the definition of a "poverty line." As Table 4.1 indicates, the official budget standard and an alternative relativistic definition use widely differing cutoff points. Using the official definition of the Bureau of the Census, one would class a family of four which had an income in 1981 of less than $9,287 as "poor."[1] Using the relative definition of poverty first advocated by Fuchs (1967) one would class such a family as poor only if its income was less than $13,162—a difference of $3,875 or over 41%![2]

Naturally, such widely varying definitions of the "poverty line" imply that a much larger percentage of the American population would be classed as poor under a relativistic definition of poverty than under the official definitions. These different classifications of the "poor" and "nonpoor" tend to shape our perceptions of the entire issue of poverty. In 1974, the revised official count of the poverty population indicated that 23,370,000 people were poor (11.2% of the population) (Bureau of the Census, C.P.R., P-60, 134:22) while a relative definition would count 41,267,000 people as poor (19.6% of the population) (U.S., Department of H.E.W., 1976:54-55). Whether one sees poverty as a large and continuing problem of society or as a small and diminishing aspect of it will be greatly influenced by the percentage of the population which is classified as living in poverty. Our perception of the trends, the nature, and the extent of

Table 4.1

Poverty Lines—1981

Family Size	Official Definition[a]	Relative Poverty[b]
	(3 × 1963 subsistence food budget × inflation)	(one-half median)
	Weighted average	
1	$ 4,620	$ 6,555
2	5,917	8,397
3	7,250	10,275
4	9,287	13,162
5	11,007	15,559
6	12,449	17,545
7	14,110	21,668
8	15,655	22,187
9	18,572	26,321

Sources: [a]Bureau of the Census. C.P.R. P-60-119, p. 206, and C.P.R. P-60-134, p. 31.
[b]Bureau of the Census. C.P.R. P-60-134, p. 19. One-half 1981 median for 4-person households, weighted for family size in same way as official measure.

poverty will also be shaped by our choice of definition. If one adopts a relative definition, poverty did not diminish during the 1970s, but the official definition implies both that the poverty population declined steadily until 1974 and then fluctuated around 24 million until 1978, when it began an upward climb, reaching 31,822,000 in 1981 (C.P.R., P-60, 134:22).

How do these discrepancies arise? How can it be that something as real as poor people can appear and vanish in a statistician's definition? To see why, we must examine how these poverty lines were set and how they are adjusted.

Figure 4.1 illustrates what will happen to the poverty line, over time, if it is increased only by the rate of inflation. Suppose that the poverty line was initially drawn at $3,000 per year or one-half of the median family income of $6,000 per year. If there is real growth of 2% per year (as in the United States from 1963 to 1978) but no inflation of prices (Fig. 4.1(a)), in fifteen years the income of the median family will be $8,099 but the poverty line will (since we have assumed zero inflation) still be $3,000— i.e., now only 37% of the median.

More realistically, we can assume inflation is, for example, 5%—i.e., approximately the compounded U.S. inflation rate from 1963 to 1978— Fig. 4.1(b). The poverty line then grows at 5% per year (since it is adjusted for inflation) but median incomes grow at 7% (5% inflation plus 2% real growth). In fifteen years the poverty line will grow to $6,351 but median money income will grow to $17,145—i.e., after fifteen years the poverty line has still fallen to 37% of the median. The fraction of the population defined as "poor" will therefore have a tendency to fall. This process occurred during the 1960s and early 1970s, and, relative to the median income, the poverty line was cut by roughly three-tenths from 50% to 35% of median family income.

4.3 What Is Poverty?

The official definition of poverty is based on calculations done by Mollie Orshansky in 1963 at the Social Security administration. Using the "economy food plan"[3] of the Department of Agriculture as a base, she calculated the cost of such a food plan for various family types. Since the average food expenditure of families was then roughly one-third of family income, the cost of the economy food plan was multiplied by three to give the estimated "poverty line." Since food intake was calculated to differ not only by family size but also by the age and sex of the household head and by the number of children present in it, and since the cost of food differs between farm and nonfarm families, the "poverty line" differs for different family types. In fact, until 1980 there were 124 poverty thresholds identified (see U.S., Department of H.E.W. 1976:29/30) for different possible combinations of size, sex of head, number of children, etc.

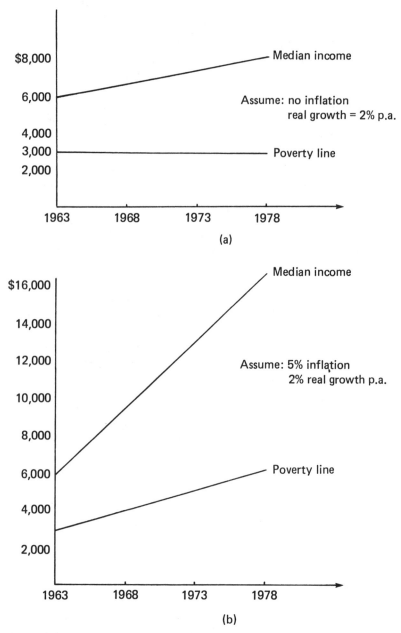

Figure 4.1

Initially, these calculations implied that an average family of two adults and two children needed an income of $3,130 in 1963 to stay above the poverty line. In 1963, the "official" and "relative" measure of poverty in fact very nearly coincided, since median family income was then $6,249—implying a "relative" poverty line of $3,125. The difference between these conceptions of poverty has arisen solely because the official definition has been updated only by the rate of inflation, and, as a result, the standard of living of the officially poor fell further and further below that of the rest of society.[4]

As we discussed in Chapter 2, the quintile shares of money income have remained fairly constant over this period as the entire distribution shifted up with economic growth. Figure 4.2 represents this upward shift in the income distribution and P_1 and P_2 represent poverty lines drawn at half the median income for each year. If the poverty line is frozen at P_1 (as the official poverty line has been) the upward shift in the distribution obviously means that fewer people will be counted as poor. The problem of poverty will then seem to be a diminishing one. What is less obvious is that the nature of the poverty problem will also seem to change. Those people who had incomes below P_1 in 1978 were the very poorest, those least likely to have an attachment to the labor market, those with the least resources. If we had drawn a poverty line at 37% of the median income in 1963, as at P_0, we would likewise have isolated the least fortunate of the poverty population. The people above 37%, but below 50%, of the median

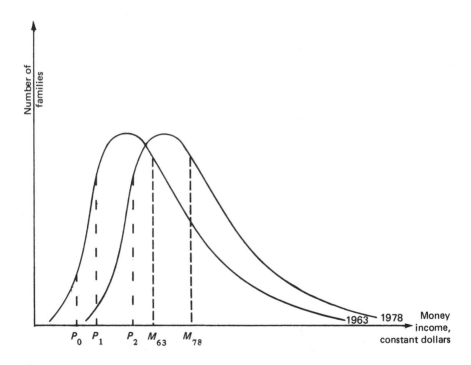

Figure 4.2

income (i.e., between P_0 and P_1 in 1963; between P_1 and P_2 in 1978) are much more like the rest of the population in age, labor force attachment, family type, etc., than those in the extreme lower tail. As a result, freezing the poverty line at P_1 meant progressively isolating the worst cases of poverty. As the problem of poverty appeared to be declining it therefore also appeared to be becoming less amenable to traditional sorts of public policy. The issue of how one draws the poverty line is therefore highly important for social policy since a perception that the poverty population was small and declining in size, with severe and intractable problems, may have led some to simply wash their hands of the whole issue. (Since 1978, of course, the combination of unemployment, de- creased transfers, and less-than-inflationary wage gains has pushed an additional 7,325,000 Americans below the official poverty line.)

It has been argued that "all the numerous economic definitions of poverty contain one common element; they consider poverty a condition of having insufficient funds to maintain a (socially) acceptable standard of living" (Perlman, 1976:3). The disagreement is about whether this "ac- ceptable" standard of living should be defined *relative* to the "incomes of the rest of the community" or whether it should be set at an income sufficient to meet basic "needs." What is the rationale for these different approaches?

The method of establishing a poverty line by construction of a minimal subsistence budget has a long history. As an early researcher wrote, "My primary poverty line represented the minimum sum on which physical efficiency could be maintained. It was a standard of barest subsistence rather than living. In calculating it the utmost economy was practiced. . . . A family living upon the scale allowed for in this estimate must be governed by the regulation, 'nothing must be bought but that which is absolutely necessary for the maintenance of physical health, and what is bought must be of the plainest and most economic description' " (Rowntree, 1941:102).

One criticism of this "budget standard" approach is that although skilled nutritionists and expert budget planners might be able to maintain adequate nutrition within a severe budget one cannot assume that real live poor people will be able to. Cooking, as we all know, is something that many people at all income levels do not do very well. Where income is more uncertain and families live closer to the margin it may also be more difficult (even if more essential) to learn budgeting skills than in middle- class families where income arrives dependably in regular and foreseeable installments. Finally, the monotonous virtue of the careful planning involved in these budget calculations ignores a very central part of the human makeup. As Orwell said (in response to a 1937 newspaper article suggesting that the unemployed of England could live quite nicely if they ate more wholesomely and saved fuel by eating raw vegetables), "The ordinary human being would sooner starve than live on brown bread and raw carrots. . . . When you are unemployed, which is to say when you are underfed, harassed, bored and miserable, you don't *want* to eat dull wholesome food. You want something a bit 'tasty.' There is always some cheaply pleasant thing to tempt you" (Orwell, 1937:86).

In comparing definitions of the poverty line the "budget" methods of calculation have an appearance of objectivity which explains much of their widespread acceptance. This appearance is, however, largely illusory. Even Rowntree's strict regimen included an allowance for tea—an item with no nutritive value. Such an item may be a social necessity but it is not a physical one. In fact, as Rowntree himself recognized, the definition of a "necessity" and of the "minimum" family budget must necessarily be relative to a particular society at a particular time.

Deciding which are the "necessities" of life is a difficult task. Our most basic need is probably food, but the minimum daily caloric requirements of an individual depend on sex, age, body size, level of physical activity, climate, and kind of housing, as well as on whether one wishes to set a standard, as in concentration camps, which is just sufficient to prolong life or one which is adequate for health and resistance to disease. Level of physical activity alone can vary the needs of adult men from as low as 1,750 to as much as 5,000 calories per day (McKenzie, 1970:70). Even if one could define unambiguously the chemical requirements of humans in terms of calories, vitamin units, and grams of protein, humans, unlike other animals, are not indifferent as to the form in which these nutrients are delivered. A minimum-cost diet would, for example, have no place for meat—a relatively high-cost protein source. Would most Americans today consider a diet based *solely* on potatoes and beans to be a socially acceptable standard of life?

Once one moves beyond food, it becomes even more difficult to define a minimum standard of living since, as many suggest, "the luxuries of yesterday become the comforts of today and the necessities of tomorrow." Indoor plumbing was not, a hundred years ago, viewed as a necessity—today, a home without indoor plumbing in almost any city in the United States would be condemned as substandard accommodation and ordered demolished. The construction of a "minimum" budget must inevitably take into account prevailing standards in the community in which it is to be used. As Adam Smith wrote, over two centuries ago, "Custom has rendered leather shoes a necessary of life in England. The poorest creditable person of either sex would be ashamed to appear in public without them. . . . In France they are necessaries neither to men nor to women; the lowest rank of both sexes appearing there publicly, without any discredit, sometimes in wooden shoes and sometimes barefoot. . . . Under necessaries, therefore, I comprehend not only those things which nature, but those things which the established rules of decency have rendered necessary to the lowest rank of people" (1776:399).

And, in fact, established standards of decency influence very strongly the construction of minimum standards. As an aid to determining eligibility for charity and welfare, charity institutions in the early 1900s and, since 1920, the Bureau of Labor Statistics have constructed subsistence-level household budgets for U.S. families. Since the criterion involved in these budgets was "to provide simply the minimum of food, clothing and so forth necessary to keep someone alive and functioning during the 'emergency' that has made him seek charity" (Rainwater 1974:45), one would expect these budgets to remain roughly constant, *if* poverty is an absolute concept. In fact, "subsistence" levels more than doubled, in constant dollars, over the period during which these budgets were being revised (see Table 4.2). Comparing, for example, a subsistence budget of 1908 and 1960, Rainwater observes that the 1908 budget did not require a full bathroom, made no allowance for electricity, and involved a diet very heavy in breads and cereals while the 1960 budget allowed for a full bathroom, for enough electricity for lights, an iron, and a refrigerator, and for a diet with substantially more protein. In 1960, as in 1908, it was certainly possible to survive without these things but the social standard of what a minimally decent life required has changed considerably in the interim—in terms of constant 1981 dollars, by 113%.

Changes in social standards have two components—changes in the level of consumption of goods (such as meat) available both in 1908 and in

Table 4.2

"Subsistence" Standard of Living Budgets 1905-1963

Period	"Subsistence" Budget Amount* (converted to 1981 dollars)	Average Percent of 4 × Per Capita Disposable Income
1905-1909	4,469	39%
1910-1914	5,406	39%
1915-1919	5,657	41%
1920-1924	5,901	44%
1925-1929	6,170	43%
1930-1934	6,345	53%
1935-1939	5,613	40%
1940-1944	7,299	32%
1945-1949	8,047	38%
1950-1954	8,510	37%
1955-1960	8,583	35%
1963	9,525	37%

Source: L. Rainwater (1974:46). Reprinted by permission of Basic Books, Inc., Publishers, New York.
*I.e., maximum amount subsistence budget reached during period.

1960 and changes in the goods which are generally available over the period 1908 to 1960. Changes in the general level of nutrition have changed our norms as to a minimal diet, but in addition changes in the goods most people consume may make some goods increasingly unavailable to the poor. For example, in 1908 the general absence of automobiles meant that cities tended to be smaller and urban mass transit was generally available—the entire spatial pattern of shopping, recreation, trips to work, etc., was oriented to a population without cars. By 1960, the vast majority of families had automobiles, cities had expanded enormously in size, and mass transit in most cities had become much more inconvenient and often unavailable. The orientation of urban structure to those with cars has meant that those without cars face, on average, a substantially more difficult life now than in 1908. It is thus not much consolation for America's poor to know that in most of the rest of the world the possession of any sort of automobile is a privilege reserved for the elite—the poor here need transportation. Similarily the poor have to live somewhere, and increased legal requirements for housing standards (e.g., indoor toilets) are reflected in higher rents—another example of the increased costs of living which must be incorporated into increasing "subsistence" budgets.

As Rainwater concludes, "Expert judgments concerning living levels ranging from minimum subsistence to comfort showed remarkable stability in relation to the general level of affluence of society over the first half of the twentieth century and into the present" (1974:47). Over the period 1905 to 1963, the subsistence budget averaged 39.8% of average disposable family income.[5] Unfortunately, once three times the subsistence food budget became enshrined in 1963 as the poverty line, it has become very difficult to make the periodic revisions to the subsistence budget which were normal before 1963. As a result, "subsistence" as *officially* defined has fallen further and further below the average American's standard of living.

Public attitudes are more generous than official budgets, but are also remarkably consistent, on a relative basis. From 1946 to 1977 the Gallup Poll asked Americans almost every year, What is the smallest amount of money a family of four needs to get along in this community? Table 4.3 presents the answers. In money terms, average incomes changed by a factor of almost five—but the social definition of a minimum required income seems to have changed much less, *relative to median male earnings*.[6]

International evidence produces much the same conclusion. In very poor countries poverty can be understood in terms of absolute deprivation of food, clothing, and shelter, but in developed economies poverty is best understood as an income sufficiently below the norms of society that a "decent" life does not appear to be feasible. These norms increase as the average income of society increases. In Table 4.4, the poverty lines

Table 4.3

Minimum Income to "Get Along" and Median Male Earnings

Year	(1) Weekly "Get-Along Income"	(2) (1) × 52	(3) Median Male Earnings[a]	(4) (2) ÷ (3), percent	(5) Column 2 in 1981 dollars
1947	45.20	2,350	2,230	105%	9,572
1948	51.93	2,700	2,396	111%	10,106
1949	49.73	2,586	2,346	110%	9,859
1950	47.98	2,495	2,570	97%	9,421
1951	55.00	2,860	2,952	96%	9,962
1952	62.00	3,224	3,105	103%	11,032
1953	59.80	3,110	3,221	97%	10,482
1954	63.85	3,320	3,193	105%	11,343
1957	74.77	3,888	3,677	107%	12,764
1958	82.17	4,273	3,743	114%	13,381
1960	81.54	4,240	4,080	104%	13,046
1961	83.23	4,328	4,189	103%	13,059
1962	83.13	4,323	4,372	99%	13,008
1963	83.24	4,328	4,511	96%	12,827
1964	85.35	4,438	4,647	95%	12,995
1967	109.16	5,676	5,553	102%	15,381
1969	119.72	6,225	6,429	97%	15,499
1970	120.00	6,240	6,670	94%	14,620
1971	126.00	6,552	6,903	95%	14,718
1972	127.00	6,604	7,450	89%	14,361
1973	149.00	7,748	8,056	96%	15,865
1974	152.00	7,904	8,452	94%	14,580
1975	161.00	8,372	8,853	95%	14,156
1976	177.00	9,204	9,426	98%	14,709
1977	199.00	10,348	10,123	102%	15,528

Sources: American Institute of Public Opinion (George Gallup, The Gallup Poll, Public Opinion 1935-1971, Vol. 63, New York, N.Y.: Random House, Inc., © 1972. Used with permission of Random House, Inc.

American Institute of Public Opinion. The Gallup Poll, Public Opinion 1972-1977, Vol. 1 1972-75 and Vol. 2 1976-77, Wilmington, Delaware, 1978. Used with permission of Dr. G. Gallup.

U.S., Department of Commerce, Bureau of the Census. Money Income in 1977 of Families and Persons in the United States. (Washington: U.S. Government Printing Office, 1979), Tables 61 and A1.

[a]Median 14 and over male full-year earnings, all industries.

The Question: What is the smallest amount of money a family of four (husband, wife, and two children) needs each week to get along in this community?

Table 4.4

Gross Domestic Product Per Capita and Poverty Norm
(excluding rent)
Selected Countries for Selected Years

	GDP/Capita U.S. Dollars	Single-Person Poverty Norm as Percentage of GDP/Capita
United States (1965)	3,240	25.8[a]
Switzerland (1966)	2,265	30.3
Canada (1965)	2,156	23.3[b]
Denmark (1965)	2,070	24.4
Finland (1967)	1,801	24.1
France (1965)	1,626	22.4
United Kingdom (1963)	1,395	32.8
West Germany (1962)	1,321	25.4
Japan (1964)	717	30.3
Ireland (1962)	639	24.3

Source: Taira (1969: Table 1, p. 37).
[a]The general assistance standard of Santa Clara County, California.
[b]The general assistance standard of the Province of Ontario.

reported were drawn by a number of different methodologies, but the "subsistence" which they represent varies relatively little as a percentage of average living standards.

In the poorest countries, the poverty line is relatively high as a fraction of per capita income, probably because of the absolutely low level of per capita income. In the richer countries, there is some variation in the "generosity" reflected in these official definitions of poverty,[7] but the interesting thing to note is how much less variation there is when poverty lines are expressed in relative terms to the average level of incomes.

If poverty is a relative concept, then the definition of the poverty line should be *explicitly* relative. A relative measure does not necessarily imply that the percentage of the population defined to be "poor" is immutably fixed; it simply implies[8] that a more egalitarian (but still less than perfectly equal) society can succeed in eliminating poverty. In Figure 4.2, for example, the dashed lines represent an income distribution with a lower incidence of poverty, and greater equality, than the current distribution of income. All that is required for the elimination of relative poverty is that the least well-off members of the society should not receive less than half the median income. A "relativistic" conception of poverty therefore implies that the issues of poverty and economic inequality are inextricably linked, not in the sense that *absolute* equality is required to eliminate poverty but in the sense that the extremes of inequality create and sustain poverty.

There is, however, a problem with any measure which is based on a *single year's* average (or median) income. If a depression cut everyone's income, yet fewer people had less than half the median, this would indicate less "poverty" and not more. Social norms are, more likely, a sort of moving average of recent living standards. The "relative" measure of poverty would therefore be improved if one defined the poverty line as one-half the median real family income of the past five years, in order to avoid "perverse" results if one year's income should be particularly below (or above) its long-run trend.

4.4 How Much Poverty Is There?

Traditionally, the amount of poverty has been measured either by counting the fraction of a country's population whose income lies below the poverty line (the so-called "head-count" method) or by calculating the ratio between the total amount by which the income of the poor falls short of the poverty line and their incomes if they were raised to the poverty line (the "poverty-gap ratio" method). Simply counting the proportion of the population below the poverty line, however, pays no attention to the *amount* by which the income of the poor falls short.[9] On the other hand, measuring poverty by the size of the "poverty gap" pays no attention to the number of people who are poor. Both the "poverty gap" and the "head-count" method of measuring the extent of poverty are therefore unreliable, *regardless* of how the "poverty line" was initially drawn.

A number of alternative measures of the extent of poverty have therefore been proposed, all of which have in common an explicit consideration either of economic inequality among the poor or of economic inequality in the larger society. Sen (1979), for example, has proposed that the incidence of poverty in a society be measured by: $p = H[1 + (1 - I)G]$ where: H = "head-count"—percentage of people below poverty line (however drawn), I = "poverty gap ratio"—total shortfall of all incomes of poor from poverty line as fraction of poverty line income for all poor people, and G = Gini ratio of income distribution of poor (see Chapter 2).

This measure of the extent of poverty is therefore a combination of a head count, the poverty-gap ratio, and the extent of inequality among the poor. Since inequality among the poor may be fairly great (e.g., between someone just below and someone far below the poverty line) this measure indicates that the severity of the poverty problem increases as inequality among the poor increases. Other measures (e.g., that of Hagerbaumer, 1977) differ in detail but the essential point remains, that an accurate measure of poverty must be linked to a measure of inequality among the poor.

4.5 Who Are the Poor?

The extent of poverty may depend upon the degree of inequality of income distribution in society, but, to make statistics more personal, who are the poor and why are they poor? Table 4.5 presents data on the distribution and the incidence of poverty in 1974 and 1981, since both the official and the relative measure of poverty are available for 1974 (the year of minimum poverty) while 1981 data are the most recent available.

There are two separate issues considered in Table 4.5: the incidence of poverty (the probability with which a particular family type will be poor) and the distribution of poverty (the percentage of all poor families who are of that particular type). Some groups may have a low *chance* of being poor but are so large that even this low incidence produces a large *number* of poor people. The incidence of poverty among families with a male head employed year round at full-time work was relatively low by either definition, but since in 1981 there were roughly 35.8 million such families they amounted to a relatively large fraction of the poverty population. Indeed, between roughly one-fifth (by the Social Security definition) and roughly one-quarter (by the relative definition) of all poor families were headed by full-time, full-year workers. Another 12 to 20% of poor family heads were over the normal retirement age of 65. By either definition of poverty, a clear majority of poor family heads under 65 worked in the paid labor market.

Stereotypes of the poor are, however, probably based more on the incidence of poverty than on the number of poor people. Most poor people are white, under 65, and in intact families, usually with a head who participates in the paid labor market—but one's *chances* of being poor increase dramatically if one is black, over 65, in a female-headed family, or out of the paid labor market. It is the latter *types* who are most often identified with the poverty issue. Also, in going from the official to the relative definition of poverty, one should note that those who thus join the poverty population are much more similar to the population at large than those below the Social Security cutoff. For example, the families that "joined" the poverty population in 1974, if one uses the relative definition, were 79% white, 75% were male-headed, and 62% of family heads worked during the past year (almost half on a full-time, full-year basis). Stereotypes of the poor as "abnormal" are much more difficult to maintain if (1) one sees poverty as a relative phenomenon and (2) if one counts the *number* of poor people.

4.5.1 Poverty among the old Aging is, of course, a normal process and it is crucial to distinguish between poverty among the old and poverty within the rest of the population. Younger people may be able to escape

Table 4.5

Incidence and Distribution of Poverty by Selected Family Characteristics—1974 and 1981

Families	1981 Official Poverty Line		1974 Official Poverty Line		1974 Relative Poverty Line		All Income Levels	
	Percent Incidence	Percent Distribution	Percent Incidence	Percent Distribution	Percent Incidence	Percent Distribution	1974	1981
All Families	11.2		9.9		16.1			
Male-headed	6.9	52.5	5.7	54	11.7	63.3	87.0	84.6
Female-headed	34.6	47.5	32.5	46	45.4	36.7	13.0	15.4
White	8.8	68.1	7.0	68.2	13.1	72.3	88.8	87.2
Black	30.8	28.8	27.8	29.9	42.3	25.9	9.9	10.5
Other	24.0	3.1	12.7	1.9	21.1	1.8	1.4	2.3
Age of Head								
Under 25	16.1	12.2	17.3	14.3	27.1	12.8	7.6	5.9
25 to 64	9.2	75.4	8.3	70.8	14.0	68.2	78.0	78.7
65+	9.1	12.4	9.5	14.9	21.5	19.2	14.4	15.4
Work Experience of Householder, all ages								
Full-time, 50–52 weeks	3.5	17.5	2.9	19.2	6.3	23.4	63.1	57.0
Less than full time, full year	18.1	33.5	15.9	34.0	28.6	34.9	19.6	21.5
Did not work	25.6	48.9	24.8	46.8	38.8	41.7	17.3	21.5
Total—million families		6.851		5.109		8.967	55.712	61.019
Unrelated Persons								
Male	18.1	34.4	20.3	33.4	32.0	32.3	41.8	44.6
Female	27.7	65.6	29.2	66.6	48.1	67.7	58.2	55.4
All persons (millions)	14.0%	31.822	11.6%	24.260	19.7%	41.167	209.343	227.157

Sources: L. Brown, *The Measure of Poverty*, Technical Paper 18. U.S. Department of Health, Education, and Welfare. (Washington: U.S. Government Printing Office, 1976) Bureau of the Census, C P R, P60, 134.

from poverty by getting a new or a higher-paying job but people over 65 are generally excluded from paid employment by regulation, custom, and physical capacity. They are, therefore, largely dependent on transfer income, savings, pensions, or the support of relatives. To the extent that their incomes while employed were not sufficient to permit the accumulation of savings for their old age or their employers did not provide pension plans, their *present* poverty is the result of the *past* operation of the labor market. Low-income workers are least able to save for retirement and also least likely to be covered by pensions.

In Chapter 11 we consider the "life-cycle" savings model and, to anticipate our conclusions then, the evidence indicates that only a small fraction of the population can accumulate enough assets while working to finance a decent retirement. Indeed, Schiller (1980:78) reports that only half of all aged families hold at least $100 in a savings account and that the average net worth of aged families was only $15,000—mostly in the form of home ownership. Private savings are insufficient for most people's retirement and so are private pension plans. Not only are high-income workers much more likely to have jobs in which private pension plans are available; they are also much more likely to actually receive the benefits of such plans. Employees who are laid off or disabled or who quit before their pension rights are "vested" typically lose their pension rights. Such job instability is greater among low-income workers, implying that relatively few low-income workers acquire entitlement to private pension plans. In addition, most private pension plans are not indexed. The net result is that in 1978 only 20% of aged households had any income from private pension plans and such plans provided only 7% of the total income of the aged (Schiller, 1980:81). The main income source of the aged poor is, therefore, Social Security and government transfer payments and they have few realistic alternatives.[10]

4.5.2 The Working Poor As has already been noted, a majority of poor adults under 65 work and a substantial fraction work full time year-round. These are the "working poor." Among this group it is primarily low wages, and not unemployment, that is the cause of poverty. The incidence of low wages is higher among unattached individuals, females, the poorly educated, Southerners, blacks, farmers, and employees in seasonal or service industries (see Chapters 7 to 10). Families with fewer earners are, of course, also less likely to be able to put together a total income package above poverty levels. Those families whose low wages are interrupted by unemployment are more *likely* to be poor but the availability of unemployment insurance lifts some such families[11] over the poverty line and lessens the poverty gap of those who remain.

Of course, looking at current earnings may be misleading. Those who are young and have skills may (like college students) expect low incomes to be a temporary thing. Garfinkel and Haveman (1977) therefore emphasized the "earnings capacity" (see Chapter 8) implied by a standard 2,000 hours of work a year and the wage that one could expect based on education, region, occupation, sex, etc.—they then compared earnings capacity with actual earnings. They concluded that defining poverty in terms of current income overemphasizes the temporarily low earnings of younger people, as well as the low current income of retired people (who may have savings to fall back on). Conversely, defining poverty in terms of current income underemphasizes the "working poor." If one examines those who are "earnings capacity" poor, they are much more likely to be fully in the labor force; indeed, in order to keep their current income above the poverty line they tend to "utilize their earnings capacity more fully" (1977:59)—i.e., work more than 2,000 hours in order to compensate for their low wages.

4.5.3 Women and Poverty The incidence of poverty is especially high for female-headed family units. Among those over 65, female poverty often arises because women typically live longer than men and, as widows, become dependent upon government transfer payments. Few widows can depend on private pensions in their old age since only a minority of workers are covered by private pensions in the first instance, and, of those, many are in plans that give no benefits whatsoever to surviving spouses. Since most women are out of the paid labor force for some years as they raise a family, their entitlement to a Social Security pension is correspondingly less. As a consequence, the poverty of older women living alone is especially severe.

Older people and low-wage workers have long composed the bulk of the poverty population but the greatest recent change in the anatomy of poverty has been the growing importance of single-parent families. Over the period 1970 to 1977, the number of female-headed single-parent families increased by 49.8% (Bureau of the Census, C.P.R., P-23, 100:81)—and roughly four out of ten such families fall below the Social Security poverty line. Child-care responsibilities often make full-time paid employment impracticable but even year-round full-time employed women typically have earnings that are only approximately 59% of male earnings (C.P.R., P-23, 100:73). Averaging employed women and those who must depend on transfer payments, one finds that households headed by females with no husband present had an average income, in 1979, that was half that of the average household (C.P.R., P-60, 126:53).

Absence from the paid labor force or discrimination within it (see Chapter 7) may prevent an escape from poverty for female-headed families but one must beware of assuming that these families are poor because they are female-headed, rather than *now* being female-headed partly because they were poor previously. Schiller (1980:98) has argued, "While at any point in time a high proportion of poor families will be female-headed, family breakup cannot be identified as a major cause of poverty. . . . Family disunity may help sustain poverty, but in most cases it appears that poverty preceded, and itself helped to cause, family dissolution." Similarily, Orcutt, Caldwell, and Wertheimer (1976:116) found that unemployment of the family head is highly significant in increasing the likelihood of divorce—a finding supported by Moynihan (1965) and Duncan and Morgan (1976). Prolonged periods of high national unemployment therefore leave a residue of broken marriages, single-parent families, and an increasing poverty population.

Of course, we all know of wealthy couples whose marriages have broken up, just as we all know of sober drivers who have had car accidents, even though drinking increases one's chances of a car accident. Similarly, economic stress increases one's chances of a marriage breakdown, and a primary cause of economic stress is low and/or uncertain family income. Broken marriages then create single-parent families, whose chances of escape from poverty are lessened by the burden of family responsibilities and by low wages for females in the labor market.

4.5.4 The Permanence of Poverty Using *annual* income as a criterion has two defects for a study of poverty—a year is both "too short" and "too long" a period of time. If we are interested in income adequacy we must recognize that a year can be a very long time for a household budget. Indeed, for those who have no money and no groceries even a week can seem like an eternity. A family whose wage earner is unemployed with no income from January to July and who then gets a job at $8 per hour may be a family whose total annual income is above the poverty line—but it is also a family which spent six months of the year substantially below the poverty line. If credit is easily available or if the family has adequate savings to rely on, we can ignore the unpredictability of some people's income and the interruptions in income others face since credit and/or savings could tide people over "temporarily" rough spots. Low-income people are, however, more likely than high-income people to experience such involuntary shocks to their financial plans as getting fired, being put on short time, or being laid off or evicted (Ehrlich, 1975). This greater instability, plus the obvious difficulty in accumulating savings from a low income, means that savings are rarely a sufficient cushion. Access to credit is, naturally, restricted to those who are most likely to be able to repay—i.e., it is very "imperfectly" available to the poor and the unemployed. Uneven income flows can therefore mean occasionally inadequate income, even for some whose total annual income puts them above the poverty line.

On the other hand, a year is "too short" a period of time if our focus is the "culture of poverty." The impacts of poverty on self-esteem, on optimism for improvement, and on ability to cope take time to have their full effect. Families which are poor for only a year or two may well escape many of the psychological costs of being poor.[12] The self-hatred, hopelessness, and depression which has been described in such classic studies as Harrington (1963) is probably more a function of expected lifetime income than of annual income in any given year. Since incomes fluctuate, some people who are poor in a lifetime sense will, in any given year, have annual incomes which are above the poverty line due to a run of good luck such as a lot of overtime at work. Conversely, some people who are not poor in any lifetime sense, and who do not basically regard themselves as "poor," will have a run of bad luck (such as a divorce or a layoff) and will fall below the poverty line for that particular year.

The number of people whom we count as poor, using either the "official" or the relativistic annual income poverty line, is thus a very imperfect indicator of the extent of lifetime poverty. We can get some idea how imperfect an indicator by examining longitudinal data on families over time, such as those of Lane and Morgan (1975:32-35). Using the "official" poverty line, they found that 39% of those who were "poor" in 1967 were also "poor" in 1972 and a further 26% were near-poor—i.e., below 150% of the official poverty line in 1972. Roughly 64% of the officially poor in 1967 had a six-year average income which was below the official poverty line, although only about 30% of the officially poor were "poor" *in all six years* 1967 to 1972.[13]

On the other hand, a more liberal definition of "poverty," one which is closer to the poverty line that would be implied by a relative conception of poverty, shows both a high incidence and a greater permanence of poverty. If we examine those who fell below 150% of the official poverty line in 1967, Lane and Morgan found that they constituted some 22% of the total population, as opposed to 11% who were below the official poverty line. Of this 22%, some 17%, or over three-quarters, had a six-year average income below this more liberal poverty line.

Another interesting finding of the Lane/Morgan study is the low fraction of families who were poor *in all six years* (8%, by the more liberal definition) and the high fraction who were poor *in one year of the six studied* (36%, again by the more liberal definition). This points up the variability in personal income that is caused by year-to-year fluctuations in overtime hours, layoffs, and new jobs and the variability in family income that comes with changes in family composition and paid labor force participation. Two classes of individuals largely escape, however, year-to-year variability in employment income—those in isolated rural areas or outside the paid labor force due to age, infirmity, or child-care responsibilities and those whose income is entirely from salary. As Lane and Morgan put it (1975:39) "Only the very well educated seem to be entirely free from occasional poverty," while those who are poor every year are overwhelmingly uneducated and black, half living in rural areas and 85% living in the South.

If we focus on those who are in the labor force, Lillard and Willis (1978) used the same years of data from the Michigan Panel Study of Income Dynamics to decompose the total variance in earnings into those differences which represent permanent differences in earnings and those which are due to year-to-year fluctuations. Some 73% of the total variance in log earnings, they found, was permanent in nature—even if measurable characteristics could explain only some 65% of the differences in the permanent earnings of whites.[14] The great importance of permanent earnings differentials means that "there is a considerable tendency for individuals to retain their position in the earnings distribution over time whether this position is in the lower, upper or middle of the distribution" (1978:1008), *but* the appreciable role of year-to-year variations among employed people means that only a minority of poor people are poor *in every year*. Since family money income can change considerably as individuals enter or leave the family or as family members enter or leave the paid labor market, there is more variability in annual family money income than in annual individual earnings. Freeman (1981), however, has recently focused his attention on "troubled" workers—those who are disadvantaged in the labor market by sex, race, or qualifications or who are displaced from relatively good jobs (e.g., by layoff, plant closing, illness, or accident). His conclusion (based on the same data source for 1967 to 1979) is that "many workers at the bottom of the income distribution are *permanently* plagued by problems of low earnings" (1981:106), due largely to low wages and the permanent losses of older workers suffering job loss. One can predict that blacks, the poorly educated, women, and those in certain industries and areas will have a high chance of low earnings, but the best predictor is simply whether a person had low earnings last year. This points up the importance of unobservable personal variables in predicting permanent earnings, and Freeman argues, "We can reasonably assume that family background is an important determinant of whether a worker is permanently in trouble in the job market" (1981:127).

To sum up, most of those who are poor in any given year are not poor *every* year. Changes in labor demand in the economy and in labor supply by families produce fluctuating incomes for the working poor. They also produce temporary poverty for some families which are not poor in any lifetime sense. These fluctuations can in addition produce income inadequacy for some months for families which are not poor even in an annual income sense. Families that are *temporarily* poor for a few months or for a year or two, but are not "lifetime income poor," are more likely to escape the psychological and social costs of poverty. Roughly speaking, one could say that some two-thirds to three-quarters (depending on the poverty criterion used) of those who are "annual income poor" are also "average income poor."

4.5.5 *Implications of Low Income* As Rainwater has put it, "Not having enough money to support a family properly means that the husband is constantly vulnerable to accusations of being inadequate or incompetent as a provider and the wife is constantly vulnerable to accusations of not being sufficiently energetic in making do. . . . These factors produce a common pattern of endemic tension and dissatisfaction within lower-class marriages" (1974:12). Marital instability is one result; significantly different patterns of child rearing are another (see Chapter 6).

Relative incomes are a vital component in the process of social stratification—what Parsons (1954:69) called "the differential ranking of the human individuals who compose a given social system and their treatment as superior or inferior relative to one another in certain socially important respects." Both social rewards (prestige, authority, status) and social sanctions (such as one's treatment by the criminal justice system) are unequally distributed across social strata. In North America, economic criteria are overwhelmingly the basis for social stratification.[15]

Since these criteria are "inculcated from early childhood and are deeply 'introjected' to form part of the basic structure of the personality itself" (Parsons, 1954:74), it is not surprising that the poor tend to have very low self-esteem and generally negative evaluations of their own capabilities (Rothman, 1978:114).

Political scientists refer to a low sense of personal efficacy among the poor, meaning that they feel it unlikely that they personally could influence political events and feel that "it doesn't make any difference anyhow." Limited personal and financial resources, plus a low sense of efficacy, mean that voter turnout and political participation in general is much lower among the poor than among other socioeconomic groups. In the 1978 elections, for example, 30.6% of adults in families with under $5,000 in income voted, but 60.1% of those in families with over $25,000 income voted (Bureau of the Census, C.P.R., P-20, 344:5). This discrepancy in voter turnout clearly limits the political constituency to which antipoverty policies might appeal. In addition, those who are poor in money are usually also poor in the contacts and skills required for political lobbying. Effective political activity at the local or the national level requires time and knowledge—or the money to purchase them. The poor, in general, lack these resources. Hence, as a freshman text on American government puts it, "The data show up a major problem of American politics: Those who need government intervention the most—the poor, the less educated, the victims of racial discrimination—are the ones who are least (politically) active. Those who need government help the least—because they are already wealthier, better educated, less discriminated against—are the most active" (Prewitt and Verba, 1979:198).

Finally, one must emphasize that the operation of the labor market is central to the poverty issue. The immediate causes of poverty (e.g., lack of a pension, single-parent status) may not lie in the labor market but these factors are, themselves, often the result of other more basic factors or processes.[16] Such "causes" of low (or high) income are probabilistic, not determinate. Factors such as low education or residence in the rural South or being black are associated with a higher chance of being poor, but exceptional (or lucky) people have always been able to surmount the odds—indeed that is what makes them exceptional! Probabilities of being poor are, however, cumulative. The woman who marries a poor husband has a somewhat higher chance of marriage breakup, a lower chance of maintaining job-relevant skills if out of the paid labor market, a lower chance of getting a high-paying job when she returns to the labor market, and a lower chance of getting adequate pension entitlement on retirement. It is the accumulation of these probabilities which determines the odds she will be poor in her old age, and it is the characteristics of the labor market which are central to determining these probabilities. A labor market which contains jobs without pension entitlements, jobs with a relatively high risk of disabling accidents, and jobs for women with pay much below that of men implies that the holders of these jobs have a higher chance than average of having low incomes and their families have a higher chance of poverty.

4.6 Summary and Conclusion

1. Sen (1979:287) has recently argued, "The measurement of poverty must be seen as an exercise of description assessing the predicament of people in terms of prevailing standards of necessities. It is primarily a *factual* rather than an ethical exercise and the facts relate to what is regarded as deprivation." There is considerable evidence, over long periods of time and across many countries, that in developed economies deprivation is a relative concept. At any point in time in any particular society, the majority of people will probably share an idea of "minimum prevailing standards." These ideas (or, as Adam Smith put it, "the established rules of decency") change slowly over time and increase in proportion to increases in average incomes. Poverty is thus a relative phenomenon, with the qualification that it is relative to long-period income norms and not simply to "this year's" average income. A nation whose average income suddenly dropped drastically as the result of some calamity could well be one where a majority fell below "prevailing standards," but those standards would change if the drop in average income were long prolonged. Conversely, a *sudden* rise in average incomes (with income inequality unchanged) may initially reduce the fraction of the population below a "common standard of necessities" but if this increase in average incomes is long-lasting social definitions of necessities will change.

Ideally, one would measure "full income" (i.e., including nonmarket production) and express the poverty line relative to, and in terms of, both monetary and nonmonetary income. In practice, only annual money data is available with sufficient promptness for policy purposes. One can usefully check how closely one's own opinion of "minimum standards" accords with the official poverty line by completing the "exercise" below, adjusted for inflation between 1981 and now.

2. Since the average income of a society can be inflated by a few very high incomes, median income is probably a better indicator of prevailing income norms than average income. One-half of the median has often been suggested as an indicator of the poverty line, although it is recognized by all that this can be only an approximation, given the tremendous variability that exists in individual needs and living costs. Drawing the poverty line for four-person families at one-half the median income of such families, and adjusting for family size, produces a poverty line that fits very closely the "minimum subsistence" estimates of budget planners over the period 1905 to 1963 but is somewhat below the opinion poll evidence on the minimum income Americans consider necessary to "get along."

3. At the time of its initial formulation in 1963, the official poverty line was drawn at the same level as that implied by a relative conception of poverty as one-half of median income—but since that time it has been increased only by the rate of inflation and has, as a result, fallen from 50% to roughly 35% of median income. Cutting the poverty line in this manner reduced the estimated size of the poverty population and produced the impression that it was a declining fraction of American society, increasingly dominated by "hard-core" poverty types. Drawing a poverty line at one-half of median income, on the other hand, implies that poverty is a continuing problem for American society, one in which the "working poor" play a substantially greater role. By either criterion, however, the period since 1978 has seen an appreciable rise in American poverty.

4. If one accepts a "poverty line" based on current income, older people, single parents, and others not in the labor force comprise the majority of the poverty population. For many of them, however, current poverty is an indirect effect of the past operation of the labor market. Most of the younger poor are "working poor" and an emphasis on "earnings capacity" would give even greater stress to their situation. Low wages are the primary cause of poverty among the working poor, followed closely by the number of earners available and unemployment.

5. Fluctuations in family income mean that a fairly high fraction of the population is poor "once in a while" but relatively few are *always* below the poverty line (although they may not move much above it either). Between two-thirds and three-quarters of the "annual income poor" can be seen as "average income poor."

6. The process of income *determination* governs the incidence of poverty but the process of income *distribution* governs the extent of poverty. If, explicitly or implicitly, we adopt a relativistic conception of the nature of poverty, then the extent of poverty in a society depends directly on the degree of economic inequality in it. The shape of the lower range of the income distribution then determines *how many* people will be

poor; *who* those people will be depends on the relative advantage which education, experience, sex, or occupation accords to individual earnings—i.e., on the process of income determination.

Exercise

In 1981, the official poverty line for a nonfarm family of four of one parent and three children was $9,287. Assume that you are a single parent of three children, aged 3, 6, and 8, and that you have no inheritances, alimony, or other outside money income on which you can depend. Calculate a "typical" month's budget for your family under the following assumptions.

(a) You normally make $5.00 per hour driving a truck and work 40 hours per week. Unfortunately, your employer had to lay you off for two weeks last February and for another two weeks last November and you could not find another job during those periods.

(b) You work in an office (as a secretary) and make $140.00 per week (i.e., $4.00 per hour for a 35-hour work week). You get two weeks paid vacation a year but no other fringe benefits.

NOTES

[1]That is, on average, they would be classed as poor since the precise official poverty line depends on farm/nonfarm residence, number of children present, and age of householder.

[2]Note that the relative poverty line of Table 4.1 is in terms of money income and is drawn by comparison with the money income of all families. Were one to draw a relative poverty line in terms of full income one would have to include in full income the value of food stamps, school lunches, subsidized housing, and Medicare/Medicaid received by low-income families *and include as well* the value of "perks" of employment (from free parking to reduced air fares), the imputed income from owner-occupied housing, employer-paid medical insurance, pension plan contributions, and capital gains—all of which are received predominantly by the more affluent. It is far from obvious that using full income as a base would decrease, rather than increase, the incidence of relative poverty—recall from Chapter 3 that privately paid fringe benefits grew slightly more rapidly than aggregated government social welfare expenditures during the 1970s.

[3]Which Perlman (1976:9) has called "an eating regimen suitable for a lifeboat."

[4]A minor amendment to inflation indexing occurred in 1969 when the relevant inflation rate was changed from food only to the all-items consumer price index and the assumed price ratio paid for food by farm families relative to nonfarm families was increased.

Beginning with 1981 data, the distinctions between farm and nonfarm, male- and female-headed households were eliminated. This statistical adjustment produced a 0.2% overall increase in estimated poverty incidence (see Bureau of the Census, C.P.R. P-60, 134:21).

[5]Since the median income for all households is less than the average, subsistence incomes are a higher fraction of median incomes—in 1978, the median income of all households was .842 the average, implying that 40% of the average is 47% of the median.

[6]Over the 1946-1977 period, female labor force participation has increased substantially, implying that female earnings are a larger fraction of family money income. As Chapter 8 discusses, however, this trend is, in part, simply a monetization of female labor since market earnings are achieved at the cost of foregoing "home production" of goods and services.

Using male earnings as a base implicitly holds roughly constant the supply of family hours to the paid labor market.

7This variation may partially reflect the timing of when poverty lines were drawn—e.g., the Canadian poverty line was initially drawn in 1961 and revised substantially in 1973.

8Other "relativistic" definitions of poverty have been proposed, and, obviously, some such definitions of "the poor" (e.g., defining "the poor" as the bottom 20% of the income distribution) do have the defect that, statistically, the poor must always be with us. In other countries, the relative poverty line has been drawn more generously—i.e., relative to *average* instead of *median* income. In Canada, Adams et al. (1971) argued that one should weight the income of a family by a system of points depending on the number of people in the family and thereby calculate the "average living standard" of Canadian families—and the poverty line should be one half of it.

9Furthermore, the paradoxical result of focusing on a "head-count" measure is that one would conclude that poverty had not increased and might even have decreased if income is transferred from a poor person to a richer one. The poor person becomes poorer, but the *number* of poor remains constant—unless the transfer is to someone just at the poverty line and pushes that person over the poverty line, in which case the number of poor declines.

10Hurd and Shoven (1982) computed the comprehensive income of all aged family units, including the value of transfers and in-kind income. In 1978, Social Security was 30% of total income, Medicare/Medicaid services were 16%, and public assistance comprised 2%, while government pensions and private pensions each provided 5% of the total income of the elderly.

11However, unemployment insurance covers relatively few of the unemployed in the United States. In October 1982, when the unemployment rate was 10.4%, only some 4.6 million of the 11.55 million unemployed received state unemployment insurance benefits (*Toronto Globe & Mail,* October 29 and November 6, 1982).

12For example, a middle-class family which is split by divorce may well produce a poor single-parent family, but remarriage or reentry to the paid labor market may, after a time, restore this family to approximately its previous socioeconomic position.

13Recall that unemployment during this period was exceptionally low—3.8% in 1967, 4.9% in 1970, and 5.6% in 1972.

14See Lillard and Willis (1978:993)—measured characteristics explained 73% of permanent variation for blacks.

15An enormous literature on social stratification exists (see, for example, Harold W. Pfautz, "The Current Literature on Social Stratification: Critique and Bibliography," *American Journal of Sociology,* Vol. 58, p. 391, with a bibliography of 333 books and articles) in which it is far from uniformly established whether it is desirable to study prestige, status, class consciousness, class existence, political power, economic power, or some combination of the above. It is, however, agreed that basic to social stratification is social inequality and the most popular single criterion of placement of individuals is occupation, as ranked by income and education. In addition, many of the other variables used to "explain" status, prestige, etc. (such as "life-style," housing type, etc.) are highly related to income and wealth.

16The poverty of the "working poor" is directly related to low wages and/or employment instability. The poverty of older people arises from their lack of pension rights or savings from their working years. Although few single parents could work full time even if offered a job, "if the men who participated in forming the families that end up on welfare were not economically marginal there would not be so many female-headed families. If economic marginality produces (1) high rates of illegitimacy and divorce and (2) a low rate of remarriage, then it is the principle cause of the welfare problem" (Rainwater, 1974:15).

5 OF LABORERS AND CAPITALISTS— THE ISSUE OF FACTOR SHARES

The produce of the earth—all that is derived from its surface by the united application of labour, machinery and capital is divided among three classes of the community, namely, the proprietor of the land, the owner of the stock or capital necessary for its cultivation and the labourers by whose industry it is cultivated. To determine the laws which regulate this distribution is the principal problem of political economy.

> DAVID RICARDO
> The Principles of Political Economy and Taxation (1831)

5.1 Introduction

During Ricardo's time, his definition of the issue of income distribution made sense on two levels—the income generated by the three factors of production, land, labor, and capital, was at the same time the income received by three distinct classes of the community. Hence his analysis of production by inputs was at the same time an analysis of distribution among people. In many less-developed countries today, the same rigid social stratification as in early nineteenth-century England draws clear lines between the social interests of large landowners, capitalists, and ordinary peasants/workers but in the developed countries these lines have become much more blurred.

With development, of course, the relative importance of agriculture has declined; hence the role of land as a productive input is no longer as important—indeed it is sometimes no longer separately mentioned in statistics on the "factoral" distribution of income. Labor and capital are the main inputs into the modern productive process but "labor" includes both minimum-wage, seasonal workers and secure professionals, like doctors or business executives. Likewise, although ownership of capital is quite concentrated today (see Chapter 3), those who live on the returns from capital include both aged pensioners and multimillionaires.

Most modern studies of income distribution in developed countries therefore emphasize the distribution of income from all sources. It is, after all, total income which enables consumption and it is not true that all wage earners are poor and all capital owners are rich. Some segments of the population, like pensioners, have relatively high wealth but relatively low current income while others with high earnings have not yet been able to acquire much wealth. On the other hand, the assets of the top 5% of adults in the wealth distribution, at a normal rate of interest, are alone sufficient to put them in the top few percentiles of the income distribution, while the bottom 40% of the wealth distribution, it is safe to say, receive virtually no capital income (see Table 3.2).

Recent literature has emphasized the division of income among persons and this book is no exception. Nevertheless, the distribution of income among factors of production is too important an issue to ignore. Section 5.2 outlines recent trends in the division between labor and capital while sections 5.3, 5.4, and 5.5 discuss alternative explanations of these trends. It will be seen that there is no consensus, even today, on the answer to Ricardo's 160-year-old question.

5.2 The Division of National Income

The total marketed output of a nation is commonly defined as its Gross National Product—the total money value of all final goods and services produced by the residents of that country. Since some capital equipment is used up in the process of production, one must subtract "capital consumption allowance" from GNP figures to get Net National Product (NNP), or the net output of the economy if capital stock is maintained intact. On the one hand, the uses of this output can be divided into the categories of consumption or investment. On the other hand, the receipts from its sale are divided among the various factors of production. Table 5.1 presents national accounts data on the share of each factor in net national income over the period since 1929. The table is presented by year for the 1970s since there are both significant long-run trends and short-run cyclical movements in the division of national income.

5.2.1 Trends Perhaps the most consistent long-run change is the decline in the share of proprietors' income—farmers and unincorporated businesses. This trend basically mirrors the urbanization of the population and the long-run trend away from self-employment. Since proprietors use their own capital as well as their own labor, a really accurate account would assign part of their income to the third row as due to the capital they use and part to the first row as due to the labor they supply. Different methods of assignment can give different answers. One can consider the labor earnings of the self-employed to be that income remaining after subtracting a market rate of return on capital or, alternatively, one can

Table 5.1

Distribution of National Income by Factor Payment: 1910-1979

Year	1900-09*	1910-19*	1920-29*	1930-39*	1950	1960	1970	1975	1979
1. Compensation for Employees	55.0	53.2	60.5	67.1	65.5	71.6	76.3	76.6	75.8
2. Proprietors' Income	23.6	24.2	17.6	16.4	16.3	11.4	8.2	7.2	6.8
Rental Income (a)	9.1	7.7	7.6	4.3	3.0	3.3	2.3	1.8	1.5
Corporate Profits (b)	6.8	9.7	8.2	5.3	14.3	11.3	8.5	7.9	9.3
Net Interest (c)	5.5	5.2	6.2	6.9	1.0	2.4	4.7	6.5	6.7
3. Total Capital Income (a + b + c)	21.4	22.6	22.0	16.5	18.3	17.0	15.5	16.2	17.5
TOTAL (1 + 2 + 3)	100.0	100.0	100.0	100.0	100.0	100.0	100.0	100.0	100.0

Sources: Bureau of the Census. Statistical Abstract of the United States: 1950-1980.
___. Historical Statistics of the United States: Colonial Times to 1970, Bicentennial Edition, Part 1. Washington: U.S. Government Printing Office, 1976.
*Average.

subtract the market value of labor supplied from total income and consider the remainder to be capital income—see Feinstein (1968) or Kravis (1959). Discrepancies between these two methods arise because the self-employed typically could not pay the going market rate for both all the labor and all the capital they use (i.e., they receive below-normal returns on labor or capital or both).

The problems involved in estimating labor and capital returns among the self-employed clearly make estimates of trends in the total share of labor and capital difficult. Another complicating factor is the year-to-year variability in factor shares during the business cycle. As a boom gets under way, output will expand and productivity will increase as existing plant and equipment are used more intensively, but the inertia of multi-year union contracts may lock many workers into fairly fixed wages. Profits will then tend to rise faster than wages and will increase as a share of national income. Conversely, in an economic downturn profits fall faster than wages and capital's share tends to decrease. It is thus usually somewhat misleading to take a single year's evidence as indicative of "labor's share" or "capital's share," since these should be averaged over the entire business cycle.

Nevertheless, some trends appear clear. Over the postwar years there has been a trend to an increased share of net interest, partially balanced by a trend to a decreased share of personal rental income. The form in which capital income is received is thus changing over time. In aggregate, the share of capital income (third row) has fluctuated from year to year, but, with the exception of a decline in the early 1970s followed by a recovery in the late 1970s, there has been no trend in capital income comparable to the long-run trends in employee compensation or proprietors' income. Both Haley (1968) and Feinstein (1968) found, for the United States and Britain respectively, that the share of labor had increased over time, at least up to the 1970s. Similarily, Atkinson (1975:168) concluded that labor's share had shown a "long-run tendency to rise over time" in most advanced countries, again up to the early 1970s.

5.2.2 Personal Income Of course, all taxpayers know that income paid is not quite the same as income received—the government steps in to take its share in the form of taxes and to make amends in the form of transfer payments. In addition, to the extent that companies retain profits for further reinvestment, the owners of capital may receive capital gains on the value of their stock holdings rather than dividends. Spendable income after tax is what concerns most people since it is the basis of a household's current consumption. Table 5.2 presents the relationship of GNP, NNP, and Disposable Income.

When we referred to the income of family units in Chapter 2 it was to the personal money income (before tax) of all members of a family unit. Table 5.3 illustrates the increasing proportion of transfer payments in the money income of family units—an increase which, as we have seen in

Table 5.2

Relationship between GNP, NNP, and Disposable Income

GROSS NATIONAL PRODUCT (GNP)
− capital consumption allowance
= *Net National Product (NNP)*

+ Subsidies less current surpluses of government enterprises
− indirect business tax and nontax liability
− business transfers
= *National Income*

− corporate retained earnings
− social insurance contributions
+ government transfer payments
+ personal interest income
− net income
+ business transfers
= *Personal Income*

− personal tax and nontax payments
= *Disposable Personal Income*

+ income in kind
+ capital gains
= *"Full Income"*

Chapter 3, has *not* been accompanied by a decrease in aggregate inequality. Naturally, Table 5.3 presents only average figures for the composition of family income and there are very significant divergences. Low-income families depend far more heavily on transfer payments while investment income is a greater fraction of income for high-income groups. Nevertheless, wages and salaries are the largest component of family income by far—even for the highest income categories recorded.

5.3 The "Neoclassical" Explanation

Free competition tends to give to labour what labour creates, to capitalists what capital creates and to entrepreneurs what the co-ordinating function creates. (J. B. CLARK, The Distribution of Wealth 1899)

As one of the originators of the "marginal productivity" approach to distribution, J. B. Clark argued that the "natural law" regulated the distribution of income between labor and capital.[1] This natural law was

Table 5.3

Personal Income by Source, 1950-1970

Personal Income	1950	Year 1960	1970	1979
Wages and Salaries and Other Labor Income	66.6	70.8	72.2	70.2
Proprietors Income	17.0	11.8	8.1	6.8
Rental Income	3.1	3.5	2.3	1.4
Dividends	3.9	3.2	2.9	2.7
Personal Interest Income	3.9	5.8	8.0	10.0
Total Capital Income	10.9	12.5	13.2	14.1
Transfers	6.7	7.2	10.0	13.1
Social Insurance Contributions	−1.3	−2.3	−3.5	−4.2
Net Transfers	5.4	4.9	6.5	8.9
TOTAL	100.0	100.0	100.0	100.0
In Current Dollars (000,000)	226.1	399.7	801.0	1,924.0
Per Capita	1,490	2,230	3,940	8,710

Source: Bureau of the Census. *Statistical Abstract of the United States: 1950-1980.*

composed of two elements: the technological relationships governing production (i.e., the engineering relationships of input to outputs) and the relative abundance of factors. Figure 5.1 illustrates Clark's view of the determination of the rate of return to capital.

In Figure 5.1 the line MP represents the marginal product of capital (strictly speaking, of capital services). Clark argued that the marginal product of capital declines as the total stock of capital increases, due to the law of diminishing marginal returns. (The *shape* of the marginal productivity schedule is governed by the state of available technological knowledge—i.e., it is seen as a purely "technical" datum.) The marginal productivity schedule (MP) represents the potential increase in total output, for a given level of supply of capital, when one additional unit of

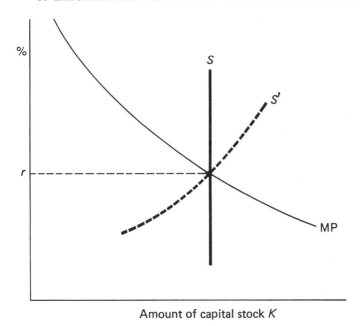

Figure 5.1 MARGINAL PRODUCTIVITY AND THE RATE OF INTEREST

capital is added. That *marginal* return, Clark argued, determines the return all capital will receive in the marketplace. The aggregate supply of capital in a society *(S)* determines where an economy will be on its aggregate marginal productivity schedule, hence determining the rate of return on capital *(r)*. In the short run, the stock of capital is fixed (at *S*) but in the long run the supply of savings responds positively to a higher rate of interest. Thus the long-run supply schedule *(S')* is sloped upward to the right.

Put somewhat differently, the marginal productivity schedule can be seen as the aggregate demand curve for capital at any given interest rate— so the rate of return on capital (*r*) is set by the forces of supply and demand. Demand (MP) is seen as determined solely by technical relations of production. Supply *(S)* is seen as determined by the past and current savings, i.e., the abstinence from current consumption of individual households.[2] The rate of return on capital (*r*) then becomes the "return for waiting." Total payments to owners of capital are then equal to the rate of return times the stock of capital (i.e., $= r \times K$). Payments to labor are similarly determined by marginal productivity; hence Clark's "natural law" argues that the shares of national income received by labor and capital are determined purely by relative factor abundance and socially neutral technological relationships.

A special case of this approach is provided by the Cobb-Douglas production function. Cobb and Douglas (1928) argued that total output can be predicted by equation (5.1).

(5.1) $Q = cL^aK^b$
           L = total labor services
           K = total capital services

The relationship $a + b = 1$ implies constant returns to scale. If the wage (W) is equated to the marginal product of labor and the rate of return (r) is equated to the marginal product of capital (as will tend to happen in competitive markets) then it can be shown that the total capital will remain constant (i.e., $wL/rK = a/b$ for any K or L). See, for example, Bronfenbrenner (1968). This "production function" relationship therefore "explained" the presumed constancy of factor shares in developed economies (more complex production functions can be used to explain a long-run movement in factor shares).

Elements of this early viewpoint can still be found in introductory textbooks,[3] but one of the theoretical advances of the 1970s has been the widespread recognition that Figure 5.1 is founded on a logical fallacy. That is, Figure 5.1 is founded on a logical fallacy if there is more than one type of capital good in existence (the only reasonable assumption), since "Capital" must be some aggregate of all the various specific capital goods in the economy. But how can one add together the services of drill presses, lathes, buildings, and computers? These can be added together to produce "Capital" only if they are measured in a common unit—but dollars will not do. If one adds up the *prices* of capital goods, one is forgetting that these prices depend on the value of the future stream of returns which each capital good is expected to generate. But the present value of these future returns depends on rate of interest[4]—hence the "amount" of the capital stock depends on the rate of interest, but the "amount" of the capital stock is supposed to determine the rate of interest.

Bliss (1975:162) therefore investigated the conditions under which capital goods can be aggregated into "Capital" (or labor types into "Labor") in a competitive general equilibrium model and concluded that these conditions were so special that "we can safely dismiss them from serious consideration" (see also Koopmans, 1977). He argues, however, that one can speak meaningfully of the marginal products of particular *types* of capital equipment and that at any point in time each capital good will generate a stream of returns over time to its owner. One cannot, however, speak in general terms of "the" rate of return on "Capital" in aggregate or "the production function" relating "Labor" to "Capital" (Bliss, 1975:238-244 and 144-195)—nor does one need to, since all the results of competitive general equilibrium theory can be obtained without specific reference to the aggregates of "Labor" or "Capital" (for a recent example see Varian, 1978).[5]

Only for convenience (e.g., in presenting a diagram) does competitive general equilibrium analysis restrict itself to the case of two goods or two inputs,[6] since discussion of n goods or m types of labor is much more realistic. In this modern view, the distinction between "Labor's" share and "Capital's" share is then meaningless. An individual's income in any period is the sum of the returns to his or her *particular capital assets* plus his or her labor earnings. There is no particular significance attached to the "factoral" distribution of income and no expectation that it can be easily explained (see, for example, Lipsey, Sparks, and Steiner, 1979:396).

5.4 The Post-Keynesian Approach

> The share of wages in the value of output varies, from one country to another and one period to another, with the strength and militancy of trade unions and the help they get from social arrangements. (J. ROBINSON and J. EATWELL, An Introduction to Modern Economics 1973)

For the "Cambridge school" of economists the proof that one cannot derive "technically" a division of national income between labor and capital was simply an indication that the division of income between laborers and capitalists is a *social* and not a technical relation. This approach starts from the money-wage bargain made between workers and capitalists and argues that capitalists typically set prices by a "markup" over their costs. Total profits are then the value of sales minus costs and are determined by volume of sales and the rate of markup. Total labor costs are determined by labor's aggressiveness in bargaining for money wages and the level of employment. The level of employment is, in turn, determined by the level of aggregate demand.

This is not a theoretical system that automatically tends to equilibrium, nor is it a system designed for a stationary economy. The Cambridge authors regard the possibility that their model can predict a disequilibrium economy, in which government fiscal policy is necessary for full employment, to be a valuable addition to its realism. Total private demand in the economy is set, in the model, by workers' consumption plus the investment decisions of capitalists. The Cambridge school argues that capitalists save out of profits and, if the savings propensities of capitalists generate the amount of investment the economy needs to stay on its long-run growth path, then and only then will the economy be in equilibrium steady-state growth. Asimakopolus (1977:341), however, argues that "capitalist development is unlikely to be 'smooth' " since nothing in the model *guarantees* that the appropriate level of investment will be undertaken.

In general, the Cambridge school argues that total income (Y) can be split into wages (W) and profits (P).

$$(5.2) \qquad Y = W + P$$

Investment (I) must equal saving (S) if the economy is to be in equilibrium. For simplicity assume that only capitalists save, at a rate S out of the profits they receive.[7] We then have:

$$(5.3) \qquad S \times P = I$$

Hence

$$(5.4) \qquad P/Y = (I/S) \times (1/Y)$$

We can then see why the Cambridge school argues that "workers spend what they get and capitalists get what they spend." The more capitalists spend, the lower is S; hence the higher is P in equation (5.4)! There is thus no abstinence, no "reward for waiting," and no natural law involved in the Cambridge model. The division of national income is dependent on the pressure of workers in bargaining their wages and on the savings and investment decisions of capitalists; it is subject to change by political or trade union action and by the unpredictable investment decisions of capitalists.

5.5 The Marxist Tradition

The value of a commodity is determined by the total quantity of labour contained in it. But part of that quantity of labour is realized in a value, for which an equivalent has been paid in the form of wages; part of it is realized in a value for which no equivalent has been paid. . . . The surplus value, or that part of the total value of the commodity in which the surplus labour or unpaid labour of the working man is realized, I call Profit. (KARL MARX, Value, Price and Profit 1899)

The Marxist approach to the division of national income is but one aspect of a many-faceted intellectual movement which embraces historical, sociological, philosophical, and political aspects, as well as the purely economic. The historical perspective of Marxism sees existing Western social institutions as but one stage in the long evolution of human history, a stage which, like European feudalism or the city states of Greece, is fundamentally transitory. The basic problem of Marxist social science is then to understand the determinants of social change, the "laws of motion" which underlie human society and human history. As a school of sociology, Marxism defines social classes in terms of their relation to the means of production[8] and argues that those who own the means of production have fundamentally conflicting interests with those who do not.

As a philosophical viewpoint, Marxists use the method of dialectical materialism. They argue that society can never be in static equilibrium; rather, throughout history each form of human society has contained within itself the contradictions, i.e., the class conflicts, whose resolution generates a new stage of historical evolution and a new set of class conflicts. The political analysis of Marxism argues that the state can never be neutral in these conflicts. Indeed, since the social institution of property can survive only with the protection of the state, the state generally serves the interests of dominant social classes. Marx argued, "The economic structure of society is the real basis on which the juridicial and political superstructure is raised, and to which definite social forms of thought correspond; the mode of production determines the character of the social political and intellectual life generally" (Marx, 1887:1:82). Here, however, we have space only for the narrowly economic aspects of Marxism—in particular, the Marxist discussion of the division of national income and the empirical measures which exist of it.[9]

Since Marxists aim at explaining the transition of capitalism, since they view the defining characteristic of capitalism as the private ownership of capital, since they see class conflict as the dynamic which engenders social change, it is natural that Marxists should see the division of national income between labor and capital as the *primary* aspect of economic inequality. Speaking loosely, this is the distribution of income into factor shares[10] but more exact Marxists refer to the "rate of exploitation." (Of secondary interest is the concentration of capital, while the distribution of income among families, Chapter 2, is of subsidiary theoretical importance.) Fundamentally, the division of national income is, in the Marxist perspective, determined by the rate of exploitation and the organic composition of capital—concepts which are defined in terms of the labor theory of value.

The labor theory of value states that the value of any commodity is determined by the socially necessary labor time required for its production. Economic activity is the process by which man creates objects of use from his natural environment, objects which require the input of human labor to be of value. At any point in time, the socially necessary labor required to produce a commodity is determined by the state of scientific knowledge and the cost of maintenance of human labor power. Labor is involved in production both directly (referred to as variable capital V) and indirectly through the use of capital equipment. In the labor theory of value, capital equipment (constant capital) is simply congealed labor, the product of man's past exertions. Through wear and tear on machinery, a certain amount (c) of constant capital is physically used up in the production process. Total labor involved in production is therefore equal to $c + V$, but in capitalist societies commodities exchange for more than the labor cost of their production; i.e., the exchange value of a commodity is given by:

(5.5) $$\text{value} = c + s + V$$

Since capitalists own not only the capital stock but also the product[11] they receive the surplus value (s). In other words, a worker produces a certain amount of value in a working day, but receives as pay only V, which covers the cost of his subsistence (i.e., is sufficient to "reproduce" labor for the next working period). Part of the working day is then devoted to producing enough output to cover wages, part to covering capital used up in production, and part to producing a surplus which is appropriated by the capitalist. The ratio between the time during which the worker produces "for himself" and the time during which he produces for the capitalist is s/V, i.e., the rate of surplus value, which is "an exact expression of the degree of exploitation of labour power by capital, or of the labourer by the capitalist" (Marx, 1887:1:218). Recently, Wolff has estimated that the rate of surplus value in the United States has risen gradually over the period 1947 to 1967 from 1.009 to 1.122. (1979b:334)[12]

The existence of surplus in the production process is a necessary condition if economic growth is to occur. Capitalists receive s, but consume only part of it and reinvest the rest. Capital is therefore the source of "self-expanding value" since this investment produces in its turn more surplus and more investment. As capitalist growth continues, increasing investment means an increase in the organic composition of capital ($c/c + V$), which in the Marxist view creates a tendency to a falling rate of profit as variable capital V (the source of surplus value) becomes a smaller part of the total. The quest for new investment opportunities makes capitalism a dynamic and expansionary social order. Backward nations are integrated into the world market as accumulating surpluses seek new opportunities for profit and expanding production seeks new markets.[13] Unless balanced by changes in the rate of exploitation, however, the increase in the organic composition of capital will periodically produce a lack of investment opportunities, a lack of sufficient aggregate demand to absorb production, and a "realization crisis" where goods remain unsold and a depression occurs.[14] This cyclical instability of capitalism is, of course, seen as a key element in the development of a proletarian movement and of political action which will spell the demise of the private ownership of capital stock.

When Marx said "the capitalist mode of production abolishes private property and private labour" (Marx, 1887: 3:266), he meant that the growth of monopoly and the concentration of capital deprives small businessmen and independent farmers and artisans of the private property which used to be the source of their independence. Increasingly, the self-employed are converted to paid employment, owning (and selling) only their labor power. Marxists therefore emphasize the concentration of capital—and the concentration of economic and political power which they see accompanying it. However, "capital" for Marxists refers to constant capital, "the raw material, auxiliary material, and the instruments of labour" (1887: 1:209) and, unlike "wealth," it includes neither the consumer durables required to reproduce labor power nor the price of unimproved land whose rents are merely a return to their scarcity—it is thus a narrower concept than either the "wealth" or the "riches" we referred to in Chapter 3. A measurement of "capital" in the Marxist sense would include corporate financial instruments (i.e., debt, equity) and that fraction of other financial assets used to finance capitalist production. As we have seen, these assets are much more narrowly held than other assets.

The differentiation of earnings is accorded a relatively minor place by Marxist writers. For Marxists, the primary contradiction of capitalism is the conflict between labor and capital. Marx himself explicitly recognized that not all labor is identical but argued that "skilled labour counts only as simple labour intensified, or rather, as multiplied simple labour" (1887: 1:84). He saw the value of skills as the value of the human labor used to produce them—a concept which is not so very far from Smith's initial view of human capital (see Chapter 8) although the value and the price of skilled labor may diverge in the marketplace. Some of the radical authors cited in Chapter 9 are attempting to integrate their insights on labor markets into a Marxist historical perspective, but the integration with a labor theory of value is much less obvious.

One must, in addition, recognize the failures of Marxist analysis. Two important predictions are a falling rate of profit and a progressive immiserization of the working class. Neither has come to pass. Wolff (1979b:340) has concluded, "Marx's law of the tendency of the rate of profit to fall is theoretically unsound and there is no support for it during my period of investigation." Real living standards have increased substantially since Marx wrote—as evidenced by, among other things, the increase in "subsistence" norms (Table 4.3). To be fair, of course, one must compare these failures with the failures of alternative viewpoints. A naive competitive general equilibrium analysis predicts, for example, that markets will clear and economies will be in stable equilibrium. Unemployment and cyclical instability therefore require "higher-level" rationalization—and confirmed Marxists have their own "higher-level" rationalizations on the falling rate of profit and proletarian immiserization.

Debate between Marxists and neoclassical economists regarding inequality often degenerates, therefore, into a dialogue of the deaf: the two schools of thought ask different questions, take different assumptions for granted, use different definitions, and give different predictions. For a neoclassical economist, the issue is to predict changes in the income distribution which arise as a result of individual or government decisions within our existing social and institutional framework. For Marxists, change in that framework is the central issue. Whereas a neoclassical economist will see the state as essentially neutral, responsive to the pressures of the majority, a Marxist will argue that the state can never be neutral in distributional issues and that in capitalist societies it generally acts in the interest of the minority who control capital. Whereas a neoclassical perspective sees interest payments and dividends as returns to a factor of production which is itself created by individual saving/abstinence, a Marxist perspective sees these payments as surplus value, created by the use of capital (congealed labor) and appropriated by capitalists. Whereas neoclassical economists view the economy as generally being either at or tending to equilibrium and social and political institutions as basically constant or changing due to their own internal logic, Marxists see the economy as developing unevenly, as inherently unstable, with an intimate connection with social and political forces. Most importantly, Marxists see the possibilities for reform which will limit the domain of inequality as fundamentally limited within existing social and political institutions; hence they argue for radical transformation of society. Neoclassical economists, however, assert that radical change in social and political institutions is probably unnecessary for the achievement of economic equality.

No book on distributional issues can do everything, and one thing this book is not going to try to do is answer the question, "What determines the rate(s) of return to capital?" Instead, this book takes the general level of the rate of return on capital as given and discusses the determinants of labor earnings (Chapters 6 through 10) and of the ownership of property (Chapter 11). It then discusses the growth/equality relationship (Chapter 12) and the impact of government on the income distribution (Chapter 13). It is true that posing the problem in this way, i.e., focusing on distribution among individuals and families rather than on inequalities among classes, has much more in common with the neoclassical analysis than with Post-Keynesian or Marxist approaches. Examining the distributional impact of existing government policies and of fairly mild reforms is likewise a familiar policy issue framework to neoclassical economists. This choice of focus, on distribution among persons and on marginal social change, is not meant to imply that the analysis of issues of class or of radical social change is unimportant or uninteresting; rather, this choice of focus is dictated by the constraints of space and the importance of the issues which remain.

NOTES

[1]Clark, himself, was very aware of the political implications of such a theory. As he wrote, "This thesis (the 'natural law of distribution') we have to prove; and more hinges on it than any introductory words can state. The right of society to exist in its present form, and the probability that it will continue so to exist, are at stake. . . . The welfare of the laboring classes depends on whether they get much or little; but their attitude toward other classes—and, therefore, the stability of the social state—depends chiefly on the question whether the amount they get, be it large or small, is what they produce. If they create a small amount of wealth and get the whole of it they may not seek to revolutionize society; but if it were to appear that they produce an ample amount and get only a part of it, many of them would become revolutionaries, and all would have the right to do so" (1899:3). In this case, as in

the post-Keynesian or Marxist analysis, there is no logically inescapable necessity to favor capitalism versus socialism if one adopts Clark's analysis of factor returns. As he argues, however, theories do differ greatly in the ethical justification, or lack thereof, which they appear to provide to the private ownership of the capital stock. One suspects that the debate on the theory of factor shares could never have acquired its current length and intensity were it not for the hidden political agenda of many of its participants.

2In a fully integrated model, these savings decisions are often formulated in a "life-cycle" framework—see Chapter 11, section 2.

3Compare, for example, the diagrams in Clark (1899:201) and Lipsey, Sparks, and Steiner (1979:370).

4See Chapter 7 for a discussion of present values and the rate of interest.

5Estimates of the marginal product of labor, as derived from production functions, indicate it to be greater than the average wages paid to workers—see, for example, Thurow (1968), Shaw (1981), Gottschalk (1978), or Appelbaum (1978).

6For a discussion of marginal analysis as a special case of general equilibrium analysis see Bliss (1975:95-118).

7Pasinetti (1974:127) shows this assumption is simplifying but not essential.

8Under feudalism, the primary means of production was land; in industrial societies it is physical capital.

9The term "Marxist" is capable of many interpretations. In practice it is used very loosely by some to mean "undesirably left-wing" and very strictly by others to distinguish between those who are "true" Marxists and all others. One must distinguish between a Marxist analysis of modern societies and a Marxist political program—neither necessarily implies the other. Indeed, the general Marxist premise that social and political institutions are ultimately based on the relations of economic life was novel in 1860 but has since been adopted by many politically conservative authors. In this chapter we refer to Marxist economic analysis and define it as "analysis of the historical process of capitalism based on the labor theory of value." It should be noted that many "Marxists" would object to the idea of considering "economic" Marxism independent from Marxism's historical and sociological perspectives.

10Strictly speaking, however, "capital" in the Marxist system does not include the value the market places on the scarcity of naturally occurring assets. Land, unlike machinery, derives its price in the marketplace from scarcity and not from the human labor which creates it.

11The Marxist idea of alienation stems from the idea that man is fundamentally a creative being, projecting himself upon the natural environment through his labor, but the division of labor in capitalist production and the workers' lack of ownership of the product of their labors mean that they are estranged from it, hence, alienated. See Marx (1844:287-301).

12The exchange value of commodities is not, in general, equal to their price in the market. The transformation of labor values into equilibrium market prices is a topic which is beyond the scope of this chapter, but a full discussion may be found in Morishima (1973).

13Hence, the Marxist theory of imperialism—see Lenin (1917).

14Obviously, this is a thumbnail sketch of Marxist economics—for a fuller picture, see Sweezy (1942) or Mandel (1969).

6 OF CHANCE AND ABILITY

6.1 Introduction

The next five chapters emphasize alternative theories of the distribution and determination of labor earnings—but not all theories can explain both. Indeed, some theories owe their continuing appeal almost solely to their ability to "explain" the one rather than the other. For example, "chance" may be able to explain the shape of the aggregate distribution of incomes, but at the cost of a highly unrealistic discussion of the determination of individual income. Section 6.2 discusses stochastic process models, their explanation of the distribution of income, and their nonexplanation of individual incomes. Genetically inherited ability is a different sort of explanation of the distribution of earnings and of the determination of individual rewards, one which has aroused a long history of passionate debates. Section 6.3 discusses the "nature versus nurture" controversy while section 6.4 offers a conclusion and summary. Chapter 7 discusses the roles of race and sex in earnings inequality, Chapter 8 outlines the neoclassical position, with its emphasis on the choices individuals make, and Chapter 9 presents the "institutional" and "radical" perspectives, with their emphasis on the constraints individuals face.

6.2 Inequality—A Matter of Chance?

One of the recurring regularities of aggregate income distribution statistics is that they reveal a distribution that is, approximately, often "lognormal"—that is, if in Figure 2.2 we had graphed the *logarithm* of income along the horizontal axis we would have observed a curve which almost fits the familiar "bell" curve of statistics textbooks.[1] The lognormal distribution, as it turns out, has some interesting mathematical properties. In particular, if income is determined entirely by chance, in the sense that one's income this year is a random fraction of one's income from last year,[2] it can be shown that the distribution of income will be, in aggregate, lognormal.[3] Recently, Thurow (1975) and Wold and Whittle (1957) conjectured that this sort of random process could be a model of the wealth distribution as well.

In addition, as we discuss in Chapter 9, section 9.2.4, the Paretian distribution has often been found to fit the upper tail of the income distribution rather well. Champernowne (1953) demonstrated that if one constructed income ranges (above some modal value) which were defined proportionately and if "the prospect of shifts upward and downward along the ladder of income are distributed in a manner independent of present income," then over time the distribution of income converges to the exact Pareto distribution.

The appeal of these approaches lies in their prediction of the *distribution* of income and/or earnings. After all, a "chance" model of income determination does not really *explain* anything.[4] How much difference is there, in effect, in saying that income distribution is due to "fate" and saying that income distribution is due to the operation of unknown random processes? Beneath the elegance of the mathematical derivation, as Sahota (1978:7) has said, "the theory provides a stamp of scientific respectability for the age old myth that the goddess of fortune is blind, poverty hits at random, none is destined to abject poverty from birth, and the sons of poor families have the same chance for success as anyone else"—despite a great deal of evidence to the contrary (see Chapters 7, 8, and 9). No one can deny that chance does affect individual incomes but, equally, there are far too many clear regularities in the determination of income for anyone seriously to take "chance" as *all* that matters.

The appeal of stochastic process models lies, however, in the fact that they offer an explicit prediction of the aggregate distribution of income which appears to be relatively close to actual aggregate data. However, even with respect to the aggregate distribution, there is the problem that random movement can generate a stable distribution of income only after an implausibly long period of time has elapsed (Shorrocks, 1976). In addition, when one examines the stable distribution which would be generated if income movement were a random process, this distribution is usually quite unlike the actual distribution of earnings (Osberg, 1977). There is clearly much more to the income distribution process than chance.

6.3 Inequality—A Matter of Unequal Ability?

When Gibrat (1931:194) discussed the mechanism by which chance affected earnings, he speculated that it might be due to a "genetic lottery." Pareto's earlier explanation of the "social pyramid" was that those who were *aptes a la lutte vitale* (fit for the vital struggle) clamber upward to form the vital elites on which the progress of society is based (1892:386). These authors, and many others, have in common an emphasis on the importance of "ability," especially genetically inherited ability, a factor which surely has some role in the determination of individual earnings. Some such theories are closely related to a chance model. If abilities are randomly and independently distributed and if they act together in a multiplicative rather than in an additive way, income can be expressed as the product of these abilities. The product of independent random variables will be lognormally distributed (Roy, 1950:489). Abilities theories, therefore, offer a more credible explanation of the determination of individual earnings and the possibility, under some circumstances, of explaining the distribution of earnings.

But what do we mean by "ability"? If we use the term to mean "the ability to earn money" then we have a prime example of a nonrefutable, circular argument since we are saying, in effect, "more able people earn more money but the only way we can tell if they are more able is if they earn more money." A theory which attempts to explain the distribution of earnings with reference to "ability" therefore faces a number of major hurdles:

(1) There must be some way of testing this presumed "ability" or "abilities" which is independent of current earnings, if the "theory" is to be more than a tautology.

(2) One must have some evidence on how this ability is distributed among the population if it is to explain the distribution of earnings among the same population. It is often presumed, for example, that intelligence is normally distributed in the general population since I.Q. scores are—but it is usually forgotten that I.Q. tests are scaled so as to produce a "normal" distribution (see Ryan, 1972). Stamp (1937) and Davis (1941) contended that mental capacity was not "normally" distributed but was highly skewed. Mandelbrot (1961, 1962) argued that each ability followed a Paretian distribution. When one does not know the true shape of the distribution of an ability such as intelligence one can hardly say it determines the shape of the distribution of earnings.[5]

(3) Even if "ability" determines earnings within a labor market the distribution of ability can determine the distribution of earnings only if everyone competes in the same labor market. Where "noncompeting groups" exist people's earnings will be determined both by their own ability *and* by the labor market they are assigned to (see Staehle, 1943). A theory of the overall distribution of income is therefore incomplete unless it can also explain the extent of the barriers which separate labor markets.

(4) As Sattinger (1975) has shown, people with different levels of ability usually have a "comparative advantage" in performing different sorts of tasks, and in general it will pay employers to assign workers to the task for which they are best suited. But what determines the productivity of different tasks? One needs a theory of tasks (i.e., of the demand for ability), as well as a discussion of the supply of ability, before one can explain how the distribution of ability determines the distribution of earnings.

(5) Many sorts of abilities can produce income. The ability to sing, to hit a baseball, to convince customers, to calculate the stresses in a bridge—these can all produce income. The overall distribution of earnings is a summation of the earnings distributions within a large number of occupations, such as singer, baseball player, salesman, and engineer. The shape of the overall distribution depends, therefore, on the correlation of abilities possessed by individuals and on the demand for them. Each occupation may have a distribution of earnings, but the aggregate distribution in society depends not only on how high and how unequal salaries are within each occupation, but also on how many there are in each occupation—i.e., the overall extent of inequality depends not only on the differences between the earnings of rock stars or major league ballplayers and those of nightclub bands or minor leaguers but *also* on how many there are of each occupation relative to engineers and salesmen. A theory of the demand side of the economy is required to predict the number in each occupation, as well as the inequality of rewards in it.[6]

One can, of course, see these difficulties as challenges. In the last decade, rich new data sets have become available and the progress of computer technology has made relatively easy a level of analysis that was previously impossible. By following a "panel" of individuals from youth and recording test scores while they are young and occupation and earnings when they are older, economists and sociologists have begun to establish the relationship between the measured "abilities" of individuals and their later economic success. This is, however, the study of *individual* earnings determination. Only under very special conditions can one extrapolate from such studies to an explanation of the *distribution* of earnings. For example, an "efficiency units" model, such as Taubman (1976), assumes that the market will always pay relative wages equal to relative "capacity"—i.e., the sum of the estimated returns to each ability. It is thus assumed that there is no "comparative advantage" for particular abilities in particular tasks and there is perfect substitutability of labor types: the relative returns to different abilities are estimated from current data. In short, one assumes a perfectly elastic demand for all types of ability—if we could all sing like Frank Sinatra we would all make millions, even if no one was listening.

As well, in order to generalize from a small sample to society as a whole about the determinants of individual earnings, one has to have data which are representative of society as a whole.[7] No one set of panel data is fully representative of the general population but Jencks (1979) has attempted to compare and condense the findings of the eleven major panel studies done in the United States to date. Two major questions have often been asked by researchers:

(1) How important is genetic inheritance vis-à-vis socioeconomic background in the production of "ability"?

(2) What is the relative importance of ability, social background, and acquired skills (such as education) in determining individual earnings?

6.3.1 Nature versus Nurture The issue of "nature versus nurture" in the creation of human abilities has an extremely long history. In recent years people such as Jensen (1969, 1970) and Shockley (1970) have argued that genetic inheritance is the primary cause of differences in intelligence (as indicated by I.Q. scores) and that these differences in intelligence are the cause of differences in earnings. If both of these statements were true then it might be thought that the existing earnings distribution was a "natural" one or that government policy should emphasize selective breeding (eugenics) to change inequality (Shockley, 1970).[8] Most social scientists, however, argue that the differences between individuals' environments are much greater than the differences between their genetic inheritances. For example, Lydall's encyclopedic study concluded that the most important factor likely to influence a newborn child's earnings is "the socio-economic class into which it is born and in which it grows up" (1968: 135).

How can we disentangle the legacy of nature from the effects of nurture? Genetic inheritance gives us the chromosomes that determine whether we will be black or white, male or female, but from the moment of their conception humans differ enormously in the nurture they receive from their environment. Smoking, alcohol and drug use, nutrition, and exercise by pregnant mothers have all been shown to affect the size and healthiness of the child they bear. Women differ widely in their awareness of these factors and their ability to afford adequate rest and nutrition. As a result, there are significant differences between social classes in the incidence of premature delivery and of abnormally low birth weight babies. As a Vancouver, British Columbia, study reported, "Low birth weight has long been recognized as one of the major causes of deaths and handicaps in infants" (Ross and Rutter, 1978:1). Vernon (1979:100) has described as a vicious cycle "the widespread syndrome of poverty, maternal ill-health and pregnancy and delivery abnormalities associated with poor growth and intellectual and emotional disorders in the children."[9]

6.3.2 Preschool When educators estimate that "about 50 percent of cognitive development of children occurs by the age of three or four" (Sahota, 1978:20 and Van der Eyken, 1977: 70), it is clear that children's preschool environment is very important to their eventual life chances. Almost all of this early environment is created by one's parents and it is in these early years that basic personality traits such as self-confidence and achievement motivation are largely shaped. Time spent in parent–child interaction has been seen as a key variable and as a significant determinant of later I.Q. scores (Leibowitz, 1974).[10] As Leibowitz (1977) has demonstrated, the vocabulary of preschoolers is positively related to their mother's education, household assets, and activities with the child. In "human capital" terminology this is seen in terms of higher income families' being able to make greater investments in "child quality" (see

Chapter 8, section 8.4), but social classes differ in much more profound ways than simply time spent with their children.

Hess (1970), for example, reports that, in a study where mothers were asked to teach their preschool children a simple task, significant differences in teaching strategies emerged, along class lines. Economically poorer mothers were, in brief, poorer teachers, more likely to become frustrated and simply to direct their children. These differences in maternal control techniques arise, argues Hess, out of quite understandable adaptations of the mothers to their own life situations (i.e., endemic economic stress and general powerlessness) but produce in their children a frustration with learning situations and an expectation of failure. Conversely, middle-class mothers who verbalize their instructions more effectively and who appeal to specific arguments rather than direct commands appear better able to set up effective learning situations—and the success a child achieves in such a situation is a strong positive reinforcement for attentiveness and effort in a future learning situation.[11]

Social classes differ in their language uses, in their emphasis on control versus autonomy in child rearing, in the value they place on inhibition/reflection versus impulsiveness/expression, and in their possession and use of books, newspapers, and other informational media. Many of these differences (such as discipline strategies or language usages) are imitated by children and passed on quite unconsciously by parents while some differences (such as encouraging reading or controlling television viewing) are conscious parental choices. Whatever the cause, however, when children arrive at school, "middle class children are advantaged not merely in such surface characteristics as better clothing or a different speech accent; they are also much more fluent and grammatical in expressing ideas, they have had a lot of experience at home in school-type tasks, and they are generally more cooperative with teachers and accepting of school aims; they will, therefore, settle down to learning more readily" (Vernon, 1979:124).

Some of these differences are easy to see in economic terms. Since Becker (1965), economists have seen money and time as partial substitutes, and where a family has the available income it will tend to purchase relief from the time and the hassle involved in many household chores. To put it another way, it takes time and energy to be poor—time and energy that are therefore less available for child rearing. Furthermore, it is understandable that parents pass on to their own children the value of those virtues which are rewarded in their own work place. Professors who emphasize reading skills while tolerating their children's insubordination know that the former is rewarded and the latter not much penalized in academia—but blue-collar workers know that insubordination gets you fired and reading skills don't matter much where they work. An economic perspective can see that the skills parents choose to emphasize and the resources they have available with which to pass them on clearly differ—

but it is more difficult for the economic perspective to capture the imitation and unconscious acculturation that defines "the normal." Some imitation, such as of speech patterns, produces in children a trait which may have a negative evaluation by the school system or the larger society, but which cannot be seen as intrinsically debilitating. More serious for the children of the poor is the everyday implicit lesson that one's parents cannot control the responses of the bureaucracies they deal with, cannot guarantee an adequate income, and do not have the respect of the larger community. Children who see all this are lucky if they do not also see it as normal to be powerless, insecure, and ashamed.

During the 1960s, early childhood day-care and special compensatory preschool education programs, such as Head Start, were proposed as one way of lessening the disadvantage faced by the children of poorer families. Early evaluations of some of these programs were not encouraging, in the sense that the large initial advances in measured I.Q. among some Head Start children tended to diminish later, after several years of schooling. However, more recent investigations, based on some fourteen longitudinal studies, "demonstrate that in comparison to control groups, children from low-income families who participated in carefully supervised and implemented programs in the 1960's have required over the succeeding years less special education, have been held back in grade less often and in a few of the studies have demonstrated generally more successful adaptation to the demands of schooling" (Halpern, 1982:30). As a consequence, their subsequent education is less costly to the taxpayer and simply in terms of total costs to the public education system the cost–benefit ratio of preschool programs is highly favorable (perhaps 2.4/1 or more). In addition, subsidized day-care enables families to participate more fully in the paid labor market, earning wages (and paying taxes) rather than relying on social assistance. Subsidies to enriched preschool day-care can therefore promote both efficiency, in the sense of net decreases in the costs of government and increases in earned incomes (Zigler, 1979), and equity, in the sense of partially remedying some of the handicaps of a disadvantaged social background.

6.3.3 The School System Early social reformers saw education as "the great equalizer of the conditions of men—the balance wheel of the social machinery" (Mann, 1839), but do all children receive equal opportunities once they are in the school system? First, one must ask, Do they all go to school? Secondly, which school system do they enter, public or private? Thirdly, one must examine the school board and school they go to. Fourth, one must look at which class within their school they are assigned to. Fifth, one must examine whether teachers treat children from different backgrounds within the same class in an unequal manner.

The Children's Defense Fund (1974) estimated that 5% of school-age children are not enrolled in school at all, and another 5% miss more than a quarter of a school year, perhaps because they drop out and are not noticed, perhaps because of school actions such as suspension or expulsion, or perhaps because of parental imperatives such as the need to care for younger children or a fear of revealing illegal alien status. Overwhelmingly such nonattendees are poor and/or nonwhite. At the other end of the scale, 1.7% of elementary and secondary students were in unaffiliated private schools and 8.9% were in church-affiliated private schools. Attendance at such fee-paying schools is positively correlated with economic success, and restricted by parental income. Nonattendance at school, on the other hand, excludes an individual from all but the worst jobs of society.

Those who do attend the public school system are generally assigned to a school board and a school on the basis of the area of their parents' residence. Since school boards' funds are largely raised from property taxes, the resources available to the school are dependent on the prosperity of the region which supports them. In 1978, Alabama spent $1,281 and Arkansas spent $1,193 on the education of each of its elementary and secondary students. New York spent $2,527 and Massachusetts spent $2,137 (*Statistical Abstract:* Table 256). In addition, school boards within each state differ, often dramatically, in the tax base and other resources available to them. Garmes and Pierce (1978:318) report that in 1975 the top two school districts in New York spent $6,327 and $4,632 per pupil, while the bottom two spent $1,453 and $1,456. Averaging across states, Harrison (1976:47) noted that typically the top 5% of school districts in a state spend 2.1 times as much per student as the bottom 5%, and, where school expenditure is low, dropout rates tend to be high. These differences in educational expenditure have a very long history. Current inequality in earnings at least partially reflects past inequalities in educational inputs: future earnings inequality will be due partially to present educational inequalities.

Perhaps just as important is the "tracking" that goes on within school boards and within schools. Tracking within schools is ostensibly done in the interests of the child, based on objective criteria, but it is hard to believe that class attitudes do not color the picture when we examine the probability of being placed in a "slow learner" stream. Not only are middle-class children more likely to exhibit behavior patterns that are favorably judged by middle-class school administrators but middle-class parents also tend to be more aware of the adverse consequences for their child of "slow-learner" placement and more able to do something about it.

The differential treatment of children within classrooms is a contentious issue, with some (e.g., Vernon, 1979) arguing that, controlling for achievement, a child's socioeconomic background does not affect teacher behavior. Rist (1970:413), however, cites some thirteen studies which indicate "that the teacher's expectations of a pupil's academic performance may, in fact, have a strong influence on the actual performance of that pupil"—i.e., teacher expectations become a self-fulfilling prophecy. His study describes the process of initial grouping of children in kindergarten into fast and slow learners, on the basis largely of language, clothing, and manners, which de facto split the class he studied by socioeconomic background. This initial grouping and the more favorable attention paid to the "fast learners" soon produced differential achievement, different responses in the classroom, and different records of inattention and indiscipline which formed an "objective" basis for streaming in later grades. Since a student's formal dossier and informal reputation went with him or her from grade to grade, it was very difficult for lower-class children to escape the results of their initial labeling.

Treatment within school interacts with the expectations of parents and peers outside school to produce lowered aspirations and goals for lifetime careers—and it is unlikely one will achieve what one has been taught not to aim at. Many have therefore seen the school system as an essentially middle-class institution in which middle-class children feel comfortable and tend to do adequately well while working-class children are, in the majority, screened out.

6.3.4 "Social" Inheritance Although lower aspirations, a higher dropout rate in high school, and financial constraints mean that only a minority of working-class children go on to attend university, clearly some do. Clearly, too, the majority of working-class children are born healthy, have attentive parents, are not assigned to slow-learner classes, and do graduate from high school—but a much larger majority of middle-class children receive these benefits. Children from middle-class and upper-class backgrounds therefore have a systematically higher *probability* of educational and economic success, since the cycle of advantage is cumulative. No single factor in the different class background of working-class children prevents, absolutely, the achievement of high incomes, but the accretion of disadvantages makes it more unlikely. Jencks concludes his summary of eleven panel studies on American men by arguing, "All aspects of family background explained about 48% of the variance in mature men's occupational statuses (and) the most important single-measured background characteristic affecting a son's occupational status is his father's occupational status" (1979:214).[12]

Brittain (1977:19) concludes in a U.S. study that family background characteristics explained 57% of the variance in a composite measure of economic status while just six *measurable* family background variables explain 44% of individual variations in economic status—i.e., there is a very strong tendency for children to inherit the economic status of their parents. His finding (1977:138) that much of this socioeconomic inheritance is mediated through the school system is very similar to that of Husen's 26-year study of 1,500 Swedish children (see 1969:158). Brittain puts his own findings in very concrete terms when he notes that a man born into the top 5%, in terms of family income, had a 63% chance of a

1976 family income of over $25,000 (which, in that year, would have meant being among the top 17.8% of families) while a man born into the bottom 10% had a 1% chance of that level of income (1977:72).

6.3.5 Genetic Inheritance The "nurture" received by children therefore differs very substantially, both within and outside the family. "Nature" also gives us different genetic endowments but assessing the relative importance of nature versus nurture in educational or economic success requires a measurement of genetic inheritance which is *independent* of social inheritance. In practice, this is impossible. Measuring the "ability" of kindergarten or preschool children measures their ability *after* the socialization of early childhood has occurred. One needs a measure of ability *before* environmental influences have come into play, but there is such an enormous natural variability in the rate at which very young children acquire skills that, although the physical and mental development of children under two years of age has been tested, such early I.Q. test scores have zero correlation with later childhood or adult I.Q. (Vernon, 1979:81). The I.Q. scores of older children are more stable, but do these scores measure one's heredity or one's environment?

"Twin studies" have attempted to resolve the nature/nurture issue by comparing the achievements of twins whose genetic endowment is identical (i.e., identical, monozygotic twins). The methodology of much of the early work in this area was to take a sample of identical twins, some of whom had shared the same family environment and some of whom had not (i.e., were separated and reared in different families). The heritability of ability was then assessed by analysis of the variance of I.Q.: if the I.Q.s of identical twins reared in different environments were more similar than the I.Q.s of randomly selected individuals, this greater similarity was seen as an indicator of the heritability of ability in the general population.

In studying separated identical twins, however, one does well to ask why they were separated in the first place. Kamin (1974) produces evidence that the most common reason for separation in early studies was economic (i.e., the family could not support both) and the most common practice was for a friend or relation to take one of the twins (i.e., their social environments tended to be quite similar). Where identical twins are placed in different homes by adoption agencies, the families to whom they are sent will have been selected by similar criteria for defining "acceptable" adoptive parents. In neither social origin nor social environment are separated twins representative of the general population. Part of the similarity in the test achievement of separated twins could then reasonably be said to be due to the similarity of their environments.

In addition, there is a stronger reason for disbelieving the early twin studies. The principal researcher in this area, Cyril Burt, believed very strongly in the importance of genetic influences—to the point of adjusting, and in some cases falsifying, his data (Hearnshaw, 1979; Kamin, 1974). Since data on separated identical twins are extremely hard to come by, many subsequent researchers relied heavily on Burt's work (e.g., Jensen, 1969) and revelation of this fraud has deprived their work of any credibility. Kamin has analyzed the work of Burt and others in this field and concluded that, *if* one were to rely *solely* on twin studies, "there is no reason to reject the hypothesis that I.Q. is simply not heritable" (1974:67). Others (e.g., Vernon, 1979) argue that genetics does influence I.Q., but to a degree that "cannot, as yet, be quantified."

The connection between I.Q. and economic success is, of course, far from obvious, since so many other abilities and other variables also affect earnings. Jencks, for example, reports that higher I.Q. correlates with higher earnings among American men, but much of this is mediated through the school system—i.e., higher I.Q. correlates with more years of education, which correlates with higher earnings (see Chapters 8 and 9). Holding constant demographic background and amount of schooling, one sees that achievement on tests of academic ability has minimal correlation with earnings for American men under the age of 30, a finding also reported by Griliches (1976). Among older men, a 15-point difference in I.Q. scores is associated with a *maximum* 14% difference in earnings of older men. Lillard (1977) argues that males with higher I.Q. do tend to do better financially later on in life and that there is a significant interaction effect between ability and education in the speed at which earnings rise with age. However, for men with a similar level of education the differences associated solely with measured I.Q. are relatively small—i.e., "the effects of test performance on earnings are not very large relative to the overall earnings gap between the rich and the poor in general" (Jencks et al., 1979:121).

6.3.6 Recent Twin Studies Taubman (1976) attempted to examine the influence of a common genetic endowment on earnings by contacting a sample of 2,000 twins (both fraternal and identical) who were about 50 years old in 1974. He argued that if genetically inherited ability is important, then genetically identical twins should have earnings which are more similar than fraternal twins. Partitioning the variance of earnings into genetic, environmental, and family influences produced his estimate that 18 to 41% of the variance in the log of earnings was due to genetics (1976:867).[13] Twins are, however, a "rather peculiar sample" (Vernon, 1979:178), whose average I.Q. is somewhat less than that of the population in general, whose parents tend to treat them more similarly than most siblings are treated, who have to share parental attention with their twin, and who may interact more with each other than siblings normally do. Assortative mating means that the genetic endowment of their parents is probably correlated rather than random, while sample attrition means that Taubman's respondents tend to be of higher socioeconomic status than the population at large. Twin studies therefore "involve as much social science theorizing as genetic theorizing" (Goldberger, 1979:336).

Since twin studies involve a large number of potential variables[14] but only a few observed correlations, a system of equations to analyze genetic influences on I.Q. or earnings is inherently underidentified. Taubman was therefore forced to make a number of strong simplifying assumptions (e.g., random mating by parents). Goldberger (1979:341), however, substituted a different set of assumptions, using the same evidence, to yield the result that 0% of the variance in socioeconomic achievement was attributable to genetic differences. His point is not that genetics in fact has zero influence, but that his assumptions can fit the data equally well.

The basic problem in this and other studies of human genetic inheritance is that we have nothing remotely approaching a controlled experiment. Assessing heritability requires the placing of identical genetic material in environments that are randomly selected on a large enough scale so that one can say with statistical confidence that differences in environment are uncorrelated with genetic differences and will average out. This is possible, if difficult, in controlled experiments in agricultural research stations but impossible in real human societies. Perhaps the safest conclusion is that for humans "precise heritability studies are out of the question" (Crow, 1970:157); Goldberger (1979) argues that there is little hope for narrowing the range between estimates of 0 and estimates of 41% of earnings explained by genetic endowment.

Goldberger's more important point, however, is to ask why we should care about how much of the variance in earnings is due to genetic factors. As he points out, "Some genetically based handicaps are remedied at low cost, some environmentally based handicaps are remedied at great cost if at all" (1979:345). Genetic inheritance may, for example, produce poor eyesight or hearing which impedes learning and productive work; hence genetic factors may imply low earnings, but eyeglasses or hearing aids are relatively cheap solutions. Conversely, some of the "environmental" handicaps of a deprived family background are extremely difficult to eliminate. There is simply no reason for accepting genetic influences on the income distribution as more inevitable or unalterable than environmental influences. Public policies to decrease inequality may be designed to mitigate genetically inherited *or* environmentally acquired individual differences *or* may be aimed at changing the environment within which individuals function: if we value equality we will presumably want to choose those policies, from any or all the above categories, which give us the greatest positive and the least negative results. It is the relative costs of particular policies, rather than the label of "genetic" or "environmental," which should guide us in this choice.

6.4 Summary and Conclusion

(a) Stochastic process models possess mathematical elegance and the ability to produce explicit predictions on the functional form of the aggregate distribution of income and/or earnings. However, these predictions do not fit actual aggregate distributions particularly well. "Chance" is an unsatisfactory explanation of the determinants of individual income or earnings—there are too many clear regularities in the determination of earnings to say that it is a random process.

(b) The idea that greater ability often pays off in greater individual earnings has an obvious ring of truth. Assessing the relative importance of ability in individual earnings determination poses, however, severe problems of definition and measurement. Assessing the role of the distributions of abilities as factors in the distribution of earnings requires in addition a theory of the relative demands for the different tasks in which abilities are used and an explanation of the barriers to mobility which may prevent the returns to particular abilities from being equalized. More progress has been made in the discussion of earnings determination than in the debate on earnings distribution. Among white males, higher I.Q. scores are associated with higher earnings, but only in later life and to a rather small degree.

(c) From the moment of conception on, humans experience substantial differences in environment. Many of these differences are correlated with the socioeconomic status of parents and can be expected to affect the academic and socioeconomic achievement of children. Differences in preschool environment affect children during a crucial phase of their learning and render it impossible to obtain a measurement of inherited ability which is not, to some degree, contaminated by environmental influences. Children are thus highly differentiated on entry to the school system, which is itself a highly differentiated system.

(d) Several authors have attempted to use data on twins to assess the relative importance of environmental and genetic influences. Studies based on Burt's data on identical twins now have zero credibility, since these data were in part fabricated. Taubman's data on identical and nonidentical twins can be fitted equally well by models which imply that 0% or 41% of the variance in earnings is due to the variance of genetic inheritance for policy purposes. Assessing the relative importance of genetic and environmental influences is, however, basically irrelevant for policy purposes.

NOTES

[1]One must say "almost fits," since the distribution of the logarithm of income is usually, in fact, more peaked (leptokurtic) and has a fatter upper tail than the normal lognormal. A lognormal distribution can be summarized in two parameters—the mean and the variance. For this reason, the variance of the logarithm of income is occasionally used as a measure of income inequality, although it does not always satisfy the "principal of transfers," as noted in Chapter 2.

[2]We postpone discussion of possible individual choice between occupations with different risks to Chapter 8, section 8.2.4.

[3]Kapetyn (1903) first suggested what Gibrat (1931) called the "law of proportionate effect." It can be expressed as:

OF CHANCE AND ABILITY / 113

(6.1) $$Y_t = P_{t-1}Y_{t-1}$$

where Y_t = income in period t
P_t = a random variable
By expansion, this becomes:

(6.2) $$Y_t = (P_{t-1}) (P_{t-2}) (P_{t-3}) (P_{t-4}) \ldots Y_0$$

where Y_0 = income in initial period
In terms of logarithms:

(6.3) $$\ln Y_t = \sum_{i=1}^{t} \ln (P_{t-1}) + \ln Y_0$$

If Y_t is an independent random variable, the central limit theorem will apply and one obtains:

(6.4) $$\ln Y_t \sim N(\mu, \sigma^2)$$

This implies that the inequality of income increases as t increases. Rutherford (1955) argued that this might be true within each age cohort, although the size of an age cohort decreases with time as its members die off.

[4]The conclusion of Jencks (1972) that chance was an important factor in earnings determination was based on the low percentage of variance in earnings explained by his regressions, which may mean that chance is responsible and may mean that the regressions have not been correctly specified.

[5]Most "ability" scores, such as I.Q. scores, are essentially ordinal and not cardinal numbers. One cannot say that a person with an I.Q. of 132 is 10% more intelligent than a person with an I.Q. of 120—if I.Q. scores measure "intelligence" (and there is a considerable debate on what it is they do measure) one can at most say that the former person is "more intelligent" than the latter.

[6]If all abilities are highly correlated, then a person who is good at one thing is good at most other things—hence one might as well talk of "ability." Or, if almost everyone is in one occupation, the number of abilities which exist hardly matters. Neither is reasonable. See Mandelbrot (1962), Roy (1950), or Osberg (1975:17-29).

[7]Taubman and Wales (1973), for example, use data on a sample of World War II Air Force volunteers who were extensively tested then and followed up in 1955 and 1969. Since they were initially selected on the basis that they were male, with above-average I.Q. and schooling, they would be expected to have above-average earnings. The segmentation perspective argues (see Chapter 9) that one could not generalize from their experience to that of the disadvantaged.

[8]That a "natural" distribution should be accepted as desirable or inevitable is far from obvious. It is natural, for example, to have spring floods but desirable and possible to build dikes to prevent them.

[9]Mental retardation is, for example, ten times more likely in low birth weight babies (i.e., those less than 5.5 pounds) than in normal babies (Perkins, 1974) and a higher incidence of motor disorders also occurs. Butler and Bonham (1963:139) report that in the United Kingdom the incidence of abnormally low birth weight was 3.6% in the highest social class and 8.2% in the lowest. These differences are not inevitable. The Vancouver project was successful in reducing the incidence of low birth weight in a high-risk sample to 2.8% (compared to a Vancouver average of 7.2%) by a combination of counseling and nutritional supplements (see Bradley, Ross, and Warnyca, 1978). Brown (1978) reports similar results for the Montreal Diet Dispensary's work in low-income areas of Montreal.

[10]Hill and Stafford have estimated that high-socioeconomic-status mothers spend, on average, 2.25 times more hours with their preschool children than low-status mothers (1977:533).

[11]Phelps-Brown (1977:220) cites similar British evidence on class differences in child-rearing patterns. Physical development also differs by social class. In a study of 10,901 Halifax, Nova Scotia, schoolchildren in 1968-69 Welch, Winson, and MacKintosh found that "socio-economic factors strongly influence the stature (height and weight) of children in the area studied" (1971:373). A recent French study examined the I.Q. and scholastic achievement of children from lower-class families who were adopted into upper-middle-class families. It concluded, "If French children of lower class parents were reared under exactly

the same conditions as the adopted children of our study, they would obtain I.Q. scores and scholastic results close to those presently observed for upper middle class children" (Schiff et al., 1982:186). Here is a great deal of evidence, from many societies, on the importance of the socioeconomic status of the family for children's later achievement.

[12]Detailed occupational social status measures are constructed from measures of average occupational education and earnings (see Coleman and Rainwater, 1978). Transitory variation in earnings and the enduring discrepancies between different members of the same occupation mean that family background explains considerably less of the variance in individual annual earnings (see Jencks et al., 1979:217).

[13]Since the estimating equations are underidentified, only an estimated range is possible and this estimate is highly qualified. Goldberger (1978) criticized the econometric specifications very severely. Even if this is a true estimate for this sample, it is highly unclear how, without consideration of demand factors, conclusions from an advantaged group of white males can be generalized to the population as a whole.

[14]Potential variables include the degree of assortative mating of parents, the relative similarity of environment of identical and nonidentical twins, the presence of additive and nonadditive genetic inheritance, the genetic and environmental component of variance, etc. Observed correlations are generally limited to those between identical twins, between nonidentical twins, or between parents and children.

7 OF RACE AND SEX

Your prospects in the labour market depend very much on *who* you are. The most basic dividing lines are between male and female workers, on the one hand, and between black and white workers on the other.

L. G. REYNOLDS
Labor Economics and Labor Relations (1974)

7.1 Introduction

For many years there have been substantial differences between the incomes of blacks and whites and between those of men and women. That these differences exist can hardly be disputed—but *why* these differences exist and what, if anything, can be or should be done to eliminate them is greatly in dispute. To set the subsequent discussion in context, section 7.2 presents a small part of the evidence on racial and sexual differences in money income. Section 7.3 presents a number of alternative theoretical models of discrimination and in section 7.4 we consider the extent to which these models of racial discrimination can be used to analyze differences in earnings between men and women. Section 7.5 offers a summary and a conclusion.

7.2 Differences in Pay by Race and Sex

Table 7.1 presents a few of the many comparisons which can be made between the incomes of blacks[1] and whites, males and females in contemporary America. Black males have weekly earnings that in 1981 were, on average, roughly 20% below those of white males, while the pay of white females averaged roughly 60% of the pay of white males. Blacks were over 60% more likely to experience unemployment in 1980 and that unemployment was, on average, some 30% longer. These are substantial differences in average pay rates and unemployment experience and these differences have a long history. They produce large differences in eco-

115

Table 7.1

Selected Statistics by Race and Sex

	Males			Females			White Female/Male	Black Female/Male
	White	Black	Black/White Ratio	White	Black	Black/White Ratio		
Median weekly earnings of wage and salary workers who usually work full time								
1967	$130	$ 90*	0.69	$ 79	$ 63*	0.80	0.61	0.70
1973	193	149*	0.77	117	107*	0.91	0.61	0.72
1981	353	274*	0.78	223	210*	0.94	0.63	0.77
Median 1981 weekly earnings by educational level (full-time workers)								
less than 4 yrs. high school	301	241	0.80	182	172	0.95	0.60	0.71
4 yrs. high school	372	294	0.79	224	209	0.93	0.60	0.71
4 yrs. college or more	490	396	0.81	326	326	1.0	0.67	0.82
Median 1981 hourly earnings (hourly rated workers)								
Age 16-24	4.44	4.11	0.93	3.76	3.70	0.98	0.85	0.90
Age 25+	8.14	6.64	0.82	4.77	4.51	0.95	0.59	0.68
Percent experiencing some unemployment in 1980	17.3%	29.4%	1.7	16.4%	26.6%	1.6	0.95	0.90
Median duration unemployment (weeks)	13	17	1.3	10	13	1.3	0.77	0.76

Sources: E. F. Mellor and C. D. Stamas (1982); S. L. Terry (1982).
*Data for blacks exclusive of other races are not available prior to 1978—hence this is "nonwhites."

nomic well-being. But do these differences represent discrimination? In part they may simply represent the unequal outcomes that one would expect to find as a result of unequal qualifications for paid employment—a crucial issue is, therefore, how much of these pay differences cannot be explained by qualifications.

If one compares black men with white men with similar education and similar years of experience, there are still substantial differences in pay. For example, black men with 16 to 20 years experience and a high-school education had a weekly wage some 71% of that of similar white men in 1977 (Taylor, 1981). However, this differential was substantially less for younger men, the black/white weekly earnings ratio for those with under six years experience being 78% for the high-school-educated and 100% for the college-educated. Smaller differentials among younger men can be explained as (a) evidence of a lessening of discrimination, perhaps because of equal opportunity legislation; (b) evidence of the increased relative quality of black education which has followed the decreased segregation of the school system; or (c) an illusion which obscures the fact that black wage rates do not increase with experience at the same rate that white wages do.

During the 1960s, the black/white earnings ratio increased for all experience/education groups. Smith and Welch (1977) ascribed relatively little of this improvement to antidiscrimination legislation but noted that school quality and school completion levels increased more rapidly for blacks than for whites. Despite the lower returns blacks receive for schooling, the net effect of improved black schooling was to reduce earnings differentials for young males. In addition, earnings differentials narrowed, particularly in the South and North Central regions. Although these results were mildly optimistic, Smith and Welch point out that, if the gains of the 1960s could be maintained, one would wait until 2040 for full racial parity. Similarly, Reich (1981) and Butler and Heckman (1977) found that racial disparities among men were narrowing over the period 1948 to 1974 at the rate of 0.4% per year. This finding implies that racial equality will not be achieved until 2070. In assessing these trends, one must remember that the postwar period saw large-scale black migration from the rural South to the North—which produced an income gain which cannot be repeated. As well, the gains of the 1960s were certainly partially due to the booming economy and very low unemployment rates (as low as 3.5%) which were characteristic of the Vietnam war era.

Boom periods have historically been times in which blacks have made gains relative to whites but it is noteworthy that even in the softer labor markets of the 1970s black male earnings have risen somewhat relative to white male earnings, especially for the young and the better-educated. Lazear (1979a), however, argues that this gain is illusory if the increase in the ratio of current earnings is achieved at the cost of decreasing on-the-job training for blacks. He argues that, although entry level wages for blacks have risen, decreased on-the-job training will imply slower promotion in future years; hence discrepancies in lifetime wealth will remain.

Many studies have found that earnings do not increase with experience for blacks (or women) in the same way they do for white males (e.g., Blinder, 1973a; Akin and Garfinkel, 1980). This has sometimes been interpreted as evidence of a lower rate of return on on-the-job training for blacks (Taylor, 1981). Alternatively, the institutional tradition (see Chapter 9) would argue that blacks are typically hired for jobs which offer little training or promotion possibilities; hence the black/white differential in average earnings largely reflects the fact that whites get promoted and blacks don't. Duncan and Hoffman (1979) tried to measure directly the amount of on-the-job training received by blacks and whites, males and females and found that the rate of return to training was roughly equal for the different groups, but that white males received significantly more years of on-the-job training. Taylor (1981) similarly found fairly equal rates of return for years of education among black and white men—indeed he found a higher rate of return to education for recent black college graduates (who are, of course, a small minority of black workers). The crucial difference is that black men still get fewer years of education[2] and they get substantially slower increases in pay as they gain work experience. Taylor estimated the rate of return to on-the-job experience for blacks at roughly 60% that of whites—and there seems little explanation for this differential other than discrimination in promotion and training decisions.

Reich (1981:74) has examined national trends in earnings disparities while also looking at racial inequality in wages within industries and regions. He argues that the movement of blacks between sectors (i.e., from the rural South to industrialized urban areas) and cyclical changes in aggregate demand explain most of the improvement in national data (which is, anyhow, fairly slow). Indeed, he turns the issue around somewhat. "The gains that have occurred seem especially small in comparison to the magnitude of black migrations, advances in the quantity and quality of black schooling, antidiscriminatory legislation and highly publicized affirmative action programs, as well as black struggles, protests, and gains in black political power that have taken place since the Second World War. These forces, one would expect, should have imparted considerable upward pressure on the relative income of blacks."

If we compare men and women, one obvious factor is the great difference in "typical" male and female occupations. Rytina (1981) points out that most employed women work in a small number of predominantly female occupations—some 40% of employed women being in occupations that were over 90% female in 1975 and over half in occupations more than 80% female. Occupational stereotyping is illustrated by Table 7.2, which presents data on a number of "female," "neutral," and "male" occupations. One can note that occupations which are more heavily male generally tend to have higher median earnings and social prestige. Within occupations (i.e., among cashiers or among lawyers) the "typical" female/male earnings ratio differs widely but it is almost universally less than unity (equality) and, overall, averages about 0.65 for full-time year-round employees. Within-occupation comparisons obscure, however, some of the differences that arise within the occupational hierarchy. Male and female school teachers, for example, are relatively close in annual earnings, but Table 7.2 indicates that most school administrators are male whereas most elementary and secondary school teachers are female. Similarly, computer programmers earn more than computer operators, accountants do better than bookkeepers, and supervisors outrank assemblers and checkers: in all these cases, the occupation with greater pay, prestige, and authority contains a substantially higher percentage of men. Differences in pay within occupations are thus combined with differences in promotion between the occupations.

In assessing the extent of sex discrimination, one has to decide how many variables to control for. "Pure" pay discrimination, in the sense of unequal wages for people with the same duties and job titles, in the same place with the same employer and the same qualifications, is too blatant and too obviously illegal. Such outright discrimination is rare—but it is not uncommon to see men and women assigned to "different" jobs with different pay or to observe different probabilities of promotion. However, does one consider a different occupation or job title evidence of different "qualifications," hence meriting a difference in pay, or evidence of discrimination at some earlier stage? The approach that has usually been adopted in economic work is to attempt to explain male and female wages in terms of observable characteristics that can reasonably claim a relation to productivity (such as schooling, occupation, or work experience) and to ascribe any residual unexplained difference in average expected wages to discrimination. Clearly, the more variables one counts as "qualifications" the more narrowly one is focusing on "pure" pay discrimination and the more chances one has of being able to explain a large fraction of the gap between male and female wages—but it is a very large gap (some 40%) and, whatever one does, one cannot explain it all.

A range of estimates of the unexplained differential thus exists in the literature. One of the lowest is Sanborn's (1964) estimate of 12 to 13%, while one of the highest is Fuchs (1971) at 40%. A number of estimates lie in the 25% to 30% range—Oaxaca (1973); Malkiel and Malkiel (1973).[3]

7.3 Models of Discrimination

7.3.1 "Neoclassical" Arguments The "neoclassical"[4] approach to economics has at its methodological core the assumptions that one can

Table 7.2

Sex-Earnings Ratios for Selected Occupations

(Full-time, year-round workers—1975; all full-time workers—1981)

	1975 Percentage Women	Average 1975 Annual Earnings Men	Women	Earnings Ratio, 1975 Women/Men	1981 Percentage Women	Median 1981 Weekly Earnings Men	Women	Earnings Ratio, 1981 Women/Men
Kindergarten teachers	99	*	9,348	*	97	*	264	*
Secretaries	99	*	8,070	*	99	*	229	*
Waiters/Waitresses	93	6,027	4,441	.74	85	200	144	.72
Bookkeepers	92	12,300	7,455	.61	91	320	222	.69
Cashiers	91	10,553	5,973	.57	85	180	166	.85
Elementary school teachers	84	12,243	10,545	.86	82	379	311	.82
Social workers	59	12,602	10,947	.87	61	358	286	.80
Assemblers	54	10,497	7,019	.67	53	297	205	.69
Checkers, examiners	51	11,964	7,353	.61	54	348	219	.63
Secondary school teachers	51	13,255	11,280	.85	49	387	321	.83
Computer operators	50	11,450	8,358	.73	63	342	232	.68

Accountants	32	15,218	10,617	.70	40	433	308	.71
School administrators (elementary and secondary)	30	19,144	13,350	.70	32	520	363	.70
Computer programmers	21	15,150	12,785	.84	28	447	329	.74
Blue-collar work supervisors	10	14,297	7,832	.55	11	409	262	.64
Managers and administrators	15	16,657	8,445	.51	28	466	283	.61
Lawyers	10	24,964	*	*	22	574	407	.71
Industrial engineers	3	17,948	*	*	3	549	*	*
Auto mechanics	1	10,488	*	*	0.7	286	*	*

Sources: N. F. Rytina: January 1981 and April 1982.
*Too few cases for valid estimates.

most usefully analyze economic phenomena in terms of individual maximization of individual self-interest and that such analysis can safely proceed in isolation from "noneconomic" or "preeconomic" variables such as social status or political power. Analysis is, therefore, focused on market phenomena as distinct from social or political phenomena, and in particular on the perfectly competitive market with many informed traders. Its most important general prediction is the convergence of the economy to a general equilibrium, in which no one can be made better off without someone else's being made worse off, but from this starting point particular qualifications are introduced into the general model in order to assess the impact of, for example, limited numbers of traders, imperfect information, or differential tastes. Firmly in this tradition is Becker's (1957) classic study of discrimination, whose focus is discrimination "in" labor markets.

If one can distinguish between prejudice (i.e., believing blacks cannot do as good a job as whites) and discrimination (preferring whites over blacks even knowing they can both do an equally good job, on average), Becker argued that discrimination in a particular labor market might be due to employer's tastes—in this case an aversion to hiring blacks.[5] In Figure 7.1(a) one might place employers in the order of their degree of aversion to hiring blacks. The vertical axis represents black wages as a fraction of white wages, and the horizontal axis measures the number of blacks (who are of the same productivity as whites). Employers who are indifferent between hiring blacks and whites (nondiscriminatory) will be willing to hire blacks when they get the same wages ($W_B/W_W = 1$). An employer with mildly discriminatory tastes would prefer whites if wages were equal, but if black wages were, for example, 90% of white wages he would hire the cheaper black labor. An employer who is strongly averse to black workers would be at the extreme right of schedule D and would hire blacks only if they received, say, 30% of the white wage.

The wage ratio between races would, in this market, be determined by the demands of the various employers and the supply of black labor. If S_1 were the supply curve of black labor, the equilibrium wage ratio between blacks and whites would be W_1. Relatively nondiscriminatory employers would hire only blacks (B_1 in total), paying them the going market rate, which is $W_1\%$ of the white wage, while more discriminatory employers would hire only whites, paying the full wage.

In Figure 7.1(b), however, we can see the impact of these discriminatory decisions on firm costs (quantity produced is measured on the horizontal axis). AC_B represents the average cost curve of a firm hiring blacks and AC_W represents the cost curve of a firm hiring whites. Firms paying the full white wage rate will have a cost disadvantage. If the product market is a competitive one, relatively low-cost (black labor force) firms will expand; hence, their demand for labor will increase—represented by the dashed demand schedule D^* in Figure 7.1(a). This

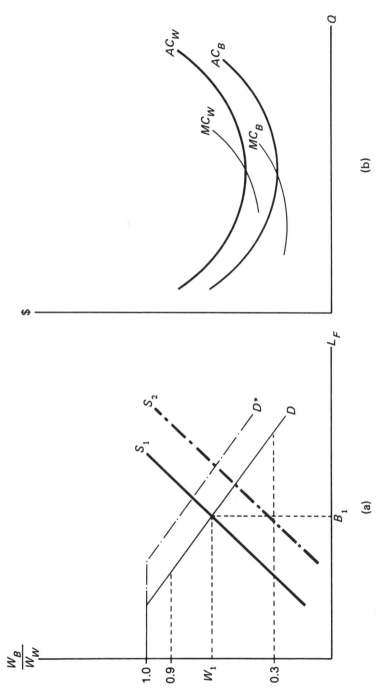

Figure 7.1 EMPLOYER DISCRIMINATION IN LABOR MARKETS

increase in the demand for black labor will, if nothing else changes, bid up its price, moving the equilibrium black/white wage ratio closer to 1/1. This "neoclassical" argument then predicts that discriminatory wage differentials will be eroded over time *if* the market is competitive (i.e., there will be more, longer-lasting discrimination in noncompetitive sectors). Since discriminatory tastes are an irrational preference, the logic of competition eventually will force discriminating employers from the marketplace. Of course, if the supply schedule S_1 of black labor shifts to S_2 and more blacks enter the labor market (perhaps as a result of their displacement from agriculture by the mechanization of southern farms), the equilibrium wage ratio may not increase and could even fall, in the short run. Unless the supply schedule keeps on shifting, however, at a faster rate than nondiscriminatory employers expand hiring, the wage ratio will move toward 1/1. This perspective therefore argues that the basic logic of capitalism is to eliminate employer discrimination and that if one wants to combat discrimination the most effective government policy is probably to encourage competition in the marketplace.

Essentially the same argument on the "weeding-out" of discriminatory employers can be extended to the elimination of "prejudiced" employers. If some employers believe, incorrectly, that blacks cannot do as good a job as whites and hire more expensive white labor, then they are making a mistake in the same way as if they paid more than they had to for any of their other productive inputs. Smarter, less prejudiced competitors will have a cost advantage and will, eventually, drive prejudiced employers, neoclassical authors argue, from the marketplace. Aigner and Cain (1977:177), for example, state that "the forces of competition would lead to an expansion of output by employers who erred the least, or not at all (in assessing average worker ability) at the expense of those who erred the most." Again, the economic policy prescription implied is to eliminate barriers to employer competition, so as to hasten the demise of prejudiced, and discriminatory, employers.[6]

7.3.2 The "Institutional" Perspective The "institutional" approach to economics (see Chapter 9) argues by contrast that the distinction between "economic" and "noneconomic" phenomena is only sometimes a useful one and that it is part of the art of political economy to know which issues can be safely analyzed in terms only of market variables and which issues require explicit consideration of social, political, and historical factors. There is a strong emphasis on the details of the mechanisms (the "institutions") which directly affect how economic events unfold and little faith that, left to itself, the economy will reach any sort of optimum in any relevant period of time.

The "institutional" perspective on discrimination argues, in particular, that most productive skills are created through on-the-job training and that wage rates are fixed by institutional rather than market forces (see section 9.2.3). This implies that the labor costs of employers increase only slightly if the employer exercises a discriminatory preference over the type of labor he desires to hire.[7] In addition, institutionalists tend to see many real-world product markets as capital-intensive, oligopolistic, and fairly noncompetitive in price terms, with most competition taking the form of product innovation and/or marketing (see Chapter 3, section 3.2). Differences in labor costs are, in many industries, of secondary importance to reputations for product quality, sophistication, or reliability of delivery (see Marris and Mueller, 1980).

Hiring black rather than white labor is therefore seen as having only a small impact on labor costs in many firms. Labor costs may not be all that large a fraction of total production costs. Variable costs may have only a marginal impact on market share, relative to the impact of product development and marketing. As a result, discrimination will evolve differently in different sectors. Price-competitive sectors where direct wages costs are large fractions of total costs may have an incentive to hire minorities, but these tend to be low-wage sectors. Labor-intensive goods production must compete with the low-wage industries of developing countries while labor-intensive personal services face, at the margin, the competition of unpaid household production. In capital-intensive goods industries wages are higher, but any black/white wage differential is a smaller fraction of total costs. Sophisticated services, such as lawyers or consulting engineers, compete in terms of reputation more than in terms of price. As a result, the latter sectors will show little tendency for discrimination by employers to be eroded over time by unaided market forces.

The erosion of discrimination is slower when employment roles resemble social roles. Writers such as Kessler-Harris (1975) argue that it is not an accident that most employed women are employed in occupations of subordinate authority, with an overtone of "nurturing" (e.g., nurse, secretary, waitress). Such "sex ghettos" accord well with traditional viewpoints on "femininity" and often have strictly limited promotion possibilities, low pay, and poor fringe benefits—partly because they are crowded with women who have few other options and partly because "women's work" is systematically undervalued in a male-dominated society (Bergmann, 1971; Weisskoff, 1972). In this view, occupational and job segregation is the primary mechanism of discrimination, both "before the market" in the socialization and training of workers (who, in general, do not *try* to enter nontraditional occupations) and "in the market" (where employers really do not believe that women and men are of equal productivity).

Since sexual and racial stereotyping is seen as the major cause of discrimination and as having little tendency to be eroded by market forces, the policy measures advocated by institutionalists are largely administrative. Antidiscrimination legislation, for example, prevents employers from specifying that they desire male or female workers and gives employees the right to sue for damages if discrimination is suspected. Somewhat stronger are mandated affirmative action plans which compel employers to make extra efforts to hire and to promote members of groups discriminated against. Stronger still are hiring and promotion quotas. All these measures are legislative "interferences" in the labor market, seen by institutionalists as necessary since the labor market is regarded as having little tendency to produce "equal opportunity" for blacks and whites or for males and females on its own.

7.4 "Before" or "In" the Labor Market?

In many analyses the discussion of black/white earnings and male/female earnings differentials has been conducted very similarly, but there are important differences. In particular, there is no reputable evidence for economically relevant physical differences between blacks and whites— but there are biological differences between men and women. Some viewpoints on sex differences in earnings are based on these biological differences. It has been argued, for example, that women who enter traditionally female occupations with little career progression are making a rational choice, given that they are biologically different from men and are the ones who bear the children. The force of this argument is, of course, very much blunted once one recognizes that bearing children takes very much less time than caring for them—and men can do just as well at caring. If an average adult work life is roughly forty-five years and a "normal" number of children is somewhat over two, the percentage of an adult woman's working life which can be expected to be spent on medically necessary maternity leave (at roughly four to six months per pregnancy) is miniscule. Absences from the workplace which are *physically* necessitated by child bearing can be compared to the time college students have for vacations. During three summer vacations a college student has available some twelve months of time. If a woman has two children and takes six months' pregnancy leave for each, the total time involved is a similar amount. Clearly, there is much more to sex role differences than would be implied if men had summer jobs while in college and women didn't, but these differences arise from the social, not biological, reasons why women spend, on average, much more time out of the paid labor force than men.

Phelps-Brown (1977:148) has argued, "Though half the intelligence of every country is in women's heads, that half does not develop the same qualifications for paid employment as the men's half." From this perspective, the main cause of different labor market outcomes for men and women is the differential experiences of boys and girls—the different "feedback" which home and school provide in early years. Differential treatment (discrimination) means that boys and girls get different amounts of education and prepare themselves for different sorts of jobs. In 1970-

71, for example, women were 50% of the high school graduating class, but only 14% of the crop of Ph.D.s. Women comprised 3.9% of those receiving master's degrees in business but 56% of those receiving them in education (Chiswick and O'Neill, 1977:151). Socialization to different norms of an "appropriate" education or occupation may explain some of these early differences in career choices but there may in addition be a motive relating more to economics.

Mincer and Polachek (1974) have argued that, as individuals look forward over their expected working life, men and women are likely to differ systematically in their career expectations. If women expect to leave the paid labor force at some future time, to have children, and to return to paid employment after an absence, then they can expect a shorter total period of return on their investment in training. They can also expect that the skills which they learn on the job will grow rusty while they are out of the paid labor force.[8] It may, therefore, make economic sense to invest less in training or to invest in training (such as teacher training or nursing) which has a high degree of "transferability" to one's work outside the paid labor force. In addition, if women expect to have to move in order to accommodate a husband's career moves, then acquiring "portable" skills makes most sense—which rules out many jobs involving highly specific training and encourages participation in such easy-entry fields as nursing or secretarial work.

All these factors can be said to influence choices made "before" one enters the labor market and Mincer and Polachek argue these are voluntary, individual choices. Although there is not much difference between married men and married women in average education, there are very big differences in average years of employment experience. Mincer and Polachek (1974:S103) argue that this accounts for some 45% of the hourly wages gap between white married men and white married women. And, of course, women's work outside the market, chiefly in the raising of children, is socially and economically productive, even if it is not paid. If the household remains intact, sex roles can be seen, in the neoclassical tradition, as reflecting comparative advantage and an efficient production of market and nonmarket goods (see Chapter 8, section 8.2.5). However, one problem is that the household often does not remain intact and that men and women bear very different shares of the economic risks involved in divorce—witness the very high probability of poverty for female-headed households (Chapter 4).

A second problem is whether women get to "choose." To the extent that these choices are made by others (e.g., parents or admissions committees) there may also be overt discrimination "before" the labor market. Young girls are offered dolls to play with while boys get base-balls—it is not long before they usually want what others see as appropriate. Economists rarely make the subtle distinction between "choice" and "socialization" in the production of different qualifications for employment. Economists have tended to concentrate, instead, on discrimination "in" the labor market, i.e., the differences in access to employment, pay, and prospects for advancement of people with equal qualifications.

The distinction between discrimination "before" and "in" the labor market is both intellectually useful and academically convenient (since it can serve to divide the turf between "economics" and "sociology") but it ought not to be pushed too hard. Unequal outcomes in the labor market will be observed by those who are about to enter it, and reasonable people will base their own decisions on what they observe happening to people like themselves. Black and white youngsters, for example, have similar scores on tests of their desire and motivation for education and high-status, high-pay jobs. They differ, however, in the jobs they aspire to (aim at) since, as Gurin (1978:19) puts it, "the one way in which black and white achievement motivation may differ is in a reality-based perception among blacks that their chances for success are relatively poor."

There are, on average, greater differences in career aspirations between men and women than between blacks and whites, but, again, if one controls for the degree of success anticipated, these differences in aspiration largely disappear (Gurin, 1978:22). Blacks and whites, men and women are therefore guided to their traditional occupations partly by their own (socialized) preferences but largely also as a response to their observation of the difficulties encountered by those who wish to enter nontraditional areas. And it is quite reasonable not to want to be the one who sets the precedent. The first blacks in all-white high schools and the first women in all-male professions pay a price for their access, in stress and in isolation, that is abnormally high. It is those who come after the precedent-setters who reap the highest net benefits—but if a rational calculation implies it is optimal to be a follower, who will *lead* in breaking down traditional barriers?

If, therefore, we cling to the notion that "before" and "in" labor market issues can be completely divorced, we will miss some of the major dynamic benefits of equal opportunity legislation. This legislation *in* the labor market is really aimed at influencing decisions on career aspiration and training which are made "before" the labor market by making it easier to take nontraditional roles and by showing that it is possible. Tradition, "the way things have always been," is after all a powerful and pervasive, if "irrational," social force.[9] Anthropologists have long observed that one society may define as "women's work" such jobs as the harvesting of particular crops while in others the same jobs may be exclusively a male role—and both patterns generally will tend to be quite stable over the generations, once they are established.

7.5 Summary and Conclusions

1. There is a very long history of substantial differences in pay between men and women and between blacks and whites. Black male

earnings are some 20% below those of white males. Female earnings are, on average, 60% of male earnings. Even after controlling for differential qualifications, differences in pay rates and career progressions remain.

2. Employer discrimination has been viewed very differently by different schools of economic thought. The neoclassical approach argues that the logic of competition will drive prejudiced and discriminatory employers from the marketplace; hence, policy measures should emphasize the improvement of competition. Institutional writers argue that in many sectors such forces can be expected to be relatively weak; hence, legislation is required.

3. Differences in qualifications for employment are sometimes ascribed to choices made "before" the labor market, but the distinction cannot be complete. Observed outcomes "in" the labor market will inevitably influence choices made "before" the labor market.

NOTES

[1]Blacks constitute some 90% of the census category "nonwhite," which also includes Indians, Japanese, Filipinos, Koreans, etc. Space precludes consideration of these other groups or of Hispanic groups (Cuban, Mexican, or Puerto Rican Americans).

[2]Boys from poorer families can expect in general to get fewer years of education—see Chapters 8 and 9—but in addition the quality of one's urban neighborhood can be very important. Datcher (1982) found that earnings and educational attainment are positively related to neighborhood income, as well as to parental education, income, etc.

[3]Clearly, the literature is much larger than this. See Gunderson (1980: 360-370) for a list of further references.

[4]The term "neoclassical" was originally coined to distinguish writers of the late nineteenth century such as Marshall, Edgeworth, and Walras from the "classical" writers of the early 1800s such as Ricardo and Malthus. It has, however, come to be a broad label which is somewhat casually affixed to many present-day academic economists and, in particular, to the perspective discussed in Chapter 8.

[5]The explanation of such tastes being seen as a "noneconomic," "before" the market issue, which can be suitably delegated to sociologists and psychologists. Other neoclassical models emphasize worker or customer discrimination—see Reich (1981).

[6]Aigner and Cain (1977) argue that predictions of black work performance may be more unreliable than those of whites and that wage differentials therefore reflect risk aversion by employers. This cannot explain why the labor demand of large employers (whose size pools the risks of assessing individually many workers) does not bid wages up to parity.

[7]Indeed, it may be less costly to "go along with the crowd" and discriminate rather than to compete on price terms with the use of lower-cost labor. If one's competitors wish to discourage such "unfair competition" as offering lower prices because of the use of lower-cost labor, they may take retaliatory action through the political system. If one has assets which are "at risk" to the political process—e.g., subject to potentially unfavorable licensing or zoning decisions, such retaliation from other business may be very costly.

[8]Clearly, black men do not expect to take maternity leave—but they may expect to be laid off more frequently by their employers, implying a similar reduction in returns to training.

[9]A theoretical model of career plans based on job information feedback has been outlined by Starrett (1976).

8 THE "NEOCLASSICAL" PERSPECTIVE: THE IMPLICATIONS OF CHOICE

When any expensive machine is erected, the extraordinary work to be performed by it before it is worn out, it must be expected, will replace the capital laid out upon it, with at least the ordinary profits. A man educated at the expense of much labour and time to any of those employments which require extraordinary dexterity and skill, may be compared to one of those expensive machines. The work which he learns to perform, it must be expected, over and above the usual wages of common labour, will replace to him the whole expense of his education, with at least the ordinary profit of an equally valuable capital. It must do this too in a reasonable time, regard being had to the very uncertain duration of human life, in the same manner as the more certain duration of the machine.

The difference between the wages of skilled labour and those of common labour is founded upon this principle.

ADAM SMITH
The Wealth of Nations (1776)

8.1 Introduction

These words of Adam Smith have been much repeated in the more than two centuries since they were penned. Today, this small paragraph has expanded into a vast and growing "human capital" literature which represents the largest and most influential economic approach to the differences of individual earnings. In this chapter we outline the "neoclassical" approach to the study of economic inequality. The theory comes in two parts—that which concerns the determination of individual earnings (section 8.2) and that which concerns the determination of the distribution of earnings (section 8.3). As we shall see, the link between these parts can be questioned. The implications of this debate extend beyond economics, in that such sociological approaches as status attainment models can come fairly close to a human capital methodology. Of course, one must stress that these models concern the distribution of earnings among individuals, and not the distribution of income among families, or economic inequality more broadly defined. Wages and salaries are the primary income source for the vast majority of people (see section 5.2), but a full theory has to consider as well income from wealth—i.e., the share of total GNP going to owners of property and the distribution of that ownership. Chapter 11 discusses the determinants of property ownership. In this chapter, section 8.4 considers the family, in terms of both total earnings and the "production" of inequality across generations. Section 8.5 presents a summary and conclusions.

8.2 The Determination of Individual Earnings

8.2.1 Human Capital Investment The crucial notion underlying the human capital model is that of the voluntary deferral of returns—i.e., investment. Becker has defined human capital investments as "activities that influence future monetary and psychic income by increasing the resources in people" (1964:1).[1] Such a deferral of returns is involved if, for example, an individual were to choose between the two occupations pictured in Figure 8.1. Choosing occupation A implies that up to age 24 one would receive lower income—e.g., $6,000 less at age 20. After age 24, those who choose occupation A begin to benefit from the choice—e.g., by $10,000 per year at age 50. The cost of the "investment" involved in choosing occupation A over occupation B is the lower income one receives up to age 24; the benefits involved are the higher income one receives after age 24. The crucial "human capital" question is, When are the costs worth the benefits?

To answer this, one must look at how much it costs an individual to wait until the age of 24 for a higher income, as well as how much higher that income eventually is. If tuition must be paid or books bought, it is quite possible that choosing occupation A might involve a period of training in which income was less than expenditures (i.e., negative) and these initial deficits must be financed in some ways. Borrowing capital involves an interest charge. Indeed, even if one does not actually have to borrow, one must still pay attention to the rate of interest since the money used to finance training could have been invested somewhere else. This time cost of money is central to the idea of discounting. If R is the interest rate per annum, one dollar today will compound to $1/(1 + R)$ in a year's time. Conversely, however, it would only take $1/(1 + R)$ today on which interest was compounded at R percent to equal $1 in one year. The *present* value of $1 received a year from now is $1/(1 + R)$, and the present value of $1 received in two years is even less. In general, the higher the rate of interest the greater is the cost of waiting, and the farther

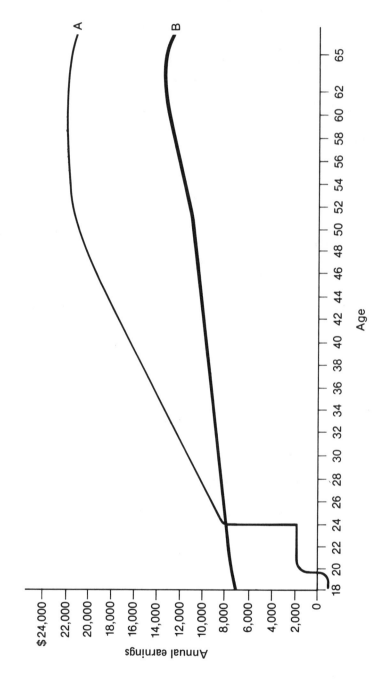

Figure 8.1 HYPOTHETICAL AGE/EARNINGS PROFILES FOR TWO OCCUPATIONS

a benefit is in the future, the less it is worth today. Discounting takes this into account and enables one to calculate the equivalent, in current income, of future returns in alternative occupations. [Mathematically, if V_i denotes a sum of money to be received in i years, that sum of money now has a present value equal to $V_i/(1 + R)^i$.]

If A_i is the earnings of a individual i years from now if that person works full-time in occupation A and B_i is a person's earnings in i years if he or she works full-time in occupation B, the differential in earnings between the two occupations in any year is $A_i - B_i$. In Figure 8.1 this is the vertical distance between the curves, and at age 20 it is equal to $-\$6,000$, while at age 50 it is equal to $+\$10,000$. An individual who is deciding between careers is assumed, in the human capital model, to be aware of the differences in earnings between occupations at different points in the future. An individual is also assumed to calculate the present value of the differential between earnings in each occupation, for each year, i.e., to calculate $(A_i - B_i)/(1 + R)^i$. Up to age 24, this will produce a negative number since the earnings in occupation B are actually higher than those in occupation A (i.e., there is a cost to choosing A). After age 24 the difference is positive, when the benefits of choosing A start to be received. A rational choice clearly involves looking at the costs and benefits over one's entire working life, i.e., adding the cost and benefits to give the net present value of the benefit of choosing occupation A.

$$(8.1) \quad NPV = \frac{E_1^A - E_1^B}{(1 + r)} + \frac{E_2^A - E_2^B}{(1 + r)^2} + \frac{E_3^A - E_3^B}{(1 + r)^3}$$
$$+ \frac{E_4^A - E_4^B}{(1 + r)^4} + \ldots + \frac{E_n^A - E_n^B}{(1 + r)^n}$$

8.2.2 Equilibrium In this example, if the net present value of choosing occupation A over occupation B was positive when the interest rate was 5%, and if one could borrow for 5% or less, someone who wished to maximize the present value of earnings would enter occupation A. The human capital model argues that we all make such calculations, implicitly or explicitly. One might then ask, if *everyone* could borrow money at 5%, wouldn't *everyone* try to enter occupation A? Wouldn't this be a disequilibrium situation? The answer is yes—but that equilibrium might occur in either of two ways: (1) interest rates might rise to the point that the advantage of occupation A, on a present value basis, would disappear, *or* (2) the higher net advantage of entering occupation A would prompt an increase in the supply of labor to that occupation and a decrease in supply of labor to occupation B.

If wages are flexible, such a change in the relative supply and demand conditions in the two occupations means that the wages in occupation A tend to fall and the wages in occupation B tend to rise, thereby decreasing the differential between the wages in A and in B. This differential will continue to narrow as long as the supply of labor to occupation A is increasing; the supply of labor to occupation A would continue to increase as long as there were net benefits, at the market rate of interest, to choosing A over B. The labor market will therefore be in equilibrium only when there are no net benefits to be obtained by choosing occupation A over occupation B, i.e., when the present value of all occupational earnings streams is equal.

Naturally, many assumptions are required for this strong result. One must assume: (a) that individuals are well informed of the future prospects of different occupations; (b) that they are of equal ability; (c) that they have the same taste for money income vis-à-vis leisure and the nonmonetary aspects of jobs; (d) that they have access to capital at equal rates of interest; (e) that they compete in labor markets where wages are flexible and (f) that occupational entry and the supply of training are unrestricted. Note, however, that even if all of these conditions hold the human capital model does *not* predict that in equilibrium all individuals will have equal annual earnings. Indeed it predicts that inequality of annual earnings will exist. In our example, an inequality of $6,000 will exist between the annual earnings of 20-year-olds and an inequality of $10,000 between the annual earnings of 50-year-olds. Since people of different ages are at different points in their earnings streams, the range in annual earnings of the entire population will be much larger. If, in our example, we considered people of all ages in occupations A and B we would observe that the range was from a high of plus $20,000 to a low of minus $1,000. If the labor market of this example is in equilibrium, however, the net present values of the two earnings streams will be *equal* at the market rate of interest.

From the human capital perspective, therefore, it is inequality in the discounted value of lifetime income which best indicates "true" economic inequality (see Chapter 3, section 3.5.4) since individuals with the same value of lifetime income may, in any given year, have unequal incomes. If the assumptions (a) to (f) listed above hold, a competitive labor market will be in equilibrium when all occupations have equal net present value. As a result, occupations which involve a long period of training must have higher annual wages in order to compensate for the low income of training years. Of course, such a theory can explain only the demand for training by individuals who are induced (by variations in wages) to enter different occupations. Where the supply of training is restricted, i.e., assumption (f) does not hold, training will acquire a scarcity value and wages in that occupation will rise above that which is strictly required to entice entrants. Occupations will then differ in net lifetime present value as a result of a "market imperfection" in the supply of training. As Friedman and Kuznets (1954:132) observed in their pioneering work on the incomes of independent professionals, restriction of supply by organizations such as medical associations can produce substantially larger differentials than can be explained by period of training or unpleasant working conditions. Moreover, as Blaug (1976) has pointed out, in most countries there is not much of a market mechanism for the supply of training, since governments largely fund education and determine its priorities.

The United States, with its many privately funded universities and training institutes, probably comes closer than most nations to possessing a market mechanism for the supply of training, and it is there that the human capital school has its greatest influence. Scores of studies—Blaug (1976) and Mincer (1970) provide partial lists—have found that, in general, those who are more highly educated and have more work experience have higher earnings (see section 8.3.2).

In 1978, however, the average salary of American college professors was somewhat less than the average earnings of coal miners or automobile workers (Blumberg, 1979), despite the long years of formal education required to become an academic. Is this because coal miners and auto workers are highly unionized whereas American professors are not? Or is it because in such aspects as social status, risk of injury on the job, freedom from direct supervision, job monotony, and working conditions, it is much more pleasant to be a professor than to be a coal miner or an auto worker? Is this the reason why Taubman and Wales (1973) found the rate of return to a B.A. degree to be 11% but the rate of return to a Ph.D. to be only 4%? The lower wages of academics could be seen as due to a combination of a lack of union power (another market imperfection) or to the existence of "compensating differentials" in pay which enable more pleasant occupations to attract labor even at a lower wage.

8.2.3 Compensating Differentials The idea of compensating differentials goes back, again, to Adam Smith, who argued that "the whole of the advantages and disadvantages of the different employments of labour and stock must, in the same neighbourhood, be either perfectly equal or tending to equality." Wages are, of course, only part of a job's attractiveness or unattractiveness—a point recognized explicitly by Becker in his definition of "human capital" by his emphasis on "monetary and psychic income." Figure 8.1 really represents, then, the special case where occupations A and B are similar enough on balance in nonmonetary characteristics that an individual chooses only on the basis of money income. More normally, occupations differ substantially in nonmonetary aspects and people choose career paths on the basis of "the whole of the advantages and disadvantages," both monetary and psychic. There would therefore be nothing irrational, for example, about a person's choosing to be a jazz musician for $10,000 a year for the rest of his or her life rather than an accountant for $30,000 or more, *if* that person loved music and hated accounting.

Clearly, "compensating differentials" are a powerful idea. If Adam Smith's statement were true and the whole of the advantages and disadvantages of employment were in fact equal, then the inequality of money incomes which we observe would be highly misleading, since "compensating differentials" would mean that "total" incomes (money income plus psychic income) were really equal. If this were true, then a government policy to increase the money income of the poor (defined in money terms) would *increase* inequality, by raising their "total" income *above* that of everyone else. If one really believed in the theory of compensating differentials one could, for example, argue that a Mississippi sharecropper with a money income of $8,000 and a New York office worker earning $35,000 are equally well off, since the sharecropper has nicer weather and lives in a more tightly knit community.

But do nonmonetary aspects of jobs *accentuate* or *reduce* the inequality of pay? Is a doctor burdened with responsibilities and pressures and an orderly carefree and easygoing? Or does the doctor love the power and status of his profession and the orderly hate cleaning bedpans? "Compensating differentials" could be used to "explain" *either* a higher wage for orderlies *or* a higher wage for doctors. Clearly, there has to be some way to *test* the existence of "compensating differentials" or they may simply become a way of "explaining" everything that has no other explanation.

One problem with tests of the idea of compensating differentials is represented in Figure 8.2, where the horiziontal axis measures the number of workers in job A, which involves "outside work," and the line W represents the money wage available in "all other jobs" which demand similar qualifications. The supply curve for job A is represented by SS, which slopes upward to the right. Some people *prefer* outside work and would accept a lower money wage in A in preference to working elsewhere, whereas others dislike it and would demand a wage premium. What will the "compensating differential" be? It depends on whether demand for this job is high (D') or low (D''). In the former case a wage premium must be paid in job A since the marginal person hired into the job dislikes it; in the latter case the wage in A is less than that paid elsewhere since the marginal person actually prefers the job. The tastes of the marginal person can rarely be predicted unambiguously and the characteristics of actual jobs are hard to quantify in all but a few dimensions, so tests of the theory of "compensating differentials" are, to date, "inconclusive with respect to every job characteristic except the risk of death" (R. Smith, 1979: 347).

The risk of death on the job can be quantified (from accident statistics) and can unambiguously be said to be disliked. Figure 8.3 represents one view of the trade-offs involved, for individuals and for firms. If we graph wages vertically and risk of injury horizontally, individuals will prefer less risk of injury and more wages and one can present those combinations of risk and wages offering equal total utility as indifference curves (the dotted lines). Individuals who seek to maximize

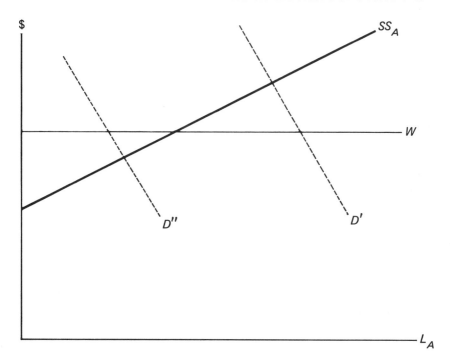

Figure 8.2 COMPENSATING WAGE DIFFERENTIALS FOR "OUTSIDE WORK"

utility are represented as attempting to be on the highest possible indifference curve—but individuals also differ in their tastes for income vis-à-vis
risk. The indifference curve U_{II} represents the tastes of a person who is
less averse to risk of injury, while U_I represents a more cautious individual. At the same time, of course, firms face a trade-off between spending
on safety measures and spending on wages. If they spend more on safety,
they may be able to attract labor at a lower wage. The solid lines are "iso-
profit lines"—those combinations of safety spending and wages spending
which offer the same level of total profit. If firm A and firm B are in
different industries, one can reasonably expect them to have different
risks of injury and to face different costs of installing safety measures—
hence, the difference in iso-profit lines.

   If we put the two together, the prediction is that more cautious
individuals will maximize utility by working at firm A (at lower wages W_I,
with risk of injury P_I) and less cautious workers will choose firm B (at
wage W_{II} and risk of injury P_{II}). Of course, one can only reasonably apply
this model where risks are of a well-understood type (e.g., the risk of a
highway accident). Where the risk involved is of an occupational hazard,
such as the risk of cancer caused by vinyl chloride, which is of recent
discovery and hotly debated by experts, it is unreasonable to expect that

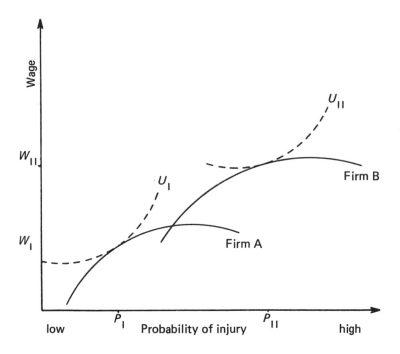

Figure 8.3 RISK/WAGE TRADE-OFFS

production line workers are making informed choices. We can also safely assume that some jobs now perceived as safe will, in future years, be revealed as dangerous. Nevertheless, hazardous jobs do tend to have a small wage premium (Viscusi, 1978) and tend to be filled by workers with fewer assets—i.e., the poor tend to do more hazardous jobs (at somewhat higher wages) while the more wealthy can "afford" to "purchase" more job safety. Otherwise, however, there is no strong evidence to support the theory of compensating differentials as a general explanation of unequal money wages[2]—and one ought to mention that the "dual labor market" theory discussed in Chapter 9 predicts that disagreeable jobs will be paid less (not more) than average.

    8.2.4 Uncertain Rewards—Risk and Inequality A particular case of the general "compensating differentials" argument is that jobs, careers, and occupations differ in the uncertainty of their rewards—a fact on which Friedman (1953) based a theory of the extent of inequality in general. Friedman argued that if each individual had a choice of occupations which had different degrees of riskiness in their returns (e.g., movie actor versus policeman), then people who liked risk would tend to choose occupations with a chance of a few high rewards as well as the chance of many low rewards whereas "risk-averters" would choose occupations whose possible returns were all very similar. If everyone had the same options but each person chose separately and their choices did not affect one another, then societies where many people were risk-lovers would, he argued, have more unequal income distributions (because more people would be in the risky occupation) while societies with a "risk-averting" population would be more equal. This is an important prediction since, as Friedman put it, "inequalities resulting from deliberate decisions to participate in a lottery clearly raise very different normative issues than do inequalities imposed on individuals from the outside" (1953:290). He went on, in another work, to argue that "much of the inequality produced by payment in accordance with product reflects 'equalizing' differences or the satisfaction of man's taste for uncertainty" (1962:148). If inequality is conjectured to arise from deliberate participation in a lottery, on equal terms with all others, one's perception of inequality clearly changes. Money incomes may be unequal but "life-chances" were assumed equal—Does inequality "really" exist? If people have different likings for job lotteries, should the state restrict their choice of lotteries by equalizing money income?

Even aside from the issue of whether people actually get to make such choices, Kanbur (1979) has recently shown that Friedman's predictions were based on highly restrictive assumptions—i.e., they depend entirely on a partial equilibrium approach. In a general equilibrium framework, the average return in risky occupations will be forced down when more people enter those occupations. Average incomes in a society with more "risk-lovers" will then tend to be lower and overall its degree of inequality *cannot be predicted a priori.* As Pissarides (1974:1264) has also concluded, "There is no simple relationship between the degree of risk aversion (in a society) and the extent of income and wealth inequalities." One cannot predict, from theory, that societies where people are more risk-taking will be more unequal; they could be *less* unequal—hence Friedman's position is more a personal point of view than a general proposition of economic theory.

8.2.5 Inequality of Outcome Up to this point we have used the terms "wages" and "earnings" fairly interchangeably, but this is really only valid if we are always talking of a constant number of hours of work per year. If individuals can choose their number of hours of work per year, then one must distinguish between "full income" (Becker, 1965, i.e., the money which an individual could earn by working continuously) and the money income that individuals do earn, given that they decided to take some leisure time. As well, an individual might decide to engage in nonmarket work, or "household production" using his or her own time to produce directly such things as a new coat of paint on the house, a home-cooked meal, or a handmade dress.

Figure 8.4 represents a way of analyzing choices among nonmarket work, market work, and leisure, under the simplifying assumption that all work (market or nonmarket) is of equal disutility. Both market and

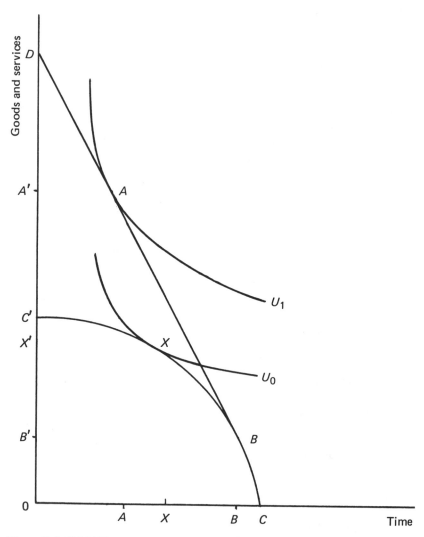

Figure 8.4 MARKET WORK AND ITS ALTERNATIVES

nonmarket work produce goods and services (vertical axis), which the individual trades off against leisure (horizontal axis). The curved line $CBXC'$ represents an individual's productivity in "home production," i.e., productive activity for one's own consumption with no explicit monetary wage. It is curved, concave to the origin, to represent the diminishing marginal productivity of household labor—and one can think, for example, of how much difference the first hour makes when one cleans house and how little difference the seventeenth hour makes. If one's only option is home production, utility is maximized (U_0) at point X, implying a division of the day into $0X$ hours of leisure and XC hours of nonmarket work.

The neoclassical view of labor markets is that they offer individuals the chance of trading their time for market goods and services, at a rate which is the hourly wage. The amount of one's human capital is seen as determining the available hourly wage, and the availability of possible market trades increases an individual's consumption possibilities, as represented by a shift of the budget line from CBC' to $CBAD$. The line segment BAD has a slope equal to the hourly wage rate and is tangent to the individual's "household production possibility curve" at point B. Point B represents the point at which an individual is just indifferent between work in the marketplace and work at home, because the hourly money wage is just equal to his or her marginal product of time used in household production. In this perspective the individual maximizes utility (U_1) at point A and divides his or her time ($0C$) into $0A$ hours of leisure, ab hours of market work, and bc hours of home production.

The reason for going into all this in a book on inequality is that the total goods and services potentially available to the individual is determined by that person's productivity at home and the hourly wage rate; in the diagram it is the distance $0D$. However, in practice the individual foregoes $A'D$ of goods and services (preferring to consume $0A$ hours of leisure) and produces some goods and services ($0B'$) at home. The market income of the individual is the distance $A'B'$ and it is this market income which we measure in income distribution statistics.

One implication of the fact that income distribution statistics measure money income is that they tend to overstate the increase in family economic well-being that has occurred as women have entered the paid labor force. (For other implications see Gronau, 1977.) If an individual enters the paid labor market and utility increases from U_0 to U_1, money income increases from zero to $A'B'$, but the increase in goods and services is smaller than this, by the amount of $B'X'$, so that the true net increase in goods consumption is $A'X'$, *not* $A'B'$. In addition, one must consider that this increase in goods consumption was achieved at the cost of a decrease in leisure—i.e., from $0X$ to $0A$. Figure 8.4 therefore merely represents graphically what many two earner families know intuitively— they are working harder, making and spending lots more money, but the quality of their lives has advanced only fractionally.

Similarly, if the wage rate (after tax) of an individual were to increase, not only would there be some change in hours of leisure, but there would also be a tendency for hours of housework to drop, meaning that some of the increase in market income is obtained by sacrificing goods which the person would otherwise produce for himself or herself.

However, unless individuals have *very* large differences in their capability at housework (which seems unlikely), the main factor determining their potential consumption, or "full income," is their hourly wage. Maximizing the present discounted value of lifetime wages can be expected to be roughly equivalent to maximizing the present discounted value of lifetime full income—which is the maximand of the human capital investment decision. This analysis therefore argues that we should compare potential hourly wage rates (or, what amounts to the same thing, annual income standardized for hours of work) if we want a "true" picture of earnings inequality at any point in time. "True" inequality of outcome in incomes would then be inequality in the present discounted value of lifetime wages (or constant hours annual income).[3] If we want to measure inequality of outcome in utilities, we should then adjust this for "compensating differentials" for different types of work—but since compensating differentials are ambiguous and impossible to quantify, in practice, we will have enough problems to keep us busy if we stop at "true" inequalities in income.

To sum up, in neoclassical analysis the individual is seen as making three sorts of choices: (1) an investment choice which determines his or her stock of human capital and the market wage he or she can command in any period; (2) a type of work choice which determines the hourly money wage the individual does receive, as well as psychic income from work; (3) a labor/leisure choice in which the individual chooses between the pleasures offered by leisure and those offered by goods and services. If we follow this perspective, inequalities in the present discounted value of potential wages over a lifetime are the appropriate measure of inequalities of outcome.

8.2.6 Inequality of Opportunity Writers in the human capital tradition tend to emphasize the choices people make and to see the unfettered market as the best mechanism available for those choices, but individuals may differ in their constraints—in particular in their access to the funds required for investment in the human capital market. The education of some students is paid for by their parents, others must borrow, and still others find it impossible to finance further training. Such inequalities of opportunity can be seen as differences in the cost of acquiring human capital—and many policy recommendations for equalizing opportunity are simply ways of equalizing the costs of human capital investments.

Inequality of opportunity can be represented in Figure 8.5 by the existence of different supply schedules of funds for different individuals.[4] An individual who faces S_1 can acquire financing for training only at a high initial interest cost and finds, relatively early, that it is impossible to borrow further (i.e., he or she faces an infinite interest rate beyond Y_1). An individual who faces supply schedule S_2 can finance further years of training but at steadily increasing marginal costs, perhaps because he or she has to turn to progressively more expensive sources (from family funds and low-cost government loans, for example, to bank loans). The fortunate individual facing supply curve S_3 can obtain low-cost funding (e.g., from family funds) for as many years of training as desired, with only gradually increasing costs.

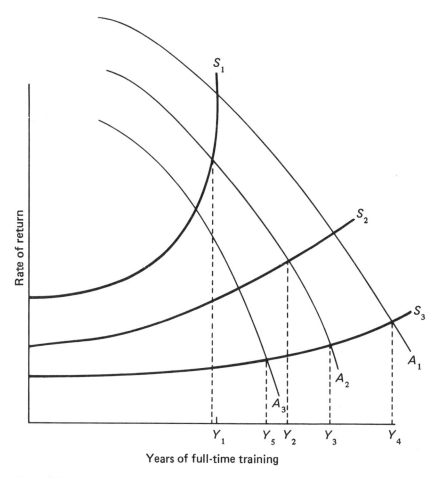

Figure 8.5

A person who wished to maximize wealth would invest in training until his or her marginal costs equaled the marginal return from training. If A_2 represents the marginal rate of return from each year of training for a person of average ability, it is reasonable to expect A_2 to be downward sloping. Initial years of education teach such invaluable skills as literacy and numeracy—which have very high returns. Later years of education and training may yield smaller increments in useful knowledge and hence have a lower marginal rate of return. A rational person of average ability who was from a poor background (faced supply curve S_1) would then acquire Y_1 years of training as marginal cost = marginal return at that level of training. A rational person of average ability from a middle-class background (i.e., curve S_2) would acquire Y_2 years of training while someone from a well-off background (curve S_3) would acquire Y_3 years of training; i.e., controlling for ability, people from more advantaged backgrounds would acquire more training as youngsters and hence would have higher earnings as adults.

A rational person will acquire training to the point where the marginal return equals the marginal cost *if* that person actually makes the decisions involved. If someone else makes the decision, the answer is less clear and early writers (e.g., Pigou, 1932:493) were concerned that parents made "human capital" decisions for their children, but did not have to bear the consequences of those decisions. As Chapter 6 discussed, the preschool and early childhood years are important ones for human capital formation; if conscious decisions are made at this point, they are made by parents, not children. Let us then distinguish between K_1, human capital acquired in childhood, and K_2, human capital acquired as an adult. Figure 8.5 is therefore a better picture of adult decision making in human capital investment (i.e., with respect to K_2) than of the total process of human capital formation $(K_1 + K_2)$.[5] "Equal opportunity" to acquire adult human capital would mean that everyone faced the *same* supply schedule for funds for investment in human capital—"leveling up" would imply that everyone has the advantages of S_3.

8.2.7 Inequality of Ability Inequality of ability can also be represented in Figure 8.5, by curves A_1, A_2, and A_3. A person of high ability (A_1) might be hypothesized to benefit more (i.e., have a higher marginal rate of return) from each additional year of training; a person of lower ability (A_3) might get a lower marginal rate of return.[6] If we had instituted effective equal opportunity (i.e., if everyone faced S_3) but people were of unequal abilities, then society would have become an educational meritocracy, where high-ability people have Y_4 years of training, average people have Y_3, and low-ability people have Y_5.

In fact, we have both unequal opportunities and unequal abilities in the real world. Figure 8.5 therefore illustrates nine possible combinations of ability and background, and the intersection points of A_1, A_2, A_3 and S_1, S_2, S_3 represent nine among the many possible combinations of rates of return and years of training, any of which might be selected by a rational individual, depending on his or her particular combination of abilities and opportunities. Mincer (1974:27) in fact argues that empirically "there is little if any correlation between rates of return and quantity invested"[7] since both inequality of opportunity and inequality of ability are important.

8.2.8 Summary The "human capital" approach to earnings inequality argues that higher earnings are the result of past investments and that people choose which human capital investments to make in themselves on the basis of their own individual preferences and circumstances. Human capital authors tend, as Mincer put it, to define economics as "the analysis of constrained choices" (1976:137) and see labor economics as the analysis of constrained choice with respect to human resources—with the emphasis firmly on the choices rather than the constraints.

Predictions as to the result of these choices are, however, greatly complicated by the existence of "psychic income," the empirical ambiguity of compensating differentials, and the simultaneous presence of inequality of opportunity and of ability. Nevertheless, one important prediction is fairly clear—even if labor markets possessed no institutional imperfections and if all individuals had equal opportunity to finance their training, still some inequalities in the net present value of lifetime monetary earnings would persist in a market system. This remaining "inequality of result" would, in the human capital view, be attributable either to differences in rewards arising from unequal ability (about which, they argue, one cannot do very much, without deserting the market mechanism) or to differences in individual tastes, for leisure and for compensating differentials (about which, in the libertarian view point, one *ought not* to do very much).[8]

8.3 The Distribution of Earnings

8.3.1 A Simple Model If one ignores the complications of unequal hours, psychic income, risk, tastes, etc., the human capital school predicts that individual earning capacity will be determined by equation (8.2).

(8.2) $$E_j^* = E_0^* + r_j HK_j$$

where E_j^* is the earnings capacity of the j-th individual.

In other words, earnings capacity (E_j^*) is the sum of the earnings capacity of unskilled labor (E_0^*) plus the rate of return (R_j) times the stock of human capital an individual possesses (HK_j). If we assume (a) that actual earnings are equal to earning capacity and (b) that years of schooling represent the stock of human capital, this formula can be manipulated into the form (where S_j represents an individual's years of schooling):

(8.3) $$\ln E_j = \ln E_0^* + r_j s_j$$

This is a special, very simple specification. Chiswick (1968) and Mincer (1970) have argued that it can become a model of income distribution if one takes the variance of both sides of the equation and calculates equation (8.4).

(8.4) $$\sigma^2(\ln E_j) = \bar{r}^2\sigma^2(s) + \bar{s}^2\sigma^2(r) + \sigma^2(s)\sigma^2(r)$$

Where $\bar{r}$ and $\bar{s}$ are the average rates of return and years of schooling, respectively, and $\sigma^2(r)$, $\sigma^2(s)$, and $\sigma^2(\ln E_j)$ are the inequality in (i.e., the variances of) rates of return, years of schooling, and natural log of earnings.

Although this is the simplest formulation of the human capital approach to income distribution, it still has a number of clear and important predictions. If the distribution of schooling is symmetric, the distribution of earnings will be skewed—i.e., have a long "tail" to the right as in Figure 2.2. Holding all other variables constant, equation 8.4 also predicts that as the inequality of schooling decreases inequality in earnings will also decrease; that as the inequality in rates of return to schooling decreases inequality in earnings will also decrease; that as the average level of schooling increases the degree of earnings inequality will tend to increase. The first two relationships may seem obvious, but the third may not. Inequality increases as the average level of schooling increases, ceteris paribus, since an increase in the average level of schooling magnifies the impact of any inequality which exists in the rate of return to schooling among individuals. Hence, if we observe that the inequality of schooling has decreased at the same time as its average level has increased (as has happened since World War II in North America), this model predicts that these two factors would have offsetting impacts on the distribution of income—the former tends to decrease earnings inequality while the latter tends to increase it.

Chiswick (1974) reports the results of tests of this model against U.S., Dutch, and Canadian income distribution data. Mincer's comment, however, still stands: "The heroic statistical specification of the schooling model yields very low explanatory power and biased estimates of rates of return" (1970:16).

8.3.2 A More Complex Model The simple schooling model of equation (8.3) restricts the production of human capital to years of formal education, but learning does not occur only in school. In practice, "on-the-job training" is often more important. Human capital theorists see a similar sort of investment process underway in the production of "on-the-job" training which explains, in their view, the increase in earnings with age which is observed in most occupations.

On-the-job training can produce skills which are *specific* to the firm where an individual is employed or *general* enough that they are of potential value to other employers. An example of firm-specific skill might be the knowledge of a particular firm's accounting system, whereas experience as a machinist usually develops skills valuable to several potential employers. The human capital school sees training as costly and argues that the cost of specific training will be borne by the firm. However, the firm will not be willing to bear the cost of general training since, once trained, a worker could threaten to leave and demand a wage equal to his or her marginal product; i.e, the firm gets no return on its investment in general training.[9]

Individuals are then seen as paying for "general" on-the-job training by deciding what fraction (k_t) of their time in period t they wish to devote to the production of human capital and what fraction $(1 - k_t)$ they wish to devote to the production of current income. The earnings capacity (E_{jt}^*) of individual j in period t must therefore be distinguished from actual earnings (E_{jt}).

$$(8.5) \qquad E_{jt} = (1 - k_t)E_{jt}^*$$

It is argued that k_t tends to decrease with age, since further investment in on-the-job training become less worthwhile the closer one is to retirement. The speed at which k_t decreases cannot, however, be predicted from theory and the exact functional form must be fitted by experiment. Mincer (1974:86), for example, presents four possible specifications of earnings functions, which correspond to different specifications of the human capital investment profile. The preferred specification is equation (8.6), which embodies the assumption that the fraction of time put to human capital investment (k_t) declines with experience (t) at an exponential rate (B). Neglecting the subscript for the j-th individual for simplicity, it is:

$$(8.6) \qquad \ln E_t = \ln E_0 + rs + \frac{rk_0}{\beta} + \frac{rk_0}{\beta} e^{-\beta t} + \ln (1 - k_0 e^{-\beta t})$$

assuming $k_t = k_0 e^{-\beta t}$

If one introduces the idea that a person's human capital stock "depreciates" with time at a constant rate d, perhaps due to physical aging and infirmity, or to the lapse of memory with time, or to the progress of current technology, this becomes:

$$(8.7) \qquad \ln E_t = \ln E_0 + (r - d)s - dt + \frac{rK_0^*}{\beta}(1 - e^{-\beta t}) + \ln (1 - K_t^*)$$

where $K_t^* = k_t + \dfrac{d}{r}$

There is, of course, no theoretical reason why human capital might not depreciate exponentially and/or investment ratios might not fall linearly (or otherwise).[10] In practice, the choice between these (and other) assumptions is made on the basis of which gives the better fit to the data at hand—an approach defended by Blinder (1976).

Using a human capital framework, Mincer (1974) succeeded in explaining some 55% of the variance of log earnings of white males in the United States, with a regression which used as variables only years of education, age, and weeks worked. This result is often cited as conclusive evidence for a human capital approach, although, since "full income" is what people really want to maximize, the more appropriate dependent variable is hourly wages and such regressions have much poorer results. In addition, Wolff and Bushe (1976) and Osberg, Clairmont, and Apostle

(1982) have shown that good aggregate results could just as easily be a phenomenon of aggregation of dissimilar labor market segments.[11] ("Rates of depreciation" and investment ratios are logically quite important to human capital *theory,* but do not enter the regressions since unlike current monetary earnings, experience, or education they cannot be observed directly.)

8.3.3 Criticisms Formulas such as equations (8.6) and (8.7) predict individual earnings and obviously become even more intricate when the variance of both sides is taken in order to predict the distribution of earnings (e.g., see Chiswick and Mincer, 1972).[12] At this point, some (e.g., Blaug, 1976) pause to ask whether the theory is still "scientific" in the sense that it is potentially refutable. They wonder whether the selection of functional forms to fit the data and the plethora of ad hoc assumptions mean that any "bad" empirical results can be handled by a new "technical" assumption.[13] More fundamentally, the institutionalist tradition (Chapter 9) questions the whole notion of individual decision making in on-the-job training and the reason why earnings typically increase with age—i.e., they explain Mincer's (1974) result in terms of credentials and seniority.

A final source of criticism is the viewpoint that, whatever the merits of the human capital theory of the determination of individual earnings, it cannot be a complete theory of the *distribution* of earnings. The point can perhaps be best made with the aid of a fable.

Once upon a time in the far-off land of Asif there lived a king who decided one day upon the size distribution of labor incomes F(Y). Having made his decision, he then appointed as PM (Personnel Manager) his most intelligent advisor. The PM was charged with allocation of labor, within the king's constraint, and soon found years of education to be a convenient rationing device. The limited number of high-paying positions was restricted to highly educated individuals and, with experience, the PM learned to adjust the education requirement to reduce to zero the excess supply of workers who were willing to undergo enough expensive training to qualify themselves for such jobs. The king was pleased, for his subjects' potential discontent with F(Y) was greatly lessened when they learned that it was up to individuals to decide how much education (and hence future high incomes) they should acquire. The PM was happy as he was also able to use race, sex, and age to screen individuals for desirable positions. Happy also were the academics, who became very proficient in econometrics and estimated many equations where individual income was a function of education, age, sex, weeks worked, experience, etc. Acceptable correlations were obtained and one day one

Asif academician decided to take the variance of both sides of one equation (written in log form) and thereby explain the variance of the logarithm of male earnings in Asif by the dispersion of male Asif education, age, and weeks worked per year. All the other academicians were happy with this new use of Asif methodology and they all agreed that, were the inequality of education to be decreased, the inequality of earnings would surely also decrease. This did not bother the king as he was out hunting.

A theory of distribution must predict not only that there will be rich and poor, but how many rich and poor there will be. In the mythical kingdom of Asif, people really do make investment decisions in their own future income (i.e., a human capital model adequately analyzes earnings *determination*) but the aggregate process is constrained by a very particular pattern of labor demand (i.e., a human capital model cannot adequately explain the king's decision). In less mythical kingdoms we also have to inquire as to the demand-side constraints on the distribution of earnings. Under simplifying assumptions, given interest rates and costs of training, human capital theory may be able to predict particular relative wage rates for graduates of different "training programs" but nothing in it can predict *how many* people will get work at those wage rates. Demand for training depends on wage ratios *and* tastes; demand for trained people depends on wage ratios *and* technology—neither tastes nor technology are discussed within the model.

For example, given the cost of university education and the cost of funds for training, a human capital theorist might predict that, in equilibrium, the wages of university graduates and high-school graduates would be in a certain ratio, but the theory cannot predict how many people will find it worthwhile, at that wage ratio, to go to college or how many college graduates industry will want to employ. When Chiswick and Mincer argue, for example, that "if everyone were a college graduate . . . inequality would increase by 0.1074 points" (1972, S45), they are assuming that the wages of B.A. graduates would remain the same even if everyone had a B.A.—in effect, an infinitely elastic demand for that type of labor must exist. This does not seem reasonable. Using current data one might be able to predict an *individual's* increase in earnings due to college graduation on the assumption that he or she is a small part of the total labor market and other people's behavior remains unchanged. But can one predict the result of changes in the aggregate using these marginal relationships?[14]

If we wish only to consider very marginal changes in labor supply there is probably not much error introduced if we simply assume that the return to education remains unaltered. If we wish to consider non-marginal changes in the supply of characteristics, it makes a great

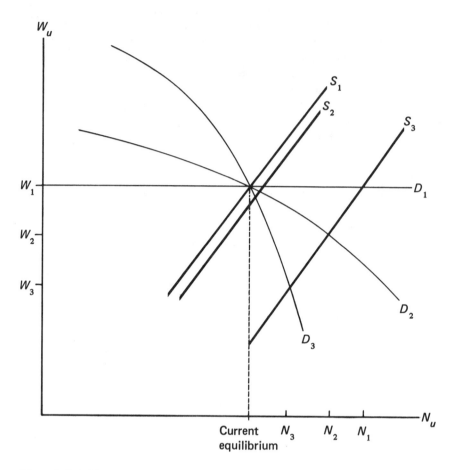

**Figure 8.6 ALTERNATIVE DEMAND HYPOTHESES
AND RELATIVE WAGES AND EMPLOYMENT
OF UNIVERSITY-EDUCATED LABOR**

difference what we assume about labor demand. In Figure 8.6, for
example, we plot on the vertical axis the relative wages of university
graduates and on the horizontal axis the number of university graduates
employed in the labor market. D_1 represents the hypothesis of a perfectly
elastic demand for university graduates—i.e., an unchanged wage which
can be estimated from current data on earnings. D_2 and D_3 represent
alternative hypotheses of declining productivity of university-trained
labor. If we consider an increase in supply from S_1 to S_2[15] there is not
much difference between the wage ratios implied by D_1, D_2, or D_3. But if
we are considering policies to deal with economic inequality (such as, for
example, an equalization of opportunity throughout the educational sys-

tem) we will often be considering shifts in labor supply such as that to S_3—when it makes a great deal of difference which demand curve is appropriate (and when we will also get little assistance from econometric estimates made in the region of S_1).

The three alternative demand hypotheses not only imply different wage rates for university-trained labor (W_1, W_2, or W_3) but also imply that different numbers (N_1, N_2, or N_3) will be employed at these wage rates. Since the aggregrate inequality of the earnings distribution depends not only on relative wages but also on the number at each wage, one cannot predict its degree of inequality until one has specified the shape of *both* the supply and the demand schedules.

Sattinger (1980) argues persuasively that, if one is to see wages as factor prices, then their level must be set by the interplay of supply *and* demand factors; hence "the distribution of earnings cannot be explained solely by reference to any set of worker characteristics, including ability" (1980:6) since worker characteristics can refer only to the *supply* side of labor markets. One must investigate as well the distribution of jobs and the assignment of workers (of differing characteristics) to jobs of differing capital intensity. Sattinger's work investigates the conditions one must impose on a macro production function if wages are to reflect solely individual characteristics[16] and finds them to be "very restrictive." In general, aggregate inequality in earnings depends not only on the distribution of productive abilities (which includes training) but also on the capital intensity of production. Sattinger also examines the influences of comparative advantage in individuals and of the scale of resources—i.e., the fact that some individuals do some things better than others and that these differences are magnified by differences in jobs, especially the amount of capital equipment and the number of subordinates with which one works. Differences in ability and in jobs create the problem of assigning workers to jobs, and differences in wages can be viewed as differences in "rents"—i.e., one's own output in a particular job over and above that of the next best candidate. In general, "the distribution of earnings depends on the distribution of capital among jobs" (1980:95). In particular, Sattinger argues that increasing capital intensity of production increases the inequality of labor earnings, and he finds "strong support" for this hypothesis in his examination of U.S. data.

8.4 Of Families

8.4.1 The Family as a Productive Unit The theory presented so far concerns *individual earnings* but Chapter 2 referred to the distribution of *income* among *households* and *families*. This section therefore outlines a generalization of the human capital approach as it is applied to family labor supply. Just as an individual maximizes utility by deciding to work for others for money when money wages are attractive and to work for himself or herself when "home production" yields a higher return, so also do families make the same decision. Household tasks (e.g., painting the garage, minding the children) are productive—some people decide to do them themselves and some people decide to hire others, while earning the money to pay for these services by their own work in the labor market. Contemporary labor economics views this decision as an economic one, where individuals choose that use of their time which gives the greatest returns—either paid work in the labor market or unpaid work at home. In a family, total income will be higher if the family members who can obtain higher money wages for outside work specialize in paid employment while other family members specialize in production within the home. Whether from discrimination or due to lower stocks of human capital, women typically face lower wages than men (see Chapter 7, section 7.4). Some theorists (e.g., Gronau, 1977) often add the assumption that women are also more efficient in such home tasks as raising the children. Lower wages outside the home and higher productivity inside it comprise the neoclassical explanation of the household division of labor, in which men typically work outside the home and women tend to alternate paid work in the labor market and unpaid work in the home.

Over a family's lifetime, the relative returns to home and market work change. The presence of young children, for example, creates additional demands on parents' time and the "economic" model argues that it is primarily relative wage rates that cause women (rather than men) with young children to leave the paid labor force. As children grow older, they grow less demanding of time, and married women tend to reenter the labor market (J. Smith, 1978).[17] Seen in dollar terms, family income obviously increases when women reenter the paid labor force, but, since the use of time in paid employment means the sacrifice of time for leisure or work around the home, the increase in family money income overstates the increase in family economic well-being. Conversely, inequality in family money income which is due to differences in the number of family earners overstates inequality in family economic well-being.[18]

Recently, Garfinkel and Haveman (1977) have used the human capital framework to try to estimate the importance of inequality in "earnings capacity" to the total inequality of money income. Arguing that individuals' potential wages can be predicted by their education, age, race, sex, and location, they compute the earnings that a family would have if both husband and wife worked 2,000 hours per year. Adding to this the family's income from other sources, such as interest or dividends (but excluding government transfer payments), they compute the family's "earnings capacity"—which section 8.2.5 argued was a better measure of "true" inequality than observed income—and compare the inequality of earnings capacity across U.S. family units to the inequality of money income across U.S. family units. Their finding is that "the distribution of earnings capacity is about four fifths as unequal as the distribution of pre-transfer income" (1977:3). The remaining 20% of inequality (as measured by the Gini index) is due to differences in "capacity utilization" either because of child-care costs or differences in tastes (i.e., lack of work effort)—and they argue that child-care costs are about two-thirds responsible.[19]

8.4.2 The Next Generation: The Intergenerational Transmission of Economic Status People often speak of being able to "afford" having children and if one is willing to see a decision to have children as conceptually equivalent to a decision to purchase a car or other consumer durable (in the sense that both are seen as yielding a stream of utility in the future) the "human capital" perspective can be also used to analyze family fertility. If children are a "normal" good, more will be desired at higher levels of income. The "price" of children is, however, expressed partly in terms of time (i.e., primarily their mother's time). This approach to fertility therefore argues that higher *family* incomes will mean that parents will have more children but that more highly educated women will have a higher "opportunity cost" of time and may tend to have fewer children. Willis (1973), Becker and Tomes (1976), and others have also argued that in deciding the size of their family parents face a "trade-off" between "child quality" and "child quantity." "Child quality" is produced, in their view, by parental purchase of such inputs as ballet lessons or private schooling or by the parents' own time. If parents have a taste for "child quality" they will, other things equal, invest more in a fewer number of children.

As a consequence their children will receive a greater endowment of childhood human capital (K_1), to which these children will add the human capital which they decide to acquire as adults (K_2)—see section 8.2.6 and Figure 8.5. Speaking very roughly, one would then see individual earnings capacity as given by something like equation (8.8).

$$(8.8) \qquad E^* = E_0 + r_1 K_1 + r_2 K_2$$

In this formulation, inequality of opportunity can therefore occur in either or both of two ways—an unequal endowment of childhood human capital (K_1)[20] or unequal access to funds with which to acquire K_2. One must, however, treat this formulation with great care since the vague and embracing category of "capital" does little justice to the many sorts of productive abilities which exist and the ways in which they are acquired. Childhood human capital is an aggregate of many skills, many of which are acquired at a very early age. Some of these skills can perhaps be acquired at any age (e.g., the ability to play the piano) but some are much more difficult, and sometimes impossible, to acquire as an adult if not acquired as a child (e.g., the ability to organize) while some childhood-acquired skills are necessary conditions if one is to acquire adult-level skills (e.g., it takes self-confidence and relatively good study habits to complete medical or graduate school).[21] In short, K_1 and K_2 are not in general perfectly substitutable—a certain amount of K_1 may be a prior requisite to acquiring K_2 and may enhance the productivity of a given amount of K_2.

Childhood-acquired human capital is, however, highly important. Writers such as Tomes (1980) have argued that parents who derive pleasure from their children's consumption (have altruistic tastes) will decide on the most effective means of passing on an inheritance—either by bequest of material wealth at their own death or by investing in their children's "quality" (human capital) over the childhood years. "Utility maximization" by parents is, in the neoclassical view, held to determine a simultaneous choice of family size, the human capital formation of children, and material bequest.[22]

Many years ago the English economist Alfred Marshall wrote:

> the investment of capital in the rearing and early training of the workers of England is limited by the resources of parents in the various grades of society, by their power of forecasting the future and by their willingness to sacrifice themselves for the sake of their children (1913:561).

Marshall saw systematic biases in parental foresight, information, effort, access to capital (and contacts), and low rates of time discount of future earnings which all favored heavy investment by "the higher grades of society" in their children's training and the opposite for "the lower ranks." As he put it:

> the professional classes especially, while generally eager to save some capital *for* their children are even more on the alert for opportunities of investing it *in* them,

while the children of the working classes "go to their graves with undeveloped abilities and faculties." Marshall emphasized, "The point on which we have specially to insist now is that this evil is cumulative" (ibid., p. 563), as poorly trained, poorly paid workers reproduce poorly trained offspring in each generation while those with better opportunities themselves tend also to invest more in their own children.

Figure 8.7 presents a simplified graphical illustration of this process. On the vertical axis we measure the value of parents' own consumption while the horizontal axis plots the value of investment in children's human capital (to keep the diagram two-dimensional, we assume here that the number of children is fixed). Investment in children has a price, which is paid partly in money and partly in time, and the relative price of parents' own consumption versus the cost of investing in children is given by the slope of the budget lines $C_1^* K_1$ and $C_0^* K_0$. The height of these budget lines is determined by parental income—parents with a higher income could consume C_1^* if they spend all their income (E_1^*) on themselves while parents with lower incomes could consume only C_0^* if they spent nothing on their children.

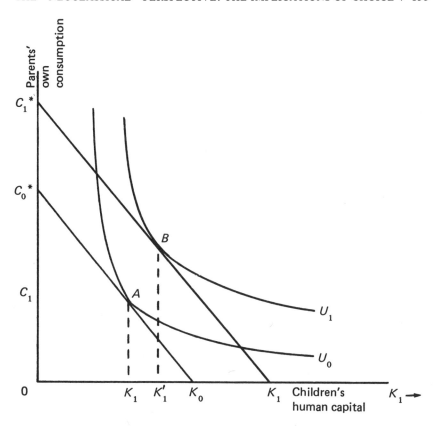

Figure 8.7 PARENTAL CONSUMPTION & CHILDREN'S HUMAN CAPITAL

Of course, parents do spend time and money on their children and in the neoclassical view this is explained in terms of parental altruism—i.e., parents have a utility function defined over both their own consumption and that of their children. Parents derive increased utility from increases in the consumption of their children and, consequently, purchase human capital for their children to enable that higher consumption. They maximize utility at points such as A if parental income is E_0 or B if parental income is E_1. A diagram such as Figure 8.7 can therefore be used to represent the importance of (a) variations in parental tastes, (b) changes in relative prices, and (c) differences in parental incomes.

More altruistic parents will, for any given income and relative prices, consume less themselves and purchase more human capital for their children. If relative prices should change—for example, if high schools should start to charge tuition—parents can be expected to purchase less human capital for their children. Probably the most important variable in practice is parents' own income, which is partially determined by the parents' inheritance of childhood human capital from their parents.

If we hold relative prices constant and denote by α the fraction of parents' potential lifetime earnings (E_p^*) used to purchase children's human capital (in Figure 8.7, α is equal to $0C_1/0C_1^*$ if potential consumption is C_1^*) we then have equation (8.9). Denoting E_M^* as mother's earnings capacity and E_F^* as father's earnings capacity produces (8.10).

(8.9) $$K_1 = \alpha \times E_p^*$$

(8.10) $$E_p^* = E_M^* + E_F^*$$

Hence,

$$K_1 = \alpha(E_M^* + E_F^*)$$

Equation (8.10) can be used to illustrate the importance of assortative mating (i.e., a high positive correlation between E_F^*, father's earnings capacity, and E_M^*, mother's earnings capacity). In addition, using (8.11) we can see clearly the cumulative importance of intergenerational social inheritance of earnings power, since part of one's parents' earnings capacity is due to *their* endowment of childhood human capital (K_{1M} and K_{1F}).

(8.11) $$K_1 = \alpha(E_{OM} + r_{1M}K_{1M} + r_{2M}K_{2M} + E_{OF} + r_{1F}K_{1F} + r_{2F}K_{2F})$$

Recently, Becker and Tomes (1979) and Loury (1981) have formalized some of these perceptions into equilibrium models of the distribution of income across generations, within a market society with private ownership (i.e., a capitalist society). Whereas Marshall argued verbally, these authors present their arguments mathematically—but with essentially the same conclusion, that families pass their status from generation to generation, largely by investing in their children. Since parenting is far from a science and since abilities of children differ, r_1 (the return realized on childhood advantages) can be interpreted as being partially random in practice. Still, the expectation of economic success is clearly passed from generation to generation.[23]

Specific predictions from models such as the Becker/Tomes model depend on the empirical values of such parameters as a family's propensity to invest in children, the heritability of endowments of "social capital" such as business connections, etc., but the general perspective is clear. If one accepts Marshall's or Becker and Tomes's analyses, they are arguing that, unless government intervenes to invest in the human capital of children and/or to provide systematic compensatory mechanisms for investment in adult life, a market economy with private ownership will be a dynastic society. The "life-chances" of an individual person will be in large measure determined by the dynasty or family line into which he or she is born, since dynasties differ in "tastes" for investment in children and in "endowment" of monetary and "social" capital. The fortunes of family lines are affected by transitory shocks such as "market luck" (i.e., variations in the returns their assets bring in the market place) and "endowment luck" (such as random fluctuations in inherited ability), so some intergenerational mobility is possible (but temporary). In general, however, there is a substantial correlation between the incomes of grandparents, parents, and children.

Of course, "equality of opportunity" in the labor market has usually been interpreted to mean that all individual persons, within a given generation, have an equal chance—in human capital terms an equal endowment of "social capital" and childhood human capital and equal costs of acquiring adult human capital. Indeed, it is difficult to see what "equality of opportunity" could mean, if it does not mean equality of opportunity for individual persons. If the Becker/Tomes model is a good representation of a capitalist market economy, it would indicate that "equality of opportunity" cannot be attained in such an economy, any more than can "equality of result."[24]

8.5 Summary and Conclusion

"Neoclassical" labor economics has been defined by Cain (1976:1216) as:

> the marginal productivity theory of demand—based on profit maximizing behavior of employers—and a supply theory based on utility maximization of workers (which) . . . takes the form of (1) investment in human capital, which determines one's skill or occupation—the *kind* of work supplied, and (2) labor/leisure choices, which determine the *amount* of one's labor supply.

The strengths of the neoclassical approach lie both in the volume of theoretical and empirical work (literally hundreds of journal articles, books, and monographs) and in its extremely wide domain, which asserts insights into health economics, criminology, sociology, religious attendance, and much else—as well as claiming to be an explanation of both individual earnings determination and the distribution of income.

The human capital approach also provides an extremely close "fit" with other areas of neoclassical economic thought. The theory of optimal investment in human capital is almost identical, formally, with the theory of a firm's optimal investment in physical capital; hence, techniques of optimization over time and under uncertainty which are used in other areas of economics can be readily transferred to this "special case." "Relative wages" in neoclassical labor models perform the same functions that relative prices do in models of the general economy as guides to optimization, embodying all the information necessary for firm and individual decision making and equilibrating supply and demand in the marketplace.[25] Most importantly, the focus of the neoclassical approach is rational individual choice. The determination of individual earnings and of the distribution of earnings is therefore seen as the result of rational individual choices—on skill acquisition, on family labor force supply, and on "investment" in children.

Other interpretations, however, exist, two of which are discussed in Chapter 9. Two general criticisms of the human capital approach are the difficulty of constructing definitive empirical tests of its theory of individual earnings determination and the incompleteness of its general model of earnings distribution. Indeed, the very plasticity of the human capital approach, its ability to generate new working hypotheses on unobservable variables to explain any and all new observations, opens it to the criticism that it has become more a working language of economists than a body of theory which can, ultimately, be refuted.

However, in Mincer's (1970:15) phrasing, one can make "important though not unconditional" statements about the perspective which a "neoclassical" approach brings to the analysis of inequality:

1. Individuals invest in their own future income, primarily by choosing to acquire schooling and on-the-job training, although the amount they invest and the return they receive is dependent both on their abilities and on their opportunities.

2. Greater schooling and on-the-job training increase worker productivity and, as a result, the potential hourly wage.

3. The higher wages of those with more education and work experience are the return to past human capital investment decisions.

4. Differences in working hours in the paid labor market reflect utility-maximizing choices by individuals and families between leisure, market goods, and home-produced goods and services.

5. Inequality in annual money incomes overstates "real" inequality. "Real" income inequality is better measured by inequality in the present value of lifetime "full income" (actual money income adjusted for differences in hours of work).

6. Inequality in money income (annual or lifetime) generally overstates inequality in utility, since low money earnings are typically compensated by high nonmonetary returns (and vice versa).

7. The aggregate degree of inequality in the earnings distribution can be seen as the summation of (past) individual decisions on human capital investments and labor supply. Hence, a more equal distribution of education will tend to equalize the distribution of earnings.

8. Family labor supply over the life cycle and male/female work roles within the family can be usefully analyzed as utility-maximizing responses to labor market conditions (and especially to relative wage rates).

9. Family income (as determined by family labor supply decisions and human capital investments) and the opportunity cost of time are important determinants of fertility and of the resources families invest in their children.

10. Since individuals have differing tastes and abilities they make

different investments in human capital—in the absence of government intervention *inequality of economic result is therefore inevitable in a capitalist market system.*

11. Since families have different resources and make different decisions on investments in their children, in the absence of government intervention which equalizes investments in the human capital of children, *inequality of opportunity is inevitable in a capitalist market system.*

In a certain sense the last conclusion may appear surprising. The literature on human capital investment in child quality has typically been approached from the viewpoint of parents, who make choices which affect their children's lives, rather than from the viewpoint of the children, whose choices are limited by the decisions and resources of their parents. Nevertheless, the implication that inequality of opportunity is an inevitable part of unconstrained capitalism has often been stated over the years (e.g., Knight, 1923, 1951). It follows directly from the inequality of result in the labor market of one generation and the constraints and utility-maximizing choices of that generation; it follows also from a very different analysis of contemporary labor markets, to which we now turn.

NOTES

[1]The concept of "human capital" is far broader than that of merely the impact of training on earnings. For a discussion of the "music capital" involved in listening to serious music or the "euphoric capital" involved in drug addiction see Stigler and Becker (1977); for a discussion of human interaction in general see Becker (1974).

[2]The Lucas (1977a) study is, for example, saturated with data problems.

[3]In sections 8.3 and 8.4 we assume constant annual hours of work.

[4]Along the vertical axis of Figure 8.5 we measure the marginal return to investment in human capital—i.e., the internal rate of return on the last year of training undertaken. The horizontal axis measures years of training.

[5]Alternatively Figure 8.5 could model the decision making of parents if one assumed that all parents had the same degree of altruism—i.e., true costs of investment were always inflated by the same fraction to yield "perceived" cost.

[6]It is not as obvious as it may seem that high-ability people benefit more from training. Presumably high-ability people may learn more in school but may need school less in order to learn. (See Bowles and Gintis, 1976:107.) In addition, Figure 8.5 implicitly defines "ability" as "the ability to make money"—for a criticism, see Chapter 6.

[7]The discussion here refers to marginal returns to training which will equal average returns to training only if either the supply or the demand schedules are perfectly elastic, i.e., S_3 or A_3 is horizontal. Equation (8.2) and almost all empirical work, in fact, refer to an individual's average rate of return.

[8]Simulation studies such as Blinder's (1974) have concluded that an appreciable portion of U.S. lifetime inequality is due to differences in taste but that "disparities in wages dominate all other causes of inequality" (p. 125).

[9]Whether the firm gets a return on its specific training when the worker realizes he is worth more to his employer than he is being paid may depend on the outcome of a bargaining process—see Chapter 9—or on the nature of long-term contracts (see Lazear, 1979b).

[10]Chiswick and Mincer (1972) in fact assume that k_i decreases linearly with time.

[11]Wolff and Bushe (1976) found that for operatives, clerical workers, and other occupations making up about one-half the U.S. labor force there is little payoff to experience or education. Osberg, Clairmont, and Apostle (1982) demonstrate that Mincer's result, or indeed even better results, can be obtained in synthetic samples by the aggregation of

dissimilar segments, none of which follow "human capital" wage relationships. In cross-sectional empirical work such aggregate results are obtained by the aggregation of sectors only some of which fit a human capital model.

[12]To make things tractable, Chiswick and Mincer (1972) must, for example, make the unappetizing assumption that an individual's rate of return to school and postschool investments is uncorrelated. Schultz (1971:27) has argued that much of the empirical success of these models of income distribution is in fact due to a "weeks worked" variable which he argues cannot be properly considered part of the human capital framework.

[13]Mincer, for example, comments, "A low correlation between investment in human capital and earnings would not constitute a rejection of the human capital hypothesis" (1974:138) since this might be "due" to unequal opportunity. Similarily the presence of "psychic returns" could "explain" almost anything—e.g., the earnings of academics, which have fallen continuously for a decade.

[14]A mathematical presentation of this argument can be found in Lucas (1977b). At the theoretical level the human capital response is to argue that the return to each unit of human capital is determined by aggregate supply and demand in the market for human capital regardless of the holdings of particular individuals (Ben-Porath, 1967)—i.e., the human capital of individuals differs in quantity but not in kind.

[15]Figure 8.6, in presuming an upward-sloping supply curve of labor, assumes that wages alone do not govern entry into the university graduate labor market, or else the supply curve would also be horizontal if discount rates were uniform. One must appeal to unequal time preferences, the differential tastes for nonmonetary attributes of jobs, or to inequalities in access to funds to derive an upward-sloping supply curve—but if one does not, the predicted solution becomes completely indeterminate.

[16]This is known as the "efficiency units" assumption, i.e., that one can calculate all wages as the summation of returns to individual attributes, which returns are exogenous market prices. It is widely used (e.g., Taubman, 1977) even outside strictly human capital work.

[17]Women do not reenter the labor market at the same wage as men of the same age, human capitalists argue, since their absence has cost them some years of on-the-job training. Indeed, those women who anticipated, as children, these absences from the labor market would have had less incentive to invest initially in human capital of all sorts (see Chapter 7).

[18]In practice, increasing female labor force participation has tended to reduce the measured inequality of family money incomes, by increasing the share of low-income families in money income.

[19]Among adult males Mirer (1979a) found utilization of earnings capacity to be lower for lower-income groups, implying that the variance of the log of earnings capacity was some 8% less than the variance of log earnings.

[20]When one is a child, others are responsible for the major decisions which affect one's life while as an adult one is responsible for one's own decisions; exactly when this transition occurs is the subject of many family and scholarly debates. Perhaps one should recognize that in practice an intermediate period of joint veto generally exists but basically this is an age-old and universal problem. Anglo-American jurisprudence attempts to solve this problem by specifying an "age of majority" (now generally 18), before which one is "a child" and after which one isn't—although this age of majority often differs for different classes of acts (e.g., criminal offenses versus property transactions).

[21]Not to mention the fact that childhood-acquired skills demand inputs of material resources and parental time in differing proportions.

[22]The "economic" approach to fertility is seen by the unsympathetic as the development of a new language to describe old facts. "Tastes" can be so easily respecified, e.g., to incorporate social norms which emphasize the importance of male offspring, that virtually any real-world fertility behavior can find an explanation. The differences between childhood environments (see Chapter 6, section 6.3) have been reduced to a "tractable" two-dimensional quality/quantity choice but some, e.g., Ryder (1973), wonder if this new language creates or obscures insight.

[23]The major innovation in Becker and Tomes (1979) is the suggestion that the impact of progressive income taxes in one generation has an impact on inequality in the succeeding generation that is theoretically indeterminate; i.e., progressive taxation could increase inequality. Kanbur (1979: 791) derives a similarly ambiguous result within one generation, arguing that the impact of progressive taxation on inequality depends on society's degree of

risk aversion. The presentation of these counterintuitive theoretical possibilities illustrates the importance of empirical evidence in economics. Davies (1982) has shown that the Becker/Tomes conclusion regarding progressive income tax is highly sensitive to the parameter values chosen to represent the degree of parental altruism and the rate of interest relative to the economy's growth rate and indeed that a disequalizing effect requires implausible values of these variables. Reasonable parameter values imply the reasonable result that redistributive taxation produces a more equal income distribution.

[24]Opinions on the desirability of "equal opportunity" may differ. Marshall, in his use of the word "evil" to describe this intergenerational transmission process, certainly left no doubt as to where he stood on the issue.

[25]The market for human capital, like the market for automobiles, doesn't really require that *everyone* be perfectly informed if it is to function effectively. If enough consumers at the margin respond to relative wages, relative occupational returns will tend to equalize. In addition, since discounting implies that returns which will be received in thirty or forty years are heavily deflated in terms of present value, it is not really necessary for individuals to have firm forecasts of earnings in the far distant future.

9 STRUCTURAL INTERPRETATIONS: THE IMPORTANCE OF CONSTRAINTS

9.1 Introduction—An Analogy

Suppose that, instead of being determined by complex market processes, individual earnings were determined by one's success at a simple task, such as hitting a baseball. In particular, suppose that at age 21 you faced a pitching machine which threw one thousand baseballs over the plate and your earnings for the rest of your life were determined by the number of hits you obtained. Those who hit home runs every time become billionaires. Those who strike out become skid row bums. The rest of us are somewhere in between.

Such a process might generate a distribution of earnings not unlike our own and analysis of it could be approached from different angles. Those who emphasize ability (see Chapter 6) would argue that genetically inherited ability is the primary reason for the inequality of batting averages and of income which one would observe. Tests of eye/hand coordination, reflexes, and strength and their similarity between parents and children might be used to test this theory. The policy implications would be ambiguous—some might argue that one cannot do much to remedy inequalities in reflexes and coordination and therefore not much to equalize the distribution of income, but others would argue that one ought, for example, to provide eyeglasses to those with genetically weak eyesight.

By contrast, human capital theorists (see Chapter 8) would examine the time that individuals had spent practicing before the age of 21 and would argue that this investment of time would largely explain the differences one observed in batting averages. "Equal opportunity" would mean that every child is excused from household chores for an equal amount of batting practice time and all have equal access to expert coaching—but, if people prefer not to practice, that of course is their business. A human capital theorist would argue that, even with equal opportunity, some inequalities of incomes would remain, as a result of differences in tastes and abilities which society should not seek to alter.

162

Most of the authors cited in this chapter would, however, wonder whether the others have taken too much for granted. Does the machine pitch the ball at the same speed to everyone? Is the ball always the same size? Does everyone receive a bat of the same size to swing with? All these variables clearly affect the probability that any individual will be able to connect, regardless of inherent ability or how hard the person practices. In the extreme, those who are swinging with a broom stick handle at a marble which is traveling at bullet speed have the odds stacked against them! They will have to be of *exceptional* ability and perseverance if they are not to strike out.[1] For the vast majority the differences will be less large and in some cases quite subtle—e.g., the difference between hitting a hard or a soft ball. If, however, people come up to bat in groups and if each *group* faces the same speed of pitch and size of ball, then individuals will never observe how difficult it is for people in the *other* groups to hit the ball. Members of more advantaged groups will then find it hard to understand the low batting average of less advantaged groups— except in terms of a presumption of their own greater ability and training.

"Structural" approaches to the determination of income[2] emphasize the systematic differences in the probability of economic success which different individuals face. Whereas a neoclassical perspective views outcomes as the result of choices, a structural perspective sees outcomes as the results of the choices made among perceived available alternatives. They would emphasize that people differ in the options available to them, in their perception of the options available to them, and in the results they can expect from similar actions.[3] Although individuals do make choices, and although those choices are important to them, they are choosing from a restricted set of alternatives. How and why these sets of alternatives differ among people is, in the structural perspective, more important in practice than the choices open to individuals.

Emphasizing the constraints rather than the choices alters both the measurement and the interpretation of inequality of outcome and of inequality of opportunity. The emphasis of neoclassical theory on the distribution of the present value of lifetime full income as a measure of inequality of outcome was based on the idea that individual labor/leisure choice of paid working hours (H) and individual choice of human capital investment program (implying the current wage, w) together determine annual earnings $(= w \times H)$. But when working hours are fixed or unemployment is involuntary, hours of work are not solely determined by individual choice. And when wages over time are not determined by human capital investments, individual choice is only part of the picture of wage determination. A structural approach emphasizes the demand side of labor markets, with the result that observed annual money earnings partially regain their place as a rough measure of inequality of outcomes and without the idea that individuals are alone responsible for their place in the distribution of outcomes.

In looking at inequality of opportunity, a structural approach would similarly downplay the role of conscious parental choice. Unconscious parental imitation of the "appropriate" way to rear children, learned in part from the larger society but mostly from their own upbringing, is seen as much more important. Intergenerational transmission of economic status is thus seen as much more an issue of social class than of investments in childhood human capital. What one can do about it is another issue altogether, and here the two strands of a structural approach, the "institutional" and the "radical," diverge quite sharply. They are, therefore, presented separately—the "institutional" in section 9.2 and the radical in section 9.3. Section 9.4 offers a conclusion.

9.2 Neo-Institutionalists

In many ways, the institutionalist approach to labor economics is a uniquely American school of thought. Although one can trace some antecedents in the German historical school, still the American writers of the late 1800s (e.g., R. M. Smith, H. C. Adams, and especially R. T. Ely) represented a sharp and original break from the abstract conjectures of the then-dominant English tradition in economics—and their approach became for many years *the* way to approach labor studies. McNulty (1980:139) characterizes their approach as comprising "a historical and comparative approach to the study of labor institutions and organizations, an inductive study of labor's actual economic position and the effects of labor's policies, an espousal of the ideal of an interventionist state in labor matters and an emphasis on the actions of groups rather than of individuals."

During this period, the boundaries demarcating academic disciplines were not as tightly defined as they are today, and these writers and their successors of the early 1900s (e.g., J. R. Commons, R. F. Hoxie, T. S. Adams, H. L. Summers, W. C. Mitchell, S. Perlman) often ranged widely in their writing over areas that would now be seen as parts of sociology and history. In many cases (especially Ely and Commons) an interdisciplinary approach to labor studies was combined with an acute interest in economic policy and an urge to reform existing economic and social institutions. In addition, "the earliest labor economists were generally unequivocal in their rejection of economic theory" (McNulty, 1980:163) due both to its underemphasis on group behavior and its prediction, belied by the unemployment of the Great Depression, of full employment equilibrium.

Such economists as Kerr (1950) and Reynolds (1951) were thus heirs to a long tradition in emphasizing the "imperfections" of real-world labor markets and the importance of considering social factors and specific circumstances in the analysis of earnings determination. During the 1960s this school of thought was largely submerged by an onrushing tide of "human capital" literature whose stress lay, as we have seen, on the utility-maximizing decisions of individuals over time.[4] In 1971, however, Doeringer and Piore resurrected the notion of an "internal labor market," which they defined as "an administrative unit within which the pricing and allocation of labor is governed by a set of administrative rules and procedures" (1971:2). They estimated that over 80% of U.S. workers were members of "internal labor markets" and argued that in emphasizing "external" labor markets contemporary labor economics was largely missing the boat on the real determinants of earnings.

9.2.1 *The Internal Labor Market* In Figure 9. 1 we present a schematic diagram of labor organization in a chemical plant. This plant is part of a larger organization and, as is normal, contains several operating sections. Within each section a number of "job ladders" exist and we have presented two of the job ladders of the production department in some detail.[5] Typically, individuals are hired at a "port of entry" (usually at the bottom of a job ladder) and progress with experience, with increasing pay and responsibility at each stage. In blue-collar internal labor markets the primary criterion for promotion is seniority while managerial internal labor markets lay greater stress on ability (but balance that, usually, with an implicit guarantee of employment).[6]

Underlying the internal labor market is, in Doeringer and Piore's view, the technological fact of job specificity. They argue that the highly specialized nature of most modern production means that productivity improvements at the plant level usually come from a process of minor production modifications and adaptations to the idiosyncracies of local conditions. Knowledge of these locally made improvements and an awareness of the different operating characteristics of particular pieces of equipment is not easily codified; in practice nobody knows these details of work better than the workers themselves. Promotion up a job ladder means learning the skills of your new job and teaching your old skills to your replacement. In general it is not feasible for formal educational systems to perform this training function since the skills involved are so specialized. On the job, workers can learn by "osmosis," by filling in during vacations or illnesses, and by informal demonstration (methods which can often be more effective than highly verbal classroom instruction).

But note that the "human capital" emphasis on individual decision making regarding on-the-job training has vanished. On-the-job training is seen as a relatively costless by-product of employment, with management making such decisions as exist.[7] However, on-the-job training cannot exist without employment stability and it will not exist if the instructors (other workers) are reluctant to pass on their knowledge. As Williamson, Wachter, and Haris (1975) have argued, the standard market solution cannot provide motivation for instruction since there are only a small number of participants involved in each training situation (due to speciali-

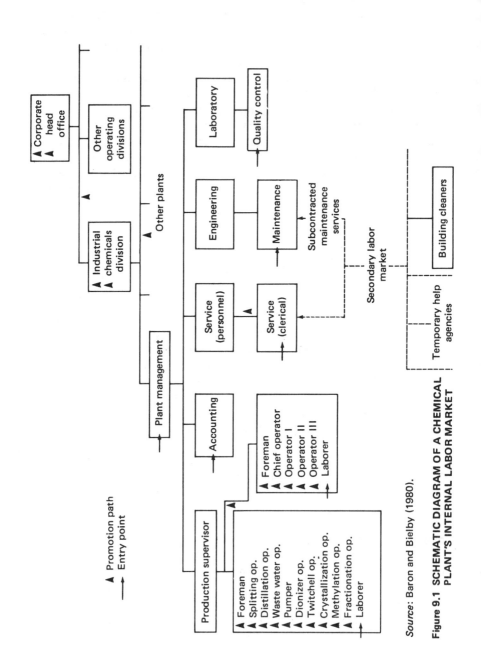

Source: Baron and Bielby (1980).

Figure 9.1 SCHEMATIC DIAGRAM OF A CHEMICAL PLANT'S INTERNAL LABOR MARKET

zation). Any attempt to create a price mechanism to reward workers for training their subordinates would soon degenerate into unproductive haggling over the "appropriate" price.[8] Any success in creating a competitive labor market within the firm would simply dry up the supply of training entirely. If worker A knows that passing on his knowledge of the job to worker B enables B to compete for A's job (e.g., by offering to do it at a slightly lower wage), then he is unlikely to help put himself out of a job by sharing knowledge. Yet increased productivity depends on effective transmission of these highly specialized skills. Technically sophisticated firms therefore have strong practical reasons for instituting seniority systems or employment guarantees which guarantee the individual worker that he can safely pass on his skills. In a seniority system, someone with lower or higher seniority is neither a threat nor threatened themselves by the competition of other workers; hence nothing is lost if one helps another to do his job—and no work group can function without some cooperation.

Stability of employment also means that people at a work site have an ongoing relationship with each other; i.e., they form a social group. As social animals, humans who interact with each other for any length of time tend to develop patterns of behavior and to evolve group norms about the customary way of doing things. Patterns such as the normal length of a coffee break or the expected time to quit work are usually based mainly on the way things have been done in the past but they can become very deeply ingrained—indeed Doeringer and Piore refer to them as the "customary law" of a workplace. Transgressing this "customary law" produces morale problems, which can have financial consequences. It is rarely sufficient for management to gain "perfunctory compliance" (indeed "working to rule" almost invariably brings an organization to its knees) since beyond the most routine tasks it is usually impossible to formally describe all of a job's duties. Without some degree of internalization of the firm's goals, authority could not be delegated and unexpected developments could not be handled. Even firms without unions therefore tend to exhibit a tendency for "past practice" to continue, although a certain degree of codification of work rules is usually implied in a collective agreement.[9]

Pulling these ideas together, Thurow (1975:79) argues that 60% of U.S. workers acquired *all* their job skills on the job and that "the labor market is not a market where fully developed skills bid for jobs. Rather it is primarily a market where supplies of trainable labor are matched with training opportunities that are in turn directly associated with the number of job openings that exist. Training opportunities only occur when there is a job opening that creates the demand for the skills in question." Turning the supply-side orientation of human capital analysis neatly on its head, Thurow argues that typically a demand schedule exists for a job but there is no independent supply schedule! In contrast to a neoclassical approach (which can be called a "worker sovereignty" model) he therefore sees the effective locus of decision making on training (and relative wages) as being at the firm, rather than the individual, level.

If the dynamic efficiency gains (in long-run technological innovation and improved morale and labor productivity) of maintaining employment security in an internal labor market typically dominate short-run efficiency gains from hiring in an external labor market, people outside the internal labor market are simply shut out. Hence, for example, the existence of unemployed economists does not produce a bidding down of all economists' current wage rates and a new "market-clearing" equilibrium where business and government replace existing personnel from the pool of the unemployed. Instead, a variety of institutional mechanisms (tenure, Civil Service regulations, de facto employer policies—what Freedman, 1976, calls labor market "shelters") protect those currently employed, and they in turn continue to use their very specialized areas of expertise for their employer's benefit.[10] Once we look inside the internal labor market (a faculty or government or business department) notions of parity with similarly qualified personnel (i.e., "wage contours") tend to dominate wage increases—e.g., a university wage settlement which provides the same percentage increase for all departments, regardless of the current supply/demand situation of biologists vis-à-vis economists.

Many of the authors cited in Chapter 8 would, however, argue that none of this is really new; it is rather simply a *description* of the process of on-the-job training which they acknowledge to be important.[11] Nor do Doeringer and Piore deny totally the influence of market forces. The points at issue for earnings determination are really rather subtle: the speed with which wage rates adjust to excess supply (or demand) of particular types of labor, the importance people ascribe to relative wages compared to the absolute level of wages, and the degree of individual choice involved in the on-the-job training process. Neo-institutionalists argue that the internal wage structure of an establishment changes very slowly, that relative wages are extremely important, and that there is in fact little individual choice involved in the on-the-job training process— while "neoclassical" writers, for the most part, take the opposite tack. In addition, institutionalist writers stress the importance of "past practice" for work organization and productivity. However, there is no clear criterion for determining when, for example, wages within a firm move "so slowly" in response to outside pressure as to be "rigid" or "quickly enough" to be "responsive" to market forces. One's choice of perspective is, therefore, largely a matter of judgment at the present time.

9.2.2 The Role of Education The institutionalist viewpoint argues that one's initial port of entry into the internal labor market is crucial to one's lifetime career. The main function of education is, in this view, that of screening workers for different possible levels of entry into the world of work. Even if almost all the skills people actually use in their jobs are learned on the job, still a *relatively* high level of education may indicate the *relative* ability of individuals, in particular their ability to absorb training. When technological progress is rapid and only dimly foreseeable beyond the short run, the ability to absorb new training or to adapt to new, as yet unknown, techniques becomes highly important. Access to management jobs, for example, will then tend to be restricted to those with a *relatively* high level of education. Hiring at this entry port will be determined, in large measure, by credentialism. The absolute level of education is not nearly so important as one's *relative* level of education—when only 5% of the population had B.A.s, they were the ones hired as trainee managers in business and government; when 20% of the population has a B.A. it is the 5% who have M.B.A.s who are hired.

Then B.A. graduates are pushed farther down in the educational queue, receiving the lower wages which accompany lower positions rather than a "general" rate of return on human capital. Inflation of education qualifications which occurs throughout the job pyramid, from the increased education required of potential policemen to the increased credentials required for elementary school teachers, produces a competitive scramble in which more education is a "defensive necessity" for each individual to secure his or her place in the job queue. Institutionalists argue, however, that the job hierarchy is not changed by all this jostling in the queue for desirable jobs—hence the considerable equalization of education since World War II has produced no corresponding change in the inequality of income distribution.

Formal models of labor markets where education is mainly a "signal" of potential ability have been developed by Arrow (1973), Spence (1974), Stiglitz (1975a), and others.[12] A common conclusion of these models is that "economies with imperfect information differ in fundamental ways from economies with perfect information" (Stiglitz, 1975a: 269). Several different equilibrium positions may exist in these models and in some equilibria everyone may be worse off—there is no guarantee that unaided market forces will push an economy to its "optimum" allocation of resources. These multiple equilibria differ in income inequality as well as in average income. What determines which equilibrium the model converges to? Past history (Spence) or particular parameter values (Arrow, Stiglitz), which may be determined institutionally, are crucial. These models, if taken seriously, then point to the role played by expectations formed on the basis of past behavior and "arbitrary" social institutions in determining the degree of economic inequality.

In general, the "screening" perspective—that *relative* education indicates *relative* ability but does not change productivity—implies that equalization of opportunities for education will *not* equalize the distribution of earnings. It also implies that increases in the average level of education will not aid economic growth to any appreciable degree. "Investment in education" is therefore attacked on two fronts, and it is argued (e,g., Taubman and Wales, 1973) that the "social" rate of return (in terms of increased output to society) to investment in education is less than the private return to the individuals involved. Part of the justification for the expansion of colleges and universities in the 1960s lay in the human capital arguments that increased growth *and* equality would result—hence the screening/human capital controversy is of considerable importance for policy.

Does education primarily create credentials or primarily impart skills? Obviously the issue is highly important. Wolff and Bushe (1976) have demonstrated that only in a limited number of occupations does education affect earnings directly, as opposed to its general importance in limiting *entry* to an occupation. Riley (1979) comes to much the same conclusion but Layard and Psarchopoulous (1974), among others, disagree. One can be *certain* the controversy will continue, but basically it is now a controversy over the *degree* to which education creates credentials versus skills—few would contend that it does not do some of both.

9.2.3 Discrimination Since the institutionalist view is that hiring decisions are largely based on estimated *potential* for future training rather than current skills, employers may well believe that "background characteristics" such as age, previous employment history, general personal demeanor, or race or sex are good predictors of future trainability. The standard neoclassical approach to such discrimination (see Chapter 7) is that if an employer is factually wrong in his belief he must pay for the privilege of discriminating, via higher wages unbalanced by higher productivity. The institutionalist perspective is that, where there is in fact little difference in potential trainability and where wages are generally fairly rigidly set by the "wage contours" of the internal labor market, there is little cost to the employer in exercising a preference for a particular type of worker. Spence (1973) and Starrett (1976) have argued as well that an observed preference for, for example, whites over blacks in managerial positions will create informational feedbacks which decrease the perceived payoff for blacks to invest in education, thus decreasing their average level of education and reinforcing the stereotype of uneducated blacks.[13]

In addition, personal contacts (what economists tend to call "informal information networks"—see Rees, 1966, or Granovetter, 1974) may well be the determining factor in which job a person entering the labor market actually gets. Accepting that initial job forecloses some options and opens up others. It is usually very difficult for an individual to evaluate fully the complex tree of decisions and future options involved, but those who have "better" contacts are clearly better off.

Therefore, the institutionalist model of individual income determination stresses education, seniority, background characteristics, personal contacts, and an element of luck.[14] Their model of the income *distribution* stresses technology and the sociology of wage determination. If we refer again to Figure 9.1, institutionalists tend to see the demand for these specific occupations and the job-ladder relationships between them as largely determined by technology. The state of technical and management knowledge at any point in time determines the number of possible choices of technology, plant layout, capital equipment, etc., open to a firm but, once made, that choice determines a matrix of labor inputs required.[15]

9.2.4 The Wage Structure The technology of production may determine the number of people at each point in the job hierarchy, and "progression" up a job ladder may imply some increase in pay, but how much? It is the sociology of wage determination which, in the institutionalist view, determines relative wages within an internal labor market. They argue that relative wages depend heavily on notions of equity and "fair" treatment with respect to the custom of a workplace. Relative wages are thus heavily influenced by past history; the exact level of differentials is somewhat arbitrary, yet highly resistant to change once established. Past practice tends to define what is a "fair" remuneration for different shifts, for varying degrees of responsibility, or for unpleasant working conditions, and job evaluation schemes both codify and lend an air of objectivity to these judgments. Institutionalists argue that employers are loathe to risk the morale problems caused when an established wage structure is tampered with.

Lydall's (1959) model of the wage structure of a hierarchic organization argued that firms can be seen as composed of levels of supervisors, each of whose wages is proportionate (by a ratio p) to the total wages of the people under him. If the "span of control" of a supervisor (i.e., the number of people who report to him or her) is typically n and the wage of the i-th level of supervisor is written as x_i, this amounts to equation (9.1).

(9.1)
$$\frac{x_{i+1}}{nx_i} = p$$

Hence:

$$\frac{x_{i+1}}{x_i} = pn$$

The wage differential for responsibility is therefore dependent on n, which Lydall assumes is technically determined, and by p, which he argues is due to expectations—i.e., the sociology of the workplace.

Pareto's law has long been known to be a reasonable approximation to the upper end of the distribution of wages and incomes.[16] Where y is the number of incomes exceeding any level of income x, and b and a are constants, it states (in its simplest form):

(9.2)
$$y = bx^{-a}$$

Lydall proves that $-a = \log p/\log (np)$—i.e., that under the assumptions of his model the shape of the upper tail of the wage distribution is

172 / ECONOMIC INEQUALITY IN THE UNITED STATES

given by a combination of technology and the expectations of rewards for responsibility.[17]

There are fundamental differences between the way "neoclassical" and "neo-institutional" authors view the setting of wages. The neoclassical tradition argues that it is a reasonable approximation to say that supply and demand determine wages—labor demand is determined by marginal productivity[18] and labor supply by individuals maximizing their utility, subject to their own budget constraint, independent of the income of others. Thurow's verbal model (1975) and Stiglitz's (1975a) or Arrow's (1973) mathematical models argue that the marginal product of an individual is often very difficult (expensive) to calculate and may in fact be unknowable if the joint production of a group of workers is involved.

Thurow goes on to argue that, even if constant returns to scale prevailed and marginal products were ascertainable, a profit-maximizing firm might not use them to construct a wage schedule, if such a schedule offended the norms of pay held by its labor force. (The cost of morale problems might mean the firm would be better off paying its traditional scale.) In contrast to a neoclassical approach, he feels that preferences are largely interdependent and that people care deeply about relative incomes;[19] hence institutional mechanisms are required for wage setting.

9.2.5 The Secondary Labor Market Up to this point, we have basically been discussing the "primary" labor market where jobs are relatively well paid, with good fringe benefits, relatively pleasant working conditions, employment security, and clearly defined grievance procedures/work discipline regulations. Institutionalists argue that this desirable package of employment rewards arises when the profit maximization of firms entails stable employment patterns and well-defined internal labor markets, but a second major theme of early work is the presence of a "secondary labor maket" whose jobs are much less desirable. Piore, for example, argues (1975:141), "Most industries appear to be operating as if they consistently faced a choice between two different techniques of production." One technique is capital- and technology-intensive, uses specific skills and highly differentiated work roles, and is well adapted to long, stable production runs (hence it generates stable employment and well-developed internal labor markets). The other option is less capital-intensive, uses more general skills and more adaptable capital equipment, and, being more flexible, can better cope with instabilities in market demand (hence it generates unstable employment). In the "secondary" or "dual" labor market, jobs are typically short term, unstable, with low pay, poor working conditions, arbitrary work discipline, and few fringe benefits. Casual employment, subcontractors of business services, marginal suppliers in unstable industries, and some retail and service establishments are cited as examples.

A segmentation perspective on labor economics has at least as long a pedigree as an institutional viewpoint. John Stuart Mill emphasized the existence of "non-competing groups" and wrote, "The really exhausting and the really repulsive labours, instead of being better paid than others, are almost invariably paid the worst of all, because performed by those who have no choice" (Mill, 1848:372). Marshall referred to the occupational structure as a series of steps. He argued, "The dirtiness of some occupations is a cause of the lowness of wages in them" (1920:558), since they would be filled only by unskilled workers with no other options; he saw "no more urgent social need" than the elimination of such jobs. The modern version of "dual labor market" analysis developed, however, in the late 1960s out of a perception of the employment problems of blacks in the urban ghettos of the United States. The quintessential secondary labor market employers, in this view, are the hiring halls for temporary labor which can often be found gathered around the edges of urban American ghettos. These hiring halls typically pay cash, by the day, for unskilled or at best semiskilled labor on a first-come, first-served basis. No promise of work tomorrow is made by either party. More common (but less extreme) are the seasonal or short-duration jobs, from fish plant worker to security guard to gas station attendant, which offer little or no on-the-job training or prospects of advancement.

A major feature of this analysis is its emphasis on "feedback" effects—from jobs to work attitudes and from past work history to future job options. Low pay and poor prospects for advancement mean that there is little payoff to an individual in cultivating a good work record. As a result, habits of absenteeism and tardiness may become established and voluntary job changes may restore some of the variety in work experience that the more fortunate members of the primary labor market achieve by progression up a job ladder. As the saying goes, a worker may become "jack of all trades, master of none." Instability of employment can thus create a vicious circle where there is little incentive for an employer to invest in on-the-job training and little incentive for a worker to stay, without prospects of future advancement. High turnover may also mean that work relationships appear arbitrary, since there is no chance for customs to become established among a stable social group. Bad morale and a general pattern of "negative exchange" or guerrilla warfare between management and workers exacerbate the problem of low employee productivity.

Why would workers stay in the secondary labor market, if they had a choice? For some, membership in the secondary segment of the labor market may be voluntary. Students (who are in it only for the summer), housewives (whose family roles may take priority), and temporary migrant workers may have no desire for employment stability or long-term prospects of advancement. Others may not have a choice. Sexual or racial discrimination, the lack of educational credentials, unstable prior work history, a criminal record, or the bad luck of a layoff during a period of high unemployment may well trap an individual in a succession of low-wage, dead-end jobs interspersed with spells of unemployment. From the segmentation viewpoint, this is the basic problem of the working poor.

Piore (1979) has also emphasized the role of migrant workers, both the legally resident "Gastarbeiter" of Western Europe and the illegal aliens from Mexico, the Carribbean, and Latin America who may number as little as 2% or as much as 12% of the U.S. labor force (Piore, 1979:26). In both cases, foreign workers provide a virtually inexhaustible supply of labor which can fill the menial and short-term jobs inherent in the "flux and uncertainty of all economic activity." Only part of the aggregate demand of advanced economies is stable and predictable and can generate stable, long-term employment. In capitalist economies, cyclical fluctuations, changes in fashions and technology, seasonal variability, and a host of other influences generate an unavoidable instability in production and, therefore, in demand for labor.

In a "pure" capitalistic system, all labor is "at risk" in this process but Piore argues that advanced industrial nations are only "quasi-capitalist" in that native labor has, by and large, managed to insulate itself from this insecurity (through its struggles for the seniority system in the United States and redundancy pay and employment guarantees in Europe). Pools of malleable migrant labor therefore allow the system to cope with its inevitable instability and to fill its menial jobs while offering stable employment and relatively good jobs to many of its native sons. Migrants accept their place in such a scheme of things where native workers would not precisely because most migrants initially view their move as temporary. Hence, they can function as pure "economic men," doing work that they would find demeaning, as well as living under conditions that they would find intolerable, if they had to do so in their home communities. Frequent visits home enable them both to maintain a psychological distance from the work which they do in the developed nations and to ride out temporary downturns in labor demand. The contradiction in this process is the growth of community among migrant workers in the advanced nations. The growth of social ties, assimilation, and long-term residency create, over time, permanent inhabitants rather than temporary sojourners—and consequent pressure for upward occupational mobility.

In summary, a "dualist" approach differs from the "human capital" analysis of Chapter 8 on three important grounds:

(a) it argues that "bad" jobs are not paid more but rather are paid less than "good" jobs (hence, inequality of utility is greater than inequality of money incomes would suggest);

(b) it feels that one's analysis should "make both technology and tastes integral parts of the economic process" (Piore 1974: 685), since there are substantial feedback effects between these variables and labor market outcomes;

(c) it postulates that one should see the labor market as composed of segments between which both outcomes and "rules of the game" differ.

9.2.6 Criticisms Our discussion of "compensating differentials" noted, however, how difficult it is to define unambiguously "good" and "bad" jobs from first principles alone. At the level of anecdote, both "dualists" and "neoclassicals" can offer examples of highly paid *and* poorly paid jobs which have poor working conditions, unstable employment, and few fringe benefits. Since these characteristics do not always point to the same classification, the description of secondary jobs above must be seen as an "ideal type." As a result, in empirical work different writers in the dualist tradition emphasize different criteria—e.g., Piore (1975) stresses employment instability while Gordon (1980) focuses on workers' control over their own working time, and Edwards (1979) emphasizes job security. These different criteria blur the focus of a segmentation approach and expose it to the criticism that it lacks a unified theory.

The argument that technology necessarily splits possible production processes into two major options is probably as difficult for most people to swallow whole as a literal interpretation of the smooth "isoquant" of neoclassical microeconomic theory (which implies that an infinite range of production combinations exists). Interpreting these theories as "metaphors," however, would have the segmentation approach arguing that there are "only a few" processes which are viable options while the neoclassical approach feels there are "quite a few."

It is the identification of "feedback" effects, which workers cannot foresee, from a firm's choice of technology which the critics of a dualist approach (Cain, 1976; Wachter, 1974) identify as one of its main theoretical contributions. A firm's choice of technology determines many aspects, such as stability, of the employment it offers. Stability of employment and conditions of work affect the psychology and abilities of its employees (their "tastes" in the language of Chapter 8) and these changes in employee attitudes and the work histories they acquire will affect their future employment prospects—and, Bowles and Gintis (1976) argue, the way they raise their children. Once we recognize that it is very difficult to foresee the future, we can see an individual's initial choice of job as analogous to the choice of which door to enter as one enters a maze of mirrors.[20] None of us can see more than a little way along each of the passages we initially face, but our initial choice predetermines our future choices, and we never get to go back and start over.

One's "choices," of course, are structured by one's labor market segment, and "segments" are an idea which many economists find hard to accept. Many argue, with Marshall, that "nature does not make jumps" and feel that, since there are usually fine gradations between ideal types, one should more appropriately think of a continuum. They wonder also what defines the segments and what prevents people from moving between them.[21] (One might agree that blacks and women receive different treatment in the labor market, but argue that the dividing lines there are at least fairly clear and that such discrimination is a smaller topic than dualism claims to be.[22]) It is also frustrating that there is no common operationalization of the idea of "segments"—segmentation writers speak of segmentation of jobs (e.g., Edwards, 1979), segmentation of occupations (e.g., Piore, 1975), segmentation of industries (e.g., Osterman, 1975), and segmentation of establishments (Clairmont, MacDonald, and Wien, 1980)—or combinations thereof (Freedman, 1976). Hence many economists view segmentation as "a rich and provocative set of loosely connected empirical hypotheses" (Wachter, 1974:680), which is "not a threat" to established theory (Cain, 1976).

In response, segmentation writers argue that "dualism" of the labor market is a metaphor which is a useful starting point for analysis—much as "perfect competition" is seen by neoclassicals as a useful starting point for analysis, but is not generally defended as a completely realistic picture of the world. More complex revisions are necessary if a more realistic analysis is to be had. Piore (1975) and Edwards (1979) both now argue that one should think of three segments—in Edward's terms the secondary, subordinate primary, and independent primary, each of roughly equal size. The secondary market is characterized by its low-wage, casual, low-skilled nature (e.g., security guards, waitresses), the subordinate primary segment offers somewhat better paid, somewhat more secure jobs (e.g., auto workers), and the independent primary segment contains supervisors and professionals who have "career" prospects (1979: 162-183). Gordon (1980) argues from a radical perspective that the degree and type of labor market segmentation changes over time as economies develop and historical and political trends evolve. Other reformulations are sure to arise as the approach matures—but these reformulations expose the segmentation perspective to the same criticism we made of the neoclassical perspective, that it can be reformulated to cope with almost any empirical event and is more of a "working language" or "research tradition" than a strictly refutable theory.

9.2.7 Summary The "neo-institutionalist" approach is composed of a number of strands of thought and a general perspective. It argues:

(a) that institutions (internal labor markets) generally allocate labor and set wages for most workers, without "much" pressure from market forces except at ports of entry;

(b) that education serves mainly as a credential to gain access to desirable jobs; hence equalizing access to education will have little effect on earnings inequality;

(c) that there is little tendency for market forces to eliminate discrimination;

(d) that wage inequality is heavily influenced by historically determined wage patterns and the sociology of the workplace;

(e) that the labor market should be thought of as split into segments, within which outcomes differ greatly and between which little mobility is possible.

Rather than emphasizing the choices individuals make, its general perspective is to emphasize the constraints individuals face. Technology and social attitudes are therefore seen as the chief factors governing the degree of earnings inequality we observe, and their explanation must be found in engineering and sociology.

Institutionalists argue that the possibilities for reducing inequality are illustrated by the one major decline in economic inequality of recent times—i.e., that which occurred in North America during World War II (Haley, 1968; Ostry and Zaidi 1979: 222) as a result, Thurow argues, of wartime wage controls' reducing differentials but the new wage differentials' becoming, over time, accepted as "normal."

In methods of analysis, conclusions, and policy implications neo-institutionalism offers a different viewpoint from that of Chapter 8, but *if taken separately* its components can often be incorporated into neoclassical models. In its own way, it is "optimistic" on the subject of inequality—i.e., it sees greater equality of opportunity and greater equality of result as achievable, within present-day capitalist market systems, by a process of institutional reform (see Chapter 13, section 13.4.2.)

9.3 A More Radical Interpretation

Edwards (1975) and Bowles and Gintis (1976) are representative of a group of radical writers who argue that it is not technology but the social relations implied by capitalism which create job ladders and segmented labor markets. These writers agree with the institutionalist description of primary and secondary labor markets and they agree that ascriptive characteristics such as race, sex, or age and credentials such as education ration access to the job ladders of the primary market. Where they disagree with the institutionalists is in their conception of the role of technology. Institutionalists tend to see technology as an essentially neutral, exogenous element whose development depends largely on the inherent logic of scientific discovery. Radicals emphasize that the choice between existing techniques of production and that between competing research and development projects for the development of new technology are both under the control of existing elites. They argue that the owners of industry have two main aims—to maximize profits and, more fundamentally, to maintain the control of the means of production which ensures they will continue to receive those profits.

Explaining the maintenance of social control is thus a key issue in the analysis of radical writers. As a result, their discussion is broadened to include issues of the distribution of political power, of the historical development of institutions, and of the impact of work on individuals and their families which are generally not touched on by other authors. Concentration of wealth and of control over industry (see Chapter 3, section 3.2) inevitably implies, in their view, a parallel concentration of effective political power. Formally, however, modern democracies have given most adults the right to vote. Centralized control and the growth of large corporations mean that economic organizations are authoritarian, that work is hierarchically organized, and that any individual worker tends to lose touch with the final product. Normatively, however, the values of equality, of freedom, and of finding a sense of satisfaction in one's work are deeply engrained. How do capitalist societies deal with these contradictions?

Bowles and Gintis argue, "In capitalist society, to make the hierarchical division of labour appear just is no easy task; the autocratic organization of the enterprise clashes sharply with the ideals of equality, democracy and participation that pervade the political and legal spheres" (1976:83). Yet the stability of any social system depends on its acceptance, i.e., the socialization of most individuals into values and perceptions which imply that the existing order of things either should not or cannot be changed. In capitalist societies, the school system plays a key role in educating children to what Bowles and Gintis call the "technocratic-meritocratic" perspective—i.e., the perception that the inequalities of economic life are technically necessary and that assignment to positions in the economic hierarchy is largely made on the basis of personal merit.

Radical writers tend to see few purely technological imperatives in the organization of work.[23] They admit that technology has developed so that most production processes are fragmented into many separate operations but they deny that technology had to develop in this way or that work relationships have to be organized in hierarchies of authority. They argue that experiments in work reorganization and in industrial democracy[24] indicate that productivity may well rise when workers share in decision making and tasks are less finely divided. Following Marglin (1974), Bowles and Gintis argue that the primary purpose of the divisions of labor established during the Industrial Revolution was not to ensure efficiency but to guarantee that the capitalists controlled the whole production process and could collect their profits. Following Stone (1975), they argue that the internal labor market arose during the late nineteenth century as a mechanism to differentiate jobs that were essentially equal and thus fragment the working class into "dissimilar" segments. The dividing line between "primary" and "secondary" employment is seen as a function more of class conflict than of technology. Union organization can change "secondary" jobs into "primary" jobs[25] and employers can shift jobs from primary labor markets to secondary, unless they are prevented, but these changes are seen as merely manifestations of the current state of the class conflict.

When characteristics such as sex or race are, in practice, used to assign people to work roles and job ladders, and when status and pay are clearly differentiated within job ladders, the development of "class consciousness" is greatly impeded. These labor market mechanisms have, in the radical view, therefore played a key role in preventing the emergence of the revolutionary proletariat of which Marx wrote but the stability of capitalism also requires that individuals are, on average, reconciled to their *personal* lot in life. Partly this reconciliation is accomplished by the different norms and aspirations acquired through one's family[26] but largely it is accomplished through the school system.

The school system is supposed to offer equality of opportunity to all but in practice treats children of different backgrounds unequally (see Chapter 6). Unequal treatment by the school system helps to ensure intergenerational transmission of status but the unconscious "choices" of parents on discipline strategy, life-style, and values also create distinct class and neighborhood cultures which children acquire "by osmosis" and which guide them to particular occupational slots. One's family and neighborhood generally form the reference groups within which the returns to individual ability and effort are assessed but between which inequalities of life-chances are very significant. Indeed, Bowles and Gintis argue that those people who move up the occupational ladder must adopt the mannerisms of their new socioeconomic class (such as wearing a tie to work) if they are to "fit in" and that the real function of such mannerisms is to reinforce the authority relationships of a hierarchic society. Class differences in culture, in treatment by the school system, and in access to jobs predetermine chances of economic success independent of individual "choices." Radicals therefore argue that inequality of opportunity is inevitable in a capitalist society for people of different class backgrounds.

In addition, an important function of school is as a paradigm for later life—to convince the child that he or she is competing on an equal basis with peers and is assessed according to objective criteria and that those who are smarter and work harder are the ones who get the top marks (incomes). Failure is, therefore, important since it teaches a student to lower his or her aspirations. Repeated failure can well convince students that they are not cut out for the upper echelons—but remember that the institutionalists argue that the skills used there are very often learned on the job. Bowles and Gintis argue that the most important lessons taught in school are the implicit ones. The importance of being on time and of obeying authority is emphasized in primary grades and in working-class high schools—together with basic literacy and numeracy, they are the requirements of lower-level jobs in the economic hierarchy. Elite colleges and select private schools, on the other hand, emphasize self-direction and create a social milieu where students come to expect that they will achieve an elite position later in life. The educational system thus creates not only the credentials which allocate individuals to entry ports but also the habits and expectations which see this allocation as legitimate.

The radical analysis therefore addresses the issues of why the existing distribution of income is not equal, why this distribution is tolerated, why some individuals "get ahead" of others, and why children tend to inherit their parents' socioeconomic status. It does not address the issues of why the income distribution has a particular *degree* of inequality or why it is different in different countries other than to say that the degree of inequality in a capitalist society depends on its history and on the level of class consciousness and class struggle in that society.[27]

9.4 Discussion

Much of the radical analysis of modern labor markets is identical to that of neo-institutionalists (hence the same criticisms can be made) but their *perspective* is different. Whereas neo-institutionalists see technology as a relatively neutral but crucial force and are relatively optimistic that political actions could reduce inequality, radicals emphasize the distribution of economic power in modern societies (see Chapter 3, section 3.2) and argue that fundamental institutional change is required to produce appreciable decreases in inequality.

The "radical" and "neoclassical" approaches have both similarities and differences. Their methods of analysis could not be more different— the one verbal, inductive, and sometimes "dialectical," the other mathematical and deductive—but one will look in vain for an empirical test which could conclusively test (and possibly reject) either approach as a scheme of thought. "History" or "class-consciousness" in radical thought and "tastes" or "technology" in neoclassical thought are sufficiently loosely specified concepts so that either approach can elaborate explanations for almost any conceivable event. In some respects they can both best be seen as "working languages" or "frameworks" for discussion—and some things are easier to say in one language than in another.

Some things take on different names in the two languages, but remain the same empirical events. The advantaged "class background" referred to by Bowles and Gintis (1976) is the same advantage in parental attention, superior neighborhood and schools, and possible "connections" that Becker and Tomes (1979) refer to as a family's "endowment of social capital" and "investment" in their children. Empirically, radicals and neoclassicals disagree on whether to expect "breaks in the data" to exist which show clear differences between social classes, and how many borderline cases there are in a classification of class. They differ also in their emphasis on how many of the decisions which affect a child are under the conscious control of parents or under the control of others (such as school administrators) and they differ on the degree to which people can be said to make conscious "decisions" on their children's or their own future. Nevertheless, from the point of view of the child, it does not make much difference if the choices are conscious or unconscious and

STRUCTURAL INTERPRETATIONS: THE IMPORTANCE OF CONSTRAINTS / 181

both agree that the family into which one is lucky (or unlucky) enough to be born exercises a major influence on eventual economic success.

What is perhaps most surprising, given the great differences in theoretical starting points and methods, are the common predictions—that a market system with private ownership, i.e., a "capitalist" system, will produce neither equality of opportunity nor equality of result. Since "radical" writers have generally attempted to integrate political and historical factors into their analysis, the "capitalist market system" as they see it *includes* the state and its operations. In their view the state is an indispensable part of modern economic life, training workers, providing "public goods," and, most importantly, safeguarding property rights. They see political influence as being in large measure determined by economic power. Hence radicals argue that the contemporary operation of the state perpetuates inequality of opportunity and inequality of result and that radical political change is necessary to change this bias.

Neoclassical economists have generally left political analysis to the political scientists; hence their analysis tends to be subtly different. There is a literature on voting models of redistributive government actions (e.g., Stigler, 1970) but it is ambiguous in its predictions and often neglected. More normally, neoclassical writers tend to define the "capitalist market system" as limited to the operation of markets, with private ownership of property where government intervention, if it is considered at all, appears exogenously. They tend not to discuss *why* the state intervenes in those markets. If parents (whose wealth is unequal) are the only ones to decide how much to "invest" in the early "human capital" of their offspring, then inequality of opportunity is inevitable in a pure "capitalist market system."[28] If the state intervenes (e.g., by providing subsidized, enriched day-care for preschool children or by subsidizing university education) this intervention may reduce, or may accentuate, inequality of opportunity (see Chapter 13, section 13.2). Which type of intervention to expect in a capitalist market system is not clearly stated by "neoclassical" authors.

In practice, of course, the state intervenes in both ways. The real world is not, and never has been, a pure capitalist market system where all privately consumed goods (including education) are privately purchased and privately supplied. The state in fact always has intervened extensively in economic life, sometimes accentuating and sometimes diminishing inequalities of opportunity and of result. The interesting questions, in a world where governments always do intervene in some manner or other, therefore concern the *balance* of government actions, the marginal improvements which can be achieved by piecemeal reform, and the real extent of the differences which could be expected were society to be fundamentally changed.

NOTES

[1]Hank Aaron is reputed to have practiced, as a boy, by hitting bottle caps over his house with a broomstick handle—economic success is not impossible for the disadvantaged, just much more difficult and improbable.

[2]Note that a theory of income determination only has to predict the batting average of an individual while a full theory of income distribution must predict as well the number of hitters at each batting average.

[3]For example, one can generally choose whether to work hard or not so hard, but, as the old saying goes, "A hard-working boss gets to be vice-president; a hard-working miner gets to be a hard-working miner."

[4]The victory of the human capital paradigm produced a drastic change in the tools of labor economists. Where institutionalists tended to use a direct survey methodology, to reason inductively from the evidence, and to express their arguments verbally, their "human capital" successors have emphasized deductive, highly formalistic argument and indirect inference from secondary data. Woodbury (1979) argues that this methodological difference remains the major gulf separating the two research traditions.

[5]Figure 9.1 draws heavily on the work of Baron and Bielby (1980), who drew this particular case from a job analysis prepared by the U.S. Department of Labor in California in 1968.

[6]A third sort of internal labor market is operated through the "hiring halls" of craft unions—for example, in the construction trades. Elaborate rules decide which tradesmen will be allocated to which jobs, at which rate of pay, when tradesmen from outside the hiring hall's jurisdiction will be allowed to work on jobs in the area, etc.

[7]The neoclassical reply is to argue that individuals choose firms which offer more or less on-the-job training, hence decide indirectly on investment in on-the-job training. Institutionalists tend to see this as highly unrealistic, arguing that the required information for such choices is usually not present and that jobs with training opportunities often pay more, not less, than jobs without them.

[8]Where large numbers of market participants exist, a competitive market generates a clear signal; where only a few are present, bargaining is inescapable.

[9]As the almost universal existence of "past practice" clauses in collective agreements indicates, however, union agreements codify only part of the "customary law" of a workplace. By formalizing grievance procedures and by providing a mechanism for trading off benefits in one area for desired changes in work practices in other areas, unions may, in some instances, actually increase work flexibility—see Freeman (1980a).

[10]Competition certainly exists in the economist labor market, as in many others, at ports of entry, in the sense that real wages fluctuate but excess supply/demand may not be totally eliminated. Hall (1982) emphasizes that although the U.S. labor market has high turnover and unemployment rates it also provides stable near-lifetime employment to an important fraction of the labor force—e.g., 40% of workers over 30 are in jobs that will last 20 years or more.

[11]For example, they argue that labor market "shelters" are due to firm-specific human capital, which an employer does not want to lose.

[12]All these authors would probably call themselves "neoclassical economists" if they had to pick a label.

[13]For a discussion of statistical discrimination see Aigner and Cain (1977).

[14]"Luck" might include, for example, the phase of the business cycle when an individual enters the labor market. Institutionalists argue that employers react to booms and scarce supplies of labor by relaxing hiring qualifications, rather than by increasing entry level wages (raising wages would have a "ripple" effect on wages above the entry level). Members of minority groups or the poorly educated may be hired in such periods and if they accumulate enough seniority will escape layoff in the recession. When labor is easily obtained employers tend to demand higher qualifications, in many cases higher than some of their current workers could meet.

[15]Baron and Bielby (1980) give examples in which apparently similar California plants have different job structures. Phelps-Brown (1977:34), comparing similar French and German factories, notes that the French use a higher ratio of nonmanual to manual workers despite higher relative salaries of nonmanual workers. Dore (1973) gives a fascinating account of the substantial differences in work organization between British and Japanese

factories producing electrical generating equipment, which likewise escape simple explanation by relative wages or technological determinism. "Technology," therefore, seems to impose fairly broad constraints, within which past practice, both national and company, play a significant role.

16Pareto (1896:305) himself believed it to be applicable to the entire distribution of income, but was misled by his data (income tax returns) since income tax was then paid only by upper income groups.

17The theory of optimal hierarchy and control structures for a profit-maximizing firm has been discussed by Stiglitz (1975b) and Calvo and Wellisz (1979).

18Strictly speaking, the marginal revenue product of labor equals the marginal cost of labor in profit-maximizing equilibrium, but the potential qualifications of imperfect product and/or labor markets are often ignored. As Oi (1962) and Lazear (1979b) have noted, when firm-specific human capital and long-term employment relationships are involved the equation $W = MP$ holds only in an expected value sense over the likely tenure of the job, not necessarily at any particular point in time.

19To take a particular example, independent preferences imply that doctors are indifferent as to how much plumbers make while interdependent preferences imply that doctors get very upset if they think that plumbers make a higher hourly wage. One can test the realism of either assumption by querying any random sample of M.D.s.

20Not all of us, of course, get to choose from the same set of doors.

21Mayhew and Rosewell (1979) report finding substantial mobility in a U.K. study.

22Leigh (1976, 1978) presents some of the few detailed empirical studies of dualism done by a nonconvert. His largely negative conclusions are, however, based on the assumption that black workers are all "secondary" and whites are all "primary"; since virtually no dualists would agree with this specification, they tend to ignore his results.

23Neoclassical writers share this scientific optimism but argue it is relative prices which determine choice of technique.

24For references, see Virmani (1979) or Newton and Leckie (1977).

25As when the United Farm Workers organized California farm workers, previously a "classic" competitive labor market, and won higher pay, a seniority system, improved working conditions, a hiring hall system, and grievance procedures.

26Bowles and Gintis argue that the greater value placed on obedience, neatness, etc., and the conformity to external authority emphasized by working-class parents merely represent the lessons they have themselves learned in their jobs, while the emphasis on responsibility, internal control, etc., of higher-status parents reflects the attributes valued in their own occupational roles—hence the transmission of different family values tends to ensure an inheritance of socioeconomic status (1976:146).

27The constancy of the U.S. income distribution is noted by Bowles and Gintis as an indicator of the failure of increased educational equality to promote meaningful social change, but they do not really explain it.

28Loury (1981) argues, however, that, if parents cannot borrow to finance their children's human capital acquisition, universal public education will both increase average incomes and decrease the inequality in incomes. If parents are risk averse they will all be better off under some redistributive policies.

10

AN ECLECTIC SUMMARY

It has now become certain that the problem of distribution is much more difficult than it was thought to be by earlier economists, and that no solution of it which claims to be simple can be true. Most of the old attempts to give an easy answer to it, were really answers to imaginary questions that might have arisen in other worlds than ours, in which the conditions of life were very simple. The work done in answering these questions was not wasted. For a very difficult problem can best be solved by being broken into pieces; and each of these simple questions contained a part of the great and difficult problem which we have to solve.

ALFRED MARSHALL
Principles of Economics, 8th edition (1913:510)

10.1 Explanations: The Problem of Choice

10.1.1 Income Determination and Income Distribution Chapters 2 through 4 discussed the extent of economic inequality and poverty; Chapters 5 through 9 presented some theories. There are two sets of questions to be asked. First, what factors are responsible for the distribution of economic resources in America? In particular:

A. Why does this degree of economic inequality exist?

B. Why has income and wealth inequality been so constant over the period since World War II?

C. Why do differences in inequality exist between countries and between regions of the same country?

A second set of questions revolves around the factors which determine the economic resources of particular individuals and families. Specifically:

A. Why do the children of poor parents have a greater chance of being poor themselves? How do the children of advantaged families "inherit" the status of their parents?

184

B. Why do people with more education or more work experience tend to earn more than people with less education and less work experience?

C. Why do women tend to earn less than men, blacks less than whites? Why do some people work all their lives for low wages?

Throughout the literature there is frequent confusion between theories which can answer either or both of these sets of questions—i.e., between theories which explain the *determination* of individual income and theories which explain the *distribution* of income. Not all theories can do both. If, for example, income were determined purely by a lottery, it would be a true theory to say that an individual's income was determined by whether or not he or she held a winning lottery ticket. A further theory, however, would be required in order to explain why there were a particular number of first, second, and third prizes and why they had those particular values—i.e., why a particular income *distribution* existed.

To cite a more realistic instance, one can consider the impact of unionization on individual earnings and on the distribution of income. A major aim of unions is to raise their members' wages and several studies indicate that the average union/nonunion wage differential is somewhere between 8% and 15% (Lewis, 1963:194; Rees, 1962:79; Starr, 1973, 1975).[1] If one examines the determinants of individual income, as, for example, in the estimation of an equation predicting individual wages, union membership enters with a significant and positive sign. One might then think that, if a union were to organize a group of low-paid workers and to succeed in raising their wages relative to nonunionized workers, the distribution of income would become more equal—i.e., low-paid workers would now earn something closer to an average wage while wealthy capitalists would receive lower profits.

Within the neoclassical framework, however, Johnson and Mieszkowski (1970) argue that it is not necessarily the case that a wage increase due to unionization increases the share of labor and that union wage gains may be largely at the expense of nonunion labor. In a general equilibrium framework, a wage increase in the union sector will cause prices to rise and demand to shift away from the goods the union sector produces. Only if the union sector is capital-intensive will total returns to capital fall, since in this case unionization prompts a shift in demand toward relatively labor-intensive production (hence labor's share rises in aggregate and capital's share falls).

In this model the impact of a variable (unionization) in the individual earnings determination process may be quite different from the impact of a general change in its level on the aggregate income distribution, once general equilibrium effects are taken into account. [Johnson and Mieszkowski (1970:547) even suggest that partial unionization of the labor force may, under some assumptions, decrease absolutely the wages of *both* union and nonunion labor, even though union members continue to earn more, *relative to* nonunion members.]

As one can recall from Chapter 5, there is no consensus on the theory of the "functional" distribution of income, and the Johnson/Mieszkowski position is thus far from universally accepted. Certainly the "post-Keynesian" and Marxist perspectives would disagree, arguing that unionization more typically shifts factor shares in favor of labor. For the present discussion, however, the important point of this "neoclassical" argument is that the effect of a variable in determining relative individual earnings may not be generalizable to the distribution of income.

Similarly, men commonly earn more than women, but would an end to discrimination and equality of result between men and women in the labor market mean greater equality of earnings? Or would equality of result simply mean that more men become low-paid secretaries and more women become high-paid executives? One must distinguish between theories which can explain the income distribution and theories which can explain individual income determination—only under such special assumptions as an infinitely elastic demand for all types of skills or human capital can the same theory suffice for both. A complete theory of income *distribution* must include a theory of individual income determination; hence both sorts of theories must be discussed. In practice, however, theories of individual income determination are much farther advanced than theories of the distribution of income and wealth.

10.1.2 Choosing One's Perspective Our understanding of why individuals "get ahead" and why inequality exists is central to our understanding of the society around us and it is a truism that there is no real agreement. Chapters 8 and 9 presented some very different viewpoints on the determination of earnings, ones which will lead those who tend to value equality to very different conclusions about desirable social policy. Some of the chance or genetically based theories outlined in Chapter 6 have been used to support the idea that not much can be done about earnings inequality; hence policies which attempt to alter distributive shares can do no good and may do much harm. As has already been noted, such a conclusion does not follow and neither does it follow that the racial and sexual differences in average earnings discussed in Chapter 7 are immutable. The "human capital" viewpoint of Chapter 8 argues, however, that changes in the distribution of education and training can produce changes in the distribution of earnings, within our existing social and political structures. This "reformist" perspective is attacked by many of the radical writers cited in Chapter 9, who argue that earnings inequality is not inevitable, but that fundamental social and political changes are required in order to alter it.

How do we choose between these perspectives? In practice, many elements enter: the views of our family and the other social groups with whom we associate, our own social values on other issues, our degree of ignorance of the alternative theories which have been proposed and even such trivia as whether we like or dislike the individuals we meet who espouse a particular viewpoint. Ideally, however, we would choose "scientifically." Most economists would argue that the criteria we should apply in a scientific choice are: (a) that a theory be logically consistent, i.e., not be self-contradictory (which implies that it be framed in specific enough language so that one can tell); (b) that a theory produce predictions about the real world which are consistent with observed facts; (c) that a theory be at least potentially refutable.[2] Applying these criteria we may well find that none of the available theoretical alternatives is completely satisfactory—in particular, one can argue that such key concepts as "ability," "human capital," or "segments" can be defined in such a way as to enable theory to fit reality, whatever the reality.[3] Each of us must then make an individual judgment as to the least unsatisfactory approach or the "most promising" avenue for future research. Hopefully it will be an informed judgment.

In Chapters 6 and 7, we examined the role of chance, ability, race, and sex in earnings determination. Chapter 8 discussed the neoclassical school, whose focus is the choices individuals make as to the supply of skills to the labor market, whereas Chapter 9 presented a number of "structural" approaches which argue that the constraints individuals face and the demand side of the economy (and especially the decisions on labor market policy made by firms) are the paramount factors determining income and wealth distribution. To some extent these theories simply emphasize different aspects of the earnings determination process but they were posed separately, as alternative viewpoints, because they are often viewed as such by their exponents. Pragmatists may try to combine their insights, in the same way as one would make a stew of many ingredients, but one must do so with care. Those who have no dislike for the taste of illogic or inconsistency can combine these theories in virtually any fashion they desire, but others will notice the occasional incompatibility of assumptions between the different approaches. Tolerance or distaste for theoretical vagueness or the possibility of contradiction differs among economists, but in practice relatively few are total purists in their explanations of economic inequality. Even relative pragmatists, however, may disagree violently on what is the real "meat" of the inequality issue and what is the inessential flavoring which surrounds it.

10.2 An Eclectic Summary of Earnings Determination

Theory aside, the empirical discussion of earnings determination can perhaps best be summarized in a path diagram such as Figure 10.1. The determination of individual earnings is influenced by many factors, and this implies that individuals both enter the labor market with very different characteristics and have different experiences within it—i.e.,

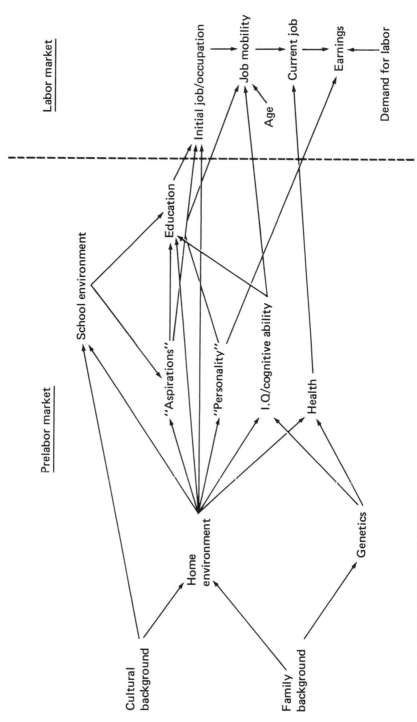

Figure 10.1 INFLUENCES ON INDIVIDUAL EARNINGS

different wage rates, unemployment experiences, and total earnings. Of course, the determination of family income depends also on inherited wealth, the returns to past savings, and the earnings of all family members. Hence, this diagram, complex as it is, is not complex enough to summarize the determination of family income.

Under the heading of "cultural" influences, we can discuss the association between an individual's background, outside of his or her immediate family, and eventual earnings. Numerous studies (e.g., Jencks et al., 1979; Lillard, 1977) have observed differences between racial, religious, and ethnic groups in average earnings. The foreign-born and individuals from rural backgrounds also tend to earn less than native-born individuals from urban backgrounds. People in the South have lower average earnings than people from the rest of the country. These differences mirror the differences in opportunity faced by people from different backgrounds—in general, the cultural environment of one's home is determined not simply by the idiosyncracies of one's parents, but also by the social community of which they are a part.

Among the measurable variables on family background, the most important seems to be the father's occupation. More generally, as Brittain (1977), Jencks et al. (1979), and many others have noted, there is a strong tendency for children to inherit the economic status of their parents, as indicated by relative family income and parental education. This inheritance process is largely mediated through the school system (Husen, 1969), through a cumulative series of educational decisions which are strongly and consistently influenced by family factors (Parsons, 1975). There appears to be some tendency for first-born children to do better economically and for children from very large families to do somewhat more poorly—these tendencies have often been explained in terms of the amount of parental attention available.[4] Parents combine to produce an individual's genetic endowment, but this comprises only part of "ability." Jencks' evidence (1979:121) indicates that measured cognitive ability has a relatively small *independent* effect on earnings while Griliches (1976) and Lillard (1977) argue there is an association with earnings in later life, if not among young men.

"Home environment" is thus a complex entity with manifold impacts on future earnings. As Forcese (1975) noted, it interacts with school environment to shape an individual's aspirations as well as having a primary role in forming personality and influencing health and cognitive ability.

The layman's term "personality" is typically disaggregated by economists into "tastes" and "abilities." One's taste for risk, one's tolerance (or desire) for change, and one's preference for the monetary versus the nonmonetary aspects of jobs affect career decisions at each fork in the road. All these tastes are systematically influenced by home environment—Bowles (1972), for example, conjectures that upper-class children are socialized to value more highly the nonmonetary aspects of jobs.[5] Tastes for leisure versus monetary income also differ among individuals and influence their choice both of jobs and of hours worked within those jobs. "Abilities," as in irritability, dependability, the ability to get along with others, the ability to delegate, the ability to organize/plan, are also often thought of as part of "personality" and largely formed within one's home environment.[6]

In some occupations, strength and dexterity are important for earnings, whereas in others physical stamina may be important; clearly "health" is an important component of one's "human capital." Despite the great importance of personal decisions (e.g., the self-inflicted wounds of smoking or alcohol abuse), a substantial fraction of one's health and physical constitution is shaped by one's genetics, early nutrition, and the presence or lack of remedial medical attention in childhood.

The effect of home environment on cognitive ability and school achievement has been discussed in Chapter 6, section 6.3.4, but in addition one's home environment may play an important role in initial job placement. The first job an individual obtains carries with it not only current wages but also a package of on-the-job training opportunities, promotion possibilities, and an implied degree of job security. The formal qualifications required almost always include a minimum level of education and/or a field of special training, but, since novice job seekers are often very poorly informed about alternatives, their access to information is also important. Rees (1966) and Granovetter (1974) have discussed the "informal" information networks of family, friends, and neighbors and have emphasized that "contacts" are important in a majority of hiring decisions.[7]

Once within the labor market, an individual's earnings are heavily affected by his or her degree of job mobility—geographic, occupational, industrial, and hierarchic. Geographic mobility is very high in America and many (see Greenwood, 1975) have argued that much of it is a response to economic incentives—i.e., a person who is willing to move tends to receive higher earnings. Occupational mobility, mobility between industries, and job mobility as a result of seniority all are associated with higher average earnings. However, the most important factor for the majority of the labor force that is employed in "lifetime jobs" (Hall, 1982) is the increased pay and benefits individuals receive as they move up a hierarchy of skill and responsibility with their individual employer. At the top of the earnings pyramid most earnings are almost totally defined by one's place in a hierarchic structure (as per Lydall, 1959).

Figure 10.1 is more complex than similar diagrams in Lydall (1976), Atkinson (1975), or Canterbery (1979), although less complex than Meade (1976: 147), but it is still highly reductive. Its essential point is that many influences operate on individual earnings, both before and within the labor market and both directly and indirectly. Unraveling the relative importance of these influences is a very highly complex task.[8]

"Luck" enters at every turn—e.g., the good luck of being placed with an exceptional early teacher who may encourage a child to persevere in education or the bad luck of a disabling accident. (Of course, some schools have a higher proportion of good teachers and some jobs have a higher risk of disabling injuries.) At most one can hope to estimate the relative probabilities of different levels of earnings of a person with given characteristics. The most important characteristics determining individual earnings are, however, basically set at birth—socioeconomic background, race, and sex.

10.3 Earnings Distribution—An Unresolved Issue

Figure 10.1 omits many[9] of the complexities of the supply side of labor markets and it omits also the complexities of the demand side. It illustrates only the influences of the characteristics individuals bring with them to the labor market, but the price those characteristics command depends also on the nature of labor demand. Labor demand is, in Marshall's phrase, the "other blade of the scissors." The degree of wage inequality is thus due to the interplay of supply *and* demand factors. Figure 10.1 cannot, therefore, be taken to imply that differences in earnings are solely due to differences in personal characteristics, since such differences can be only part of the answer.

Models of the distribution of earnings in the human capital tradition such as those of Chiswick (1974) or Mincer (1974) focus on the acquisition of education and explanation of the age/earnings profile in terms of on-the-job training. Consequently, their empirical work is restricted to the examination of variables measuring the level and distribution of schooling and the level and distribution of work experience. There is a substantial body of empirical work in this tradition which argues that, comparing states or countries, smaller inequalities in schooling attainment are associated with smaller inequalities in earnings[10] but there is more to the labor market than the supply of schooling.

Once one admits that supply-side influences can be only part of the story,[11] one needs a way to incorporate demand-side influences. Beach (1981) argues that "the demand for and supply of task performance determine a hedonic wage function that associates a wage rate with each labor supplier and with each job." The use of the hedonic price framework (see Rosen, 1974) has meant an increase in the number of variables economists have felt able to include in their regressions, but it has not produced any increase in the number of refutable hypotheses. Many characteristics of workers and of jobs can be measured, but the theory of compensating differentials (see Chapter 8, section 8.2.3) does not predict unambiguously whether these characteristics will be associated with higher or with lower wages. Neither does the hedonic price literature offer any prediction as to the frequency distribution of incomes or earnings.

Two of the few theoretical and empirical attempts to marry the supply and demand sides of the labor market are the work of Tinbergen (1975) and Sattinger (1980). Tinbergen argued that an individual's utility from a job depends not only on his income but also on any divergence between his training and that required by the job. Sattinger considered the comparative advantage individuals have in specific tasks and the assignment problem of placing individuals in jobs. He argued that the "rents" (consumer's surplus) people receive on the job depend on their task productivity relative to that of the next best worker and that this rent is a function of machine size—i.e., the capital/labor ratio. His prediction is unambiguous: "Increasing concentration of capital among jobs over time can be expected to result in greater earnings inequality" (1980:135). He tested this hypothesis on cross-section and time series data for U.S. states and found "a strong association between capital intensity in the economy and the amount of income inequality" (1980:152). Sattinger argues that the failure of income inequality to decline in the United States since 1945, despite increased average levels of schooling and decreased inequality of schooling, is due to the inequality-reducing impacts of these educational changes' being balanced by the inequality-increasing effects of capital accumulation and increased capital concentration.

10.4 Summary

(a) Students of economic inequality usually wish to know not only why a society has a particular degree of aggregate inequality but also why specific sorts of individuals receive higher income or earnings than others. The former issue refers to the causes of the income *distribution;* the latter is that of the process of income (or earnings) *determination.* Only under highly restrictive assumptions can the theories which explain the latter be directly generalized to the former.

(b) Since a variety of explanations of the earnings determination process exist, one has the problem of the choice of one's theoretical perspective. One can ask that such choice be based on reasonably full knowledge of the alternatives and that it be made in the light of specified and defensible criteria, but ultimately the choice is a personal one. As an empirical matter one can state with certainty that there are knowledgeable and intelligent people in all the intellectual camps discussed.

(c) As discussed in Chapter 9, section 9.4, different theoretical perspectives sometimes agree on a common prediction, probably because they must attempt to "explain" the same empirical regularities. Although different theories offer different interpretations they must all face the fact that socioeconomic background, race, and sex are systematically and strongly associated with differences in individual earnings.

(d) Theories of earnings determination are much more fully worked out than full-fledged theories of earnings distribution—indeed most of what now passes for a discussion of earnings distribution is really overly hasty generalization from the theory of earnings determination. The distribution of earnings is determined by the interaction of demand and supply in a large number of particular micro-markets for labor—earnings are likely to be more unequal where schooling is more unequal, where employment experience is more unequal, and where the capital intensity of production is greater.

NOTES

[1]There are, of course, several estimates of average influences outside this range and much evidence that union impact differs widely between sectors. In addition some argue that higher wages may help cause unionism, in the sense that highly paid, highly productive workers organize to protect their rights rather than simply going elsewhere—Freeman (1980b). Another argument is that higher union wages may mean higher qualifications demanded; hence on an "efficiency-units" basis, in the long run, unions don't raise wages. Obviously complex controversies continue—for useful summaries see Addison and Siebert (1979: 279-291) or Gundersen (1980:307-324)—but for the present argument we need only assume that unions have some positive impact on their members' relative wages.

Freeman and Medoff (1979) argue that, although unions may increase wage inequality by creating a union/nonunion differential, they also decrease wage inequality by standardizing wage rates within companies and/or industries—on balance, unions reduce wage inequality. See Freeman (1982) and Hirsch (1982) for evidence that unions reduce earnings inequality.

[2]An example of a nonrefutable, and hence nonscientific, theory is, "Everything that happens is God's will." This theory explains everything but it predicts nothing. No skeptic can be convinced of the truth of this theory by an appeal to empirical evidence, since, by construction of the theory, empirical evidence cannot refute the theory. Hence, belief or nonbelief is a matter of faith.

[3]Hutchison (1960), Koopmans (1957), and Kuhn (1970) are all classic statements regarding the problems of evidence and inference in economics.

[4]Since the trend to smaller families seems rather universal and the effect of family size becomes noticeable only with four or more children (see Phelps-Brown, 1977:221), perhaps the family size influence is largely dying out on its own.

[5]Which implies that eventual money income underestimates the differences in options open to upper- and lower-class children. See the survey evidence of Yankelovich (1974) for some support of Bowles's conjecture.

[6]Lydall (1976:29) emphasizes the "D" factor—drive, dynamism, determination, energy, industry, self-discipline—which is a combination of both personal abilities and aspirations. Jencks et al. (1979, Chapter 5) discuss possible measures of "personality" and conclude that "leadership" as a student may be an important predictor of eventual adult earnings.

[7]Having fewer contacts black youth make greater use of "formal" information networks such as state employment exchanges.

[8]Economists tend to use multiple regression analysis, at various stages of sophistication, while the preferred technique of sociologists is that of "path analysis," which imposes the restrictive assumption of linear relationships between all variables and an absence of interaction effects. In addition to the problem of appropriate specification of variables, functional forms, and estimating technique (e.g., Griliches, 1977), Chapters 10 and 11 of Jencks et al. (1979) discuss the differences in parameter estimates, *with identically specified regressions,* which different surveys and research styles generate. Parameter estimates are thus a function not only of statistical technique but also of data collection and manipulation methods.

[9]For example, Taubman (1977:438) mentions that nepotism may be important in determining earnings on the basis of the finding that one's father-in-law's education was a significant determinant of male earnings in the sample he studied. Any possible direct impact of family background on job mobility has been ignored in Figure 10.1 on the

presumption that the most important effects of family background are felt before most individuals enter the labor market. Figure 10.1 also neglects, in an attempt to avoid excess complexity, most feedback effects. Physical health, for example, determines whether one can pass the medical examination that many employers impose before hiring; hence health affects earnings, but job-related injuries or diseases such as the coal miners' "black lung" imply that one's job may also affect one's health, and eventual earnings.

[10]The evidence is more ambiguous on whether higher average schooling is associated with higher inequality. See Sattinger (1980:263,/81); Chiswick (1968 and 1974:152).

[11]Osberg (1975:192-196) included variables reflecting the industrial structure of employment in a study of earnings dispersion in a sample of U.S. counties. He found industrial structure variables to be highly important in determining inequality as well as finding negative, not positive, relationships between the dispersion of education and of earnings within counties.

11

THE ACQUISITION OF PROPERTY

11.1 Introduction

Chapters 6 through 10 have discussed the determination and the distribution of labor earnings but inequality of earning is only part of economic inequality. As Chapter 3 indicated, the inequality of wealth in America is considerably greater than the inequality of earnings. This wealth produces income and its ownership is particularly important for the top end of the income distribution. One must therefore ask how property is acquired and why its ownership is so unequally spread if one is to get a full picture of economic inequality. Section 11.2 discusses the "life-cycle" model of wealth accumulation, which argues that most property is acquired by individual saving from labor earnings. Section 11.3 presents the theory of inheritance, and sections 11.4 and 11.5 discuss the evidence which exists on the presence of large inheritances and inheritance in general. The social institutions of property and inheritance have been among the most hotly debated of economic issues for generations, so in section 11.6 we discuss a few of the many ethical issues involved. Knowledge about the real world, theory about how it operates, and values about how one wants it to operate are the ingredients of public policy. Section 11.7 presents some of the policy options which have been discussed regarding the institutions of property and inheritance.

11.2 The Life-Cycle Savings Models

In its simplest form, the one-generation "life-cycle savings model" argues that individuals accumulate a stock of capital while working in order to finance their consumption after retiring. Their wealth will therefore be at a maximum just before retirement and will decrease throughout their old age. Figure 11.1 graphs a "typical" individual's net worth according to this theory. Over the period $0S$ (which may be very short) the individual is going into debt in order to acquire human capital and to finance consumption during early periods of low earnings—hence his net

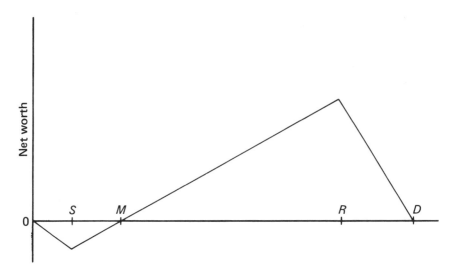

Figure 11.1 THE LIFE-CYCLE SAVINGS MODEL

worth is negative. At S, the individual begins to pay off these debts and by age M has succeeded. Over the period MR the individual saves for his retirement (at age R) and for the rest of his life lives on his savings.

Figure 11.1 presents a highly simplified version of the model since the exact pattern of wealth accumulation will depend on the rate of interest, on whether the individual wishes to maintain a constant, increasing, or decreasing level of consumption over time, and on the number of family members to be supported (Irvine, 1978). The great function of capital markets is, in this view, to enable individuals to spread their consumption more evenly over their lifetimes. Over the period MD, individuals are net lenders on capital markets—usually through intermediaries such as banks or pension funds but ultimately to investors in human or physical capital. This model is then used as an explanation both of the aggregate level of wealth in a market society and of the distribution of income from wealth.

The specific predictions of the life-cycle model are that net worth will increase with age and that the distribution of net worth will be more equal within age cohorts than within the general population. Although a small percentage of the population (the elderly) will own most of society's wealth, people of the same age will be at roughly the same point in the wealth accumulation process and will therefore have roughly equal net worth. One must say "roughly" since differences in ability will imply differences in lifetime earnings and differences in individual tastes will lead some people to consume more now and less in retirement (i.e., save less) while others accumulate more for their old age. The inequality of property ownership which we observe is therefore explained as due to a combination of individual tastes, lifetime earnings, and the natural cycle of life through which we all pass.

As tests of the theory, however, one must ask:

(a) Can it explain the total capital stock and the volume of private savings which we observe?

(b) Can it explain the inequality of wealth which we observe?

(c) Is it in accordance with the savings behavior which we actually observe among individuals?

(d) Is it true that wealth inequality within cohorts is less than that in the population as a whole?

With respect to the aggregate level of private savings, White's recent (1978) simulation study indicates that the life-cycle model can only be part of the picture, explaining, at best, about 42% of annual private saving in the United States. Kotlikoff and Summers (1981:722) estimate that at best 19% of total U.S. wealth in 1974 can be explained by a life-cycle model. (Note that these are the "best cases" that these authors can make for the life-cycle models.) With regard to the aggregate inequality of wealth, Davies (1979:241) notes, "Only 5 percent of the total (Canadian) wealth inequality on a per adult basis is due to differences between 10 year cohorts."[1] Among cohorts, Atkinson (1975:141) also concludes, "concentration of wealth within age groups is not markedly less than in the population as a whole." (See also Chapter 3, section 3.2.2.)

It is true that average wealth increases as individuals age, but the life-cycle model cannot explain the large fraction of the population who have very low net worth at all ages. Neither can the simple life-cycle savings model explain the existence of very large fortunes (see Chapter 3, section 3.3), since these are far too large to be explained by savings from labor earnings. The one-generation life-cycle model is also inadequate as a general picture of savings behavior. Brittain (1978:59-66) has noted that top wealth holders in the United States continue to save well after retirement, contrary to a simple life-cycle model. Mirer (1979b) found that the aged, in general, do *not* run down their wealth during their lifetimes. Wolff (1981) has examined wealth holdings in the population as a whole as well as among the "nonrich" population—i.e., excluding the top 5% of wealth holders. He finds that the life-cycle model is not at all an appropriate model for the top 5%, nor does it fit nonwhites, rural families, or non-high-school graduates. Indeed the only group whose behavior is modeled at all well by the life-cycle hypothesis is urban, college-educated whites— and even then only if one looks at holdings of housing, durable goods, and cash. As he puts it, "Essentially, the validity of life-cycle accumulation models must be restricted to the white, urban, educated middle classes and their accumulation of housing, durables and cash. The rich have very different motives for saving, while the poor do not earn sufficient income over their lifetime to accumulate any non-negligible wealth" (1981:75).[2] Over the population as a whole there is simply not enough individual saving from earnings, on average, to generate the amount of capital which we observe. Kotlikoff and Summers (1981:730) conclude, "The evidence rules out life-cycle lump savings as the major determinant of capital accumulation in the U.S. economy. Longitudinal age–earnings and age–consumption profiles do not exhibit the kinds of shapes needed to generate a large amount of life-cycle wealth accumulation. The view of U.S. capital formation as arising, in the main, from essentially homogenous individuals or married spouses saving when young for their retirement is factually incorrect." Since the life-cycle savings model fits neither the few who are rich nor the many who are poor,[3] it is probably best to think of it as a model of middle-class behavior.

Overall, "neither the U.S. nor the British evidence proves a wealth–age relationship of the life-cycle type to be a major factor in generating inequality" (Brittain, 1978:71). To quote Kotlikoff and Summers (1980:730) again, "Economic models of savings that stress the homogeneity of agents and the importance of the demographic structure should give way to models that emphasize the rather massive intergenerational transfers in the U.S. economy and the apparent concentration of these transfers among the very wealthy."

11.3 The Theory of the Inheritance of Property

Discussion of the inheritance of property is crucial to a study of economic inequality because property carries with it more than just income. Property gives security—to a far greater extent than the wealth reflected in human capital, which is subject to the hazards of disease and accident. It gives flexibility and, if one has enough of it, it can give power. Wealth in the form of property is also qualitatively different from "human wealth."[4] The "human wealth" of an individual refers to the value of his or her potential future earnings, and one must work in order to avail oneself of that potential. Salable property, on the other hand, represents actual current command over resources. If one compares an individual whose training commands $20,000 per year in the labor market to a person whose property assets yield the same amount, it is clear that the option of leisure or a change of job or occupation is open to someone who owns property but not (i.e., not without sacrifice) to persons who have only their skills to rely on. Income from property has therefore long had a different ethical status from income from labor earnings—and especially if that property was inherited. As the old saying goes, "It is one thing for everyone to stand on his or her own two feet, and quite another for some to stand on their parents' shoulders."

Given the distribution of property ownership among one generation, however, what impact will inheritance produce on the wealth distribution of the next generation? As usual, the answer depends on a variety of factors.[5] In particular one must ask:

(a) How much wealth is passed from generation to generation?
(b) To whom are inheritances left?
(c) How are inheritances combined in current families?
(d) What is the rate of accumulation of inherited property?

Of course, one could also ask, "Why do people leave inheritances at all?" We all know that "you can't take it with you," so one might expect people who wanted to maximize their own utility to spend all their wealth in their own lifetime (or, at least, to die trying). However, although death is certain, its timing, of course, is not. Even those people who planned to spend it all before dying will include some who overestimate the years remaining to them and leave estates inadvertently (but only to the extent of their overoptimism—probably not very large estates on average).[6]

Most inheritances are, however, probably not the result of an accidental early meeting with the grim reaper. There appear to be a number of motivations. Firstly, there may be an unselfish, altruistic desire to increase the utility of someone else (usually one's children). In this case, one's bequest will tend to be greater the greater is one's own human and property wealth, the greater the degree of empathy one feels with one's heirs, and the more they "need" an inheritance (i.e., the lower their income in the absence of an inheritance) (see Shorrocks, 1979). A less admirable motivation, however, may be aged individuals' desire for power over potential heirs in their last years. Alternatively, an individual may have a "dynastic" sense of self and feel it important that both forebearers and heirs occupy a certain social position. In this last case, an individual may have a "target" bequest which he or she wishes to pass on, to "set the children up 'right,' "[7] but whatever the motivation it is the tastes of the elder generation which govern the inheritances of the younger.

The "neoclassical" approach to the inheritance process is represented in Figure 11.2. Figure 11.2(a) represents the parental choice between own consumption (vertical axis) and bequest to children (horizontal axis).[8] If parents are altruistic, their utility depends on both their own consumption and that of their children and their relative tastes (represented by U_0 and U_1), combined with the budget constraint they face (C_0^*) and C_1^*), together determine the amount of bequest (I_0 or I_1). In Figure 11.2(b), the vertical axis represents the rate of return on inheritances received as a function of the amount received (horizontal axis).

In Figure 11.2, the line RAP represents the rate of return in money on inheritances received in the form of property. If capital markets are competitive, the rate of return will be a constant at the rate R. The marginal net return on investments in children's human capital (after allowing for the disutility of different sorts of work) is represented by the line HAL. One would expect the marginal net return to initial investments in human capital to be rather high, but to decrease as investment increases. One would also expect it to vary with the ability of the child (see

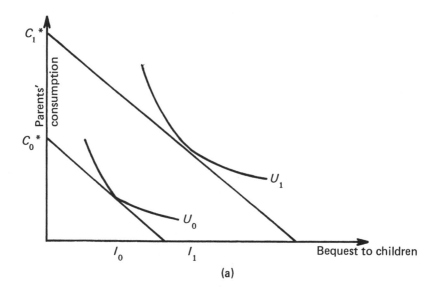

(a)

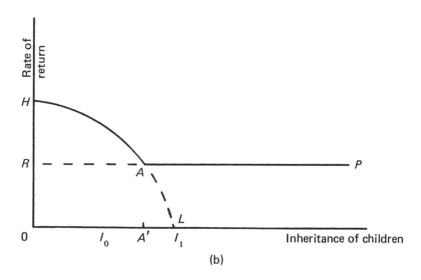

(b)

Figure 11.2 INHERITANCE—A DIAGRAMMATIC APPROACH

Figure 8.5). Point A represents the point at which the marginal return to investment in human capital is equal to the market rate of return on property; over the range $0A$ the rate of return on human capital exceeds that on property. Consequently, parents who pass on less than $0A$ to their children will, if they are efficient about the bequest process, leave a zero inheritance of property but invest I_0 in their children's earnings capacity.

Since human capital dominates property as an asset type up to an inheritance of $0A$, this model can explain why most people receive approximately nothing as an inheritance of property.[9] Richer parents, on the other hand, will leave both human capital and property—an inheritance such as I_1 will be composed of $0A'$ invested in human capital and $A'I_1$ left as property.

Figure 11.2 can be used to illustrate the implications of inheritance taxes, differences in parental tastes, and changes in interest rates, but it ignores distinctions between property and human earning power and obscures somewhat the importance of consumer durables and housing in inheritance. Assets such as furniture, cars, or the family home will typically be both a source of utility to parents throughout their lives and an eventual transfer of wealth to children. It is these sorts of assets which comprise most of the wealth of most Americans.[10] Nevertheless, Figure 11.2 does highlight, in a "neoclassical" fashion, two important predictions:

(a) Most people will receive from their parents either a zero inheritance of property or an inheritance composed of depreciated consumer durables and/or housing.

(b) The children of more wealthy families will receive an inheritance partly in the form of human capital and partly in the form of property; at the margin inheritances are solely property.

Given a certain aggregate "taste" for bequests, Figure 11.3 illustrates the importance of alternative social patterns of inheritance, fertility, and marriage for intergenerational stability of the wealth distribution. (It assumes that consumption equals only the interest on inherited property, so the principal neither grows nor diminishes.) In some societies, primogeniture has been the rule—i.e., the eldest son inherits all the family's property and other children receive either nothing or only minimal shares. This is the surest way to perpetuate the existence of large fortunes as each generation's eldest son simply passes his inheritance, intact, to his own eldest son. Although prevalent among the nobility of Europe during the period when land was the primary form of wealth, there is little evidence that such an inheritance pattern is typical today, at least in developed countries.

If all children share their parents' estate, one must examine the size of each share and how many children there are to divide the inheritance among. Menchik (1980) argues that the norm, in the United States at least, is equal sharing. Figure 11.3(a) embodies as well the assumption that each generation has two children, one male and one female. If equal sharing is the rule, the solid boxes illustrate the spreading of the original Smith family fortune among children and grandchildren which occurs with the passage of generations. Obviously, the greater the average size of family, the smaller the average share of each succeeding generation.

If a society's norm is equal sharing, however, both husbands *and*

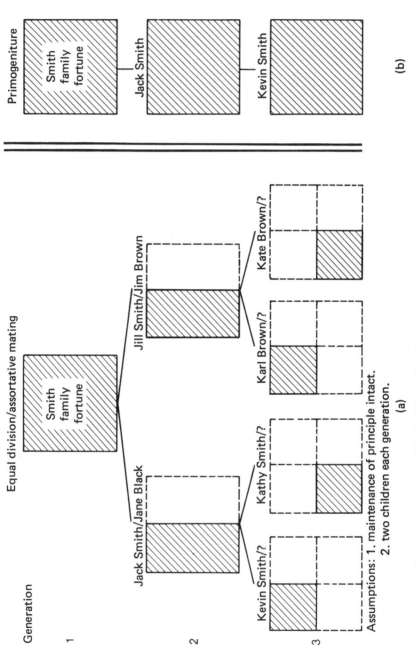

Figure 11.3 THREE GENERATIONS OF INHERITANCE

wives will receive inheritances. "Assortative mating" refers to the tendency for individuals to marry people from similar social backgrounds. Perfect assortative mating implies that individuals always marry people with the same amount of family wealth; hence husbands and wives both have inheritances of equal size from their own parents. The dashed lines of Figure 11.3(a) represent inheritances received by the spouses of Smith offspring. As the sizes of the total boxes indicate, the combination of perfect assortative mating and equal sharing among children implies inherited fortunes will not diminish; i.e., the same tendency for the perpetuation of wealth inequality will exist as under primogeniture. Under primogeniture, the Smiths, the Browns, the Blacks, and other families not pictured in Figure 11.3 would pass their fortune intact to their eldest sons. Their daughters would have to take their chances in the marriage lottery—and would normally be introduced only to well-born males and hence be married into inherited wealth. Under equal sharing with assortative mating, sons have to share their parents' estate with their sisters, but they marry their "socioeconomic sisters," who bring a similar amount of property with them into the marriage. With perfectly assortative mating, the distribution of total inheritances by families is the same in both cases. Equal sharing is, however, substantially easier to accomplish when most wealth is financial, since in that case wealth can easily be recombined into new holdings. By contrast, primogeniture was long defended in Europe as a way of preventing the division of large landed estates, at a time when land was the primary source of both wealth and influence.

However, if the children of well-off families "marry beneath themselves" (to use a Victorian term), family fortunes are fragmented over generations and wealth will tend to be spread more equally over the population. The more random (in the socioeconomic sense) are marriages, the greater the tendency for the distribution of inherited property to be equalized over generations.[11] And, although it is more romantic to think of peasants marrying princesses and millionaires marrying their maids, it is much more likely for people to marry someone with broadly similar attitudes, habits, and assumptions about day-to-day style of life. Residence in the same neighborhood, attendance at the same schools and universities, and membership in the same social network of clubs, fraternities, sororities, etc., all help to ensure that people are exposed during their marriageable years to compatible prospective mates. Some indication of this is given by the correlation of socioeconomic status scores, which among the fathers of U.S. couples is between 0.39 and 0.70 (Blinder, 1973b:625), and the correlation of spouses' educations, which in Britain is about 0.56 (Layard, Zabalza, 1979).

Finally, one must examine the rate of accumulation (or decumulation) of inherited wealth. Figure 11.3 embodies the restrictive assumption that each generation consumes only the interest on its inheritance and maintains the capital intact for future generations. If a heir's rate of consumption is particularly high, even the largest of fortunes can be squandered in a remarkably short period. (Tebbel, 1962, cites the dissipation of the Dodge fortune, as well as some other highly entertaining examples.) On the other hand, large fortunes generate large incomes (which are particularly large if the rate of return received by large investors is greater than that received by small savers).[12] The total stock of inherited fortunes will increase over time only if, on average, heirs realize a rate of return greater than their taxes and their consumption.

We can now add two more predictions to a "neoclassical" approach to the study of inheritance:

(c) Where equal sharing among children is the norm, the concentration of inherited property will decrease over time to the extent that marriages are random or negatively assortative.

(d) To the extent that the propensity to consume of heirs is abnormally high and exceeds their return on assets, inherited wealth will diminish over time.

Would "radicals" disagree with any of these predictions? Certainly they would agree with (a), that most people get very little, if any, inheritance of property, and with (b), that large inheritances are composed primarily of financial assets. They would probably put some ideas in different terminology, preferring to talk, for example, about "class cohesiveness" rather than "assortative mating"—but with the same prediction, that marriage patterns and inheritance norms can greatly influence the importance of inherited wealth. However, radicals would think it very unlikely that unequal societies would typically have random mating. While they would not deny that wastrels exist, they would see it as unusual for heirs to dissipate their wealth. In short, although the emphasis and the "tone" of the discussion would differ, the content of both "radical" and "neoclassical" analyses would be substantially similar.

If, however, one is interested in assessing the fraction of wealth that has been inherited and the fraction which is "self-made," it is difficult to classify those fortunes that are currently large but which accumulated rapidly from relatively small inheritances. The original John D. Rockefeller or, more recently, John Paul Getty or Howard Hughes all received inheritances as young men and with ruthless energy turned them into much larger fortunes. In one sense, they realized a very high rate of return on their capital, which was originally inherited. Others in similar situations have, of course, failed. Like a high-stakes poker game, success in finance depends on both ability and luck and "you can't win if you can't bet."

Thurow (1975) explains the making of very large fortunes as the result of a "random walk" where luck dictates that some able, hardworking individuals are in the right place at the right time and realize very high rates of return on their assets. Thurow argues that many people have ability and work hard but when we examine large fortunes we do not observe the efforts or skills of the unlucky—only the lucky. In his view, large fortunes arise when markets capitalize the high rates of return lucky enterprises generate. (In the next generation their heirs normally diversify their portfolio to avoid risk and their holdings become stable, inherited fortunes).[13] Drilling for oil is the classic example. It offers spectacular returns for the fortunate and bankruptcy for the unlucky. In 1982, when *Forbes* magazine published a list of America's billionaires, thirteen of the fourteen on the list had inherited all or most of their wealth, and eleven of the thirteen family fortunes involved had their origins in oil (see *Forbes*, September 13, 1982).

Many businessmen argue that acquiring one's initial stake is the greatest obstacle to success, since without inheritance of some sort one must do it by patient saving from labor earnings. This takes time, and a person who has to save for some years to start a business obviously has that many fewer years to make the business grow. The "initial conditions" of Thurow's random walk may be the inheritance of an estate which is much smaller than the fortune to which it grows. Families in the top 5% or 10% of the wealth distribution may move up much more easily if inheritance gives one generation the start it needs in business. Alternatively, if family contacts enable a business to start or to grow, inheritance may take the form of access to capital rather than capital itself.[14] Inheritance may therefore play a very complex role in wealth distribution, but even the simpler case of direct property transfers on death is difficult enough to estimate empirically.

11.4 The Inheritance of Large Fortunes

> In the great majority of cases, the large fortunes of one generation belong to the children of those who possess the large fortunes of the preceding generation (J. WEDGEWOOD, The Economics of Inheritance, 1929: 164)

As is clear from Wedgewood's emphasis on "large fortunes" there has always been great interest in the inheritances of the very rich. The possession of vast amounts of property carries with it "riches," in the sense of large amounts of discretionary purchasing power (which excites the envy of the less fortunate), and "power," in the sense of the ability to wield economic influence (which can arouse anxiety among the less favored). There are therefore really two issues in the study of inheritance: first, what fraction of "large fortunes" is inherited and, second, what the impact of inheritance is on the distribution of income and wealth in general. One problem with studies of inheritance is that some techniques are better suited to address the first issue and some better suited to address the second.[15]

"Self-made" fortunes can arise in a number of ways. Atkinson (1975) has argued that first among these is the development of a new process (e.g., microelectronics, Xerox machines) which is immensely profitable.[16] If a large fortune is to be accumulated from small beginnings, a very high rate of return is required on investment. In some industries, the high rate which we observe to have been made on existing fortunes is more like the winning ticket of a lottery than the average return for the industry in question. Quite a few prospectors, for example, die poor for every one who "strikes it rich." The average rate of return for an industry is the average of both those who make very little and those who make a great deal. Some industries may, however, have an above-normal rate of return as the result of technical innovation or a secular shift in demand patterns. Railways in the nineteenth century, the auto industry in the early twentieth century, and microelectronics in postwar California are all examples of industries which grew rapidly in a relatively short period, where individual entrepreneurs had an especially good chance to accumulate large stocks of capital. If the economy is a competitive one, these opportunities for extraordinary profit are essentially transitory, but if barriers to entry prevent, for a time, outside competitors from joining the industry and thereby diluting the bonanza, much larger fortunes may be acquired.

Historically, many of the polemics directed against capitalism have been attacks on monopoly profits and the concentrations of wealth they create. Recently, Comanor and Smiley (1975) have attempted to estimate the impact of monopoly profits on the distribution of ownership of property, arguing that the future monopoly profits of corporations are capitalized into the prices of the shares of those corporations and thereby influence the distribution of wealth in the economy as a whole. Under alternative assumptions concerning the degree of monopoly in the United States, they argue that the presence of monopoly elements in American industry has a substantial impact on the distribution of wealth. Their estimate is that between two-fifths and two-thirds of the wealth of the top 0.27% of households is capitalized monopoly profits and between 20% and 50% of the wealth share of the top 2.4% is similarly due to the presence of monopoly.[17] It is precisely these top wealth holders for whom inheritance is most important. Osman (1977:49), for example, argues that "intergenerational wealth transfers are not an important asset source for 97.5% of the population; however, for the top 2.5% of U.S. consumer units, who own 43% of the nation's wealth, they appear to be an important asset source, and an important possible reason for the persistent inequality in the distribution of wealth observed from generation to generation."

In Britain, Wedgewood (1929) and Harbury (1962, 1973, 1976) have traced the antecedents of large fortunes using estate data. Harbury's technique was to draw a sample of the names of deceased males who left net worth of £100,000 or more from the registry of wills probated in 1956, 1957, 1965, and 1973 (this is approximately the top 0.1% of estates). Harbury then identified the fathers of these men and searched estate records, until he located details of the estates left by them. By comparison of the estate of the father with that of the son, he sought to examine the importance of initial inheritance to wealth accumulation. He concluded that no very appreciable change had occurred in the relative fraction of self-made fortunes between Wedgewood's similar studies of the 1920s and the mid-1950s or the mid-1960s. Over all, some 67% of sons leaving an estate greater than £100,000 had had fathers whose estates were at least £25,000 (in constant prices)—although less than 1% of the population at large had fathers with that much wealth. By 1973, some decrease in the percentage of wealthy sons who had wealthy fathers had occurred (a reduction to 58%), but Harbury is unsure as to whether that reflects a real decrease in intergenerational wealth transmission or simply a growth of gifts, trusts, and other methods of estate tax avoidance (Harbury and Hitchens, 1976:326). Harbury was also able to establish that about one in eight of top wealth leavers may have had poor fathers, but were able to marry into money. Harbury qualifies his conclusion by noting that he has not been able to consider gifts between living persons, trusts, or "social inheritance" but his primary conclusion is that inherited property remains the most significant determinant of large fortunes.

In the United States, Menchick (1979) has somewhat reversed Harbury's procedure by starting from a sample of the large estates which were left in the 1930s and 1940s and examining the probate records of the estates left by their children. He finds that wealthy children tend to have wealthy parents, although there is a tendency (which depends partially on how many children there are in a family to share the inheritance) for children not to have quite as much wealth as their parents.[18] There appears to be some "regression to the mean"—if your parents left an estate 100% larger than my parents did, on average you will leave an estate some 75% larger than mine.[19] Menchick speculates, however, that the inheritance of earnings capacity and that of property are correlated and can reinforce one another to produce more similarity between parent and child wealth than either would produce alone. But examination of the impact of inheritance *in general* demands that we examine more than just the estates of the wealthy.

11.5 Inheritance and the Distribution of Lifetime Resources

Concentrating attention on "large fortunes" emphasizes only part of the total picture of income and wealth distribution. The majority of people die leaving either no estate or an estate comprised largely of such assets as a house, a car, home furnishings, and, perhaps, a small amount of cash. Indeed, in many ways, it is more accurate to think of many individuals as leaving "negative bequests," since those people who require financial assistance in their old age are receiving wealth transfers *from* their children rather than bequeathing property to them.[20] Taking the population as a whole, what impact does inheritance have on the entire distribution of wealth and lifetime income?

Since to acquire property legally one must either inherit it, receive it as a gift, or save it from one's own current income, Oulton (1976) followed Atkinson (1975) and argued by elimination that inheritance must be a major source of inequality in the distribution of wealth. Oulton argued that, if we take the simple life-cycle model of section 11.2 seriously, inequality in wealth holdings is created by inequalities in earnings, the rate of return on savings from those earnings, and one's position in the lifetime accumulation/decumulation process. He calculated the distribution of wealth which the life-cycle model would imply under alternative assumptions about these variables and observed that inequality in the resulting estimated distribution of wealth in the United Kingdom (measured by the coefficient of variation) was, if interest rates were equal, less than 20% of the inequality observed in reality. The residual he ascribed to the inheritance of property. Davies and Shorrocks (1978) agreed with Oulton that the life-cycle model does not adequately explain the distribution of wealth but argued that his methodology ascribed all remaining, unmeasured influences to inheritance, ignored possible interaction effects between the inheritance of earnings and of property, and was potentially sensitive to the measure of inequality adopted. Indeed, any simple model of only two or three variables which "explains" the distribution of wealth is always open to the criticism that it has omitted the "most important" factor. Davies (1980) therefore set out to model explicitly the process of the acquisition of property and to assess rigorously the contribution of inheritance to overall inequality.

Availability of data is a severe constraint in such an exercise. In the United States, estimates of the wealth distribution are very often made by the "estate multiplier" method (see Chapter 3, section 3.3), since only a few irregular direct surveys of the general population's wealth have been done—see Projector and Weiss (1966) and Lininger, Vaughan, and Whiteman (1981). The "estate multiplier" method can be used to estimate the upper tail of the wealth distribution but cannot help us in estimating the wealth of the majority who leave an estate which is too small to be subject to tax. Davies uses the micro-data of the Canadian *Survey of Consumer Finance* (SCF). Unlike the United States, Canada gets its data on the wealth distribution from a series of periodic surveys of the general population.[21] Such sample surveys are reasonably accurate for middle- and lower-income households but face very serious problems of nonresponse and response error among rich households. Davies therefore had to adjust SCF figures substantially (see Davies, 1979b), especially in the upper tail.

Davies's simulation[22] study takes a great many variables into explicit account within a basically "neoclassical" methodology. Using a life-cycle, intergenerational utility-maximizing framework, Davies performed the conceptual experiment of asking what the distribution of wealth would look like: (1) if inheritance of property were equalized; (2) if the institution of unequal inheritances were abolished; and (3) if unequal opportunity were eliminated. Unequal inheritance, by itself, appears to have an impact on the distribution of wealth of the same order of magnitude as differences in tastes, rate of return on assets earnings, and age. Davies argues that all of these factors have distinct impacts on the distribution of wealth and it is difficult to rank their importance if one controls for each separately. Eliminating the *institution* of unequal inheritance has a much greater impact, however, since it implies that not only do people receive the same amount from their parents but they also bequeath the same amount to their own children (consequently, higher-income families accumulate less wealth themselves). Davies concludes that "equalizing inheritances for *both* parents and children has such a large impact that one would be justified in attributing to the *institution* of unequal inheritance a dominant effect on the distribution of wealth" (1980:24).[23] Eliminating unequal inheritance from one's parents and inequality in the rate of return on assets has an impact on the distribution of wealth "almost as large" as eliminating the institution of inheritance.

Since income from property is only part of total income, it may be more meaningful to examine the impact of the inheritance of property on the present value of lifetime resources (i.e., total lifetime earnings discounted to the age of 20 plus the discounted value of inherited property). The importance of inheritance is lessened by the fact that wages and salaries comprise, for most people, the largest part of lifetime resources. Discounting, moreover, implies that inherited property received late in one's own life has a much lower present value at age 20 than its current dollar value when it is received. If one's parents die at 70, for example, one can usually expect to be at least 40 before receiving inherited property—discounting the value of this inheritance to age 20 will usually produce a fairly low present value. For the bulk of the population, therefore, inherited wealth has a fairly small impact on the present value of total lifetime resources evaluated at age 20. It has a somewhat larger impact on the extremes of the distribution. In Davies's simulation, the equalization of inheritances from one's parents would produce a decrease in the share of the top quintile in total lifetime resources from 40.4% to 38.1% and an increase in the share of the bottom 20% of the population from 5.3% to 6.5%. Inequality as measured by the coefficient of variation or the Gini ratio would decline by approximately 10%. This small impact of inheritance must, however, be interpreted with some caution since it is partially a function of the point in time at which comparisons are made. Discounting at 3.6% per year (as in Davies) implies that a dollar received at age 45 has a present value at age 20 of roughly 41 cents. Any inequality in inheritances received at 45 is thus "scaled down" in comparison to inequality in current earnings, if lifetime resources are calculated as at age 20. If one calculated the impact of inheritances on the inequality of resources, for the rest of their lives, of people aged 45, it would be larger than the impact on lifetime resources, discounted to age 20.

Should one evaluate the impact of inheritance as of the point most individuals become "adults" or as of the point they receive their inheritances (if any)? Does the knowledge that an inheritance is coming, or that family financial resources are available in an emergency, offer a security to those from wealthy families that others do not have? Lifetime income, discounted to age 20, will not guide us on these issues,[24] but one can note that equalizing *earnings* would decrease the share of the top 20% of families to 23.3% of lifetime resources and increase the share of the bottom 20% to 18.8%—fairly close to absolute equality. As both "neoclassical" and "radicals" would predict, for the bulk of the population (although *not* for the inheritors of large fortunes) inherited property is a significant cause of economic inequality, but one which is very much smaller in importance than the inequality of earnings in the labor market.

11.6 On Property

The discussion up to this point has concluded that the inheritance of property is chiefly important for the top 2.5% or so, the "upper tail" of the distributions of income and wealth. For the vast majority, and thus for the distribution as a whole, the inheritance of earning power is far more important than the inheritance of property. But the astute reader may perhaps have asked, "What is property?"

Property is clearly not things themselves (since they exist regardless of whether anyone owns them) nor is it the possession of things (since one can use what is not one's property).[25] Rather, as Macpherson puts it, "What distinguishes property from mere momentary possession is that property is a claim that will be enforced by society or the state, by custom or convention or law" (1978:3). Private property is then a person's socially enforceable claim to use, or to exclude others from the use of, or to receive the benefits of, certain rights. Or as Tawney put it,

> Property is the most ambiguous of categories. It covers a multitude of rights which have nothing in common except that they are exercised by persons and enforced by the State. Apart from these formal characteristics, they vary indefinitely in economic character, in social effect, and in moral justification. They may be conditional like the grant of patent rights, or

absolute like the ownership of ground rents, terminable like copyright, or permanent like a freehold, as comprehensive as sovereignty or as restricted as an easement, as intimate and personal as the ownership of clothes and books, or as remote and intangible as shares in a goldmine or rubber plantation. It is idle, therefore, to present a case for or against private property without specifying the particular forms of property to which reference is made (1920:136).

Property as an enforceable claim implies that there must be someone to enforce it, which in modern times means the state. It is therefore both a political and a social phenomenon and its definition varies across societies and, over time, within the same society. Many African tribal societies, for example, conceive agricultural land as being held "in trust" by the current generation for the benefit of a community which consists of both this generation and past and future generations—they recognize private property rights in land, but only so long as the land is being productively used and not sold outside the community (Elias, 1962). English and Scottish landlords used to possess, along with their land, the right to nominate the priest for the parish which it comprised (Cohen, 1927). The modern institution of property is shorn of these appendages. Modern property rights are not conditional on any social function, nor do they exclude the right to dispose of as well as to use.[26]

Any social institution, such as property or the inheritance of it, requires some ethical justification. Tawney argues that the primary justification of property is a functional one—that it contributes to human happiness by guaranteeing the security of man's labor, by ensuring that individuals can prosper from their own exertions. He traces the history of its justification in recent times to the defense of the right of English farmers and working men to receive the product of their labors. Land or tools which were used by the owner for the purposes of production were plainly indispensable to the primary social purposes of providing food and clothing. The security which came with an assurance, via the institution of property, that improvements to them would yield benefits to their owners in future years was both a benefit to most individuals (at a time when ownership was widely dispersed) and a condition of the increasing prosperity of the nation.

To the extent that they have any property, it is this sort of "active" property that the vast majority of Americans are familiar with. Indeed, if the life-cycle savings model were an accurate picture of the wealth generation process in total, all wealth would be the product of individual saving from the earnings of their own exertions and this historic justification of property would be applicable to the present day. But the life-cycle savings model can explain only a small part of the aggregate distribution of property. And the "functional" justification of property is a two-edged sword, since it does *not* justify "passive" property, or property as pure ownership unlinked to the performance of any social function. As John Stuart Mill argued (1848: 359), "Private property, in every defence made of it, is supposed to mean, the guarantee to individuals, of the fruits of their own labor and abstinence. The guarantee to them of the fruits of the labor and abstinence of others transmitted to them without any merit or exertion of their own, is not of the essence of the institution, but a mere incidental consequence, which when it reaches a certain height, does not promote, but conflicts with the ends which render private property legitimate."

In the incomes of the very wealthy, some income arises from their labor and some income arises merely from their possession of wealth. In American society, while the makers of high-level business decisions are often very well rewarded,[27] as we saw in Chapter 3, section 3.2, they are not often the *owners* of major corporations. When the ownership and the control of the modern corporations are separated, "management becomes, in an odd sort of way, the uncontrolled administrator of a kind of trust having the privilege of perpetual accumulation. The stockholder is the passive beneficiary, not only of the original 'trust' but of the compounded annual accretions to it" [Berle, 1968:xx]. Share ownership carries with it the expectation that a portion of after-tax corporate profits will be received in the form of dividends, but the diffusion of ownership implies that the individual shareholder plays no part in the management of assets or the creation of further wealth. Indeed, since corporate investment is primarily financed from retained earnings, the major function of the trading of property rights in future profits on stock exchanges is not the raising of *new* investment; rather, it is to ensure the liquidity of *existing* property rights. This raises, as Berle (1968:xxiii) puts it, "a problem of social ethics"—i.e., "Why have stockholders? What contribution do they make? Stockholders toil not, neither do they spin—they are beneficiaries by position only." Berle's own answer is that the justification of such wealth "turns on the distribution as well as the existence of wealth. Its force exists only in direct ratio to the number of individuals who hold such wealth—the privilege to have income and a fragment of wealth without a corresponding duty to work for it cannot be justified except on the ground that the community is better off—and not unless most members of the community share it." But we saw in Chapter 3, section 3.3 that the inequality of share ownership is extremely high—most people do *not* have a share.

The inheritance of such passive property can therefore be judged somewhat differently from the inheritances with which the vast majority are familiar (i.e., nil or, for the more fortunate, the family home or farm, the home furnishings passed down through generations, or, perhaps, the small family business). In part, the law recognizes such a distinction. Such property as the family farm or family home receives special tax consideration. Other countries exempt entirely estates under a certain amount from taxation.[28] Many societies therefore draw ethical and legal distinctions between types of inherited property which, although somewhat vague, do roughly correspond to our empirical distinction between the inheritance of "large fortunes" and inheritance in general.

11.7 Public Policies

If competitive capitalism can be described as a race, then "equal opportunity" would imply that we all should start from about the same place. Chapter 6 discussed the "head start" that a good family background can give a child even before he or she enters the labor market but these advantages are often subtle and not easily quantified. By contrast, the inheritance of large fortunes gives some individuals a very clear and obvious lead in the economic race (see Table 3.1). Public policy has occasionally tried to intervene to even these odds—not really because of the quantitative importance of large fortunes to the distribution of economic welfare (see section 11.5) but more because of their symbolic importance for the myth of "equal opportunity" and because of a continued anxiety about the impact of a hereditary class of privilege on democratic institutions.[29]

Most often, estates have been taxed by the state. In the United States, nominal rates of taxation were as high as 77% on estates over $10 million (Cooper, 1979:1). These high rates might be thought enough to ensure that large fortunes are broken up over time but Cooper (1979) has argued that loopholes in the law were sufficiently numerous to ensure that these rates were largely cosmetic. The du Pont fortune, for example, which dates from the founding of the family firm in 1802, is still approximately $500 million and has paid an effective estate tax, over the two last generations, of only about 5% (Cooper, 1979:1). A cynic might claim that such "laws with loopholes" kept both rich and poor happy—the rich because in fact they paid little tax and the poor because they thought that justice was being done. However, as a result of the 1981 changes in tax law, "the government has virtually abandoned all pretense of taxing transfers of wealth between generations" (Tobin, 1981:13).

One alternative to estate taxation might be to encourage wealthy individuals to divide their estates into more separate pieces. Mill (1848: 378) argued that society should set a ceiling on the maximum bequest a person could make to any heirs, implying that no individual could inherit excessive wealth and large fortunes would be divided among many heirs. Alternatively, if inheritances were taxed as income in the hands of individuals, rather than estates' being taxed before division among individuals, there might be some incentive for donors to split their estates among more people, thereby hastening the process of the fragmentation of large fortunes over generations. In essence, the higher the tax rate on inheritances the higher is the "price" to put $1 in the hands of one's heirs. If the size of the estate as a whole is taxed, then heirs are paid from what remains after the tax is paid and the "price" of a $1 bequest is the same no matter whom it goes to. If the inheritances of individuals are taxed and if that tax depends on the individual's income, then a higher-income individual will pay a higher inheritance tax—i.e., the "price" of bequeathing $1 to that person will be higher than the "price" of leaving $1 to someone else with lower income. The difference in "price" will be approximately the difference in their marginal tax rates.

Hence the impact on inheritance patterns of an inheritance tax system versus a succession duty system depends on the "price-elasticity" of bequests and the difference in "prices" among one's potential heirs, as well as on the utility which the donor derives from the future utility of his or her heirs. If there is a tendency for parents to favor in their wills those of their children who have lower expected earnings (see Tomes, 1980), taxing inheritances as income might encourage this tendency—but the net effect is likely to be very small. After all, in section 11.5 we concluded that the inheritance of property is a small fraction of lifetime resources for most of the population; indeed, in many families net bequests are zero or negative.

The family, as a social institution, will have a partially equalizing influence on income distribution if inheritances of siblings are unequal and if they are negatively correlated with the earnings of siblings (Griliches, 1979). However, parents who want to preclude disharmony among their children after their death have strong reason to simply divide estates equally. Unequal division is thus likely only where such gross and obvious differences in siblings' earnings exist that the children will accept the "fairness" of "compensatory" inequalities in bequest. Unequal division matters only in cases where there is something to divide, and only to the extent that the estate is large relative to the lifetime earnings of children; as we have seen this occurs only in a very small fragment of the population. On the other hand, the "large fortunes" of Chapter 3, section 3.4 are so large that they dwarf any possible difference in lifetime earnings. "Redistribution within the family," via unequal inheritance, is therefore an interesting theoretical idea (see Sheshinski and Weiss, 1982), but it is not empirically important either for the very rich or for the poor and the middle classes, or for those upper-middle-class families where siblings have roughly similar fortunes[30] —i.e., it is an issue "of the second order of smalls."

If excessive concentration of wealth is to be diminished a tax on wealth can be imposed, much as we already impose municipal taxes on the value of one's home and some jurisdictions (e.g., Connecticut) also tax the value of one's car. These sorts of property taxes fall on the gross value of the assets in which the *poorest* 80% of families hold most of their wealth but Norway, Denmark, Sweden, and now France do it the other way around—they impose a comprehensive wealth tax, but exempt wealth under a certain level. Potentially, this is a powerful tool for the equalization of the wealth distribution[31] since, like the income tax, it can have exemptions large enough to leave most life-cycle savings untouched or rates progressive enough to bear most heavily on the largest fortunes (e.g., a tax of 0% on net worth under $250,000, 0.5% on net worth between $250,000 and $1,000,000, and 0.75% on assets over $1,000,000, etc.).

The nationalization of large enterprises—i.e., the (forced) purchase of the shares of all large companies—has also often been proposed as a remedy for inequality. As a remedy for inequalities of wealth, however, such a measure would be effective only if compensation payments were substantially below the market value of the shares purchased. If government bonds were, for example, issued to pay for the shares purchased, nationalization with full compensation would simply change the financial portfolios of the previous owners, replacing shares with bonds. As a remedy for inequalities of income, nationalization would have an effect only if the rate of return on bonds issued as compensation payments was substantially below the rate of return previously obtained on shares. Some differential in rate of return would be "fair," since the new assets (bonds) are risk-free while the old assets (shares) were exposed to the risk that companies would go bankrupt, but full compensation would imply that the differential in rates reflects only the change in risks associated with the two types of assets. Okun (1975: 53) estimates that nationalization (with compensation) of all U.S. corporate assets would imply a net transfer of income away from former property owners of roughly 1% of GNP. If added entirely to the incomes of the poorest 20%, this is not insignificant. It is, however, less than the normal year-to-year changes in the economy's growth rate.[32]

The real issue in nationalization is, however, not inequality of income or wealth but inequality of power. Socialists argue that great inequalities of economic power (see section 3.2) necessarily produce inequalities in effective political influence.[33] By now, there has been sufficient international experience with nationalization that socialists rarely see nationalization as a panacea. In addition, the easy acceptance by early socialists of centralized ownership has given way to an emphasis on dispersed ownership by worker cooperatives or local or state governments (see Carnoy and Shearer, 1980). Most socialists therefore see nationalization as enabling, but not guaranteeing (i.e., a necessary, but not sufficient, condition for) a more democratic organization of work and an emphasis on values such as workplace safety or a clean environment which are not adequately reflected in the monetary profit-and-loss calculations of capitalism. Socialists (e.g., Bowles and Gintis, 1976) also argue that only if the public owns and controls productive enterprises can one make a reasonable start on reducing inequalities both of "result" in the workplace and of opportunity outside it—i.e., the reforms necessary for meaningful equality of opportunity in the labor market run against the interests of capitalists in maintaining a hierarchical pattern of organization.

Nationalization without compensation, i.e., confiscation, is a more radical brand of socialism but is hard to envisage in a nonrevolutionary situation. A revolutionary situation, however, would require a drastic change in economic and social conditions (e.g., a depression which reduced the income share of the majority to less than half of what they now have). It is therefore somewhat unreal to estimate the impact of confiscation on the *current* distribution of income or wealth since it is clearly not going to happen in the near future and, if it ever did happen, the impact of confiscation would be relative to those distributional shares which would produce it as a response.

11.8 Summary

(a) The life-cycle savings model argues that individual savings for the retirement years accounts for the bulk of private wealth and that inequality of property ownership is largely due to age and individual tastes.

(b) The one-generation life-cycle savings model can explain only a small fraction of the capital stock, only part of private savings, and only a small portion of the inequality of property ownership. It provides a poor picture of savings behavior except for the urban, educated white middle class which tends to save in the form of durables, housing, or cash.

(c) Both the "radical" and the "neoclassical" approaches would predict that most people will inherit very little property, other than consumer durables and possibly housing. "Neoclassical" authors would ascribe this to the relative advantage of human capital as a form of bequest, at least for "small" bequests. "Radicals" would argue that it simply reflects the fact that most parents do not typically have much else by way of assets. Both schools of thought would predict that children from wealthy families would inherit both earnings capacity and property.

(d) The tendency for inherited property to become concentrated or be fragmented over generations depends on average family size, social patterns of inheritance, the degree of assortative mating, and the rate of return (minus consumption) on inherited wealth.

(e) Inherited property is an important part of the assets of the top 2.5% to top 5% of the wealth distribution, but for the *vast* majority of the population the inheritance of property is a fairly small part of lifetime economic resources.

(f) A substantial portion of the population, perhaps a third, own very little personal property at any age. A small fraction (2.5% to 5%) inherit most of their property and are joined at the top of the wealth pyramid by a few "self-made" fortunes. For the remainder, the acquisition of personal property (houses, automobiles, consumer durables, bank balances) over the life cycle and the building up of pension rights provide the main sources of wealth.

(g) Since the inheritance of property is highly important for a small wealthy minority and fairly unimportant for the large majority, it is less important than inequalities in earnings for many measures of *aggregate* inequality.

(h) Property is a social institution whose definition changes over time. There is a long history of ethical distinctions' being drawn between different types of property—in particular between property acquired by savings from labor earnings and property acquired by inheritance.

(i) Estate duties, inheritance taxes, wealth taxes, nationalization, and confiscation are some of the measures that have been proposed to prevent a concentration of inherited property.

NOTES

[1] Based on 1970 SCF data, using the coefficient of variation to measure inequality.

[2] In other words, professors, and their college classmates, are precisely the sort of people for whom life-cycle models of savings are the most appropriate—but they are not a representative sample of the population: an example of the dangers of introspection as a source of hypotheses.

[3] Preliminary evidence from the 1979 ISDP Research Panel indicates that 32 to 34% of households in the 45 to 64 age group had under $1,000 in financial assets (Radner, 1981a). Most of the net worth of older families is tied up in houses and not directly available to finance current consumption. However, Sobol (1979) examined the total assets of men approaching retirement, i.e., aged 50 to 65, in 1969. Some 6% of older whites and 25% of blacks had no assets or were in debt, while 68.4% of blacks and 28.9% of whites, that is, roughly 35% of the total population, had *total* assets of less than $10,000.

[4] The term "wealth" is used in a variety of different senses in the literature. Sometimes it is used to mean only the ownership of property rights (such as those enumerated in Chapter 3, section 3.3) and sometimes it is used to mean the present value of all expectable future income streams. We have used the term "wealth" in the former sense, but to avoid any possibility of confusion we henceforth refer primarily to "property," alternating only to avoid tedium where the context should be clear.

[5] Wolfson (1977) examines these and other factors in a complex simulation model.

[6] In theory, individuals who are uncertain about their own life span could use their stock of wealth on retirement to purchase an annuity (i.e., a promise by a financial institution to pay a certain sum of money every year until their death). This demand for annuities should impel financial markets to supply a menu of annuities with different terms (perhaps including inflation indexing). In practice, financial markets do not offer a menu of inflation indexed annuities, perhaps because of "market failure" in the sense of Akerlof (1970). See also Davies (1981).

[7] For example, a farmer whose family has farmed the same land for generations may feel it his duty to leave the farm to his children in the same relative condition as it was left to him.

[8] Clearly, it is very similar to Figure 8.7; the two can be combined very easily.

[9] In the District of Columbia an inheritance tax return must be filed if the estate exceeds $1,000. Smith (1975b) examined the estates of whites (whose average wealth is considerably greater than that of blacks) which were probated in 1967. About half the white decedents did not file returns and among those who did file the median net estate was less than $24,000— i.e., for roughly 75% *of the white population* the net estate was under $24,000. If a $24,000 estate is equally divided between two children and is invested at a real rate of return of 5%, each child receives an inheritance worth roughly $600 per year. For the vast majority of people the inheritance of property is unimportant as an income source. See also Tomes (1981).

10One can ignore consumer durables and housing as a distinct asset class in inheritance only if the equity in those assets can effectively be dissipated—e.g., through nonrepair or use as collateral—without imparing parents' use during their lifetime. This seems a poor assumption.

11If marriages are in fact negatively assortative—i.e., rich men systematically marry poor women and poor men systematically marry rich women—then the distribution of inherited wealth will equalize very rapidly. Blinder (1973b) argues that the degree of assortative mating or social stratification in marriage is in practice a more important determinant of wealth equalization than societal inheritance patterns.

12Lower transactions costs for financial investments, better access to information, preferred treatment by government authorities, or the presence of monopoly profits (see Comanor and Smiley, 1975) may all contribute to higher rates of return for large investors.

13Footnote 3 of Chapter 6 outlines the mathematics of the impact of a chance process on the inequality of income, or of wealth.

14Young people may, for example, just be able to make mortgage payments, but lack the down payment. Parental assistance may thus have enabled middle-class children to purchase homes, where working-class children could not. Certainly in the 1970s, homeowners benefited from capital gains and were, to an extent, insulated against inflation. Hence at the end of their own working lives people whose parents had resources to transfer will have an appreciably better wealth position than renters. In economic terms, parental assistance has earned a high rate of return.

15Survey evidence, as in Brittain (1977), for example, may be quite a reliable indicator for those who have inherited very little, but the natural human desire to emphasize one's own achievements probably produces an understatement of inheritance among the inheritors.

16The technical and material progress which this opportunity for profit is said to encourage has long been one of the main justifications of a capitalist system—see Schumpeter (1942).

17These estimates have been questioned by Thomas (1980).

18The raw correlation between parent and child wealth is about 0.5, but, if account is taken of the biases introduced when a truncated sample is drawn, Menchick argues the true correlation is more likely about 0.8—i.e., very high.

19Recall from Chapter 3 that Cooper (1979) has called the U.S. estate tax a "voluntary" tax and that inheritance tax rates increased over this period. Increased sophistication in tax-free intergenerational wealth transfers could produce an apparent, but illusory, "regression to the mean" in estates.

20Clearly there are limits on the extent to which one can rely on the charity of one's children; hence, models of intergenerational wealth transfers, such as Shorrocks (1979), constrain the possibility of leaving negative bequests. A "choice" model of this situation may, however, be quite misleading since, although most people probably have a very strong desire "not to be a burden on their children," some may have no other option.

21The "estate multiplier" option is not available since, unlike the United States, nine out of the ten Canadian provinces have no inheritance tax.

22Simulation models involve the creation of an artificial panel of households whose different statistical characteristics resemble the differences in the population at large, as well as the "calibration" of assumed decision rules (such as for savings as a percentage of income) which govern their future behavior. In such a computer simulation, each member of a panel is "aged" one year at a time and his or her new characteristics noted (for example, after one year's savings a household's stock of wealth has increased). The total simulated behavior of the sample is then checked against real data (e.g., the total simulated savings of all households in the artificial sample is compared to actual total savings) and if there is a discrepancy the assumed decision rules (for example, the savings rate) are changed. The final result of a successful simulation, after a large number of calibrating runs, is a computer model whose aggregate characteristics mirror those of the actual economy fairly closely. Hence one can evaluate the impact of a variable (such as inheritance) by making new and artificial assumptions regarding it and comparing the new behavior of the panel of households with the households' behavior under "normal" conditions.

23If the institution of unequal inheritance were abolished Davies's simulation indicates that the share of the top 1% in the wealth distribution would be 6.3% (compared to the actual

19.6%), the share of the top 10% would be 33.6% (actual 58%), and the share of the top 20% would be 52.3% (actual 74%).

[24]Using lifetime resources discounted to age 20 has the paradoxical implication that, if all inheritances were received at age 20, Wolfson (1977) shows that the aggregate inequality of the wealth distribution would decrease (since 20-year-olds have, on average, less wealth than older groups). However, the impact of inheritance on the distribution of lifetime resources (as measured by Davies) would increase since inheritances would no longer be "scaled down" and inequality of lifetime resources would, therefore, increase!

[25]Ownership and "property" are not restricted to material objects—you, the reader, now have this book in your possession but it may be owned by a library. M. E. Sharpe, Inc., owns the copyright to the book while I (Lars Osberg) own the right to receive royalties from its sale. Ownership rights in modern society are thus highly complex, but none of these rights has any value unless enforced by the state.

[26]See Macpherson (1978:10). Any social institution changes over time and property rights are no exception, as witness antipollution laws which increasingly restrict an individual's right to physically dispose of his or her assets.

[27]In 1980, T. B. Pickens (Mesa Petroleum) received $7,865,831, Clifton Garvin (Exxon) got $3,347,983, D. S. Lewis (General Dynamics) got $3,020,794, and G. T. Schaffenburger (City Investing) was paid $5,165,892. The average compensation of the chief executives of the 818 largest U.S. firms was $559,263 (*Forbes* magazine, August 6, 1981:114). Whether these salaries and bonuses are "too high" for the social function performed, whether the positions were unfairly obtained, and whether society is best served by "top-down" business decision making are serious questions but in the text we address only the issue of economic returns to pure ownership.

[28]Estates under $120,000 in the United States were not taxed (Harrison, 1979), even before the 1981 amendments to the Tax Act. By 1987 all estates under $600,000 will be exempt from estate tax.

[29]The small financial yield of estate duties is thus largely irrelevant to whether they should be imposed, just as a small number of heroin dealers convicted is a poor argument for heroin legalization.

[30]Even when siblings have unequal money incomes, parents who feel that these differences reflect equal psychic income or who feel their children had *equal chances* will tend to leave equal inheritances of property. If, for example, there were two children, A and B, and although A had better school marks at the age of 21 he became a college professor while B became a plastic surgeon, what is an "equalizing" parent to do? Does "equalization within the family" imply a greater bequest to A (since his money income as an adult is less than B's) or equal transfers to both (since both had equal opportunity and received equal years of education) or a greater bequest to B (since at the age of adulthood A had better "life chances")? The simplest solution is to divide evenly.

[31]Although in some countries underreporting of wealth appears significant (Harrison, 1979:1).

[32]If government bonds received as compensation can be left as inheritances, the problem of inherited wealth is not solved by nationalization, although it would probably become easier to collect estate taxes.

[33]Those who believe that markets are highly competitive and provide severe constraints on economic power and/or that economic power cannot be translated into political power obviously find such arguments unconvincing. See Chapter 3.

12 GROWTH AND/OR EQUALITY?

12.1 Introduction

The connection, if any, between economic growth and economic inequality has fascinated economists for generations. It is probably fair to say that most have agreed with Dalton (1935:21) that absolute economic equality would impede economic growth. However, as he notes, "The rejection of crude egalitarianism does not take us far, though there are some who seem to think that, when they have disposed of the argument for absolute equality, they have disposed also of all arguments for reducing existing inequalities." The more important question, since all societies are to some degree, by some definition, "unequal," is whether more unequal societies will grow more quickly or, to pose the issue somewhat differently, whether efforts to produce a more equal society will also produce lower rates of growth of average incomes. Several recent writers (e.g., Okun, 1975) have argued that society faces a "trade-off" between growth and equality—Taubman (1978:5), for example, puts the point unambiguously: "Policies to redistribute the economic pie as measured by market production also cause the pie to be reduced."

A major theme of Chapters 2 and 3 was, however, that what one means by "the economic pie" and how one measures the inequality of its division is not in general an unambiguously obvious issue. Even if one is considering only inequalities of economic outcome and not those of economic opportunity, it matters a good deal which variable one selects for examination (e.g., annual money income, annual "full" income, lifetime income, wealth, etc.) and how one measures its dispersion (e.g., Gini ratio, Theil index, etc.). "Growth" and "efficiency" are also terms which need to be defined carefully. Broad assertions that a trade-off exists between "equality" and "growth" may therefore reflect accurately a certain attitude of mind but they are difficult to evaluate dispassionately until the terms involved are carefully defined. More usually, they are very vaguely defined and the "trade-off" is asserted as virtually a self-evident proposition.

220

If there is, however, an unambiguous "trade-off" between "equality" and "growth" it should show up in comparative international statistics and the particular measures used should not matter much. Section 12.2 therefore presents some of the evidence which is available on comparative international trends—in which evidence one finds no support for the idea of an unambiguous "trade-off." Section 12.3 examines the theory which would predict that "equality" must be traded off against "growth"—theory which is in general much more ambiguous in its predictions than is commonly realized. Section 12.4 offers a summary and conclusion.

12.2 Inequality and Economic Development

Inequality in the United States may be greater than in most other developed nations but it is much less glaringly obvious than inequality within the less developed countries. American cities have few counterparts to the homeless families of Calcutta, who sleep on the streets only yards from the walled gardens of the wealthy, or to the shanty towns of Rio de Janeiro, within shouting distance of luxury apartments and villas. One of the most shocking aspects, to many Americans, of travel in the Third World is the contrast between the life-styles of the elite, who may live on a scale unknown in servantless North America, and the masses, whose poverty is hard to describe.

In the very poorest countries, however, the elite is only a tiny fraction of the population and, if the great majority of the rest of the population are more or less at a subsistence level of living, *their* incomes will be roughly equal. Hence statistical measures of inequality, such as the Gini index, will show a relatively low level of inequality. This is "equal hardship" for most, but, statistically, the smaller the elite, the smaller is its weight in the index of aggregate inequality. As growth occurs, however, some of the population climb above bare subsistence, while some remain behind. The *share* of the poorest in total income then tends to fall, even if their absolute income may not (see Ahluwalia 1976a). As development proceeds, a larger and larger fraction of the population becomes educated and urbanized, employed in the modern cash economy rather than working in subsistence peasant agriculture. If the economy can make the transition to developed status, the number of prosperous peasants and skilled urban workers may grow to the point where the income share of the poor starts to rise and inequality begins to fall.

Kuznets (1955) therefore hypothesized that the structural changes associated with development (chiefly industrialization, increased education, and urbanization) would produce first an increase, then a decrease in inequality as average incomes rose (i.e., a graph of inequality against average income would resemble an upside-down U). By this argument, Marx's prediction of the "immiserization of the proletariat" and an increase in inequality refers only to the initial stages of capitalist development; eventually we will have more equality *and* more growth.

Figure 12.1 is taken from Ahluwalia (1976b), who examined the relationship between average income and income shares for a sample of sixty-six countries. Ahluwalia examined as well the impact of an economy's structure on inequality. Socialist countries had considerably less inequality at all income levels, and higher education levels also produced a decrease in inequality—but heavier dependence on agriculture is associated with more inequality. Inequality thus depends, to some degree, on structural variables and political decisions. There is some mild support for the Kuznets hypothesis in Figure 12.1, but the share of the top 20% falls quite gently as incomes rise above $400 per capita and the share of the bottom 40% rises with equal slowness.

Although theoretical arguments can be mustered in support of the Kuznets hypothesis (see Robinson, 1976), Kuznets himself proposed it only as a historical generalization. As Fei, Ranis, and Kuo (1978) point out, income is the sum of returns to different factors; hence, income inequality is a weighted sum of inequality in factor returns. The impact of development on inequality depends on how the inequalities in the ownership of land, labor, and capital change relative to one another as well as on the changes in relative returns to each. The aggregate impact of development on income inequality is thus necessarily complex and depends on the specific trends in factor returns in each country. In some cases, such as Taiwan, increasing income equality has accompanied growth throughout the transition from a peasant agriculture, surplus labor economy to an industrializing one (see Kuo, Ranis, and Fei, 1981, and Loehr, 1980).

In his comprehensive study, Fields (1980) examined both the cross-sectional evidence which compares different countries at different levels of development and the time series evidence on the performance of the same countries over time. He found some support in cross-sectional evidence for the inverted-U hypothesis but comments, "The proportion of variation in inequality explained by income level is small, which suggests that the initial stage of rising inequality is avoidable" (1980:122). Examining individual countries over time produced a very mixed picture—some high-growth countries had low inequality and some high-growth countries had high inequality, while some others had low growth and low inequality.

There is, therefore, nothing inevitable about inequality's "having to get worse before it gets better." In a primarily agricultural economy (as most less-developed countries are), land ownership is the key to inequality among the rural population, i.e., among most of the population. Landless farm laborers and tenant farmers are the poorest of the poor while, especially in Latin America, great landowners may live in almost feudal splendor. Land reform and an emphasis on rural development can be key factors enabling growth with equality. As Johnston and Kilby put

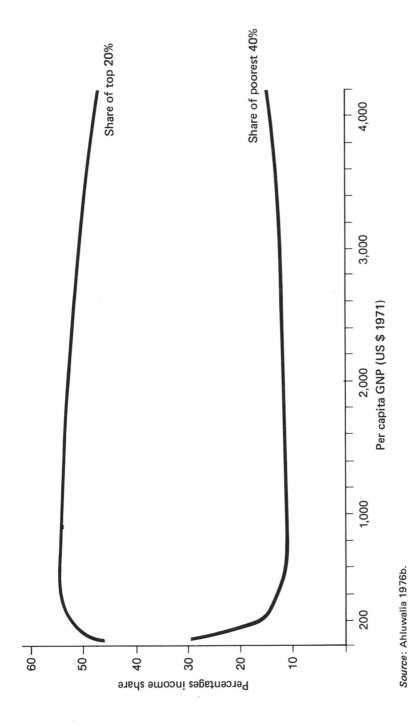

Source: Ahluwalia 1976b.

Figure 12.1 VARIATIONS IN INCOME SHARES

it, "There is now a general consensus that almost never does land reform decrease production; occasionally it has a neutral effect; most often it has a positive impact" (1975:162).

Land reform is, however, certain to affect the structure of consumer demand in less-developed countries. Where income is concentrated in a few hands, the bulk of the population will have little income available for anything but subsistence goods while the "elite" will have the income, and the inclination, to attempt to emulate the consumption patterns of North Americans and Europeans. Automobiles, stereos, and other luxury consumer goods are very unlikely to be domestically produced in most less-developed countries—the market for them is too small and the technology they embody is too complex. One implication of a highly unequal income distribution in a less-developed country is, therefore, a tendency toward a higher propensity to import.[1] By contrast, where land reform spreads income more evenly it may help to create a local mass market. Typically, the light consumer goods and simple producer goods demanded by peasants—the bicycles, tin roofs, textiles, and agricultural implements—are considerably less sophisticated technologically and can be domestically produced. Johnston and Kilby (1975) and Mellor (1966), therefore, argue that more egalitarian agricultural development strategies typically create more "backward linkages" between the agricultural and industrial sectors, so that as the agricultural sector expands industrial output also increases.

In addition, for many services such as medical care, an equivalent amount of resources provides considerably greater total benefits if it is more equally spread among the population (e.g., in rural dispensaries or public health programs) than if concentrated in a few high-cost locations (such as sophisticated urban hospitals). Less-developed countries face cruel choices. The opportunity cost of an operating room, which may save scores of lives a year, is the clean water one could provide to fifty villages, saving hundreds of lives a year. Even though governments may know that clean water offers greater total benefits it will be difficult to resist the demands of elite groups to provide them with quality health care. Economic inequality therefore affects the structure and effectiveness of development policies. Many (e.g., Chenery et al., 1976) argue that land reform, an emphasis on agricultural production, and egalitarian social policies are the most rapid path to economic development.

12.3 Equality and/or Growth?

Here, however, a myth has become entrenched in the body politic—namely, that governments have increasingly redistributed income toward the poor (see Chapter 13 for a discussion of the evidence). In the popular press this myth has often formed the basis for an "analysis"—that redistribution has gone "too far" and is the cause of current low growth rates. The argument has been made (e.g., by Gilder, 1981) that greater inequality is necessary for greater growth. Up to now, improvements in the standard of living of "middle America" have come with a constant share of a growing pie—do the poor and the middle class have to accept a smaller share if they want to have a growing pie?

As Cornwall (1977) has argued, until the 1970s economic growth meant that an expansion of public services (such as health care and old-age pensions) could be achieved at the same time as increases in individual incomes. Growth therefore enabled the preservation of social harmony, despite a commercialization of society which has undermined traditional social ties. As he puts it, "With a rapidly expanding output to be divided up, the traditional arguments for a redistribution of output of those with an anti-capitalist bent were blunted. The result was an implicit, if somewhat shaky, alliance not only between labor and management but also between various labor groups and different sectors of the economy. . . . However, a lack of economic growth introduces a zero sum game . . . given a declining sense of national solidarity or 'common shared experience'; increasing class, group, occupational and sectoral antagonisms can only be expected . . . (with) a higher risk of political instability" (1977:210).

Is there a trade-off between equality and growth?[2] Ahluwalia concludes his cross-sectional study of sixty-six countries by saying, "The cross-section evidence does not support the view that a high rate of economic growth has an adverse effect upon relative equality. Quite the contrary, the rate of growth of Gross Domestic Product (GDP) in our sample was positively related to the share of the lowest 40%, suggesting that the objectives of growth and equity may not be in conflict" (1976b:17). Of course, it might be objected that his study includes so many less-developed countries that the regression results are dominated by them. Hence, perhaps one ought not to generalize this conclusion to developed nations. Figure 12.2 therefore presents a plot of the inequality (as measured by the Gini index) within OECD nations (see Table 2.3) compared to their per capita growth rate. If there is a relationship, it is not nearly as obvious as the myths would have it. The country with fastest growth (Japan) has roughly average inequality, as does the country with slowest growth (the United Kingdom). The country with the greatest equality (Holland) has the third highest growth rate, but not that much higher than the most unequal nation (France).[3]

Although there is no obvious pattern to the relationship of growth and economic inequality among OECD nations as a whole, it might be objected that inequality within European nations should not be compared to that within the United States, since these nations are smaller in size and population and may be more homogenous. Their economic systems are also often quite different—France's high growth rates are, for example, the product of a highly centralized system of "dirigisme" or state plan-

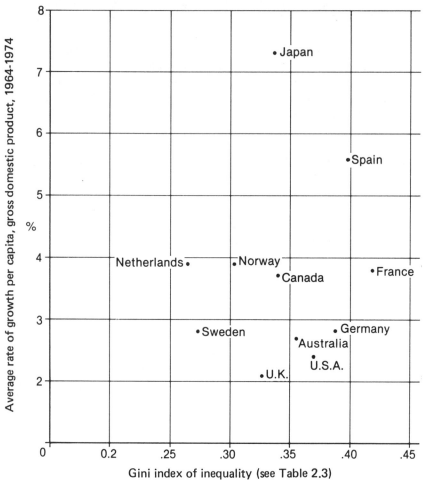

Figure 12.2 EQUALITY AND/OR GROWTH

ning, which is quite unlike U.S. economic management. It might therefore be objected that one should compare similar countries over a long period of time (to obviate differences in business cycle) and that productivity trends are as important as national income trends. In geographic size, in history, and in social institutions the country most similar to the United States is Canada. From Table 2.3, one can recall that Canada has an unambiguously more equal income distribution than the United States.[4] Canada has also had higher rates of growth in per capita income and in labor productivity—from 1960 to 1979 output per man hour in manufacturing grew by 2.6% per year in the United States and by 3.8% per year in Canada. National income per capita over the same period grew by 2.5% per year in the United States and 3.0% per year in Canada. In short, whether one examines global evidence, the data on developed countries, or just North America, international comparisons do not reveal any "trade-off" between economic growth and economic equality.

But, of course, one can turn the issue around and ask, Why would we expect more unequal societies to grow faster? The one-word answer is usually "incentives"—incentives to save and invest more, to work longer, and to be more entrepreneurial. Let us examine each in turn.

12.3.1 Incentives to Capital Ensuring an adequate supply of capital, it has been argued, is one reason for decreasing the tax burden on upper income groups. Low-income groups must consume almost all their income; hence the greater part of private savings comes from the top end of the income distribution. A larger share of income for them, it is argued, would increase savings, increase the incentive to invest, and thereby increase growth. Okun, for one, categorically rejects this argument as a fake—"the nation can have the level of saving and investment it wants with more or less redistribution, so long as it is willing to twist some other dials" (1975:99). Government budget surpluses and corporate retained earnings, as well as private savings, are the sources of domestic savings in the economy as a whole. *If* particular redistributive measures decrease total private saving, adjustments in other tax or spending measures may become necessary, but there need be no effect on long-term capital formation. *Even if* we restrict our attention to private savings, there is no reason to accept the proposition that more inequality is required to ensure more private savings. Tax policy is potentially a rather sophisticated instrument. At any given level of marginal tax rates its detailed provisions provide strong incentives for saving or for current consumption.

For example, when interest payments are deductible from taxable income (as in the United States), the net cost to a taxpayer of borrowing in order to finance current consumption is: $(1 - \text{marginal tax rate}) \times$ interest paid. Since gross interest paid normally includes an element which is the compensation for expected inflation, tax deductibility of interest can mean a *negative* effective rate of interest for borrowers, i.e., a government-financed subsidy to present consumption. For example, if nominal interest rates are 13% and inflation is 10%, the "real" return to the lender is $+3\%$. The borrower who is in a 50% tax bracket will, however, write off $(0.5 \times 13 =)$ 6.5% against taxes, leaving a nominal interest cost of 6.5%—which is 3.5% *below* the rate of inflation. When interest payments are not deductible (as in most other OECD nations) the borrower must pay the full cost of interest payments out of after-tax income. In the United States, the cost of borrowing for current consumption is therefore cushioned by the ability to write it off for taxes (a cushion which is greatest for upper income groups).[5]

In a country such as Canada there is a much stronger incentive to save before purchasing or to save in order to pay off debt (such as home mortgages). Over the five years 1976 to 1980, the personal savings of Canadian households averaged 10.2% of personal income while American households saved, on average, 5% of personal income.[6] Canada's distribution of income is more equal than that of the United States, but in Canada the "dials" of tax policy were set, in the 1970s, to encourage savings rather than current consumption.

12.3.2 Incentives for Effort Increased incentives for "effort" are also often advanced as a justification for decreased emphasis on equality. If income tax rates are high, is this not a disincentive to work more hours, hence a disincentive to expanded output? Shouldn't a decrease in income tax rates, especially for upper income groups, increase their supply of labor (and hence their output)? But might not things work the other way— might not a cut in income taxes mean that one can finance the same style of life with fewer hours of work and have more hours of leisure to enjoy? The effect of a change in income tax rates on labor supply is theoretically quite indeterminate, depending entirely on an individual's tastes.

Figure 12.3 illustrates the simplified case of a "flat-rate" income tax (a constant percentage of income) and compares two persons' ("Alan's" and "Bob's") supply of labor before and after a cut in income tax rates, on the assumption that they can freely vary their hours of work. Indifference curves, their personal trade-offs between income and leisure, are graphed as U_0 and U'.

The market work/home production/leisure framework has been presented in Chapter 8, section 8.2.5 and Figure 8.4, but, to recapitulate, prior to the income tax cut both "Alan" and "Bob" face the same after-tax wage rate, $w_1 = w(1 - t)$, and the same productivity in home production. Their consumption possibilities are therefore represented by the line *CBD*. Before the tax cut, each divides his day into $0a$ hours of leisure, ab hours of market work, and bc hours of home production. A cut in income tax, to $t_1 < t$, is equivalent to an increase in their after-tax wage rate $[= w (1 - t_1)]$ and is represented by an increase in consumption possibilities to *CB' D'*. After the income-tax cut, they each divide their day into $0a'$ hours of leisure, $a'b'$ hours of market work, and $b'c$ hours of home production. The question is, Will market work effort be greater or less after the tax cut? It depends entirely on the shape of individual indifference curves. Alan reacts to the cut in income tax rates by increasing his demand for leisure from $0a$ hours to $0a'$ hours and decreasing his market work effort ($a' b' < ab$). Even though the higher after-tax wage rate means it is more lucrative to "substitute" work for leisure at the margin, still his tastes are such that he prefers to take some of his potential higher income in the form of increased leisure (i.e., the income effect outweighs the substitution effect). Bob reacts differently and increases his market work effort ($ab < a'b'$)—the substitution effect dominates.

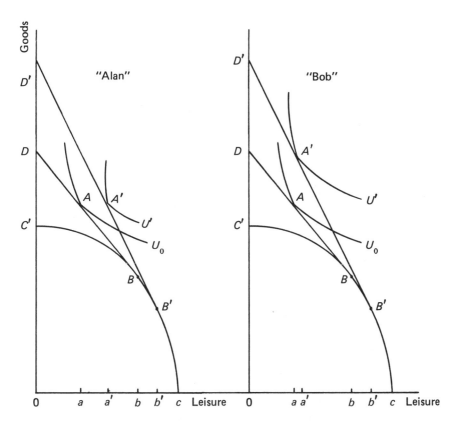

Figure 12.3 REACTION TO AN INCOME-TAX CUT

The crucial issue, of course, is which of these theoretical possibilities is more common in reality. Studies of highly paid professionals (who can vary their hours of work) and of samples of the population at large do not produce any evidence of substantial "disincentive" effects of high income-tax rates on working hours. A recent graduate text in labor economics (Addison and Siebert, 1979:87) cites, for example, six studies showing that income effects typically dominate substitution effects[7] (see also Break, 1974; Pechman, 1971:66). Thurow puts the point unequivocally, "High (income) taxes either do not affect work effort or might even increase work effort among executives and professionals. People work as hard or harder (after a tax increase) to restore their previous incomes or to obtain their income goals" (1975:49).

12.3.3 Incentives for Entrepreneurs The supply of entrepreneurial ability is an especially important aspect of the supply of labor, but one that is not as well understood by economists as it should be—perhaps because in a perfectly informed, perfectly competitive market there is really no room for entrepreneurship. Leff (1979) notes that the issue has "virtually disappeared from the literature" in recent years, although it had been prominent in the discussion of development economics. He argues that the supply of entrepreneurship in developing economies is not a serious constraint to development, although entrepreneurial activity has taken a wide variety of institutional forms, in both public and private ownership of industry.

Schumpeter, however, (1934:74–94) put the entrepreneur, the person who puts together *new* productive combinations, at the center of his theory of economic development. He argued, however, that the entrepreneur's motives could not be analyzed in terms of careful marginal calculations of benefit and cost. Rather, Schumpeter saw the entrepreneur's function as that of economic leadership and his motivation as the desire to found a private (economic) kingdom of power and independence, a will to conquer, and the joy of creating and getting things done. There are complex motivations, only tenuously linked to the careful labor/leisure choices pictured in Figure 12.3.[8] Break (1974:90), among others, has argued that it is the details of tax legislation, such as its treatment of capital gains in new small businesses, which may affect the supply of entrepreneurship, rather than the aggregate degree of progressivity in the tax schedule or the overall degree of posttax income inequality.

Consider, for example, an engineer who has the choice of continuing in secure paid employment or starting a small business to develop a new process, with some risk of bankruptcy attached but some hope of spectacular profits. Very conservative or very daring individuals will, of course, probably go their ways regardless of tax considerations but at least some potential entrepreneurs will look carefully at the after-tax difference in financial returns from the two alternatives. Such people will consider not only the nominal marginal tax rates of the income tax schedule but also the tax breaks, exemptions, and deductions for which they would be eligible *as self-employed entrepreneurs*. (They will consider also, in the United States, the fact that the absence of a national health insurance plan means that as self-employed individuals they will typically lose their medical insurance coverage.) An employed taxpayer whose income is in the form of salary has very little room for tax avoidance, but a self-employed individual has far more room for maneuver—the increased value of his or her company can, for example, be realized as capital gains, rather than paid as salary, and as such will be taxed at reduced rates.

Consider, then, the impact of a general increase in tax rates on upper-income groups on inequality and on the supply of entrepreneurship. Since most upper-income people are, and remain, paid employees, aggregate inequality will probably tend to decline. However, higher nominal taxes may widen the dollar differential between one's potential after-tax earnings as an employee and those as an entrepreneur—hence the supply of entrepreneurs may well increase![9] It is thus not necessarily true, in a world where effective tax rates depend partially on employment status, that more progressive income tax rates imply a decrease in entrepreneurial activity.

Entrepreneurial risk-taking is, therefore, especially influenced by the detailed provisions of tax legislation and may bear an ambiguous relationship to the overall progressivity of the tax structure. Even, however, were the income tax to be as free of loopholes as theory might assume, entrepreneurial risk-taking will not, in general, necessarily decline as the progressivity of the tax structure increases. Neither do inequality and risk-taking move unambiguously in the same direction. In general a change in tax progressivity will change both the level and the dispersion of returns to entrepreneurship, as more or less people decide to become entrepreneurs. The total number of entrepreneurs will depend on the distribution of abilities and of attitudes toward risk. The total effect of a tax change on inequality will depend on the changes both within and between groups. Kanbur (1982:17,19) sums up the issue by noting that "the *general equilibrium* feedbacks consequent upon a change in (tax) policy can destroy the simple links between risk-taking, inequality and public policy which have been postulated in the literature up to now. There is no such thing as a *general* policy conflict between the fostering of entrepreneurship and the reduction of inequality."

12.3.4 The Institutionalist Viewpoint Institutionalists, however, have no sympathy for the view that existing incomes are based on the rational decisions of well-informed individuals operating in perfectly competitive markets with equal opportunity. Rather, they see a world of unequal opportunity and highly imperfect markets, and therefore a world where there is nothing "optimal" about the existing income distribution, in either equity or efficiency terms. If many people now work in jobs that use only a fraction of their abilities, improved access to training and education will aid both growth and equality. If a substantial "underclass" is trapped in the secondary labor market, accelerated growth is necessary to draw them into primary labor market jobs and start them in the process of on-the-job training which produces future productivity growth—and greater income equality. In this view, economic inequality represents, at least partially, wasted economic potential—increases in the "earnings capacity" of low-income people and the "good jobs" capacity of the economy can give us both more growth and more equality.

12.4 Summary

(1) Comparison of countries at different levels of development indicates a weak tendency for inequality first to increase, then to decrease, with higher levels of average income. Countries with incomes above $400

(1971) per capita tend to have somewhat less inequality. However, examination of individual countries over time reveals no clear tendency—high-growth and low-growth countries have both high and low inequality.

(2) There is no good international evidence to support the view that there is a general "trade-off" between growth and equality. International comparisons do not reveal any tendency for high-growth countries to be more unequal. Most of the OECD nations are more economically equal than the United States and are also growing faster than the United States.

(3) Economic theory, either neoclassical or neo-institutional, offers no unambiguous prediction as to whether inequality and growth will be positively or negatively correlated.

(4) The tax system can be a powerful mechanism for reducing inequality, and it has the potential to be a very sophisticated instrument. For example, eliminating the tax deductibility of interest payments would strongly encourage savings, would increase posttax equality, and would also reduce the government deficit. The encouragement or discouragement of specific activities such as savings or entrepreneurship is compatible with different degrees of overall tax progressivity or regressivity. There is no necessary conflict between the objectives of equality and encouraging savings or entrepreneurial behavior.

(5) Economic growth may therefore be necessary if the current degree of economic inequality is to be tolerated, but there is little evidence that such a degree of economic inequality is necessary for economic growth.

NOTES

[1]Import controls may protect local luxury goods producers, such as the Indian automobile industry, but this has the considerable cost of creating an uncompetitive industrial sector.

[2]As Okun says, "Tradeoffs are the central study of the economist" (1975:1)—perhaps so central that economists may see tradeoffs even where none exist.

[3]From Chapter 2 one will recall that several aggregative measures of inequality exist, which may rank inequality differently. Indeed, Roberti (1974) has examined the details of movements in income shares in OECD nations and cautioned against the use of any single summary statistic. Growth in GDP per capita is also less than satisfactory since it may reflect such good fortune as favorable movements in international terms of trade or the finding of North Sea oil. The rate of growth in total factor productivity is what one would really like to relate to inequality, but its measurement is at least as controversial as that of inequality. Figure 12.2 is meant merely to indicate the lack of a simple partial relation between growth and inequality.

[4]Chiswick (1974) comments that the Canadian income distribution is no more equal than the U.S. if one omits the South from calculations of U.S. inequality, since the South has a lower average income and greater inequality than other regions of the United States. However, Canada is no more homogeneous regionally than the United States and dropping the Maritime region (which has lower mean and greater variance in incomes) would similarily "improve" the Canadian inequality figures. Canadian inequality figures would (for the same reason) look still better if one also excluded French-speaking Quebec, on the grounds that it forms a distinctive society with little geographic mobility to other Canadian regions.

⁵The revenue loss to the U.S. Treasury of the deductibility of mortgage and consumer interest has been estimated at $35.12 billion in 1983 (Aaron et al., 1982:266). Okner (1966:46) estimated that over half the total revenue loss accrued to the top 22.4% of income-tax filers.

⁶Note that these are substantial changes from the 1966-1970 period when U.S. savings rates averaged 6.8% and Canadian savings rates averaged 5.9%. Two trends were at work in Canada: (1) an early 1970s package of revisions to the Income Tax Act (1971)—which among other things introduced capital gains taxation; increases in unemployment insurance coverage and benefits (1971); extensions of old-age security (1972) and increased family allowance (1973); and, conversely, (2) the gradual tightening up of social programs (e.g., Unemployment Insurance) in the later 1970s. Dodge (1975) estimated the original changes to be substantially and unambiguously redistributive from rich to poor, while Gillespie (1980:31) has calculated, "For the 1970-1977 period federal budgets have not substantially altered the economic position of lowest income relative to highest income families." The chief point is that a substantial *increase* in savings rates was *not* based on a redistribution of income from poor to rich.

In general, marginal tax rates on Canadian incomes are higher than those on U.S. incomes (depending somewhat on income level, state/province of residence, and family status) but Canadian tax law provides a number of tax shelters for savings (such as Registered Home Ownership Savings Plans) which also encourage personal savings.

⁷In life-cycle labor supply models with perfect foresight (e.g., Smith, 1978), lifetime income is known from the start and only substitution effects, between work at different ages, exist. This literature is not relevant to the issue of tax changes, which do affect net after-tax lifetime income.

⁸Schumpeter's analysis has been recently resurrected by Gilder (1981)—but Gilder replaces Schumpeter's dispassionate analysis of the strains engendered by capitalist growth with an exhortation to "have faith."

⁹Suppose that Y_s represents gross expected future income as a salaried employee and Y_e represents gross expected income as a self-employed entrepreneur ($Y_e > Y_s$). An individual who recognizes the greater risk attached to being self-employed might well require a net advantage of X dollars in order to "take the plunge" and become an entrepreneur.

If we represent nominal tax rates on Y_s and Y_e as t_1 and t_2, respectively ($t_1 < t_2$), and the fact that self-employed individuals can tax plan so as to pay only $X\%$ of the taxes of employed individuals (i.e., no loopholes at all implies $X = 1$; in general, $X < 1$), then the net returns of the two alternatives are:

(1) net income salaried = $(1 - t_1) Y_s$

(2) net income self-employed = $(1 - X t_2) Y_e$; the differential (D) is $(1 - X t_2) Y_e - (1 - t_1) Y_s$.

We assume that if $D > \overline{D}$, the individual becomes an entrepreneur.

Let us assume that tax rates are raised to some multiple, t, of current rates ($t > 1$). The tax schedule is therefore becoming more progressive, and the new differential is $D = (1 - X tt_2) Y_e - (1 - tt_1) Y_s$.

To see the impact of increasing tax rates, evaluate

$$\frac{\partial D}{\partial t}$$

This will be positive, implying that increasing nominal tax rates increases the incentive to become an entrepreneur, if $X < t_1 Y_s/t_2 Y_e$. Of course, since X is also a policy parameter of government, it is always possible to ensure that this is true; whether it is desirable depends on one's judgments on horizontal tax equity versus the encouragement of entrepreneurship.

13 GOVERNMENT AND INEQUALITY

13.1 Introduction

Some of the roles played by government in influencing economic inequality have already been alluded to. The state plays a major role in financing the education whose attainment is a major element of earnings determination (see Chapters 6 through 9); it safeguards the property rights which distribute income from property (Chapters 5 and 11), and its redistributive policies have been blamed, unfairly, for slow growth (Chapter 12)—to name only a few of its impacts on economic inequality. In Chapter 9 we also noted that opinions may differ as to what kind of action to expect from government. In this chapter we do not attempt to outline a political theory of what actions governments will take on the issue of economic inequality. Rather, we consider only the impacts of the actions they have taken (13.2 and 13.3) and a few of the actions they could take (13.4).

The analysis of government's impact on economic inequality in the United States is greatly complicated by the speed with which it is currently changing. From the mid 1960s until 1980 changes in governmental distribution policy came relatively slowly, within a broadly accepted legislative consensus. The inauguration of the Reagan Administration has, however, produced dramatic changes in tax and expenditure incidence. At the time of writing (spring 1982) only a limited number of studies of the impacts of the 1981 legislative changes are available and it is unclear how much of the proposed 1982 budget will survive in its current form. Section 13.2 therefore concentrates on the tax and expenditure incidence of government prior to 1980, while section 13.3 presents some preliminary evidence on the impacts of the 1981 revisions. Section 13.4 considers two policies, manpower training and incomes policies, whose aim is greater equality of wages, as well as two which are more directly redistributive—the negative income tax and taxable family allowances. Section 13.5 is a summary and conclusion.

234

13.2 The Pre-1980 Distributional Incidence of Government

The most visible tax is probably the personal income tax, and such government expenditures as Social Security or welfare likewise attract widespread attention. Thus there is a widespread perception that government in the United States broadly acts to equalize the distribution of income. On the other hand, sales taxes and fees such as motor vehicle licenses are expenses which comprise a larger fraction of the incomes of the poor than of the rich while the progressivity of the income tax is eroded by loopholes such as the deductibility of interest expenses and the favorable treatment of capital gains. Government expenditures also include subsidies to sectors such as air travel, higher education, and the performing arts, which tend to be more than proportionately consumed by higher income groups, as well as expenses such as defense or police protection whose benefits are difficult to allocate.

Who gains the most on balance? It is unreasonable to examine only a few tax and expenditure programs in isolation and unrealistic to consider only the federal government, and not state or local governments as well. A reasonable answer must add up the direct receipts of transfer payments and the value of services and subsidies received from all levels of government. One should then subtract the cost of taxes paid to the various levels of government to get an estimate of net benefits received. A host of calculations is involved and prior to the development of computer technology it was basically impossible to keep track of them all—Okner's (1966) study was one of the first to use data on individual tax returns to compute the income distributional incidence of federal tax provisions.

The basic method of this and subsequent studies has been to express both total taxes paid and expenditures received by an individual household (i.e., total net benefits) as a fraction of the original income from factor payments of that household (wages, salaries, dividends, rents, etc.), in order to get an estimate of the net fiscal incidence of government. This can be expressed as in the formulas of equation (13.1).

(13.1)
$$E_i = B_i + R_i$$
$$\text{Net Benefits}_i = E_i - T_i$$
$$\text{Net Fiscal Incidence}_i = (E_i - T_i)/Y_i$$

where B_i = cost of government services or subsidies received by households in incomes group i

R_i = transfer payments received by households in income group i

T_i = taxes paid by households in income group i

E_i = government expenditures benefiting households in income group i

Y_i = average private factor income of income group i

Table 13.1, in the lines numbered 7 and 7a, presents Ruggles and O'Higgins's (1981) estimates of the total net benefits received by the various deciles of the U.S. income distribution in 1970 and the net fiscal incidence of government on the income distribution. One must caution, of course, that these figures represent net redistribution at a single point in time and *not* the redistribution that would occur over time between different individuals. Over the life cycle, an individual would typically draw net benefits in some periods and pay net taxes in others. While young, most people would typically receive net benefits largely in the form of government expenditure on education. Then would follow a period in which they were working and paying income taxes and Social Security premiums, followed by a period of retirement and receipt of Social Security, Medicare, etc. Some government-run "social insurance" programs redistribute income between different periods of the same person's life, while other programs redistribute income between individuals of the same generation and still others redistribute income between different generations. Indeed, different aspects of the same program may have all three effects—a case in point being the Social Security system.

The Social Security system is in part a social insurance program in which individuals draw benefits based on past contributions (thereby transferring income from one period to another period of the same person's life), and it is in part a system of redistribution since some features, such as the minimum benefit, are of special benefit to low-income individuals. In addition, it is financed on a pay-as-you-go basis, so that those who are now working pay the benefits of those who are now retired. Looking at a single year's data, Social Security will appear quite redistributive (from rich to poor) since those who are now working and paying premiums have higher incomes than those who are now retired and drawing pensions. In a lifetime sense, however, the redistributive element should be seen as only that part of benefits which differs from the annuity which could have been purchased with the premiums which retirees have paid in the past. Burkhauser and Warlick (1981) have recently computed the annuity component and the redistributive component of Social Security payments in 1972 and have compared the "actuarily fair" Old Age and Survivors' Insurance (OASI) pension, based on past contributions, with that actually received, by preretirement income class. They found that 27% of benefits, in aggregate, represented the annuity value of contributions; i.e., 73% of reported benefits represented intergenerational transfers. These very large intergenerational transfers were distributed in roughly constant dollar amounts, among all the various preretirement income classes. Social Security was thus a redistributive program, but the *intergenerational* transfers involved dwarfed the *intragenerational* transfers. Current Social Security recipients are thus receiving transfers, but primarily from the currently working generation and not from the members of their own generation. In the future, as Burkhauser and Warlick

Table 13.1

Net Benefits by Decile of Original Income: U.S. Summary Figures, 1970

	All Categories	Lowest Decile	2nd Decile	3rd Decile	4th Decile	5th Decile	6th Decile	7th Decile	8th Decile	9th Decile	Highest Decile
Number of households (Percentage)	69,240 (100.0)	7,030 (10.2)	6,879 (9.9)	7,090 (10.2)	6,920 (10.0)	7,020 (10.1)	6,930 (10.0)	6,780 (9.8)	6,920 (10.0)	6,790 (9.8)	6,900 (10.0)
Mean original income (in dollars per year)	9,685	1,018	2,385	3,930	5,693	7,429	9,228	11,030	13,142	16,244	27,288
1. Local taxes	2,099 (21.7)	614 (60.3)	867 (36.4)	1,225 (31.2)	1,546 (27.2)	1,809 (24.4)	2,163 (23.4)	2,402 (21.8)	2,772 (21.1)	3,230 (19.9)	4,446 (16.3)
2. Federal taxes	3,254 (33.6)	765 (75.2)	951 (39.9)	1,321 (33.6)	1,864 (32.7)	2,455 (33.0)	3,150 (34.1)	3,708 (33.6)	4,457 (33.9)	5,489 (33.8)	8,518 (31.2)
3. Local expenditures	2,515	2,344	1,700	2,365	2,158	2,199	2,608	2,563	2,859	3,089	3,161
4. Federal expenditures (population basis)	2,917	1,451	2,636	3,250	3,217	3,014	2,985	3,010	3,135	3,093	3,402
4a. Federal expenditures (income basis)	2,917	688	1,978	2,521	2,572	2,530	2,623	2,967	3,456	3,875	6,300
5. Local net benefits	416 (4.3)	1,730 (169.9)	833 (34.9)	1,140 (29.0)	612 (10.8)	390 (5.2)	445 (4.8)	161 (1.5)	87 (0.7)	-141 (-0.8)	-1,285 (-4.7)
6. Federal net benefits (population basis)	-333 (-3.4)	685 (67.3)	1,685 (70.6)	1,928 (49.1)	1,352 (23.7)	599 (7.2)	-165 (-1.8)	-698 (-6.3)	-1,322 (10.1)	-2,396 (14.8)	-5,115 (-18.7)
6a. Federal net benefits (income basis)	-333 (-3.4)	-77 (-7.5)	1,027 (43.1)	1,200 (30.5)	708 (12.5)	75 (1)	-527 (-5.7)	-741 (-6.7)	-1,001 (-7.6)	-1,974 (-12.1)	-2,218 (-8.1)
7. Total net benefits (population basis)	83 (0.9)	2,415 (237.2)	2,518 (105.6)	3,068 (78.1)	1,964 (34.5)	949 (12.8)	280 (3.0)	-537 (-4.9)	-1,235 (-9.4)	-2,537 (-15.6)	-6,400 (-23.5)
7a. Total net benefits (income basis)	55 (0.9)	1,653 (16.2)	1,860 (77.9)	3,140 (79.8)	1,320 (23.1)	465 (6.3)	-82 (-0.8)	-580 (-5.3)	-914 (-6.9)	-2,115 (-13.0)	-3,503 (-12.8)

Source: Ruggles and O'Higgins (1981).

Note: For entries with two figures, top figure is mean tax or expenditure benefit in dollars per year. Figure in parentheses is mean tax or benefit as a percentage of mean income. For example, in row 5, column 4, $1,140 is mean local net benefit and (29.0) is $1,140 as a percentage of mean income. Percentages may fail to add to indicated sums due to rounding error.

(1981:414) put it, "Those who, in a lifetime sense, have received less than fair returns through OASI will be counted as positive recipients of government transfers in old age."

The same problems of simultaneous interperiod, intergenerational, and intragenerational transfers are present in a great many activities of governments, from education to basic research to highway construction. The current state of the art allows us, however, only to estimate the redistribution of resources at a given point in time. One must be aware that these estimates will in general substantially overestimate *lifetime* redistribution between individuals.

The lines numbered 1 and 2 of Table 13.1 indicate that the tax system did not take a higher overall share of the income of upper-income tax payers than of lower-income groups. Local taxes in fact were somewhat regressive (i.e., as income increased they declined as a percentage of income) since state and local governments depend so heavily on sales and property taxes. If the residential property tax is seen as a tax on shelter, this shelter expense will be a larger fraction of the budget of the relatively poor. Sales taxes on personal consumption likewise bear more heavily on those who consume all their income. On the other hand, some tax sources, such as the federal corporate income tax, may be partially shifted forward to consumers (in the form of higher prices), or partially shifted back onto employees (in the form of lower wages) and only a remainder will be borne by shareholders (in decreased dividends). One can debate the proportions of such taxes which are shifted but some (e.g., Gillespie, 1980) argue that alternative reasonable assumptions on corporate tax shifting make relatively little empirical difference to these sorts of estimates. However, payroll taxes with a taxable ceiling (such as Social Security) definitely comprise a higher fraction of low incomes than of high incomes. The mix of such regressive taxes with the income tax, which has progressive tax rates but numerous regressive deduction provisions, produces a federal tax structure that, in 1970, was in aggregate roughly proportional over the top 80% of households.

Government expenditures on education, public assistance, or hospitals can be allocated to families on such bases as the number of school-age children, the presence of public assistance receipts, or the number of hospitalizations per household, since these services and transfers are consumed by particular, identifiable households. Especially for the poor deciles of the population who are often retirees, most allocable expenditures are Social Security payments—for the poorest 20% of households, 79% of allocable federal expenditure is Social Security. One may not be able to estimate very precisely the public benefit involved of some services, but at least one knows the costs involved and there is a reasonable basis for allocating these expenses among households. Expenditures such as those on highways or air traffic control are more debatable, since they benefit a number of classes of consumer and one must assume some division of the costs involved. Table 13.1 embodies, for example, the assumption that two-thirds of the costs of roads and highways ought to be assigned to automobile owners and one-third to consumers in general, since all consumers benefit from the truck transportation network.

Some government expenditures, such as national defense, police protection, and general government administration are almost pure "public goods"—i.e., if there is a benefit, it is for everyone in general and no one in particular. It makes a considerable difference to one's perception of government's impact on income distribution how one assigns these expenditures to households. If one assumes that these costs should be equally assigned to all citizens (line 4 of Table 13.1), then the value of, for example, defense services received by the poorest decile will be quite a high fraction of their original income. The net benefits (line 7) of government to the poor will then appear quite high and government will appear to be fairly redistributive. On the other hand, if one adopts a "willingness-to-pay" criterion for the supply of public goods, government will appear less redistributive. High-income households, with a lower marginal utility of income, will be willing to spend more for pure public goods (Aaron and McGuire, 1970); hence one should assign these expenditures on the basis of income (line 4a), implying a lower net cost of government to high-income groups (line 7a) and a much lower redistributive impact.

One must note that these sorts of fiscal incidence studies are calculated on the assumption that private incomes remain unchanged. Kuznets (1966:197) is among those who have argued that expected redistribution by government may alter pretax payments to individuals. Massive alterations to government's tax or expenditure role would also be likely to set off chain reactions of impacts on the private sector, whose net distributional impact, both on private incomes and government activity, is difficult to foresee. Until general equilibrium models of fiscal incidence acquire much more detail than they presently have, we will have to be content with a "first-round" computation of benefits and costs such as that of Table 13.1. These calculations do, however, indicate:

(a) that the aggregate federal tax system was proportional rather than progressive in 1970;

(b) that there was a net redistribution of resources from rich to poor in 1970;

(c) that the estimated size of net redistribution by government depends in a crucial way on how one assigns the benefits of pure public goods.

During the 1970s the growth of government expenditures was accompanied by a shift of government priorities. The share of the federal budget which was devoted to defense fell from 40% to 30% and total public expenditure on income maintenance, health education, and welfare rose from 14.9% of GNP to 18.9% of GNP.[1] Over this period it would be reasonable to think that the net incidence of government became somewhat more egalitarian.[2] However, as Danziger and Haveman (1981) point out, this was also a period in which the distribution of market income was becoming more unequal, so the effect of increased government transfers was not to produce a more equal distribution of income; rather, it was to arrest a trend to increasing inequality. Nevertheless, it is undeniable that the expanded benefits and increased coverage of programs such as Medicare and food stamps brought great benefits to many poor and near-poor families. A steadily decreasing number of people had incomes below the Social Security poverty line, indicating that absolute poverty declined even if relative poverty did not (see Chapter 4). However, this decline in absolute poverty can be attributed entirely to increased government transfers (see Gottschalk, 1981). The calculations of Danziger and Haveman (1981) indicate that from 1970 to 1978 the fraction of the population that was poor (by the Social Security definition) if only market income is counted actually increased from 18.8% to 20.2%, but the fraction defined as poor after receiving government cash transfers fell from 12.6% to 11.4%.

If one counts the cash value of in-kind transfers (as in subsidized housing) and *if* one uses an absolute standard of poverty, such as the Social Security definition, government transfers pushed the incidence of poverty even lower—some estimates are in the 4% to 6% range (see Danziger, Haveman, and Plotnick, 1981:1009). However, as argued in Chapter 4, if poverty is a relative concept these estimates will vastly understate its extent—it is more useful to look at the impact of transfers on inequality and the income share of the poorest quintile. Here, again, government transfers have had an effect. Comparing the pretransfer and posttransfer income distribution, Danziger, Haveman, and Plotnick (1981) report that transfers produced a 19% decline in the Gini coefficient of the U.S. income distribution and comprised most of the total income of the bottom quintile. Income inequality and poverty, both "relative" and "absolute," would have been very substantially greater in 1980 if government transfer programs had not been in effect.

13.3 The 1981 Legislative Changes—General Distributional Impact

As Tobin (1981:13) has noted

Wealth breeds wealth and poverty breeds poverty. Despite legendary examples of spectacular social mobility, the unequal outcomes of one generation are generally the unequal opportunities of the next. Here, as in other democracies, governments have sought to arrest the momentum of inequality by free public education, social insurance, "war on poverty" measures, and progressive taxation.

The US budget and tax legislation of 1981 is a historic reversal of direction and purpose.

The wisdom of the simultaneous massive shift to defense expenditure and of the combination of substantial budgetary deficits and tight money will be debated for decades. Here, however, we consider only the preliminary evidence on the distributional impact on individual households of the tax and expenditure changes implemented in 1981, relative to a "base case" of the continuation of previous legislation (Table 13.2).

Since the incidence of the corporate tax is so open to controversy, the changes referred to in Table 13.2 do not reflect the many changes in the corporate tax law which could be expected to largely eliminate the corporate income tax as a major source of revenue. The figures do, however, reflect the decrease in tax rates spread over 1981 to 1984, the indexing of income-tax brackets from 1985 on, and the introduction of a special married deduction for two-earner families. These tax changes will substantially erode the progressivity of the federal income tax since they are all of greater financial value to higher-income groups. In addition, since income which can be classified as long-term capital gains will now face a maximum tax rate of 20% (the 40% of long-term gains subject to tax times the new maximum 50% marginal tax rate) one can expect that there will be a steady movement toward schemes of payment which so classify income. Upper-income groups who receive mostly property income thus receive especially large tax gains from the 1981 amendments—gains which are now easier to pass on to one's heirs due to the virtual elimination of estate and gift taxes.[3]

On the other hand, the reductions in benefits which were enacted in 1981 are concentrated among lower-income households. The largest part of the decreases in cash benefits were the cuts in Social Security, food stamps, and unemployment insurance, but in addition the cuts in Aid to Families with Dependent Children (AFDC) were of special importance for the very poorest households. In aggregate the U.S. Congressional Budget Office (1982a:15) estimated that two-thirds of total cash savings (i.e., $6 billion out of $9 billion) came from reductions affecting households with under $20,000 in income. In addition, cutbacks in in-kind benefit programs (school lunches, Medicaid, Medicare, etc.) were estimated to total $3.95 billion in 1982, of which 60% was absorbed by families with incomes under $20,000.

Altogether, a wide variety of changes were made in at least eighteen different programs which involve cash or in-kind benefits to individuals. They ranged from eligibility restrictions and reduced subsidies for subsidized school lunches to increased copayment by Medicare recipients to a restriction of eligibility to benefits for compensation from black lung disease. The average loss of benefits per household presented in Table 13.2 is, therefore, a bit misleading in that some people will lose benefits

Table 13.2

Net Change in Taxes and Benefits per Household by Income Category: Calendar Years 1982-1985
(in current dollars)

	All House-holds	Household Income (in 1982 dollars)				
		Less Than $10,000	$10,000-20,000	$20,000-40,000	$40,000-80,000	$80,000 and over
Percent of Households		22.5%	24.8%	35.2%	16.3%	1.2%
1982						
Cash benefits	−110	−210	−100	−70	−60	−110
Taxes	450	70	220	450	750	8,430
Net	340	−140	120	380	690	8,320
In-kind benefits	−50	−60	−60	−40	−40	−40
Net, including in-kind benefits	290	−200	60	340	650	8,280
1983						
Cash benefits	−140	−270	−140	−90	−70	−70
Taxes	940	120	440	950	1,830	15,250
Net	800	−150	300	860	1,760	15,180
In-kind benefit	−60	−90	−80	−50	−60	−50
Net, including in-kind benefits	740	−240	220	810	1,700	15,130
1984						
Cash benefits	−130	−290	−130	−70	−50	−70
Taxes	1,280	170	590	1,280	2,520	19,350
Net	1,150	−120	460	1,210	2,470	19,280
In-kind benefits	−70	−100	−90	−50	−70	−50
Net, including in-kind benefits	1,080	−220	370	1,160	2,400	19,230
1985						
Cash benefits	−120	−290	−110	−50	−40	−50
Taxes	1,600	250	760	1,650	3,100	21,950
Net	1,480	−40	650	1,600	3,060	21,900
In-kind benefits	−80	−100	−90	−60	−70	−40
Net, including in-kind benefits	1,400	−140	560	1,540	2,990	21,860

Source: U.S., Congressional Budget Office (1982a).

from a number of programs while others may lose little or nothing.[4] Still, the cuts in AFDC and food stamps are of special importance to many poor people and, although the existence of some cuts is generally known, the size of the cuts and of the disincentives to work they have created is not generally recognized.

Table 13.3 therefore presents a comparison of the benefit entitlement, under the pre-1981 law and under the 1981 enactments, of a single-parent family with three children (including one preschooler) for the food stamp and AFDC programs. The three examples chosen are from Texas, Oklahoma, and California since these states are broadly representative of states with low, average, and high payments under the AFDC program.[5] Since the receipt of food stamps means that one can spend on other things the money one would have had to spend on food, food stamps are treated here as broadly equivalent to cash. Columns (4) and (7) therefore present the total value of food stamps and AFDC payments for which this family would have been eligible, in January 1982, under the pre-1981 and the post-1981 regulations.

The first thing to notice about the numbers in Table 13.3 is that they were very low in most states, even under the pre-1981 law, and were made lower by the 1981 enactments. (And it is worth noting that, since the states did not raise AFDC grants in line with inflation during the 1970s, the real purchasing power of average AFDC benefits for a family of four had already fallen by 28% from 1972 to 1981—Aaron et al., 1982:10). In the abstract, as numbers on a page, they are much like any other set of numbers. It is only when one computes a monthly budget and adds up the costs of rent,[6] groceries, utilities, and clothing that these budget totals acquire real significance. For most readers, this will be an academic exercise, but for the roughly 11 million people in receipt of AFDC benefits[7] it is everyday reality.

The second thing to notice is the always-positive work incentive built into the prior law. Since AFDC recipients were allowed to disregard $30 plus 30% of any earnings in computing benefits under AFDC, payments were not cut dollar for dollar and net income, in every state, always increased as work effort increased. Personal capabilities, child care responsibilities, and the availability of jobs will, of course, always limit the amount one can expect AFDC parents to earn and, indeed, only about 13% of AFDC households, at any given time, have adult members who are employed. The AFDC system has been greatly criticized but it does seem clear that the incentive structure of a welfare system should reward, not discourage, greater work effort and longer job tenure. Given the child care responsibilities for preschoolers of many AFDC single parents, it may not be realistic always to expect them to carry full-time jobs, but incentives to retain part-time jobs not only lessen their dependence on government; they also keep job skills from getting rusty and make it much easier to make an eventual transition to full-time employment.

Table 13.3
Work Incentives and
The Impact of Social Welfare Legislation
(Family of 4, Selected States, 1982 Benefits)

	(1) Hours Worked per Month	(2) Monthly Earnings @ $5 hr.	(3) Child Care Costs	Prior Law			1981 Enactments		
				(4) AFDC + Food Stamps*	(5) Net Income (2) − (3) + (4)	(6) Implied Hourly Wage 5 ÷ (1)	(7) AFDC + Food Stamps*	(8) Net Income (2) − (3) + (7)	(9) Implied Net Hourly Wage (8) ÷ (1)
Texas	0	0	0	383	383	—	351	351	—
	40	200	100	343	443	$1.50	223	323	negative
	80	400	100	207	507	$1.60	175	475	$3.80
	120	600	100	159	659	$3.80	126	626	$3.77
Oklahoma	0	0	0	529	529	—	495	495	—
	40	200	100	490	590	$1.52	373	473	negative
	80	400	100	348	648	$1.45	190	490	negative
	120	600	100	207	707	$1.47	126	626	$1.09
California	0	0	0	705	705	—	669	669	—
	40	200	100	666	766	$1.52	547	647	negative
	80	400	100	524	824	$1.45	364	664	negative
	120	600	100	383	883	$1.48	201	701	$ .26

*After 4 months' employment.

Part of the 1981 package of amendments was, however, the limitation of the earnings disregard for AFDC to the first four months of employment. In addition, changes included basing earnings disregard on net rather than gross earnings, allowing food stamps to count as income in computing AFDC, and decreasing the earnings disregard (from 20% to 18%) in the computation of food stamp benefits. Each of these changes, by itself, is small, almost petty, but the cumulative impact is not. If one supposes that the adult in the example family has the option of working at an hourly wage of $5, column (7) shows what AFDC and food stamp benefits will be, after four months of employment. For most states, the cuts in payments exceed increases in earnings up to an earnings level of about $400 per month—i.e., one is now worse off the harder one works. For Oklahoma and California one's total income increases, if one works over 120 hours per month, but the implied net hourly wage (column 9) is very small indeed.

The third point of Table 13.3 is, therefore, that the cumulative impact of many small and unrelated changes in welfare rules can be not only that benefits are reduced but also that work incentives are decreased. Presumably, the intent was to restrict benefits to the "truly needy" and to encourage work and reintegration into the paid labor force, but the effect is to discourage people from taking jobs, and especially longer-term jobs. Work disincentives are also created, in twenty states, by the fact that people whose earnings are high enough to disqualify them for AFDC also lose their eligibility for Medicaid, the ceiling for which has just been lowered.[8] A responsible parent who considers the chances that his or her children will need medical care in the future will think carefully before surrendering such access. In addition, when unemployment is high and jobs are uncertain one must weigh the chances that a job which is now available may not last—in which case it may be difficult and time-consuming to establish reentitlement to benefits.

The particular point of all this is that the 1981 amendments hurt those who cannot help themselves and discourage those who can. The general point is that a patchwork quilt of social legislation, as in the United States, will have a host of social implications, many of them bad. It is, however, an interrelated system. The "stacking" of programs means that a decrease in benefits due to increased earned income may occur in a number of programs at the same time, producing very high *cumulative* decreases in benefits. Changes in eligibility for one program (e.g., unemployment insurance) may well put people in a situation where they have to resort to another program (e.g., welfare). Eligibility changes and benefit changes ought, therefore, to be considered both in their cumulative effect on work incentives and in their impacts on the case load of other programs. As a result, ill-considered, piecemeal "reform" efforts can easily make things worse, rather than better.

The 1983 budget carried the process even further. Aaron et al.

(1982:150) have argued that it "must be viewed as the boldest and most controversial attempt in fifty years to roll back the place of the federal government as a guarantor of equal opportunity and provider of social services." Funding for food stamps and other income-tested nutrition programs was to be cut by 32%, aid to families with dependent children by 27%, and energy assistance to low-income families by 39% (1982:108). Changes in the definition of family needs and available family income account for most of the savings in the AFDC program. Similar "technical" changes are relied on to spending under the food stamps program but with differing impacts. Turning federal nutrition assistance programs into (reduced) block grants will affect particularly the most disadvantaged, the very young and the very old. Increases in the benefit reduction rate (the "tax" on earnings) will affect primarily the working poor, who will also lose out as CETA (Comprehensive Employment and Training Act) jobs are eliminated. It will be more difficult for them to find other jobs, since funding for the U.S. employment service is to be halved. In addition, cuts in urban programs affect disproportionately areas of the country with high concentrations of poor people, necessitating decreased public services and/or increased local taxes. Cuts of 14% and 6% in Medicaid and Medicare, "because federal programs focus on vulnerable populations, notably the aged disabled and poor, will cut the access of these groups to medical care" (1982:131). Finally, federal spending on elementary, secondary, and vocational education, the purpose of which is to reduce somewhat the inequalities in quality of education across the nation (see Chapter 6, section 6.3.3), was to be cut from 1981 levels, in constant dollars, by some 55% by 1985 (1982:137).

By depriving the working poor of income supplements and increasing further their effective "tax" rates these changes (1) increase inequality between high-wage and low-wage workers, (2) increase the incidence of poverty, and (3) decrease the income gap between low-income families with wage earnings and those without. The United States will therefore have more inequality, more poverty, and less work incentive. However, the extent of the 1981-83 funding cuts really raises an issue which is deeper than the issue of the technical effectiveness of particular "reform" measures. Budget cuts have gone beyond "tinkering" and beyond the elimination of waste. The real issue now is whether the federal government should intervene at all to mitigate inequality of outcomes and to improve equality of opportunity. And since the federal government took on these responsibilities due to the inability of the private sector and of local and state governments to provide adequate resources, one cannot pretend that others will do what the federal government leaves undone. Private charity is no more likely to be sufficient in the 1980s than in the 1930s. State and local governments not only differ enormously in the wealth of their tax base; they also face a competition of miserliness since higher taxes to pay for greater transfers to the poor may encourage both the immigration of the poor and the emigration of the rich. There is, therefore, a national choice which has been put into fairly clear terms by the Reagan administration—does inequality matter?

13.4 What Could Government Do?

In a market economy, where income is the sum of labor earnings, capital income, and net transfers to/from government, one can fairly easily categorize the possible options for redistributional policy. One series of options emphasizes the distribution of earnings, a second series affects primarily the distribution of capital income, and a third series looks at the net fiscal incidence of government. Since we have already looked, in Chapter 11, at some of the policies which might affect the ownership of property, we focus here on the distributions of earnings and of net transfers. Of the large number of possible policies in each area, we discuss in particular two contrasting views on how one might produce greater equality in the distribution of wage rates—a subject on which the contrasting perspectives of Chapters 8 and 9 have very different answers. However, egalitarian wage policies will only marginally assist those low-income families whose age, child-care responsibilities, or infirmities bar them from the paid labor market. Some sort of transfer policy is needed for such people and, bearing in mind the possibility of work disincentives such as those already discussed, many have proposed some form of negative income tax. However, a more modest program, with many of the same impacts, would be a taxable family allowance system.

13.4.1 Contingent Tuition Repayment Schemes If one emphasizes the view of a labor market where wages generally equal the productivity of individual workers, then one argues that decreases in wage inequality can occur only if there are decreases in the inequality of worker productivity. Okun (1975) is one of the many who have argued in this tradition that the ends of both equity and efficiency are served by moving closer to the ideal of "equal opportunity" in access to higher education. In his view, inability to finance higher education means able people from poor backgrounds are less productive workers than if they could attend college.

One possible remedy is to enable students to borrow the tuition and expenses of their training (either university or technical college) by agreeing to pay a small increase in their income tax rate in later life. Those who do financially less well after training are therefore not burdened with a load of debt, while the increase in taxes is calculated so that taking the ne'er-do-wells and the affluent among the graduates together, on average, each year's university class will pay for its own education expenses.

This plan therefore enables students from poor backgrounds to finance their education and removes much of the financial risk of going to college—both of which are likely to be important for a student from a poor background. If tuition fees were increased to cover the whole of university expenditures, it would also mean that the recipients of the financial benefits from the education obtained would, as a group, pay for those benefits. As well as equalizing the "result" both by equalizing earnings and by reducing tax inequalities, such a program is intended to equalize the opportunity of people from different socioeconomic backgrounds to enter upper-level administrative and professional positions.

Many sociologists argue, however, that streaming, or tracking, in primary and high school has largely foreclosed the option of a college education for many working-class children well before they could benefit from such a plan. Even were this not the case, if education is largely a credential, one can expect little impact on inequality of result if other people also increase their supply of credentials (see section 8.2.2). Thus institutionalists doubt whether such a program would materially affect either inequality of opportunity or inequality of result.

13.4.2 An Egalitarian Incomes Policy For institutionalists, the lesson to be learned from the decline in earnings inequality during the wage control period of World War II is:

> If the public does in fact want a more equal distribution of earnings, the public can quickly have it at very low cost. Wages can be equalized without massive long-run investments in education and manpower programs. The wage structure can be quickly altered the way it was during World War II to reflect a new pattern of interdependent preferences. To some extent the wage policies of World War II were a deliberate—and successful—attempt to change the sociology of what constitutes "fair" wage differentials. (Thurow, 1975:192)

The key is "whether the public wants it." Under wartime conditions a consensus for equal sharing of a national effort may enable substantial changes in relative wages, and the new wage structure will "stick" when it has persisted for a few years. Under peacetime conditions a "solidaristic" wage policy (as in Sweden or Holland—see Ulman and Flanagan, 1975) may set national pay scales, with somewhat larger percentage increases for the lower paid. Over time this will compress wage differentials and lessen earnings inequality. Over time, public attitudes on "appropriate" pay differentials will also change as the new pay structure is accepted as "normal." In time, a more equal earnings distribution will become entrenched. If, however, the speed of compression of wage differentials outpaces the rate of change in public attitudes, discontent may emerge. One may then have, as in Sweden, strikes of the university educated which aim to maintain or increase their earnings differential over lower-paid workers.

An egalitarian incomes policy is thus a gradualistic method for decreasing earnings differentials. To the extent that "wages drift" (local pay settlements above the national scale) favor the highly paid, its impact on the earnings distribution will be blunted.[9] Incomes policies have, however, been widely adopted, and their rationalization has often been that of equity—i.e., in attempting to limit inflation and control more strictly the earnings of upper-income groups, it is argued that incomes policies decrease the inequality of the distribution of real income.

To this argument, and especially to controls on wages and prices, many economists have a vehement reaction. Lipsey's (1977) discussion of controls is a case in point. He argued strongly that controls are at best temporarily effective in delaying inflation (i.e., a temporary reduction of at most 1% to 2% in the inflation rate) and that in general prices are much more difficult than wages to control. As a result of wages' being held down while prices continue to rise, controls tend to mean a shift in the distribution of national income from labor to capital. For this reason, controls in capitalist societies are often opposed by trade union groups.[10] In the longer run, Lipsey argues, controls introduce distortions into the economy which decrease allocative efficiency and, therefore, growth. He argues they produce a more politicized income distributions process in which "he who makes a big noise gets" (Lipsey, 1977:11). The politically inarticulate and the unorganized therefore get, he feels, a smaller share of a smaller pie (and one can recall from Chapter 4 that low-income groups now tend to be less politically active). From his perspective, egalitarian attempts to control incomes have very high costs and very uncertain benefits.

The institutionalist reply is, of course, that market forces presently play a fairly weak role in the determination of most people's relative wages; hence there is little loss in allocative efficiency when institutional mechanisms are, in effect, coordinated at a national level. In addition, if there is a strong desire to control inflation, one must compare the costs of alternative policies. If the alternative to an incomes policy is inducing a long and severe recession, then incomes policies may involve some allocative inefficiencies, but the alternative is likely to cost a great deal more in forgone output and social stress. Indeed, on these grounds, Lipsey (1981) has largely reversed his previous position. However, national coordination will produce a more equitable income distribution only if this is the demand of the political process to which the incomes policy must be responsive. Incomes policies are therefore not a panacea, since to be effectively redistributive they require a prior set of political changes.

13.4.3 Negative Income Tax Proposals On tuition payment plans or income policies there is little agreement, but many economists of varying views have supported some version of a "negative income tax," in part because of a dissatisfaction with the disincentives to work that are often present in the current welfare system. Although a wide variety of programs exists in all fifty states and the District of Columbia, typically they each embody a reduction in benefits as earned income increases. Since an individual may be in simultaneous receipt of benefits from several programs (e.g., public housing, Social Security, and food stamps), the benefit reduction of each is added to the benefit reduction of the other. This "stacking" of programs and their sensitivity to earned income can produce very substantial benefit reductions—i.e., a very high implicit tax rate. In Table 13.3 one can note that, even under the pre-1981 law, a welfare recipient kept only about $1.50 from every $5 earned—i.e., he or she faced a 70% marginal tax rate, considerably higher than the maximum 50% tax on earned income. Since the Reagan reforms, of course, the implicit tax has, in many cases, increased to over 100%.

Obviously there are severe disincentives to work built into such a situation. Part-time or limited temporary low-wage work is the only thing that pays at all, but such work generally does not generate the experience or on-the-job training required for the stable, high-paying jobs which would enable one to escape welfare altogether.

As a reform, "guaranteed annual income" or "negative income tax" schemes have often been proposed. Many variants exist, but they have in common the feature that government would guarantee a minimum level of income to all and make payments of that full amount to those with no earnings. For those with earnings, government payments would be reduced by a "tax rate" on money earnings. Such a scheme is often called a negative income tax scheme since above a certain "break-even" level of income an individual makes positive tax payments to government while below it he or she receives transfers ("negative" tax payments).

If, for example, such a scheme had been in place in 1979 with a tax credit or "guarantee level" of $600 per month for a family of four (i.e., an income just below the Social Security poverty line) and a "tax rate" on earnings of 50%, the total income of a family with no earnings would be $7,200. A family with earned income of $5,000 would get $9,700 while a family with earnings of $14,400 would be at the "break-even" point and would neither receive payments nor pay taxes. Higher income families would pay tax. If the scheme were administered through the income tax system, all three families would fill out the same forms. Some would get checks in the mail, some would send them in, but there would be no stigma to receiving a tax credit and no nosey welfare officers to supervise the lives of the poor. No one would have to declare himself or herself an "economic failure" to gain benefits. In an "automatic" program the arbitrary criteria which exclude many "working poor" from benefits would disappear, which would have the incidental benefit of easing the resentment toward those on "welfare" felt by many of today's working poor.

Gains in self-respect are impossible to quantify but money income would be given by the formula:

(13.2)

Net income = [Guarantee level − (tax rate × earnings)] + earnings

The combination of tax rate and guarantee level which is chosen sets the crucial economic parameters of a negative income tax system. Together they determine the break-even point, and hence the fraction of the population which receives payments under the scheme. The lower the tax rate on earnings, the greater are work incentives but the greater also is program cost. A tax rate of 50% and a guarantee level of $7,200 together imply a break-even point of $14,400, which in 1979 would have implied that roughly 25% of four-person families would receive net payments.[11] A lower tax rate, or a higher basic guarantee level, would have implied that more people would be net beneficiaries—e.g., if the break-even had been $20,000 in 1979, 40% of four-person families would have received payments. Either a $10,000 guarantee with a 50% tax rate *or* a 35% tax rate with a $7,200 guarantee would have produced a $20,000 break-even point.

Society thus faces a three-cornered choice between maintaining minimal adequacy, providing work incentives, and restraining program cost. Indeed it is unlikely that a negative income tax (NIT) could ever replace all current social welfare programs, since what is adequate for some is inadequate for others (e.g., the physically handicapped, who may need medication, wheelchairs, etc.). In addition, the details of payment mechanisms and payment period (monthly, quarterly, yearly?) are crucial to many households. As well, whenever payments increase less than proportionately to household size (as is the case with the Social Security poverty lines) there is a financial advantage to the (apparent) splitting up of households, since two apparently single people get more than one couple. If this is not to occur, a "family" must have a clear definition (do we count only legal marriage, or common-law, long-term relationship as well?) and the definition must somehow be policed—but the NIT was supposed to avoid the administrative costs and the invasions of privacy of current welfare schemes. Finally an NIT, if it is to be administered via the income-tax mechanism, must be "harmonized" with tax law and the current tax scheme adjusted, if people are not to be receiving negative tax supplements while paying ordinary income tax.

A variety of NIT schemes have been introduced in planned experiments (see Hum, 1980, for a brief description) and such "housekeeping" details have been shown to be quite important to the plans' impacts. Economists, however, have tended to emphasize the issue of whether a NIT would substantially reduce labor supply, since if it did the economic consequences (in reduced output) and the political fallout (in resentment at "welfare bums") would be serious.

Clearly the size of the impact of an NIT on labor supply depends on the particular program parameters adopted—the level of tax credit guarantee set implies an "income" effect (i.e., people who are now better off may consume more leisure) while the tax rate chosen implies a "substitution" effect (i.e., an hour of labor, at the margin, may yield a lower return). The number of experiments conducted and the variety of results obtained have by now created an entire specialist literature on these topics. Moffit (1981) provides a concise recent synopsis, Keeley et al. (1978) summarize and compare the Seattle, Denver, and New Jersey experiments, while Masters and Garfinkel (1977) offer a book-length treatment.

These studies diverge in some details but generally agree that the labor supply effects of an NIT differ significantly by demographic group. Older male workers work very nearly the same hours in an NIT experimental scheme or under "control" programs. Women, especially married women with children, and some younger men may reduce their paid work hours more substantially, but, since they tend to work less to begin with, their reduced labor supply is a smaller fraction of total labor supply. In aggregate, Masters and Garfinkel estimate an NIT with a poverty line base and a 50% tax rate would reduce paid work hours in the United States by 2.5% to 4.3% (1977:239), while the point estimate of Keeley et al. is 3.5% (1978:19). Since the people involved get lower-than-average wages, the net money earnings forgone is somewhat less (1.2% to 2.1% of earnings) and some of that loss is undoubtedly balanced by an increase in (uncounted) home production. Masters and Garfinkel therefore argue the labor supply effect is "small" relative to the costs of the general reductions in work hours achieved during the past few decades due to a shorter work week.

In terms of lost output to the economy, a labor supply decrease of 3.5% could be achieved by a 1/30 decrease in everyone's work hours or achieved by 3.5% of the labor force's ceasing work entirely. A negative income tax lies between these extremes since only part of the population is directly affected at all. Keeley et al. (1978:19) place the labor supply reduction of program participants (for poverty level guarantee and 50% tax rate) at 6.2% for husbands and 22.7% for wives, while Masters and Garfinkel put it at 20% for young single men, 3.3% to 4.9% for healthy married men, and 18.6% to 31.2% for wives, depending on age (1977:231). The labor supply effects are, therefore, concentrated on particular, identifiable groups.

Economists may propose "anonymity" as an ethically desirable attribute of income redistribution schemes, in the feeling that there should be no distinctions drawn between persons, but in fact the absence from paid employment of different groups excites quite different public reactions. In political terms, society draws distinctions between the "leisure" of different ages and sexes, and between the absence from paid employment of those with and without child-care responsibilities. There is little resentment, for example, at a 70-year-old who lives on Social Security or a deserted mother who receives family benefits—but considerable animosity exists toward able-bodied males of working age who do not seriously try to find a job. Social judgments are much harsher on those who could make an effort, but do not support themselves, than on those who do make an effort, but cannot support themselves. A negative income tax predicated solely on current money income will provide transfers to some, e.g., university students from advantaged backgrounds, who would not, by most "common sense" criteria, be in need. Akerlof (1978) suggested that a welfare system that "tags" identifiable groups as eligible for particular programs may be more efficient than a universalistic program such as the negative income tax. It may also be more politically acceptable.

13.4.4 Taxable Family Allowances The United States is the *only* developed nation without a universal child allowance program, and perhaps it does not deserve this distinction. A "family allowance" or "child allowance" system is extremely simple, paying a flat grant to the legal guardian of each child from birth until the age of majority. It is very cheap to administer,[12] creates no stigma to recipients, and is conveniently available in a monthly check, which is usually addressed to the mother. Since the size of the check depends only on the number of children in the family it is not affected by living arrangements. There is therefore none of the bureaucratic requirement that income be provided only if there is no man in the house—a requirement which has been, in the past, so destructive of family life among the U.S. poor. For low-income families, a child allowance can be an important income source—in Belgium, for example, such cash payments were, for two children, 13.6% of the gross earnings of an average production worker in 1972 (OECD, 1976:27).

In addition, a taxable child allowance can have most of the features of a negative income tax (although, of course, it is restricted to families with children). If the child deductions, from taxable income, which are now available were abolished that revenue would be available to meet program costs. The current system of deductions from taxable income is of greatest value to high-income households but the net benefit of a child allowance to upper-income taxpayers declines as taxable income increases (since the tax rate on the child allowance payment also increases). The redistributive impact of a child allowance can be increased still further if it is required that child allowances received be "grossed up" before being added to taxable income from other sources. For example, counting one dollar in child allowance received as equivalent to two dollars in other income (a gross-up factor of 2) would imply a sharply progressive tax on this income—a family in the 50% tax bracket would get zero net benefits. However, no family would face a higher tax on an additional dollar of earned income than that now in force in the Income Tax Act.

This scheme is thus fairly similar to a negative income tax for families with children, and one can have a fairly clear idea of where its labor supply effects would probably be felt. Younger women with pre-school-age children would be those most likely to reduce hours of paid employment—but remember that this would largely be a shift from out-of-home work to household production (Chapter 8) and this use of time is not only productive in the short run, but it is highly valuable in increasing the skills of the next generation (Chapter 6). On the other hand, family allowance income is equally available should the male decide to stay home, or it could be used to purchase better child care if neither wishes to do so. Traditionally, child care has been "women's work" and it has been unpaid. Child allowances recognize the value of what is, after all, one of the primary needs of any society and do so in a way which is essentially sex-blind. As well, they offer a stigma-free way of alleviating the poverty of large families and single-parent households—two important parts of America's poverty population.

13.5 Summary and Conclusion

(a) If we calculate the current net flow of taxes, transfers, and benefits between households, we can estimate that the activities of governments in the United States in the 1970s were redistributive, from rich to poor—although estimates of the exact size of that redistribution are sensitive to the basis used for assigning the benefits of "public goods" such as defense or police. Government can therefore be said to have had an equalizing influence on the distribution of annual income. However, these calculations are very imperfect indicators of the impact of government on "equity" since they do not indicate directly the extent of net transfers between persons over their lifetimes and they cannot indicate how the distribution of earned income would change if there were a substantial change in governments' economic role.

(b) The period from 1965 to 1980 saw large increases in government social expenditures and transfer programs, whose equalizing tendencies were balanced by increasing inequality in the distribution of primary factor income in the form of capital income and wages. The period 1980 to 1982 has seen a reversal of emphasis in government policy. It is not at present clear whether and to what extent this new trend will continue, but the clear implication is an increase in both inequality and poverty.

(c) Over the decades a complex system of social welfare legislation has grown up in the United States. As a result, piecemeal reforms to particular programs must be very carefully analyzed since they may have unintended consequences for other programs or for the financial incentives which face individual beneficiaries. The 1981 amendments to the Aid to Families with Dependent Children program are a case in point, since these amendments decrease both benefits and the incentives to long-term paid employment.

(d) Negative income tax schemes have often been proposed as ways to maintain work incentives, eliminate bureaucracy, and remove the stigma to recipients while providing an adequate income floor for all American households. The trade-offs between adequacy, work incentives, and program cost are, however, inescapable. In addition, political acceptability may well dictate a more "targeted" approach, such as a system of taxable child allowances.

(e) There is considerable disagreement as to the most effective policy to equalize the distribution of earnings. Some economists emphasize the acquisition of training and favor mechanisms, such as the contingent tuition repayment plan, which will increase equality of opportunity in the educational system. Others emphasize measures to equalize the dispersion of wage rates, e.g., by an egalitarian incomes policy. These differences in policy emphasis stem from basic differences in their underlying models of the labor market—as discussed in Chapters 8 and 9.

NOTES

[1]Private expenditures on these items also rose over the 1970-78 period, from 6.9% of GNP to 7.9% of GNP (Cohen, 1980:490).

[2]On the other hand, over the 1970-79 period there was also a trend to decreasing federal tax rates for top income categories. See U.S., *Statistical Abstract* 1980, p. 272.

[3]The U.S. Congressional Budget Office (1982a) estimates that the estate and gift tax reductions, which are phased in over four years, will cost the treasury $2 billion in 1982 and $6.6 billion in 1985. Since these taxes only raised $5.8 billion in 1980, it looks as if they will largely disappear.

[4]In addition, cuts in federal grants are likely to cause state and local governments to increase taxes and/or decrease services, but the incidence of such changes is not yet apparent.

[5]AFDC benefits under the prior law for a family of four with no earnings would have been $141 per month in Texas, $349 in Oklahoma, and $601 in California. These state payments are 50% cost-shared with the federal government.

[6]Only about 20% of AFDC recipients live in subsidized housing.

[7]In 1977, 3.5 million families with 7.8 million children were AFDC recipients (U.S., *Statistical Abstract* 1979, Table 574).

[8]In the remaining states there is the concept of "medically indigent," whose disincentive effects can be strong for those whose employers do not provide health insurance and who expect substantial household medical bills if they lose access to Medicaid.

[9]In European countries with central pay bargaining (e.g., Sweden, Germany) "wages drift" can be between 25% and 50% of the settlements agreed in central bargaining—Malles (1973).

[10]Where the capital stock is publicly owned an increased profit share may be passed back to workers in the form of a higher "social wage" of government services or in decreased taxes or it may be partially appropriated by state bureaucrats. The exact division will depend on the politics of the nation involved.

[11]Using the 1966 *Survey of Economic Opportunity,* Masters and Garfinkel (1977) estimated that 27.1% of the population would be recipients under a negative income tax with a poverty line guarantee and 50% tax rate. With a 33⅓% tax rate coverage would increase to 51%.

[12]In 1976-77 administration of the Canadian Family Allowance program cost 0.55% of program outlays—Mendelson (1979:67).

14 CONCLUSION

Our theories, regarded as tools of analysis, are blinkers in this sense. Or it may be politer to say that they are rays of light, which illuminate a part of the target, leaving the rest in darkness. As we use them, we avert our eyes from things which may be relevant, in order that we should see more clearly what we do see. It is entirely proper that we should do this, since otherwise we should see very little. But it is obvious that a theory that is to perform this function satisfactorily must be well chosen; otherwise it will illumine the wrong things. Further, since it is a changing world that we are studying, the theory which illumines the right things at one time may illumine the wrong things at another. This may happen because of changes in the world (the things neglected may have gained in importance relatively to the things considered) or because of changes in ourselves (the things in which we are interested may have changed). There is, there can be, no economic theory which will do for us everything we want all the time.

SIR JOHN HICKS
Wealth and Welfare (1981:233)

14.1 Methodological Issues

A number of methodological issues have been raised at various points in this book and this seems to be the place to draw some of them together. Some readers may be disquieted that there has been no attempt in this book to calculate a single index of "true" economic inequality and no attempt to outline a single true theory of economic inequality. Rather, I have focused on *alternative* measures of economic inequality and on the *differing* perspectives of economic theory because different measures, and different theories, are appropriate for different problems.

Chapters 2 and 3 emphasized the complexity of the measurement of economic inequality. They considered the distribution of annual money income, of lifetime income, of wealth, of economic power, and of utility equivalent annuities. If we ask "inequality of what, among whom, and how measured," the issue of what variable to consider will depend on the ultimate question one wants to ask and on the theoretical framework with which one approaches it. Measures of economic inequality are sensitive also to the choice of the recipient unit—households, families, or individuals. Social trends such as increasing divorce rates can alter the meaning of existing statistics (such as those statistics on the distribution of money income among households) and can create biases in existing techniques (such as the estate multiplier estimates of the distribution of wealth). Social trends such as increasing female labor force participation will also alter the extent to which money income inequality accurately reflects inequality in economic welfare. To add to the complexity, we noted in Chapter 4 that one ought *not* to assume that such social trends are independent of simultaneous trends in economic inequality and poverty; rather there are good grounds for believing that such social trends are partly the result of trends in economic inequality and poverty.

Finally, different technical measures of dispersion (the Gini index, the Theil measure, the coefficient of variation, or the Atkinson measure) will give differing degrees of emphasis to inequality among those at the top end of a distribution, among those in the middle of a distribution, or among those at the bottom of a distribution. As a result, these measures often disagree with one another. Even if they did agree, for example in the sense of ranking countries similarly in their degree of inequality in the distribution of annual money income, the significance of such inequality is, again, another issue. Does a given degree of income inequality reflect a process of market exchange or, primarily, mirror legislative constraints on individual freedoms (e.g., South Africa)? Are high incomes due to entrenched privileges or to the initiative and exertion of individuals? The complexities of the issue of economic inequality should teach us an important moral—to avoid simplistic slogans.

The clearest example of a simplistic notion which is now current in economic thought is the notion of a "general" trade-off between "equality" and "efficiency." It finds expression in such simple slogans as "policies to redistribute the economic pie also cause the pie to be reduced," which creates the impression that the policy choices involved in a discussion of economic inequality are easy—either "growth" or "equality." If this is interpreted to mean that any reasonable measure of economic inequality will be negatively correlated with any reasonable measure of economic progress, then it is demonstrably false (see Chapter 12). It is similarly untrue to say that policies which improve "equality" will also always decrease or impede economic growth. Enriched education for preschool children (Chapter 6) has highly favorable benefit–cost ratios and, simultaneously, decreases intergenerational inequities; an end to the deductability from personal income tax of mortgage and consumer interest payments (Chapter 12) would both increase savings and capital accumulation and decrease inequality in the distribution of after-tax income; ill-considered welfare reforms (Chapter 13) may produce more inequality, more poverty, and less incentives to work and produce. In practice, great issues, such as economic inequality, are composed of a myriad of smaller issues. In practice, the primary function of simple slogans on great issues seems to be to relieve people of the intellectual effort of thinking clearly about individual issues—as a consequence, such simple slogans are likely to be very poor guides to wise economic policy.

Simple economic theories are also inadequate to explain an issue of the complexity of economic inequality. There has been no attempt in this book to construct a single true theory of economic inequality. Rather, the emphasis has been on the insights which neoclassical, institutional, and radical authors have brought to analysis of this issue. The existence of alternative frameworks for the explanation of economic inequality creates the problem of choice, a problem which is made more difficult by the much greater role that introspection and casual evidence from personal experience plays in forming our opinions on the economics of inequality, as compared to the role which introspection and casual evidence plays in forming our opinion on the economics of energy, monetary theory, etc. Casual evidence, examples from real life, is essential to economics both in checking the initial credibility of hypotheses advanced in research and in making the classroom teaching of economics something more than a branch of applied mathematics. However, individual experiences are, of necessity, a "small sample" of the experiences of the population in general and they can be very misleading—indeed they are inevitably systematically biased by one's own position in society. These biases alter our perception of the issue of economic inequality, affect our analysis of the behavior of individuals, and are difficult to confront directly, since it is very difficult to form an understanding of how people in general got where they are economically which is totally separable from our own under-standing of how we got where we are economically.

Many researchers in the area of income distribution are likely to have had the experience of an argument with someone whose income, the researcher knows, is sufficient to place them in the top 1% of the income distribution but who cannot be convinced of that fact. Such people will often argue with great vehemence that there are many hundreds of thousands of people who are better off than they are and that they are just another member of the middle class. Of course, since 1% of the American population is something over 2 million people, they are probably right that there are a great many people who have a higher income than they do and they are also probably right that most of their friends have a similar economic status. Where they are wrong is in extrapolating from their own experience and considering themselves as "typical." Academic research-ers, like businessmen, doctors, street people, and long-distance truck drivers, are members of a particular subculture within the larger society. On average, academics accumulate wealth over the life cycle, perceive readily the benefits of education, and have children who speak standard English and enter easily into the school system. Introspection may well lead such people to overemphasize life-cycle saving and the cognitive benefits of education and to underemphasize the stratified nature of the school system.

Sociologists have argued that such beliefs as to the causes of disparities in individual economic resources can be seen as part of the "existential" aspects of culture—i.e., the set of "assertions of what man, society and nature are like" (Smelser, 1963:40). The crucial rule of "existential" beliefs arises because "within western society there is at a high level a common value base to both conservative *and* radical ideologies. Instead of attempting to undermine these high level values, the radical ideology tends to assert the unacceptability of the existing society from the point of view of values which everybody takes for granted, whereas the conservative ideology tends to assert that probably the state of society is acceptable and that deliberate attempts to usher in change would be dangerous. Thus, questions of empirical fact about the state of the society have become especially salient" (Parsons, 1954:48). Within the United States the value of "equality of opportunity" is very widely held.[1] Thus the analysis of economic inequality is of particularly great social importance.

However, one of the most interesting features of current work on economic inequality is the substantial degree of essential agreement on the basic mechanism of income determination. As Taubman puts it (1978:ix), "to a large extent parents are directly or indirectly responsible"—but this perception is sometimes wrapped in language which implies a basic acceptance of an economic system of private capitalism and sometimes it is clothed in language which is highly antagonistic to private capitalism.

A fascinating aspect of the inequality debate is the metamorphosis of the human capital tradition. Originally, the work of Mincer, Becker, Chiswick, et al. was framed in terms of models of utility maximization within a single generation. It was clearly demonstrated that, even if one assumes equality of opportunity, one will observe inequality of annual incomes. Now, however, the utility-maximizing framework is generalized to the case of several generations, with the result that the inequality of outcome of one generation produces inequalities of opportunity in succeeding generations.

This view of the American socioeconomic system is very similar, in its emphasis on the intergenerational inheritance of material and human wealth, to the perceptions of the institutional and radical research traditions. In some respects, these different approaches can be seen as alternative languages with which to analyze earnings inequality. Just as a language will evolve new vocabulary, new syntax, and new grammar for a previously unknown event, for which no term is available, so also can each of the major research traditions generate new maintained hypotheses and new theoretical models to cope with the strain of "anomalous" research results (see Kuhn, 1970). What Blaug (1976) calls the "hard core" of a theoretical approach (to distinguish it from the "protective belt" of subsidiary assumptions or working models which can easily be jettisoned) is in each case somewhat amorphous.[2] New evidence can therefore be assimilated within each major research tradition, and, just as one can trace the evolution of languages back over the generations, so also can one trace the development of the major research traditions.

Over time, a "borrowing" of vocabulary enriches languages and over time concepts such as "internal labor markets" have been borrowed from one school of thought by another. Choosing a theoretical framework or research tradition with which to analyze inequality is, at one level, therefore much like choosing which language to learn.[3] (Most learn the language they are taught in school and few take the trouble to become bilingual.) Partly, one's choice will be based on what one wants to talk about, since some things are much harder to say in one language than in another (e.g., wage rigidity and unemployment is much more difficult to explain in a neoclassical than in an institutional framework—see Solow, 1980). Partly, one's choice will also depend on whom one wants to talk to. Since the neoclassical approach dominates North American universities' economics departments, arguments framed in its terms find a readier acceptance in academia while the institutional and radical approaches have more currency elsewhere. A final factor may be one's aesthetic sense of which language offers greater clarity and ease of expression, which "tells us the most in the fewest words," and which produces the most "useful" conjectures to test against the data.

At another level, however, one must be aware that one's choice of research tradition may create or accentuate bias. Within the neoclassical tradition, for example, the fact that it is difficult to define or to speak of "exploitation" or "power" may mean that it is easier to study other issues. Since it appears to be human nature to emphasize the importance of one's own work, such a choice may, over a period of time, subtly mold one's perspective on events to the conclusion that "exploitation" or "power" are relatively unimportant (or even nonexistent) phenomena. An analysis which emphasizes only the choices people make rather than the constraints they encounter faces the danger that it will interpret every outcome as a "choice," even if it is the outcome of poverty.

Most economists would argue that one's choice of theory should depend on how well a research tradition stacks up when measured against the evidence. The pure theory of choice, however, offers no clear prediction until one specifies the constraints to which choice is subject. The pure theory of class struggle offers no clear predictions until a specific historical context is provided. Pure theory of any description does not offer unambiguous predictions. Applied theory of any description must be framed so as to be consistent with the same underlying social reality. Thus, while the applied theory may use different terms and offer different interpretations, it must still produce the same generalizations.

A recurring regularity in the study of inequality is the similarity of economic position of parents and children (see Chapter 6). One may explain this in terms of parental investment in "child quality" or in terms of the inheritance of class status. One may interpret this in terms of the choices parents make or in terms of the constraints parents face. To the child, of course, it makes little difference. To fit the data, meanwhile, one's theories must produce the same prediction: a substantial correlation between parent and child in socioeconomic status. The most striking conclusion of Chapters 8 and 9 is that, despite their vast methodological differences, both the "radical" and the "neoclassical" approach argue that inequality of result and inequality of opportunity are inevitable in an unconstrained capitalist market system.

However, inheritance between generations is most "convenient" (Knight, 1923) when it takes the form of the transfer of property. The inheritance of property has therefore long been of concern for those who value "equality of opportunity" and Chapter 11 examined the role of inheritance versus "life-cycle" saving in the accumulation of property. "Life-cycle" saving may be a reasonable picture of wealth acquisition for the "middle"classes, and especially for their ownership of housing and consumer durables. However, this sort of wealth is only about half of U.S. tangible wealth (see section 3.3.2) and these sorts of people, although a very large group, do not include the 35% of the population with nil assets or the 5% of the population with substantial holdings of financial assets. For the very rich, the inheritance of property is of the very greatest importance, but the noninheritance of earning power is what dominates the lives of the relatively poor.

The problem of choice of research tradition is thus made easier by the essential similarity of their discussions of the process of income and wealth determination. It is made more difficult by their advocacy of differing policies to deal with the issues of poverty and income distribution. There may be a large measure of agreement as to what has happened in the past, but there is very little agreement as to what should be done in the future. This disagreement is doubtless related to the fact that none of the major research traditions has a really satisfactory explanation of the *distribution* of income and wealth. The determination of individual income and wealth has been greatly studied, and, with the aid of extreme assumptions, models of individual income determination have been generalized into models of the distribution of income. However, the missing link in neoclassical models is a general, predictive theory of labor demand, and the radical and institutional traditions have no clear explanation of trends in the class struggle or in the sociology of wage determination. These lacunae will surely be the focus of much research in the years to come.

14.2 Does It Matter? A Personal Opinion

One of the earliest observers of the American scene emphasized the importance of a general equality of economic conditions and spoke of "the prodigious influences that this primary fact exercises on the whole course of society: it gives a peculiar direction to public opinion and a peculiar tenor to the laws; it imparts new maxims to the governing authorities and peculiar habits to the governed; it creates opinions, gives birth to new sentiments, founds novel customs and modifies whatever it does not produce" (Tocqueville, 1840:2). Alexis de Tocqueville's observations on the importance of equality and democracy in America were colored by the fact that the United States was, in 1840, far more democratic and substantially more economically equal than the nations of Europe. However, although the self-perception of Americans may continue to be influenced by memories of how much more equal America was than Europe, history has evolved somewhat differently over the last century in Europe than it has in the United States.

Perhaps partly to ward off some of the social discontent that might arise in societies where the presence of hereditary aristocracies has long belied the myth of equal opportunity, European nations made an early start on the welfare state. Flora and Alber (1981:37) argue "the modern European welfare states really began in the last two decades of the nineteenth-century,"[4] while comparable American legislation was delayed until the 1930s. European social welfare legislation expanded dramatically during this period from 1945 to 1960, to a degree which the American expansion in 1965 to 1980 did not approach. Redistributive taxation, in-kind transfers such as National Health Insurance, and financial transfers such as family allowances are by now integral parts of the European social scene. As Chapter 2 discussed, most European nations now have more equality of economic outcome[5] than does the United States.

The American emphasis has historically been on equality of opportunity, rather than on equality of outcome.[6] Even though native-born Americans have always had an economic advantage over the foreign-born, immigrants have historically been willing, as newcomers, to accept a relatively disadvantaged initial position. The "American dream" was born of the substantial economic advance that immigrants experienced during periods of high economic growth and of the promise for upward social mobility in the native-born second generation. In an economy whose population was growing rapidly from natural increase and successive waves of in-migration, this promise of upward mobility was very often kept. In the postwar period, from 1945 to 1973, high rates of economic growth and a substantial migration from rural to urban areas continued to fulfill some of the same promises of individual economic advancement.

But when population size begins to stabilize, the issue of inequality of opportunity from generation to generation must be faced more squarely. In a new society, as Touqueville put it, "new families are constantly springing up, others are constantly falling away and all that remain change their condition; the woof of time is every instant broken and the track of generations effaced. Those who went before are soon forgotten; of those who will come after no one has any idea; the interest of man is confined to those in close propinquity to himself" (1840:119). However, as America becomes an older society, one can expect increased interest in issues of intergenerational transfer. One can also expect that the idea that inequalities of opportunity are in practice separable from inequalities of outcome will be less and less often believed.

As Milton Friedman puts it, "Much of the moral fervor behind the drive for equality of outcome comes from the widespread belief that it is not fair that some children should have a great advantage over others simply because they happen to have wealthy parents. Of course it is not fair" (1979:127).[7] Fairness is, however, important. It is important because it is only the fairness of the rules of a game that can secure our voluntary acceptance of those rules. Of course, it is relatively easy to be tolerant of the unfairness of the rules of the game if one is also a winner. And to exactly the extent that society is unequal there will be many "losers" and a few "winners." However, if one has lost out in life's initial lottery, and if one realizes that the rules of the game are unfair and that there is no serious effort being made to reform those rules, then why should one obey or respect the rules?

There are never enough police to enforce the laws, whether of property or of morals, if these laws lose their legitimacy among substantial segments of the population. The United States has no state religion which might lend its moral authority to the justification of the economic position of the wealthy. It has a tradition of law-abidingness, but that tradition has been eroding over time.[8] Among the various schools of thought discussed in this book, only the radicals ask the questions, "Why do the disadvantaged tolerate economic inequality? Why do they obey the laws that protect other people's property?"

The answer, radicals suggest, lies in a widespread perception, up to now, that the rules of the game are basically "fair." In particular, they emphasize the perception that the school system has offered a measure of "equality of opportunity." Nobody has seriously suggested that all people could have *identical* opportunities open to them at birth but, even if perfect equality of opportunity is an unattainable ideal, it still matters a good deal what the order of magnitude is of the differences in opportunities which face individuals. To the extent that education is taken out of the market and provided "equally" to all, the ways in which parents can transmit earning power to their children are reduced. There is a random element to these inheritances—some people from deprived backgrounds do manage to surmount their obstacles and some of the children of the best-intentioned parents do not do well in later life. These differences are also of an understandable order of magnitude among families—certainly far less than the differences we observe in property ownership. And most liberals would also argue that the community should intervene to prevent child abuse or gross neglect and to assist those who are in deprived environments. However, to the extent that education enters the market and its purchase depends on the financial resources of parents, inequalities of opportunity increase by several orders of magnitude. And, of course, all these inequalities in opportunity to acquire earning power are dwarfed by the inequalities in inherited property.

Most people are not purists and they are not unreasonable. We all know of differences between parents in the attention they lavish on their children and we all know that absolute equality of opportunity is an unattainable ideal—but that does not mean that we should not strive to limit the domain of inequalities of opportunity. Similarly, we almost all know some people who got ahead in life and some who inherited, pretty exactly, their parents' economic status—but that does not mean we should not strive to increase equality of opportunity.

Of course, to say that the correlation between parent and child in socioeconomic status is "high" is somewhat similar to a statement that a glass is three-quarters full. One can just as easily protest that it is one-quarter empty. The interpretation of the exact level of intergenerational mobility is inherently subjective, and it is especially subjective since it is so difficult to really imagine one's society substantially different from what it now is. However, although it may a subjective issue whether a glass is three-quarters full or one-quarter empty, it is much less a subjective issue whether the glass is being filled up or drained out. The emphasis of government policy and the *trend* of equality of opportunity, which cannot be divorced from that of equality of outcome, is just as important as the current *level* of equality of opportunity.

In modern societies, government is a large and complex set of institutions. Government provides public goods, maintains defense, provides educational and other services, redistributes income, and maintains the framework of laws which make civilized society possible. These are interrelated functions—for example, public investments in highways and research and a publicly educated labor force are essential to the production of the income which is initially distributed according to the laws of property (which the state enforces) but which is then partially redistributed by the state. The rule of law is especially crucial to the functioning of society as a whole. However, laws which produce unfair outcomes have a way of falling into disrepute. If the state is perceived as acting to increase inequalities of outcome and of opportunity, it will be acting against deeply held values of equity. More than that, in a society with a basic belief in the possibility of "progress" and a basic value that "all men are created equal," the maintenance of law and order is likely to require a continuous emphasis on equality. To the extent that government is perceived as "redistributing to the rich," it will undermine a basic part of its legitimacy.[9]

The current degree of inequality may not be necessary for the production of economic growth (see Chapter 12) but growth is probably necessary for the toleration of continued economic inequality. Marxists and Conservatives alike have emphasized that capitalism's historic justification has been the vast increase in material wealth which it has produced. But, as this is written in 1982, it appears that the prospects for ever rising average standards of living under capitalism have become rather remote. And when the engine of growth falters and individuals can no longer expect to become better off in absolute terms year by year with a constant share of a larger pie, will there not be increasing discontent with existing shares of the economic pie? If "redistribution to the rich" undermines the basic legitimacy of the mixed capitalist state and if increasing crime rates provide graphic evidence of a decrease in belief in the rule of law, what sort of political pressures will emerge? If existing economic institutions cannot satisfy the economic aspirations of much of the population, if indeed some groups are net losers in the increasing struggle over distributive shares, will there not be increasing pressure for changes in existing economic institutions?

Up to now, America has seen a radicalism of the right, rather than of the left. The period of 1980 through 1982 has seen dramatic changes in the role and size of government and a marked emphasis on inegalitarian tax and expenditure policy, under the banner of "growth, not redistribution." What this ignores is the possibility that American society might have drifted into a "prisoner's dilemma," where the pursuit of growth at the expense of equality accentuates the social strains and interest-group politics that produce even more inequality and even less growth. When those groups with greater current political and economic influence use that influence to increase their share of the economic resources of a slow-growth economy, this increases inequality of outcome and inequality of opportunity. It produces an increase, not a decrease, in the alienation of disadvantaged groups and in the possibility of political discontent and social tension.

My own opinion is that a continuous and visible attention to equity in economic issues is, in the long term, a prerequisite for the maintenance of the system of personal liberties and representative government which we know as the liberal democratic state. Social stability and respect for the rule of law cannot, I believe, survive in the long run if the rules of the economic game are widely perceived as unfair and if there is no visible attempt being made to reform them. This is not to argue that a declining belief in the legitimacy of economic outcomes will necessarily produce political movements of an anticapitalist tendency. Indeed, in a highly individualistic culture it seems to me more likely that the more probable outcome is simply a gradual increase in disregard for the rule of law. The danger then is that a myopic viewpoint will see the causes of crime as personal moral deficiency and the solutions to crime as primarily "technical" in nature. Such quick fixes as increased expenditure on police, "streamlining" of the court system, and a more "realistic" interpretation of constitutional protections have, if political discontent is, in addition, linked to subversion, very serious implications for civil liberties.

This is not a pretty scenario, but we have only to look at the Chiles and the Argentinas of this world to see that the extinction of personal liberties and economic stagnation are not unique to Eastern Europe. The social democratic "welfare states" of Western Europe have their problems, but their citizens enjoy as much liberty as, and more equality and more affluence than, people anywhere in North or South America. To me, they present much more attractive models, but it is far from clear that the United States is headed in that direction.

NOTES

[1]For survey data, see Prewitt and Verba (1979:124).

[2]Compare, for example, the concepts "human capital" and "segments"—both are capable of a great many theoretical, and even more empirical, specifications.

[3]Just as, however, the use of French words in English is often accompanied by a subtle shift in their meaning, so also do concepts originating in one theoretical context change subtly when used in another. Purists, moreover, often dislike intensely the patois which can result.

[4]Germany, for instance, first introduced health insurance in 1883.

[5]And also higher rates of productivity increase and income growth, to the extent that several have now passed the United States in per capita GNP.

[6]This emphasis found concrete expression in the earlier expansion of universal secondary education in the United States than in continental Europe, and the earlier provision of Social Security benefits in Europe than in the United States.

[7]Friedman goes on to argue that inheritance can take the form of skills, of talent, or of property and to argue that there is no ethical distinction to be drawn between them—but oddly enough he stresses the importance of equality of opportunity as "an essential component of liberty" (1979:123).

[8]As witness the decrease involved in compliance with income tax self-assessment (*New York Times,* October 4, 1982).

[9]Ehrlich analyzed crime rates from the perspective of utility maximization, which is different from the legitimacy argument developed here, but his conclusion is the same. "Our empirical investigation also indicates that the rates of all felonies, particularly crimes against property, are positively related to the degree of a community's income inequality and this suggests a social incentive for equalizing training and earning opportunities across persons, which is independent of ethical considerations or any social welfare function" (1973:561).

BIBLIOGRAPHY

Aaron, H. J., B. P. Bosworth, E. M. Gramlich, R. W. Hartman, W. W. Kaufman, D. S. Laren, and C. L. Schultze (1982). *Setting National Priorities: The 1983 Budget*. Washington, D.C.: The Brookings Institution.

Aaron, H., and M. McGuire (1970). "Public Goods and Income Distribution," *Econometrica*, 38 (6): 907-920.

Adams, I., W. Cameron, B. Hill, and P. Penz (1971). *The Real Poverty Report*. Edmonton, Canada: M. G. Hurtig, Ltd.

Addison, J. T., and W. S. Siebert (1979). *The Market for Labor: An Analytical Approach*. Santa Monica: Goodyear Publishing Co.

Ahluwalia, M. S. (1976a). "Inequality, Poverty and Development," *Journal of Development Economics*, 3: 307-342.

—— (1976b). "Income Inequality: Some Dimensions of the Problem," pp. 3-37, in Chenery et al. (1976).

Aigner, P. J., and G. C. Cain (1977). "Statistical Theories of Discrimination in Labor Markets," *Industrial and Labor Relations Review*, 30: 175-187.

Aitchison, J., and J. Brown (1957). *The Long-Normal Distribution*. Cambridge: Cambridge University Press.

Akerlof, G. A. (1970). "The Market for 'Lemons': Qualitative Uncertainty and the Market Mechanism," *Quarterly Journal of Economics*, August 1970: 488.

—— (1978). "The Economics of Tagging," *The American Economic Review*, 68 (1), March 1978: 8-19.

—— (1980). "A Theory of Social Custom, of Which Unemployment May Be One Consequence," *Quarterly Journal of Economics*, 94 (4), June 1980: 749-776.

—— (1981). "Jobs as Dam Sites," *Review of Economic Studies*, 55 (1), (151), January 1981: 37-50.

Akin, J., and I. Garfinkel (1980). "The Quality of Education and Cohort Variation in Black/White Earnings Differentials: Comment," *American Economic Review*, 70, (1), March 1980: 186-191.

Allen, V. L., ed. (1970a). *Psychological Factors in Poverty*. Chicago: Institute for Research on Poverty monograph, Markham Publishing Co.

—— (1970b). "Personality Correlates of Poverty," pp. 242-266 in Allen (1970a).

Appelbaum, E. (1978). "Testing Neo Classical Production Theory," *Journal of Econometrics*, 7: 87-102.

Arrow, K. J. (1972). "Models of Job Discrimination," in Pascal (1972).

———— (1973). "Higher Education as a Filter," *Journal of Public Economics*, July 1973.

Ashenfelter, O. (1970). "Changes in Labor Market Discrimination Over Time," *Journal of Human Resources*, Fall 1970.

Ashenfelter, O., and A. Rees, eds. (1973). *Discrimination in Labor Markets*, Princeton: Princeton University Press.

Asimakopolus, A. (1977). "Profits and Investment: A Kaleckian Approach," pp. 328-342, in Harcourt (1977).

Atkinson, A. B. (1970). "On the Measurement of Equality," *Journal of Economic Theory*, 2: 244-263.

————, ed. (1973). *Wealth Income and Inequality*. Harmondsworth: Penguin Books, 1973.

———— (1975). *The Economics of Inequality*. Oxford: Clarendon Press.

————, ed. (1976). *The Personal Distribution of Incomes*. London: George Allen and Unwin.

Averitt, R. T. (1968). *The Dual Economy: The Dynamics of American Industry Structure*. New York: Horton.

Azariadis, C. (1975). "Implicit Contracts and Underemployment Equilibria," *Journal of Political Economy*, 83 (6), December 1975: 1183-1202.

Baily, M. N. (1977). "On the Theory of Layoffs and Unemployment," *Econometrica*, 45 (5), July 1977: 1043-1064.

Baron, J. N., and W. T. Bielby (1980). "Current Research on Segmentation and Stratification: Substances in Search of a Method," paper presented at National Science Foundation (NSF) conference on "The Structure of Labor Markets." Athens, Georgia: March 1980.

Barsky, C. B., and M. E. Personick (1981). "Measuring Wage Dispersion: Pay Ranges Reflect Industry Traits," *Monthly Labor Review*, 104 (4), April 1981: 35-41.

Beach, C. M, with D. E. Card and F. Flatters (1981). *Distribution of Income and Wealth in Ontario: Theory and Evidence*. Toronto: Ontario Economic Council.

Becker, G. (1957). *The Economics of Discrimination*. Chicago: University of Chicago Press.

———— (1964). *Human Capital*. New York: Columbia University Press.

———— (1965). "A Theory of the Allocation of Time," *Economic Journal*, September 1965: pp. 493-517.

———— (1974). "A Theory of Social Interaction," *Journal of Political Economy*, 82, November/December 1974: pp. 1063-1093.

Becker, G., and N. Tomes (1976). "Child Endowments and the Quality and Quantity of Children," *Journal of Political Economy*, 84 (4), Part 2, August 1976: S143-S162.

———— (1979). "An Equilibrium Theory of the Distribution of Income and Intergenerational Mobility," *Journal of Political Economy*, 87 (6), December 1979: 1153-1189.

Bendix, R., and S. M. Lipset (1966). *Class, Status and Power—Social Stratification in Comparative Perspective*, 2nd ed. New York: Free Press.

Ben-Porath, Y. (1967). "The Production of Human Capital and the Life-cycle of Earnings," *Journal of Political Economy*, August 1967.

Bergmann, B. (1971). "The Effect on White Incomes of Discrimination in Employment," *Journal of Political Economy*, vol. 79.

Berle, A. A. (1968). "Property, Production and Revolution," pp. vii-xxvi, preface to Berle and Means (1968).

Berle, A. A., and G. C. Means (1968). *The Modern Corporation and Private Property*, rev. ed. New York: Harcourt Brace Jovanovich.

Bhatia, K. (1976). "Capital Gains and Inequality of Personal Income: Some Results from Survey Data," *Journal of the American Statistical Association*, 71, September 1976: 575-580.

Blau, F. (1972). "Women's Place in the Labor Market," *American Economic Review*, 62 (2), May 1972.

Blaug, M. (1976). "Human Capital Theory—A Slightly Jaundiced Survey," *Journal of Economic Literature*, 14 (3), September 1976: 827-855.

Blewett, E. (1982). *Measuring Life Cycle Inequality*, Ph.D. dissertation, University of British Columbia, April 1982.

Blinder, A. S. (1973a). "Wage Discrimination: Reduced Form and Structural Estimates," *Journal of Human Resources*, Fall 1973, pp. 436-455.

———— (1973b). "A Model of Inherited Wealth," *The Quarterly Journal of Economics*, 87 (4), November 1973: 608-626.

———— (1974). *Toward an Economic Theory of Income Distribution*, Cambridge, Mass.: M.I.T. Press.

———— (1976). "On Dogmatism in Human Capital Theory," *Journal of Human Resources*, 11 (1), Winter 1976: 8-22.

———— (1980). "The Level and Distribution of Economic Well-Being," pp. 418-499, in Feldstein (1980).

Blinder, A. S., and R. M. Solow, eds. (1974). *The Economics of Public Finance*. Washington, D.C.: The Brookings Institution.

Bliss, C. J. (1975). *Capital Theory and the Distribution of Income*. Amsterdam: North Holland.

Blumberg, P. (1979). "White Collar Status Panic," *The New Republic*, December 1, 1979.

Bonacich, E. (1980). "The Creation of Dual Labor Markets," mimeo; paper presented at NSF conference on "The Structure of Labor Markets." Athens, Georgia: March 1980.

Boserup, E. (1970). *Woman's Role in Economic Development*. London: George Allen and Unwin.

Bowles, S. (1972). "Schooling and Inequality from Generation to Generation," *Journal of Political Economy*, 80 (3), Part 2, May/June 1972: S219-S251.

Bowles, S., and H. Gintis (1976). *Schooling in Capitalist America: Educational Reform and the Contradictions of Economic Life*. New York: Basic Books.

Bradley, C. F., S. E. Ross, and J. M. Warnyca (1978). *Parent's Choice—A Comprehensive Perinatal Programme*. Vancouver, B.C.: Vancouver Perinatal Health Project, November 1978.

Break, G. F. (1974). "The Incidence and Economic Effects of Taxation," in Blinder and Solow (1974).

Brittain, J. A. (1977). *The Inheritance of Economic Status*, Washington, D.C.: The Brookings Institution.

———— (1978). *Inheritance and the Inequality of Material Wealth*, Washington, D.C.: The Brookings Institution.

Bronfenbrenner, M. (1968). "Neo-Classical Macro-Distribution Theory," pp. 476-500, in Marchal and Ducros (1968).

Brown, J. A. C. (1976). "The Mathematical and Statistical Theory of Income Distribution," (plus comments by Shorrocks and Muelbauer), pp. 72-97, in Atkinson (1976).

Brown, J. C. (1978). *Prevention of Handicap: A Case for Improved Prenatal and Perinatal Care*. Ottawa: Canadian Institute of Child Health.

Brown, L. L. (1976). *The Measure of Poverty: Technical Paper 18, Characteristics of Low Income Population under Alternative Definitions*, Washington: U.S. Department of Health, Education, and Welfare.

Burkhauser, R. V., and J. L. Warlick (1981). "Disentangling the Annuity from the Redistributive Aspects of Social Security," *Review of Income and Wealth*, Series 27 (4), December 1981: 401-423.

Butler, N. R., and D. G. Bonham (1963). *Perinatal Mortality: The First Report of the 1958 British Perinatal Mortality Survey*. Edinburgh and London: E. & S. Livingstone.

Butler, R., and J. Heckman (1977). "The Government's Impact on the Labor Market Status of Black Americans: A Critical Review," in Hausman et al. (1977).

Cain, G. (1976). "The Challenge of Segmented Labor Market Theories to Orthodox Theory: A Survey," *Journal of Economic Literature*, 14 (4), December 1976: 1215-1257.

Calvo, G., and S. Wellisz (1979). "Hierarchy, Ability and Income Distribution," *Journal of Political Economy*, October 1979.

Canterbery, E. R. (1979). "A Vita Theory of the Personal Income Distribution," *Southern Economic Journal*, 46(1), July 1979: 12-48.

Carnoy, M., and D. Shearer (1980). *Economic Democracy—The Challenge of the 1980's*. Armonk, N.Y.: M. E. Sharpe.

Carosso, V. P. (1970). *Investment Banking in America: A History*. Cambridge, Mass.: Harvard University Press.

Champernowne, D. G. (1953). "A Model of Income Distribution," *Economic Journal*, 63(250), June 1953: 318-351.

——— (1974). "A Comparison of Measures of Inequality of Income Distribution," *The Economic Journal*, 84, December 1974: 788-816.

Chapman, B. J., and H. W. Tan (1980). "Specific Training and Inter-Industry Wage Differentials in U.S. Manufacturing," *The Review of Economics and Statistics*, 62 (3), August 1980: 371-378.

Chenery, H., M. S. Ahluwalia, C. Bell, J. Duloy, and R. Jolly (1976). *Redistribution with Growth*. London: World Bank, Oxford University Press.

Children's Defense Fund (1974). *Children out of School in America*. Washington D.C., October 1974.

Chiplin, B., and P. J. Sloane (1976). *Sex Discrimination in the Labour Market*. London: MacMillan.

Chiswick, B. R. (1968). "The Average Level of Schooling and Intra-Regional Inequality of Income," *American Economic Review*, 58, June 1968: 495-500.

——— (1974). *Income Inequality: Regional Analysis within a Human Capital Framework*. New York: Columbia University Press.

Chiswick, B. R., and J. Mincer (1972). "Time Series Changes in Personal Income Inequality in the United States from 1939 with Projections to 1985," *Journal of Political Economy*, May/June 1972.

Chiswick, B. R., and S. A. O'Neill (1977). *Human Resources and Income*

Distribution Issues and Policies. New York: W. W. Norton and Co.

Clairmont, D., M. MacDonald, and F. Wien (1980). "A Segmentation Approach to Poverty and Low Wage Work in the Maritimes," in Harp and Hofley (1980).

Clark, J. B. (1899). *The Distribution of Wealth—A Theory of Wages, Interest, and Profit.* New York: MacMillan.

Clark, K. B., and L. H. Summers (1979). "Labor Market Dynamics and Unemployment: A Reconsideration," *Brookings Papers on Economic Activity,* (1): 13-60, Washington, D.C.: The Brookings Institution.

Cobb, C. W., and P. H. Douglas (1928). "A Theory of Production?" *American Economic Review,* 18, Suppl., March 1928: 139-165.

Cohen, M. (1927). "Property and Sovereignty," pp. 153-175, in Macpherson (1978).

Cohen, W. J. (1980). "Economic Well-Being and Income Distribution," p. 493 (comment on Blinder, 1980). New York: National Bureau of Economic Research (NBER) reprint.

Coleman, R. P., and L. Rainwater (1978). *Social Standing in America: New Dimensions of Class.* New York: Basic Books.

Comanor, W. S., and R. H. Smiley (1975). "Monopoly and the Distribution of Wealth," *Quarterly Journal of Economics,* 89, May 1975: 177-194.

—— (1980). "Quarterly Journal of Economics LXXXIX: Revisited," *Quarterly Journal of Economics,* 94 (1), February 1980: 195-198.

Cooper, G. (1979). *A Voluntary Tax? New Perspectives on Sophisticated Estate Tax Avoidance.* Washington, D.C.: The Brookings Institution.

Cornwall, J. (1977). *Modern Capitalism: Its Growth and Transformation.* New York: St. Martin Press.

Cowell, F. A. (1977). *Measuring Inequality.* Oxford: Philip Allan Publishers.

—— (1980). "On the Structure of Additive Inequality Measures," *The Review of Economic Studies,* 47 (3), (148), April 1980: 521-532.

Crow, J. F. (1970). "Do Genetic Factors Contribute to Poverty," pp. 147-160, in Allen (1970a).

Cunningham, J. (1979). "Where There's a Will There's a Way," *Manchester Guardian Weekly,* May 20, 1979, p. 5.

Dalton, H. (1935). *Some Aspects of Inequality of Incomes in Modern Communities.* New York: E. F. Dutton.

Danziger, S. (1980). "Do Working Wives Increase Family Inequality?" *Journal of Human Resources,* 15 (3) Summer 1980, 444-451.

Danziger, S., and R. Haveman (1981). "The Reagan Budget: A Sharp Break with the Past," *Challenge,* 24 (2), May/June 1981: 5-13.

Danziger, S., R. Haveman, and R. Plotnick (1981). "How Income Transfers Affect Work, Savings and the Income Distribution," *Journal of Economic Literature,* 19 (3), September 1981: 975-1064.

Danziger, S., R. Haveman, and E. Smolensky (1977). "The Measurement and Trend of Inequality: Comment," *American Economic Review,* 67 (3), June 1977: 505-512.

Dasgupta, P., A. Sen, and D. Starrett (1973). "Notes on the Measurement of Inequality," *Journal of Economic Theory,* April 1973.

Datcher, L. (1982). "Effects of Community and Family Background on Achievement," *Review of Economics and Statistics,* 64 (1): 32-41.

Davies, J. B. (1979a). "On the Size Distribution of Wealth in Canada," *Review of*

Income and Wealth, Series 25 (3), September 1979: 237-260.

——— (1979b). "Life Cycle Savings, Inheritance and the Distribution of Income and Wealth in Canada," Ph.D. thesis presented to the University of London.

——— (1980). "On the Relative Quantitative Importance of Inheritance and Other Sources of Economic Inequality," Research Report #8012, London, Ontario: Economics Department, University of Western Ontario.

——— (1981). "Uncertain Lifetime, Consumption and Dissaving in Retirement," *Journal of Political Economy,* 89 (3), June 1981: 561-577.

——— (1982). *Intergenerational Transfers: Redistribution and Inequality,* Research Report #8206, London, Ontario: University of Western Ontario.

Davies, J. B., and A. F. Shorrocks (1978). "Assessing the Quantitative Importance of Inheritance in the Distribution of Wealth," *Oxford Economic Papers,* 30 (1), March 1978: 138-149.

Davis, H. T. (1941). *The Theory of Econometrics,* Bloomington, Ind.: The Principa Press.

Dodge, D. A. (1975). "Impact of Tax, Transfer and Expenditure Policies of Government on the Distribution of Personal Income in Canada," *Review of Income and Wealth,* March 1975, pp. 1-52.

Doeringer, P. B., and M. J. Piore (1971). *Internal Labor Markets and Manpower Analysis,* Lexington, Mass.: D. C. Heath and Co.

Domhoff, G. W. (1974). *The Bohemian Grove and Other Retreats.* New York: Harper & Row.

Donaldson, D., and J. A. Weymark (1980). "A Single Parameter Generalization of the Gini Indices of Inequality," *Journal of Economic Theory,* 22 (1), February 1980: 67-86.

Dore, R. (1973). *British Factory—Japanese Factory: The Origins of National Diversity in Industrial Relations.* London.

Duncan, G. J., and S. Hoffman (1979). "On the Job Training and Earning Differences by Race and Sex," *Review of Economics and Statistics,* November 1979, pp. 594-603.

Duncan, G. J., and J. N. Morgan, eds. (1975, 1976). *Five Thousand American Families' Patterns of Economic Progress,* Vol. 3, 4, Ann Arbor: Institute for Survey Research, University of Michigan.

Dun's Review (1978). "Politics: The New Anti-Merger Strategy," *Dun's Review,* 114 (1), July 1978.

Dye, T. R., and J. W. Pickering (1974). "Governmental and Corporate Elites: Convergence and Differentiation," *Journal of Politics,* November 1974, p. 905.

Easton, L. D., and K. H. Guddot (1967). *Writings of the Young Marx on Philosophy and Society.* Garden City, N.Y.: Anchor Books, Doubleday.

Edwards, R. C. (1975). "The Social Relations of Production in the Firm and Labor Market Structure," pp. 3-26, in Edwards, Reich & Gordon (1975).

——— (1979). *Contested Terrain: The Transformation of the Workplace in the Twentieth Century.* New York: Basic Books.

Edwards, R. C., M. Reich, and D. Gordon, eds. (1975). *Labor Market Segmentation.* Lexington, Mass.: D. C. Heath & Company.

Ehrlich, E. (1975). "Involuntary Disruptions of 'Life Cycle' Plans," in *Five Thousand American Families,* Vol. 3, Duncan and Morgan (1975).

Ehrlich, I. (1973). "Participation in Illegal Activities," *Journal of Political Economy,* 81 (3), May/June 1973: 521-565.

Elias, T. O. (1962). *Nigerian Land Law and Custom*. London: Routledge and Kegan Paul Ltd.

Fei, J. C. H., G. Ranis, and S. W. Y. Kuo (1978). "Growth and the Family Distribution of Income by Factor Components," *Quarterly Journal of Economics*, 92 (1), February 1978: 17-53.

Feinstein, C. H. (1968). "Changes in the Distribution of the National Income in the United Kingdom since 1860," pp. 115-138, in Marchal and Ducros (1968).

Feldstein, M. S. (1973). *Lowering the Permanent Rate of Unemployment*, Washington: Joint Economic Committee, Government Printing Office.

Feldstein, M. S. (1976). "Social Security and the Distribution of Wealth," *Journal of the American Statistical Association*, 7 (356), December 1976: 800-807.

Feldstein, M. S. (1980). *The American Economy in Transition*. Chicago: University of Chicago Press.

Fenn, D. H. (1979). "Finding Where the Power Lies in Government," *Harvard Business Review*, September/October, 1979, pp. 144-153.

Fields, G. S. (1980). *Poverty Inequality and Development*. Cambridge: Cambridge University Press.

Flora, P., and J. Alber (1981). "Modernization, Democratization and the Development of Welfare States in Western Europe," pp. 37-80 in Flora and Heidenheimer (1981).

Flora, P., and A. D. Heidenheimer (1981). *The Development of Welfare States in Europe and America*. New Brunswick, N.J.: Transaction Books.

Forcese, D. (1975). *The Class Structure in Canada*. Toronto: McGraw-Hill & Ryerson.

Freedman, M. (1976). *Labor Markets: Segments and Shelters*. New York: Allanheld Osmun & Co., Universe Books.

Freeman, R. B. (1973). "Decline of Labor Market Discrimination and Economic Analysis, *American Economic Review*, 63 (2), May 1973: 280-286.

——— (1977). "The Decline in Economic Rewards to College Education," *Review of Economics Statistics*, 59 (1), February 1977.

——— (1980a). "The Effect of Unionism on Worker Attachment to Firms," *Journal of Labor Research*, 1 (1), Spring 1980: 29-62.

——— (1980b). "The Exit-Voice Tradeoff in the Labor Market: Unionism, Job Tenure, Quits and Separations," *Quarterly Journal of Economics*, 94 (4), June 1980: 643-674.

——— (1981). *Troubled Workers in the Labor Market*, Working Paper 816. Cambridge: National Bureau of Economic Research, December 1981.

——— (1982). "Union Wage Practices and Wage Dispersion within Establishments," *Industrial and Labor Relations Review*, 36 (1), October 1982: 3-21.

Freeman, R. B., and J. L. Medoff (1979). "The Two Faces of Unionism," *The Public Interest*, No. 57, Fall 1979.

Friedman, M. (1953). "Choice, Chance and the Personal Distribution of Income," *Journal of Political Economy*, 61 (4), August 1953: 277-290.

——— (1962). *Capitalism and Freedom*. Chicago: University of Chicago Press.

——— (1979). *Free to Choose*. New York: Avon Books.

Friedman, M., and S. Kuznets (1954). *Income from Independent Professional Practice*. New York: NBER.

Fuchs, V. R. (1967). "Redefining Poverty and Redistributing Income," *The Public Interest*, 8, Summer 1967: 88-95.

274 / ECONOMIC INEQUALITY IN THE UNITED STATES

———— (1971). "Differences in Hourly Earnings between Men and Women, *Monthly Labor Review*, 94, May 1971: 9-15.

Galbraith, J. K. (1967). *The New Industrial State*. New York: Signet Books.

Gallman, R. E. (1969). "Trends in the Size Distribution of Wealth in the Nineteenth Century," pp. 1-30, in Soltow (1969).

Garfinkel, I. and R. H. Haveman (1977). *Earnings Capacity Inequality and Poverty*. New York: Academic Press, Institute for Research on Poverty, Monograph Series.

Garmes, W. I., and L. C. Pierce (1978). *School Finance: The Economics and Politics of Public Education*. Englewood Cliffs, N.J.: Prentice-Hall Inc.

Gibrat, R. (1931). *Les Inegalites Economiques*. Paris: Sirey.

Gilder, G. (1981). *Wealth and Poverty*. New York: Basic Books.

Gillespie, W. I. (1966). "The Incidence of Taxes and Public Expenditures on the Canadian Economy," *Studies of the Royal Commission on Taxation*, (2), Ottawa: Queen's Printer.

———— (1976). "On the Redistribution of Income in Canada," *Canadian Tax Journal*, July/August 1976, pp. 419-450.

———— (1978). *In Search of Robin Hood: The Effect of Federal Budgetary Policies during the 1970's on the Distribution of Income in Canada*. Montreal: C. D. Howe Institute.

———— (1980). "Taxes Expenditures and the Redistribution of Income in Canada, 1951-1977," pp. 27-50 in *Reflections on Canadian Incomes*. Ottawa: Economic Council of Canada.

Gini, C. (1912). *Variabilita e mutabilita, contributo alla studio delle distrubugioni e della relazioni statistiche*. Bologna.

Goldberger, A. S. (1978). "The Genetic Determination of Income: Comment," *American Economic Review*, 68 (5), December 1978: 960-969.

———— (1979). "Heritability," *Economica*, 46: 327-347.

Goldsmith, R. W. (1940). *The Distribution of Ownership in the 200 Largest Non-Financial Corporations*, Washington, D.C.: [U.S. Government Printing Office] Temporary National Economic Committee, Monograph No. 29.

Gordon, D. M. (1972). *Theories of Poverty and Underemployment*. Lexington, Mass.: D. C. Heath & Company.

———— (1980). *Labor Market Segmentation in American Capitalism*, Paper presented at NSF conference on "Labor Market Segmentation," Athens, Georgia: February 1980.

Gordon, D. M., R. Edwards, and M. Reich. *Labor Market Segmentation in American Capitalism*. Cambridge: Cambridge University Press, forthcoming.

Gottschalk, P. T. (1978). "A Comparison of Marginal Productivity and Earnings by Occupation," *Industrial and Labor Relations Review*, 31 (3), April 1978: 368-378.

———— (1981). "Transfer Scenarios and Projections of Poverty into the 1980's," *Journal of Human Resources*, Winter 1981, 16 (1): 41-60.

Granovetter, M. S. (1974). *Getting a Job: A Study of Contacts and Careers*. Cambridge, Mass.: Harvard University Press.

Greenberg, D., R. Moffit, and J. Friedmann (1981). "Under-reporting and Experimental Effects on Work Effort: Evidence from the Gary Income Maintenance Experiment," *Review of Economics and Statistics*, 63 (4), November 1981: 581-590.

Greenwood, D. (1983). "An Estimation of U.S. Family Wealth and Its Distribution from Micro Data, 1973," *The Review of Income and Wealth,* Series 29, No. 1, March 1983: 23-44.

Greenwood, M. F. (1975). "Research on Internal Migration in the United States— A Survey," *Journal of Economic Literature,* 13 (2), June 1975: 394-434.

Griliches, Z. (1976). "Wages of Very Young Men," *Journal of Political Economy,* 84 (4), Part 2, August 1976: S69-S86.

——— (1977). "Estimating the Return to Schooling: Some Econometric Problems," *Econometrica,* 45 (1), January 1977: 1-22.

——— (1979). "Sibling Models and Data in Economics: Beginnings of a Survey," *Journal of Political Economy,* 87 (5), Part 2, October, 1979: S37-S64.

Gronau, R. (1977). "Leisure, Home Production and Work," *Journal of Political Economy,* December 1977, pp. 1099-1125.

——— (1980). "Home Production a Forgotten Industry," *Review of Economics and Statistics,* 62 (3), August 1980: 408-416.

Gundersen, M. (1980). *Labour Market Economics: Theory, Evidence and Policy in Canada.* Toronto: McGraw-Hill Ryerson.

Gurin, P. (1978). "The Role of Worker Expectancies in the Study of Employment Discrimination," pp. 13-39 in Wallace and Lamond (1978).

Hagerbaumer, J. B. (1977). "The Gini Concentration Ratio and the Minor Concentration Ratio: A Two-Parameter Index of Inequality," *The Review of Economics and Statistics,* (3), August 1977: 337-339.

Haley, B. F. (1968). "Changes in the Distribution of Income in the United States," pp. 3-18 in Marchal and Ducros (1968).

Hall, R. E. (1980). *The Importance of Lifetime Jobs in the U.S. Economy.* New York: NBER, Working Paper Series No. 560.

——— (1982). "The Importance of Lifetime Jobs in the U.S. Economy," *American Economic Review,* 72 (4), September 1982: 716-725.

Halpern, R. (1982). "Surviving the Competition: Economic Skills and Arguments for Program Directors," *Young Children: The Journal of the National Association* for the Education of Young Children, 37 (5), July 1982: 25-32, 49.

Hameed, S. M. A., ed. (1975). *Canadian Industrial Relations.* Toronto: Butterworths and Company.

Harbury, C. D. (1962). "Inheritance and the Distribution of Personal Wealth in Britain," *Economic Journal,* December 1962.

Harbury, C. D., and D. Hitchens (1976). "The Inheritance of Top Wealth Leavers: Some Further Evidence," *Economic Journal,* 86, June 1976: 321-326.

Harbury, C. D., and P. C. McMahon (1973). "Inheritance and the Characteristics of Top Wealth Leavers in Britain," *Economic Journal,* 83 (331), September 1973: 810-833.

Harcourt, G. C. (1977). *The Microeconomic Foundation of Macroeconomics.* Boulder, Colo.: Westview Press.

Harp, J., and J. Hofley, eds. (1980). *Structural Inequality, The Case of Poverty in Canada.* Toronto: Prentice-Hall.

Harrington, M. (1963). *The Other America.* Baltimore: Penguin Books.

Harris, D. J. (1978). *Capital Accumulation and Income Distribution.* Stanford: Stanford University Press.

Harrison, A. (1979). *The Distribution of Wealth in Ten Countries,* Background Paper No. 7. London: Royal Commission on the Distribution of Income and

Wealth, HMSO.

Harrison, R. S. (1976). *Equality in Public School Finance*. Lexington, Mass.: Lexington Books, D. C. Heath & Co.

Hausman, L., et al., eds. (1977). *Equal Rights and Industrial Relations*. Madison: Industrial Relations Association.

Hayes, R. H., and W. J. Abernathy (1980). "Managing Our Way to Economic Decline," *Harvard Business Review*, July/August 1980: 67-77.

Hearnshaw, L. S. (1979). *Cyril Burt, Psychologist*. Ithaca, N.Y.: Cornell University Press.

Henle, P., and P. Ryscavage (1980). "The Distribution of Earned Income among Men and Women, 1958-77," *Monthly Labor Review*, 103 (4), April 1980: 3-10.

Herman, E. S. (1981). *Corporate Control, Corporate Power*. New York: Cambridge University Press.

Hess, R. D. (1970). "The Transmission of Cognitive Strategies in Poor Families: The Socialization of Apathy and Underachievement," pp. 73-92, in Allen (1970a).

Hicks, J. R. (1946). "Income," pp. 74-82, in Parker and Harcourt (1969).

Hill, C. R., and F. P. Stafford (1977). "Family Background and Lifetime Earnings," pp. 511-549, in Juster (1977).

Hirsch, B. T. (1982). "The Inter-Industry Structure of Unionism, Earnings and Earnings Dispersion," *Industrial and Labor Relations Review*, 36 (1), October 1982: 22-39.

Hoffman, S. D. (1979). "Black-White Life Cycle Earnings Differences and the Vintage Hypothesis: A Longitudinal Analysis," *American Economic Review*, 69 (5), December 1979: 855-867.

Hoffman, S. D., and N. Podder (1976). "Income Inequality," pp. 333-356, in Duncan and Morgan (1976).

Holmes, R. (1976). "Male-Female Earnings Differentials in Canada," *Journal of Human Resources*, 11, Winter 1976: 109-112.

Hum, D. P. J. (1980). "Poverty Policy and Social Experimentation in Canada," pp. 307-320, in *Reflections on Canadian Incomes*, Ottawa: Economic Council of Canada.

Hurd, M., and J. Shoven (1982). "Real Income and Wealth of the Elderly," *American Economic Review*, 72 (2), May 1982: 314-318.

Husen, T. (1969). *Talent Opportunity and Career*. Stockholm: Almquist Wicksell.

Hutchinson, T. W. (1960). *The Significance and Basic Postulates of Economic Theory*. New York: A. M. Kelley.

Irvine, I. (1978). "Pitfalls in the Estimation of Optimal Lifetime Consumption Patterns," *Oxford Economic Papers*, 30 (2), July 1978: 301-309.

——— (1980). The Distribution of Income and Wealth in a Lifecycle Framework, *Canadian Journal of Economics*, August 1980: pp. 455-479.

Jencks, C., et al. (1972). *Inequality: A Reassessment of the Effect of Family and Schooling in America*. New York: Basic Books.

——— (1979). *Who gets Ahead? The Determinants of Economic Success in America*. New York: Basic Books.

Jensen, A. R. (1969). "How Much Can We Boost I.Q. and Scholastic Achievement?," *Harvard Educational Review*, 39 (1), Winter 1969: 1-123.

——— (1970). "Learning Ability, Intelligence and Educability," pp. 106-132, in Allen (1970a).

Johnson, H. G., and P. Mieszkowski (1970). "The Effects of Unionization on the Distribution of Income: A General Equilibrium Approach," *The Quarterly Journal of Economics,* 84 (4), 539-561.

Johnston, B. F., and P. Kilby (1975). *Agriculture and Structural Transformation: Economic Strategies in Late Developing Countries.* New York: Oxford University Press.

Jones, A. H. (1980). *Wealth of a Nation To Be—The American Colonies on the Eve of Revolution.* New York: Columbia University Press.

Juster, F. T., ed. (1977). *The Distribution of Economic Well-Being.* Studies in Income and Wealth, Vol. 41, Cambridge, Mass.: National Bureau of Economic Research, Ballinger Publishing Co.

Kakwani, W. (1980). "On a Class of Poverty Measures," *Econometrica,* 48 (2), March 1980: 423-436.

Kamin, L. J. (1974). *The Science and Politics of I.Q.* New York: Halsted Press, John Wiley & Sons.

Kanbur, S. M. (1979). "Of Risk Taking and the Personal Distribution of Income," *Journal of Political Economy,* 87 (4), August 1979: 769-797.

——— (1982). "Entrepeneurial Risk-Taking Inequality and Public Policy," *Journal of Political Economy,* 90 (1), February 1982: 1-21.

Kapetyn, J. C. (1903). *Skew Frequency Curves in Biology and Statistics.* Nordhobb.

Keeley, M. C., P. K. Robins, R. G. Spiegelman, and R. W. West (1978). "The Labor Supply Effects and Costs of Alternative Negative Income Tax Programs," *Journal of Human Resources,* 13 (1): 3-36.

Kerr, C. (1950). "Labor Markets: Their Character and Consequence," *American Economic Review,* May 1950.

Kessler-Harris, A. (1975). "Stratifying by Sex—Understanding the History of Working Women," Chapter 8, in Edwards, Reich, and Gordon (1975).

Knight, F. H. (1923). "The Ethics of Competition," *Quarterly Journal of Economics,* 37, August 1923: 579-624.

——— (1951). "The Role of Principles in Economics and Politics," *American Economic Review,* 61 (1), March 1951: 1-29.

Kolko, G. (1965). *Wealth and Power in America: An Analysis of Social Class and Income Distribution.* New York: Praeger.

Koopmans, T. C. (1957). "The Construction of Economic Knowledge," in *Three Essays on the State of Economic Science,* New York: McGraw-Hill.

——— (1977). "Examples of Production Relations Based on Micro-Data," pp. 144-171, in Harcourt (1977).

Kotlikoff, L., and L. Summers (1981). "The Role of Intergenerational Transfers in Aggregate Capital Accumulation," *Journal of Political Economy.*

Kotz, D. M. (1978). *Bank Control of Large Corporations:* Berkeley, Calif.: University of California Press.

——— (1979). "The Significance of Bank Control over Large Corporations," *Journal of Economic Issues,* 13 (2), June 1979: 407-426.

Kraus, F. (1981). "The Historical Development of Income Inequality in Western Europe and The United States," pp. 187-236, in Flora and Heidenheimer (1981).

Kravis, I. (1959). "Relative Income Shares in Fact and Theory," *American Economic Review,* 49.

Kuhn, T. S. (1970). *The Structure of Scientific Revolutions,* 2nd ed. Chicago: University of Chicago Press.

Kuo, S. W. Y., G. Ranis, and J. C. H. Fei (1981). *The Taiwan Success Story: Rapid Growth with Improved Distribution in the Republic of China 1952-1979.* Boulder, Colo.: Westview Press.

Kuznets, S. (1955). "Economic Growth and Income Inequality," *American Economic Review,* 45 (1), March 1955: 1-28.

––––––– (1966). *Modern Economic Growth.* New Haven, Conn.: Yale University Press.

––––––– (1976). "Demographic Aspects of the Size Distribution of Income: An Exploratory Essay," *Economic Development and Cultural Change,* 25: 1-99.

Lampman, R. J. (1962). *A Study of Savings in the United States.* Princeton: Princeton University Press.

Lane, J. P., and J. N. Morgan (1975). "Patterns of Change in Family Income Status and Family Structure," in Duncan and Morgan (1975).

Lansing, J. B., and J. Sonquist (1969). "A Cohort Analysis of Changes in the Distribution of Wealth," pp. 31-74, in Soltow (1969).

Layard, R., and G. Psarchopoulous (1974). "The Screening Hypothesis and the Returns to Education," *Journal of Political Economy,* 82 (5), September/October 1974: 995-998.

Layard, R., and A. Zabalza (1979). "Family Income Distribution: Explanation & Policy Evaluation," *Journal of Political Economy,* 81 (5), Part 2, October 1979: S133-S162.

Lazear, E. P. (1979a). "The Narrowing of Black-White Differentials Is Illusory," *American Economic Review,* 69 (4), September 1979: 553-565.

––––––– (1979b). "Why Is There Mandatory Retirement?" *Journal of Political Economy,* December 1979.

Lazear, E. P., and R. T. Michael (1980). "Family Size and the Distribution of Real Per Capita Income," *American Economic Review,* 70 (1), March 1980: 91-107.

Lebergott, S. (1975). *Wealth and Want.* Princeton: Princeton University Press.

Leff, N. H. (1979). "Entrepeneurship and Economic Development: The Problem Revisited," *Journal of Economic Literature,* 17 (1), March 1979: 44-64.

Leibowitz, A. (1974). "Home Investments in Children," *Journal of Political Economy,* 82, March/April 1974: S111-S131.

––––––– (1977). "Parental Inputs and Children's Achievement," *Journal of Human Resources,* 12 (2), Spring 1977: 242-251.

Leigh, D. (1976). "Occupational Advancement in the late 1960's: An Indirect Test of the Dual Labor Market Hypothesis," *Journal of Human Resources,* 11 (2), Spring 1976: 155-171.

––––––– (1978). "An Analysis of the Determinants of Occupational Upgrading," New York: Academic Press.

Lenin, V. I. (1917). *Imperialism The Highest Stage of Capitalism,* New York: International Publishers.

Lewis, H. G. (1963). *Unionism and Relative Wages in the United States.* Chicago: University of Chicago Press.

Lewis, W. A. (1957). "Economic Development with Unlimited Supplies of Labour," The Manchester School.

Lillard, L. A. (1977). "Inequality: Earnings vs. Human Wealth," *American Economic Review,* 67 (2), March 1977: 43-54.

Lillard, L. A., and R. J. Willis (1978). "Dynamic Aspects of Earnings Mobility,"

Econometrica, 46 (5), September 1978: 985-1008.

Lininger, C. A., D. Vaughan, and T. C. Whiteman (1981). *The 1979 ISDP Research Panel: Scope, Coverage, and Some Preliminary Indications of Data Reliability,* paper presented to American Economics Association meetings, Washington, D.C., December 28, 1981.

Link, C., E. Ratledge, and K. Lewis (1980). "The Quality of Education and Cohort Variation in Black-White Earnings Differentials: Reply," *American Economic Review,* 70 (1), March 1980: 196-203.

Lipset, S. M. (1966). "Value Patterns, Class, and the Democratic Polity: The United States and Great Britain," in Bendix and Lipset (1966).

Lipsey, R. G. (1977). "Wage Price Controls: How To Do a Lot of Harm by Trying to Do a Little Good," *Canadian Public Policy,* 3 (1), Winter 1977: 1-13.

—— (1981). "The Understanding and Control of Inflation: Is There a Crisis in Macroeconomics," *Canadian Journal of Economics,* 14 (4), November 1981: 545-576.

Lipsey, R. G., G. R. Sparks, and P. O. Steiner (1979). *Economics,* 3rd ed. New York: Harper & Row.

Loehr, W. (1980). "Economic Growth, Distribution and Incomes of the Poor," *Journal of Economic Studies,* 7 (3): 127-139.

Lorenz, M. O. (1905). "Methods of Measuring the Concentration of Wealth," *Quarterly Publications of the American Statistical Association,* 9: 205-219.

Loury, G. C. (1981). "Intergenerational Transfers and the Distribution of Earnings," *Econometrica,* 49 (4), July 1981: 843-867.

Love, R., and M. Wolfson (1976). *Income Inequality: Statistical Methodology and Canadian Illustrations.* Ottawa: Statistics Canada, Cat. No. 13-559.

Lucas, R. E. B. (1977a). "Hedonic Wage Equations and Psychic Wages in the Returns to Schooling," *American Economic Review,* September 1977, pp. 549-558.

—— (1977b). "Is There a Human Capital Approach to Income Inequality," *Journal of Human Resources,* 31, Summer 1977, pp. 387-395.

Lundberg, F. (1968). *The Rich and Super Rich: A Study in the Power of Money Today.* New York: L. Stuart.

Lydall, H. F. (1959). "The Distribution of Employment Incomes," *Econometrica,* 27: 110-115.

—— (1968). *The Structure of Earnings.* Oxford: Clarendon Press.

—— (1976). "Theories of the Distribution of Earnings," pp. 15-46, in Atkinson (1976).

McKenzie, J. C. (1970). "Poverty: Food and Nutrition Indices," pp. 64-85, in Townsend (1970).

McNulty, P. J. (1980). *The Origins and Development of Labor Economics.* Cambridge, Mass.: The MIT Press.

Macpherson, C. B., ed. (1978). *Property: Mainstream and Critical Positions.* Toronto: University of Toronto Press.

Malkiel, B., and J. Malkiel (1973). "Male-Female Pay Differentials in Professional Employment," *American Economic Review,* 63, September 1973: 693-705.

Malles, P. (1973). *The Institutions of Industrial Relations in Continental Europe.* Ottawa: Labour Canada.

Mandel, E. (1969). *An Introduction to Marxist Economic Theory.* New York: Merits Publishers.

Mandelbrot, B. (1961). "Stable Paretian Random Function and the Multiplicative

Variations in Income," *Econometrica*, 29 (4), 517-43.

——— (1962). "Paretian Distributions and Income Maximization," *Quarterly Journal of Economics*, February 1962.

Mann, H. (1839). "Third Annual Report to the Board of Education," in *Life and Works*, Vol. 3. Boston: 1868.

Marchal, J., and B. Ducros, eds. (1968). *The Distribution of National Income.* London: MacMillan-St. Martin's Press.

Marfels, C. (1972a). "The Gini Ratio of Concentration Reconsidered," *Statistiche Hefte, Statistical Papers International Journal for Theoretical and Applied Statistics*, 13 (2), 160-179.

——— (1972b). "On Testing Concentration Measures," *Zeitschrift für Nationalakonomie*, 32: 461-486.

Marglin, S. (1974). "What Do Bosses Do? The Origin and Functions of Hierarchy in Capitalist Production," *Review of Radical Political Economy*, 6 (2).

Marris, R., and D. C. Mueller (1980). "The Corporation and Competition," *Journal of Economic Literature*, 18 (1), March 1980: 32-63.

Marshall, A. (1920). *Principles of Economics*, 8th ed. New York: The MacMillan Co.

Marx, K. (1844). *Economic and Philosophic Manuscripts*, in Easton and Guddot (1967).

——— (1887). *Capital: A Critique of Political Economy*, Vol. 1-3. New York: International Publishers, 1967.

——— (1899). "Value, Price and Profit," *The Essential Left*, London: Unwin Books, 1960.

Masters, S., and I. Garfinkel (1977). *Estimating the Labor Supply Effects of Income-Maintenance Alternatives.* New York: Academic Press.

Mayhew, K., and B. Rosewell (1979). "Labour Market Segmentation in Britain," *Oxford University Institute of Economics and Statistics*, 1979, pp. 81-115.

Meade, J. E. (1976). *The Just Economy.* London: George Allen and Unwin.

Mellor, E. F., and L. D. Stamas (1982). "Usual Weekly Earnings: Intergroup Differences and Basic Trends," *Monthly Labor Review*, 105 (4), April 1982: 15-24.

Mellor, J. W. (1966). *The Economics of Agricultural Development.* Ithaca, N.Y.: Cornell University Press.

Menchik, P. L. (1979). "Inter-generational Transmission of Inequality: An Empirical Study of Wealth Mobility," *Economica*, 46, November 1979: 349-362.

——— (1980). "Primogeniture, Equal Sharing and the U.S. Distribution of Wealth," *Quarterly Journal of Economics*, 114 (2), March 1980: 299-316.

Mendelson, M. (1979). *The Administrative Cost of Income Security Programs: Ontario and Canada*, Toronto: Ontario Economic Council, Occasional Paper No. 9.

Mendershausen, H. (1956). "The Pattern of Estate Tax Wealth," pp. 277-380, in R. W. Goldsmith, *A Study of Saving in the United States*, Vol. 3. Princeton: Princeton University Press.

Mill, J. S. (1848). *Principles of Political Economy*, Vol. 1. New York: The Colonial Press, 1900.

Minarik, J. (1979). "The Size Distribution of Income During Inflation," *The Review of Income and Wealth*, Series 25 (4), December 1979: 377-392.

Mincer, J. (1970). "The Distribution of Labor Incomes—A Survey: With Special Reference to the Human Capital Approach," *Journal of Economic Literature*, 8, March 1970: 1-26.

—— (1974). *Schooling Experience and Earnings*. New York: NBER.

—— (1976). "Progress in Human Capital Analyses of the Distribution of Earnings," p. 136, in Atkinson (1976).

Mincer, J., and S. Polachek (1974). "Family Investments in Human Capital: Earnings of Women," *Journal of Political Economy*, 82 (2), Part 2, March/April 1974: S76-S111.

Mirer, T. (1979a). "The Utilization of Earnings Capacity," *Review of Economics and Statistics*, 61, August 1979: 466-69.

Mirer, T. W. (1979b). "The Wealth Age Relation among the Aged," *American Economic Review*, 69 (3), June 1979: 435-443.

Moffit, R. A. (1981). "The Negative Income Tax: Would It Discourage Work?," *Monthly Labor Review*, 104 (4), April 1981: 23-27.

Morishima, M. (1973). *Marx's Economics*. Cambridge: 1973.

Moss, M. (1978). "Income Distribution Issues Viewed in a Lifetime Income Perspective," *Review of Income and Wealth*, Series 24 (2), June 1978: 119-136.

Moynihan, D. P. (1965). *The Negro Family: The Case for National Action*. Washington: U.S. Government Printing Office, U.S. Department of Labor.

Mueller, W. F. (1977). "Conglomerates—A Non-Industry," Chapter 13 in W. Adams, *The Structure of American Industry*, New York: MacMillan.

Murphy, M. (1982). "Comparative Estimates of the Value of Household Work in the United States for 1976," *Review of Income and Wealth*, Series 28 (1), March 1982: 29-44.

Nelson, E. R. (1977). "The Measurement and Trend of Inequality: Comment," *American Economic Review*, 67 (3), June 1977: 497-501.

Newton, K., and N. Leckie (1977). "What's QWL? Definition, Notes and Bibliography," Ottawa: Economic Council of Canada, Discussion Paper No. 100.

Niosi, J. (1978). *The Economy of Canada*. Montreal: Black Rose Books.

Nordhaus, W. D. (1973). "The Effects of Inflation on the Distribution of Economic Welfare," *Journal of Money Credit and Banking*, 5 (1), Part 2, February 1973: 465-504.

Nyman, S., and A. Silberston (1978). "The Ownership and Control of Industry," *Oxford Economic Papers*, 30 (1), March 1978: 74-101.

Oaxaca, R. (1973). "Sex Discrimination in Wages," pp. 124-154, in Ashenfelter and Rees (1973).

OECD (1976). *National Accounts Statistics of OECD Countries*, Vol. 1. Paris.

OECD (1976). *Public Expenditure on Income Maintenance Programmes*. Paris: July 1976.

Oi, W. (1962). "Labour as a Quasi-Fixed Factor," *Journal of Political Economy*, 70, December 1962: 538-555.

Oja, G. (1980). "Inequality of the Wealth Distribution in Canada 1970 and 1977," *Reflections on Canadian Incomes*. Ottawa: Economic Council of Canada.

Okner, B. A. (1966). *Income Distribution and Federal Income Tax Policy*. Ann Arbor: The University of Michigan.

Okun, A. (1975). *Equality and Efficiency: The Big Tradeoff*, Washington, D.C.:

The Brookings Institution.

Orcutt, G., S. Caldwell, and R. Wertheimer II (1976). *Policy Exploration through Micro-analytic Simulation.* Washington, D.C.: The Urban Institute.

Orwell, G. (1937). *The Road to Wigan Pier.* London: Penguin Books, 1962.

Osberg, L. S. (1975). *A Structural Approach to the Distributions of Earnings,* Ph.D. dissertation, Yale University.

——— (1977). "Stochastic Process Models and the Distribution of Earnings," *Review of Income and Wealth,* series 23, p. 205.

——— (1981). *Economic Inequality in Canada.* Toronto: Butterworth.

Osberg, L., D. Clairmont, and R. Apostle (1982). *A Segmentation Approach to Low Wage Work.* Mimeo, Dalhousie University, Halifax, N.S.

Osman, T. (1977). "The Role of Intergenerational Wealth Transfers in the Distribution of Wealth over the Life Cycle: A Preliminary Analysis," pp. 397-412, in Juster (1977).

Osterman, P. (1975). "An Empirical Study of Labor Market Segmentation," *Industrial and Labor Relations Review,* July 1975.

Ostry, S., and M. Zaidi (1979). *Labour Economics in Canada,* 3rd ed. Toronto: MacMillan of Canada.

Oulton, N. (1976). "Inheritance and the Distribution of Wealth," *Oxford Economic Papers,* 28 (1), March 1976: 86-101.

Paglin, M. (1975). "The Measurement and Trend of Inequality: A Basic Revision," *American Economic Review,* 65 (4), September 1975: 598-609.

Pahl, J. (1980). "Patterns of Money Management within Marriage," *Journal of Social Policy,* 9, Part 3, July 1980: 313-333.

Papnicolaou, J., and G. Psarchopoulos (1979). "Socio-Economic Background, Schooling and Monetary Rewards in the United Kingdom," *Economica,* 46: 435-439.

Pareto, V. (1892). *Manuel d'Economie Politique.* Paris: Librairie Droz, 1966.

——— (1896). *Cours d'Economie Politique.* Geneva: Librarie Droz, 1964.

Parker, R. H., and G. C. Harcourt, eds. (1969). *Readings in the Concept and Measurement of Income.* Cambridge: Cambridge University Press, 1969.

Parsons, D. O. (1975). "Intergenerational Wealth Transfers and Educational Decisions of Male Youth," *Quarterly Journal of Economics,* 89 (4), November 1975: 603-617.

Parsons, T. (1954). *Essays in Sociological Theory.* Glencoe, Ill.: The Free Press.

Pascal, A. (1972). *Racial Discrimination in Economic Life.* Lexington, Mass.: D. C. Heath, Lexington Books.

Pasinetti, L. L. (1974). *Growth and Income Distribution Essays in Economic Theory.* Cambridge: Cambridge University Press.

Pearl, R. B., and M. Frankel (1981). *Composition of the Personal Wealth of American Households at the Start of the Eighties.* Mimeo, University of Illinois.

Pechman, J. A. (1971). *Federal Tax Policy,* rev. ed. Washington, D.C.: The Brookings Institution.

Pen, J. (1971). *Income Distribution.* Harmondsworth: Penguin Books.

Perkins, S. (1974). *Malnutrition and Mental Development.* International Union of Child Welfare Conference.

Perlman, R. (1976). *The Economics of Poverty.* New York: McGraw-Hill.

Pfautz, H. W., "The Current Literature on Social Stratification: Critique and Bibliography," *American Journal Of Sociology,* 58; 391-.

Phelps, E. S., ed. (1970). *Microeconomic Foundations of Employment and Inflation Theory.* New York: W. W. Norton & Co.

Phelps-Brown, H. (1977). *The Inequality of Pay.* Oxford: Oxford University Press.

Pigou, A. C. (1932). *The Economics of Welfare.* London: MacMillan & Co.

Piore, M. J. (1974). "Comments" on M. L. Wachter *Brookings Papers on Economic Activity,* (3), 1974, p. 685.

——— (1975). "Notes for a Theory of Labor Market Stratification," p. 125, in Edwards, Reich, and Gordon (eds.) (1975).

——— (1979). *Birds of Passage: Migrant Labor and Industrial Societies.* New York: Cambridge University Press.

Pissarides, C. A. (1974). "Risk Job Search and Income Distribution," *Journal of Political Economy,* 82 (6), November/December 1974: 1255-67.

Prewitt, K., and S. Verba (1979). *An Introduction to American Government,* 3rd ed. New York: Harper & Row.

Projector, D. S., and G. S. Weiss (1966). *Survey of Financial Characteristics of Consumers.* Washington: Federal Reserve Board.

Radner, D. S. (1981a). "Adjusted Estimates of the Size Distribution of Family Money Income for 1972," working paper No. 24, mimeo. Washington: Social Security Administration, Office of Policy, Office of Research and Statistics, October, 1981.

——— (1981b) "An Example of the Use of Statistical Matching in the Estimation and Analysis of the Size Distribution of Income, *Review of Income and Wealth,* series 27 (3), September 1981: 211-242.

Rainwater, L. (1974). *What Money Buys: Inequality and the Social Meanings of Income.* New York: Basic Books.

Rawls, J. (1971). *A Theory of Justice.* Cambridge, Mass.: Belknap Press.

Rees, A. (1962). *The Economics of Trade Unions.* Chicago: University of Chicago Press.

——— (1966). "Information Networks in Labor Markets," *American Economic Review,* May 1966, pp. 559-566.

Reich, M. (1981). *Racial Inequality: A Political-Economic Analysis.* Princeton: Princeton University Press.

Rein, M. (1970). "Problems in the Definition and Measurement of Poverty," pp. 46-63, in Townsend (1970).

Reinemer, V. (1979). "Stalking the Invisible Investor," *Journal of Economic Issues,* 13 (2), June 1979: 391-405.

Reuss, H. S. (1981). "Inequality, Here We Come," *Challenge,* September/October, 1981: pp. 49-52.

Reynolds, L. S. (1951). *The Structure of Labor Markets: Wages and Labor Mobility in Theory and Practice.* Westport, Conn.: Greenwood Press.

——— (1974). *Labor Economics and Labor Relations,* 6th ed. Englewood Cliffs, N.J.: Prentice-Hall.

Reynolds, M., and E. Smolensky (1977). *Public Expenditures, Taxes and the Distribution of Income: The United States 1950, 1961, 1970.* New York: Academic Press.

Ricardo, D. (1821). *The Principles of Political Economy and Taxation.* New York: Dent, Everyman's Library, 1969.

Richardson, K., and D. Spears, eds. (1972). *Race and Intelligence.* Baltimore: Pelican Books.

Riley, J. C. (1979). "Testing the Educational Screening Hypothesis," *Journal of Political Economy*, 87 (5), Part 2, October 1979: S227-S252.

Rist, R. C. (1970). "Student Social Class and Teacher Expectations: The Self-Fulfilling Prophecy in Ghetto Education," *Harvard Educational Review*, 40 (3), August 1970.

Roach, J. L., and J. K. Roach, eds. (1972). *Poverty, U.K.* Penguin Books.

Roberti, P. (1974). "Income Distribution—A Time Series and Cross-Section Study," *The Economic Journal*, September 1974: pp. 629-638.

Robinson, J., and J. Eatwell (1973). *An Introduction to Modern Economics*. London: McGraw-Hill.

Robinson, S. (1976). "A Note on the U Hypothesis Relating Income Inequality and Economic Development," *The American Economic Review*, 66 (3), June 1976: 437-40.

Rosen, S. (1974). "Hedonic Prices and Implicit Markets: Product Differentiation in Pure Competition," *Journal of Political Economy*, 82: 34-55.

Rosenmayr, L. (1970). "Cultural Poverty of Working Class Youth," pp. 165-183, in Townsend (1970).

Ross, S. E., and A. C. Rutter (1978). *Healthiest Babies Possible: An Outreach Program*. Vancouver, B.C.: Vancouver Perinatal Health Project, November 1978.

Rossi, J. W. (1979). "Two Essays on Income Distribution: Problems of Measurement and Trends in Brazilian Income Inequality," Ph.D. dissertation, Dalhousie University, Halifax, N.S.

Rothman, P. A. (1978). *Inequality and Stratification in the United States*. Englewood Cliffs, N.J.: Prentice-Hall.

Rowntree, B. S. (1941). *Poverty and Progress: A Second Social Survey of York*. London: Longmans.

Roy, A. D. (1950). "The Distribution of Earnings and of Individual Output," *The Economic Journal*, September 1950: p. 489.

Ruggles, N. D., and F. Ruggles (1977). "The Anatomy of Earnings Behaviour," pp. 115-157, in Juster (1977).

Ruggles, P., and M. O'Higgins (1981). "The Distribution of Public Expenditures among Households in the United States," *The Review of Income and Wealth*, series 27, June 1981: 137-164.

Rutherford, R. S. G. (1955). "Income Distributions—A New Model," *Econometrica*, 23 (3), July 1955: 277-294.

Ryan, J. (1972). "I.Q.: The Illusion of Objectivity," pp. 36-55, in Richardson and Spears (1972).

Ryder, N. B. (1973). "Comment," *Journal of Political Economy*, 81 (2), Part 2, March/April 1973: S65-70.

Rytina, N. F. (1981). "Occupational Segregation and Earnings Differences by Sex," *Monthly Labor Review*, January 1981: pp. 49-52.

——— (1982). "Earnings of Men and Women—A Look at Specific Occupations," *Monthly Labor Review*, April 1982: pp. 25-31.

Sahota, G. S. (1978). "Theories of Personal Income Distribution: A Survey," *Journal of Economic Literature*, 16 (1), March 1978: 1-55.

Sanborn, H. (1964). "Pay Differences between Men and Women," *Industrial and Labor Relations Review*, 17, July 1964: 534-550.

Sattinger, M. (1975). "Comparative Advantage and the Distribution of Earnings and Abilities," *Econometrica*, 43, May 1975: 455-468.

———— (1978). "Comparative Advantage in Individuals," *Review of Economics and Statistics*, 60 (2), May 1978: 259-267.

———— (1980). *Capital and the Distribution of Labor Earnings, Contributions to Economic Analysis*. Amsterdam: North Holland Publishing Co.

Sawyer, M. (1976). "Income Distribution in OECD Countries," occasional paper, *OECD Economic Outlook*, Paris, July 1976.

Schiff, M., M. Duyme, A. Damaret, and S. Tomkiewicz (1982). "How Much Could We Boost Scholastic Achievement and I.Q. Scores—A Direct Answer from a French Adoption Study," *Cognition: International Journal of Psychology*, 12 (2), 1982: 165-196.

Schiller, R. (1980). *The Economics of Poverty and Discrimination*. 3rd ed. Englewood Cliffs, N.J.: Prentice-Hall.

Schnitzer, M. (1975). *Income Distribution: A Comparative Study of the United States, Sweden, West Germany, East Germany, and Japan*. New York: Praeger.

Schultz, T. P. (1971). "Long-term Change in the Personal Income Distribution: Theoretical Approaches, Evidence and Explanations." Mimeo, Rand Corporation.

Schumpeter, J. A. (1934). *The Theory of Economic Development*. London: Oxford University Press, reprinted 1969.

———— (1942). *Capitalism, Socialism, and Democracy*. New York: Harper Torchbooks.

Schwartz, J., ed. (1977). *The Subtle Anatomy of Capitalism*. Santa Monica, Calif.: Goodyear Publishing Co.

Scitovsky, T. (1976). *The Joyless Economy*. New York: Oxford University Press.

Sen, A. (1979). "Issues in the Measurement of Poverty," *Scandinavian Journal of Economics*, 1979, pp. 285-307.

Shaw, P. (1981). "A Micro-Level Test of Marginal Productivity and Human Capital Theory, M.A. thesis, Dalhousie University, Halifax, N.S.

Sheshinski, E., and T. Weiss (1982). "Inequality within and between Families," *Journal of Poltical Economy*, 90 (1), February 1982: 105-127.

Shockley, W. (1970). "A 'Try Simplest Cases' Approach to the Heredity-Poverty-Crime Problem," pp. 141-146, in Allen (1970a).

Shorrocks, A. F. (1976). "Income Mobility and the Markov Assumption," *Economic Journal*, 86, September 1976: p. 566.

———— (1979). "On the Structure of Inter-Generational Transfers between Families," *Economica*, 46, November 1979: 415-423.

———— (1980). "The Class of Additively Decomposable Inequality Measures," *Econometrica*, 48 (3), April 1980: 613-626.

Simons, H. C. (1938). "The Definition of Income," pp. 63-73, in Parker and Harcourt (1969).

Smeeding, T. M. (1981). "The Size Distribution of Wage and Non-wage Compensation: Employer Cost vs. Employee Value," paper presented at NBER conference on "Research in Income and Wealth; The Measurement of Labor Cost," December 3-4, 1981.

Smelser, N. J. (1963). *The Sociology of Economic Life*. Englewood Cliffs, N.J.: Prentice Hall.

Smith, A. (1776). *The Wealth of Nations*, ed. E. Cannan, 2 vol. London: University Paperbacks, Nuthuen, 1961.

Smith, J. D. (1973). *The Concentration of Personal Wealth in America, 1969*.

Washington, D.C.: Urban Institute Working Paper No. 1208-1, August 27, 1973.

—— ed. (1975a). *The Personal Distribution of Wealth*. New York: Columbia University Press.

—— (1975b). "White Wealth & Black People: The Distribution of Wealth in Washington, D.C. in 1967," in Smith (1975a).

—— ed. (1980). *Modelling the Distribution and Intergenerational Transmission of Wealth*. NBER, Studies in Income and Wealth, Vol. 46. Chicago: University of Chicago Press.

Smith, J. D., and S. D. Franklin (1974). "The Concentration of Personal Wealth— 1922-1969," *American Economic Review*, May 1974: pp. 162-167.

Smith, J. P. (1978). "Family Labor Supply over the Life Cycle," *Explorations in Economic Research*, NBER Vol. 4, B Spring 1978.

Smith, J. P., and F. Welch (1977). "Black-White Male Wage Ratios: 1960-1970," *American Economic Review*, 67 (3), June 1977.

Smith, R. S. (1979). "Compensating Wage Differentials and Public Policy: A Review," *Industrial and Labour Relations Review*, April 1979, p. 339.

Smith, S. M. M., J. E. Cloutier, and D. W. Henderson (1979). *Poverty and Government Income Support in Canada, 1971-1975: Characteristics of the Low Income Population*. Ottawa: Economic Council of Canada, Discussion Paper No. 130, April 1979.

Smolensky, E., L. Stiefed, M. Schmundt, and R. Plotnick (1977). "Adding In-Kind Transfers to the Personal Income and Outlay Account: Implications for the Size Distribution of Income," pp. 9-44, in Juster (1977).

Sobol, M. G. (1979). "Factors Influencing Private Capital Accumulation on the 'Eve of Retirement,' " *Review of Economics and Statistics*, 61 (4), November 1979: 585-594.

Solow, R. M. (1951). "Some Long-Run Aspects of the Distribution of Wage Incomes," *Econometrica*, 19.

—— (1980). "On Theories of Unemployment," *American Economic Review*, 70 (1), March 1980: 1-11.

Soltow, L. (1971). *Patterns of Wealthholding in Wisconsin since 1850*. Madison: Wisconsin University Press.

—— (1975). *Men and Wealth in the United States, 1850-1870*. New Haven: Yale University Press.

—— ed. (1969). *Six Papers on the Size Distribution of Wealth and Income*. New York: NBER.

Spence, A. M. (1973). "Job Market Signalling," *Quarterly Journal of Economics*, August 1973: pp. 355-379.

—— (1974). *Market Signalling*. Cambridge, Mass.: Harvard University Press.

Staehle, H. (1943). "Ability, Wages and Income," *Review of Economics and Statistics*, 25: 77.

Stamp, Sir J. (1937). *The Science of Social Adjustment*. London: Macmillan and Co.

Stark, T. (1972). *The Distribution of Personal Income in the United Kingdom, 1949-63*, Cambridge: Cambridge University Press.

—— (1977). *The Distribution of Income in Eight Countries*, background paper No. 5. London: Royal Commission on the Distribution of Income and Wealth, H.M.S.O.

Starr, G. (1973). *Union-Non-Union Wage Differentials*. Toronto: Ontario Ministry of Labour.

—— (1975). "Union-Non-Union Wage Differentials in Ontario," pp. 283-294, in Hameed (1975).

Starrett, D. (1976). "Social Institutions, Imperfect Information and the Distribution of Income," *Quarterly Journal of Economics*, May 1976: pp. 261-284.

Stigler, G. J. (1961). "The Economics of Information," *Journal of Political Economy*, 69: 213-25.

—— (1970). "The Director's Law of Public Income Distribution," *Journal of Law and Economics*, April 1970: pp. 1-10.

Stigler, G. J., and G. Becker (1977). "De Gustibus Non Est Disputandum," *American Economic Review*, 67 (2): 76-90.

Stiglitz, J. (1975a). "The Theory of Screening, Education and the Distribution of Income," *American Economic Review*, June 1975: p. 269.

—— (1975b). "Incentives Risk and Information: Notes toward a Theory of Hierarchy," *Bell Journal of Economics*, 6 (2), Autumn 1975: 552-579.

Stone, K. (1975). "The Origins of Job Structures in the Steel Industry," pp. 27-84, in Edwards, Reich, and Gordon (1975).

Sweezy, P. M. (1942). *The Theory of Capitalist Development: Principles of Marxian Political Economy*. New York: Oxford University Press.

Taira, Koji (1969). "Consumer Preferences, Poverty Norms, and Extent of Poverty," *Quarterly Review of Economics and Business*, 9 (2), Summer 1969: 31-44.

Taubman, P. (1976). "The Determinants of Earnings: Genetic, Family and Other Environments: A Study of White Male Twins," *The American Economic Review*, 66 (5), December 1976: 858-870.

—— (1977). "Schooling, Ability, Nonpecuniary Rewards, Socioeconomic Background and the Lifetime Distribution of Earnings," pp. 419-450 in Juster (1977).

—— (1978). *Income Distribution and Redistribution*. Reading, Mass.: Addison-Wesley.

Taubman, P., and T. Wales (1973). "Education, Mental Ability and Screening," *Journal of Political Economy*, January/February 1973.

Tawney, R. H. (1920). "Property and Creative Work," pp. 135-151 in Macpherson (1978).

—— (1952). *Equality*, 4th ed. London: George Allen and Unwin.

Taylor, D. E. (1981). "Education, On-the-Job Training and the Black-White Earnings Gap," *Monthly Labor Review*, 104 (4), April 1981.

Tebbel, J. (1962). *The Inheritors: A Study of America's Great Fortunes and What Happened to Them*. New York: G. P. Putnam's Sons.

Terry, S. L. (1982). "Unemployment and Its Effect on Family Income in 1980," *Monthly Labor Review*, 105 (4), April 1982: 35-43.

Theil, H. (1967). *Economics and Information Theory*. Amsterdam: North-Holland Publishing Co.

Thomas, L. G. (1980). "Monopoly and the Distribution of Wealth a Reappraisal." *Quarterly Journal of Economics*, 94 (1), February 1980: 185-194.

Thurow, L. C. (1968). "Disequilibrium and the Marginal Productivities of Capital and Labor," *Review of Economics and Statistics*, 45, February 1968: 25.

—— (1975). *Generating Inequality—Mechanisms of Distribution in the U.S. Economy*. New York: Basic Books.

Tinbergen, J. (1975). *Income Distribution: Analysis and Policies*. Amsterdam: North-Holland.

Titmuss, R. M. (1962). *Income Distribution and Social Change*. London: George Allen and Unwin.

Tobin, J. (1981). "Reaganonomics and Economics," *New York Review of Books*, 28 (19), December 3, 1981: 11-14.

Tocqueville, A. C. H. M. C. de (1840). *Democracy in America*. New York: Knopf, 1945.

Tolbert, C., P. Horan, and D. M. Beck (1980). "The Structure of Economic Segmentation: A Dual Economy Approach," *American Journal of Sociology*, 85 (5), March 1980: 1095-1116.

Tomes, N. (1980). *The Family, Inheritance and the Intergenerational Transmission of Inequality*, Research Report 8001. London: University of Western Ontario.

——— (1981). "The Family, Inheritance and the Intergenerational Transmission of Inequality," *Journal of Political Economy*, 89 (5), October 1981: 928-958.

Townsend, P., ed. (1970). *The Concept of Poverty*. New York: American Elsevier.

Ulman, G., and J. Flanagan (1975). *Wage Restraint*. Berkeley, California: University of California Press.

U.S., Congress, Senate Committee on Governmental Affairs, Subcommittee on Reports, Accounting and Management (1978a). *Interlocking Directorates among the Major U.S. Corporations*. 95th Congress, 2nd Session, Washington.

U.S., Congress, Senate Governmental Offices Committee, Subcommittee on Reports, Accounting and Management (1978b). *Voting Rights in Major Corporations*. 95th Congress, 1st Session, Washington.

U.S., Congressional Budget Office (1982a). *Effects of Tax and Benefit Reductions Enacted in 1981 for Households in Different Income Categories*. Washington: February 1982.

——— (1982b). *Cumulative Effects for Selected Households of Benefit Reductions Enacted in 1981 in AFDC, Food Stamps and Housing Subsidy Programs*. Washington: February 1982.

U.S., Department of Commerce, Bureau of the Census (1950-1980). *Statistical Abstract of the United States*. Washington: U.S. Government Printing Office.

U.S., Department of Health, Education, and Welfare (1976). *Characteristics of Low-Income Population*. Washington: U.S. Government Printing Office.

Van der Eyken, W. (1977). *The Pre-School Years*. Harmondsworth: Penguin Books.

Varian, H. R. (1978). *Microeconomic Analysis*. New York: W. W. Norton and Co.

Vernon, P. E. (1979). *Intelligence: Heredity and Environment*. San Francisco: W. H. Freeman and Company.

Virmani, B. R. (1979). *Workers' Participation in Management—A Select Annotated Bibliography*. London: Commonwealth Secretariat.

Viscusi, K. (1978). "Wealth Effects and Earnings Premiums for Job Hazards," *Review of Economics and Statistics*, 60 (3), August 1978: 408-416.

Wachter, M. L. (1974). "Primary and Secondary Labor Markets: A Critique of the Dual Approach," *Brookings Papers on Economic Activity*, (3): 637-680.

Wallace, P. A., and A. M. Lamond, ed. (1978). *Women, Minorities and Employment Discrimination*. Lexington, Mass.: Lexington Books, D. C. Heath and Co.

Wayand, O. *The Measurement of Poverty*, Memorandum No. 19, Ottawa: Social

Security Research Division, Research and Statistics Directorate Health and Welfare Canada.

Wedderburn, D., ed. (1974). *Poverty, Inequality and Class Structure*. Cambridge: Cambridge University Press.

Wedgewood, J. (1929). *The Economics of Inheritance*. London: George Routledge & Sons.

Weiss, A. (1980). "Job Queues and Layoffs in Labor Markets with Flexible Wages," *Journal of Political Economy*, 88 (3): 526-538.

Weisskoff, F. (1972). "Women's Place in the Labor Market," *American Economic Review*, papers and proceedings, May 1972.

Welch, F. (1973). "Black-White Differences in Returns to Schooling," *American Economic Review*, 63, December 1973: 893-907.

————— (1979). "Effects of Cohort Size Earnings: The Baby Boom, Babies' Financial Bust," *Journal of Political Economy*, 87 (5), Part 2, October 1979: S65-S98.

Welch, J. P., E. J. Winson, and S. M. MacKintosh (1971). "The Distribution of Height and Weight, and the Influence of Socio-Economic Factors, in a Sample of Eastern Canadian Urban School Children," *Canadian Journal of Public Health*, 62, September/October 1971, 373-381.

Whalley, J. (1974). "Estate Duty a 'Voluntary' Tax: Evidence from Stamp Duty Statistics," *The Economic Journal*, 84 (335), September 1974: 638-644.

White, B. B. (1978). "Empirical Tests of the Life Cycle Hypotheses," *American Economic Review*, 68 (4), September 1978: 547-560.

Williamson, J. C., and P. H. Lindert (1980). "Long-Term Trends in American Wealth Inequality," pp. 9-94 in Smith (1980).

Williamson, O., M. L. Wachter, and J. E. Haris (1975), "Understanding the Employment Relation: The Analysis of Idiosyncratic Exchange," *Bell Journal of Economics*, Spring 1975, pp. 250-278.

Willis, R. J. (1973). "A New Approach to the Economic Theory of Fertility Behavior," *Journal of Political Economy*, 81 (2), March/April 1973: S14-S65.

Wise, D. A. (1975). "Personal Attributes, Job Performance and Probability of Promotion," *Econometrica*, 43 (5-6), September/November 1975: 913-932.

Wold, H. O. A., and P. Whittle (1957). "A Model Explaining the Pareto Distribution of Wealth," *Econometrica*, 25, 591-595.

Wolff, E. N. (1979a). "The Distributional Effects of the 1969-75 Inflation on Holdings of Household Wealth in the United States," *Review of Income & Wealth*, series 25 (2), June 1979: 195-208.

————— (1979b). "The Rate of Surplus Value, the Organic Composition and the General Rate of Profit in the U.S. Economy," *American Economic Review*, 69 (3), June 1979: 329-342.

————— (1981). "The Accumulation of Household Wealth over the Life Cycle: A Microdata Analysis," *The Review of Income & Wealth*, series 27 (1), March 1981: 75-96.

————— (1982). "The Concentration of Personal Wealth in the United States 1969," paper presented at 7th general conference of the International Association for Research in Income and Wealth. Gouvieux, France: August 1981. Revised July 1982.

Wolff, E. N., and D. Bushe (1976). *Age Education and Occupational Earnings*

Inequality, NBER working paper No. 149, New York: National Bureau of Economic Research.

Wolfson, M. C. (1977). "The Causes of Inequality in the Distribution of Wealth, A Simulation Analysis," Ph.D. Thesis, Cambridge University, 1977.

————— (1980). "The Bequest Process and the Courses of Inequality in the Distribution of Wealth." NBER, pp. 187-210, in Smith (1980).

Woodbury, S. A. (1979). "Methodological Controversy in Labor Economics," *Journal of Economic Issues,* (4), December 1979: 933-955.

Yankelovich, D. (1974). *The New Morality: A Profile of American Youth in the '70s.* New York: McGraw-Hill.

Yntema, D. B. (1933). "Measures of the Inequality in the Personal Distribution of Wealth or Income," *Journal of the American Statistical Association,* 28.

Zigler, E., ed. (1979). *Project Head Start.* New York: The Free Press.

INDEX OF NAMES

INDEX OF SUBJECTS

transfer of, 261
Property rights, *See* Property
Proportionate effect, law of, 100-1, 112-13(n)
Psychic income, 142, 145, 160(n)
Public goods, 239
Public policy, *See* Government and politics;
  Taxes

Quintile shares, 14-16, 65

Radical approach to labor markets, *See*
  Structural theory, radical approach;
  under other subject areas
Random mating, 203-4
  See also Assortative mating
Random process, 100-1
"Random walk," 204-5
Retirement, 73, 75, 82, 84(n)
  See also Annuities; Life-cycle savings
  model; Pensions
Returns, voluntary deferral of, *See*
  Voluntary deferral of returns
Rewards, uncertainty of, *See* Uncertainty of
  rewards
Rich
  estimates of wealth, 39-42
  popular conceptions of, 45-47
  See also Fortunes; Inheritance
Risk, 138-39
  of entrepreneurs, 231
  Friedman theory of, 138-39
  and migrant workers, 174
  trade-offs of, 136-38

Savings, *See* Life-cycle savings model
School system, *See* Education
Screening hypothesis (signalling), 169-70
  See also Fable of the Kingdom of Asif
Secondary labor market, 172-74, 176
  characteristics, 176
  and class conflict, 178
  feedback effects, 173
Segmentation, 175, 177
Self-employed, 86-88
  See also Entrepreneurs
Self-made fortunes, *See* Fortunes
Sen measure of extent of poverty, 72
Seniority systems, 148, 167, 174, 190
Single-person households, 11, 60(n)
Skills, *See* Credentialism
Slavery, 47-48
Social capital, 179-80
Social control, 177-80

Social inheritance, 108-9, 112
  See also Human capital theory; Socioeconomic background
Social Security, 25, 45, 75, 84(n),
  236, 238
Social stratification, *See* Socioeconomic
  background
Social welfare, *See* Food stamps; In-kind income; In-kind transfers; Welfare
Socialism, 215-16
Socialization
  and capitalism, 178
  and choice in labor market, 127
  in employment, 167
Socioeconomic background, 84(n), 85, 94-95
  and childrearing, 104-6, 113(n)-14(n), 164
  and children's physical development,
  113(n)-14(n)
  and earnings determination, 104, 108-9,
  112, 114(n), 189
  and economic theory, 180, 259-60
  and educational opportunity, 248
  and inheritance, 203
  and marriage, 203
  neoclassical vs. radical approach to, 180
  and school performance, 106-8, 112
  and teachers' expectations, 107-8
  and twin studies, 110
  and values transmission, 183(n)
Stability (of employment), 175
Standard of living, 66-69
Statistics of Income File, 25
Stereotypes
  in occupations, 118-21, 125, 127-28
  of the poor, 73
  of uneducated blacks, 170
Stocks
  held by the rich, 40
  and inflation, 52
  ownership (general), 45
  and property rights, 212
  See also Capital gains
Structural theory, 162-81
  and childrearing, 164-80
  and choice, 163
  criticisms of, 175-77
  and discrimination, 170
  and government, 181, 248
  growth/inequality trade-off, view of, 231-32
  and human capital theory, summary of differences, 176-77
  methodology of, 182(n)

ABOUT THE AUTHOR

Lars Osberg is currently Associate Professor of Economics at Dalhousie University, Halifax, Nova Scotia. As an undergraduate he attended Queen's University, Kingston and the London School of Economics, graduating from Queen's in 1968. From 1968 to 1970 he was employed as an economist by the Tanzania Sisal Corporation, Tanga, Tanzania. He received his Ph.D. from Yale University in 1975 and was at the University of Western Ontario, London, Ontario for two years before moving to Dalhousie in 1977. He is the author of *Economic Inequality in Canada* (1981) and several journal articles.